DISPLACING THE DIVINE

Douglas Alan Walrath

To the Farmington Public Library

Religion and American Culture

The Religion and American Culture series explores the interaction between religion and culture throughout American history. Titles examine such issues as how religion functions in particular urban contexts, how it interacts with popular culture, its role in social and political conflicts, and its impact on regional identity. Series Editor Randall Balmer is the Ann Whitney Olin Professor of American Religion and former chair of the Department of Religion at Barnard College, Columbia University.

Michael E. Staub, *Torn at the Roots: The Crisis of Jewish Liberalism in Postwar America*

Amy DeRogatis, *Moral Geography: Maps, Missionaries, and the American Frontier*

Arlene M. Sánchez Walsh, *Latino Pentecostal Identity: Evangelical Faith, Self, and Society*

Julie Byrne, *O God of Players: The Story of the Immaculata Mighty Macs*

Thomas E. Woods Jr., *The Church Confronts Modernity: Catholic Intellectuals and the Progressive Era*

Clyde R. Forsberg Jr., *Equal Rites: The Book of Mormon, Masonry, Gender, and American Culture*

Andrew C. Rieser, *The Chautauqua Moment: Protestants, Progressives, and the Culture of Modern Liberalism*

Craig D. Townsend, *Faith in Their Own Color: Black Episcopalians in Antebellum New York City*

Michael D. McNally, *Honoring Elders: Ojibwe Aging, Religion, and Authority*

Nora L. Rubel, *Doubting the Devout: The Ultra-Orthodox in the Jewish American Imagination*

DISPLACING THE DIVINE

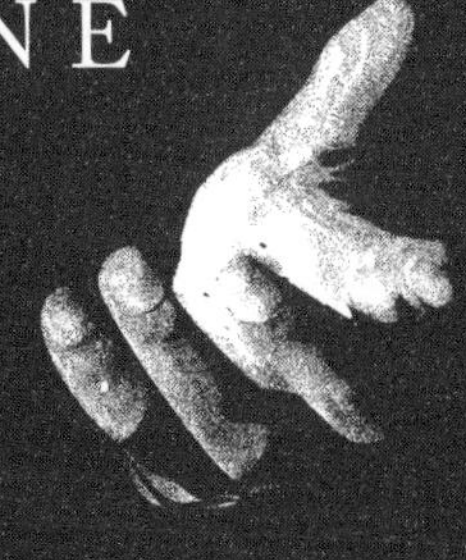

The Minister in the Mirror of American Fiction

DOUGLAS ALAN WALRATH

Columbia University Press *New York*

Columbia University Press
Publishers Since 1893
New York Chichester, West Sussex

Library of Congress Cataloging-in-Publication Data
Walrath, Douglas Alan, 1933–
Displacing the divine : the minister in the mirror of American fiction / Douglas Alan Walrath.
p. cm.—(The religion and American culture series)
Includes bibliographical references and index.
ISBN 978-0-231-15106-1 (cloth : alk. paper)—ISBN 978-0-231-52180-2 (e-book)
1. American ficiton—History and criticism. 2. Clergy in literature. 3. Christianity and literature—United States—History. I. Title. II. Series.

PS374.C55W36 2010
813'.00935823—dc22

2009045476

∞

Columbia University Press books are printed on permanent and durable acid-free paper.
This book is printed on paper with recycled content.
Printed in the United States of America
c 10 9 8 7 6 5 4 3 2 1
p 10 9 8 7 6 5 4 3 2 1

For Sherry

CONTENTS

I ask . . . to be absolved from any duty to provide orthodox morals
and consolations in my fiction.
Fiction holds the mirror up to the world and cannot
show more than this world contains.

—John Updike, "Remarks upon Receiving the Campion Medal"

PREFACE

Several years ago during the last class session of a seminary course I taught in rural and small-town culture, I asked the students to reflect on what they had learned. Looking back at his early life, one student, a middle-aged, soon-to-be Episcopal priest, burst out with his reply: "I grew up in rural culture, but I never really understood it!" I could say the same about my experience as a minister. I grew into the role, but for many years I didn't understand what caused people to view me as they did.

My first conscious encounter with the acquired public identity of a minister occurred in 1954 when I entered the seminary. My old friends from high school and college began immediately to treat me differently. For example, they apologized when they swore. When I suggested their apologies were unnecessary, they explained, "You're different; you're a minister now." I protested that I did not experience myself as different, but they insisted on seeing me as different. I now realize that my acquired identity as a minister encouraged them to look past my individual qualities and to deal with me categorically, according to a cultural image of "the minister" that told them they should not swear around ministers. In fact, once they became aware that I was studying for the ministry, all my friends automatically applied to me images of the minister that *they* accepted as valid. They ignored my protests and insisted that I would function according to their images. The cultural images they accepted overshadowed their present and prior personal experiences of me. They insisted on recasting me within their cultural images of "the minister." Many of these images seemed quite "fictional" to me, but they seemed real to my friends. Once they imaged me as a minister, I was expected to honor the cultural norms that *they* accepted. Though I was only a first-year theological student, my friends' perceptions of me were already filtered through cultural images of "the minister" they insisted I would reflect.

The excellent theological education I received offered an image of the ministry I wanted to reflect: what I was *supposed to be* like as a minister in my denomination. When I became the pastor of a congregation, I assumed that this official church image would prevail. However, I soon discovered that many members of my congregation did not accept my seminary-acquired "official" view of the ministry. A few church members and some others in the community seemed to affirm that image—or at least one that was roughly similar. Many did not. And both those who affirmed the denominational image I had internalized and those who held different images of Protestant clergy expected me to live up to *their* vision of ministers. Like my back-home friends, they had preconceived notions of what ministers are like. And they believed in them.

Of course, all of these insights are really hindsight. Only after graduate study in sociology and many years of experience and reflection did I understand why and how other cultural images of ministers can seem as significant, legitimate, and normative to those who hold them as biblically and theologically based images seem to most ministers and others for whom church culture is primary. I now recognize that even my own theologically based self-perceptions are socially conditioned. For nearly fifty years now, two perspectives, the theological and the sociological, have lived next door to each other inside of me—and not always comfortably. My thinking and writing have been informed by both of them.

In this book, I describe how American fiction reveals changing perceptions of Protestant clergy and their God in American society. The book represents much more than an attempt to understand my own experience. To be sure, I gained some self-understanding as I viewed Protestant clergy in American novels. But I also recognized that the ways I and others are and have been perceived as ministers have deep roots in American culture. Changing images of ministers reflected in American fiction mirror broader social, cultural, and theological changes in American society. I see reflections that inform my own experience when I look into the mirror of American fiction, but I also see much more. Cultural images of ministers reflected in American fiction mirror the changing character of American culture and religion during the past two hundred years. Which is why I want to share what I saw when I journeyed through this looking glass.

I am deeply grateful to friends and colleagues who encouraged and guided me during the years I worked on this book. Horton Davies in his *A Mirror of the Ministry in Modern Novels* first gave me the idea that fiction could serve as a mirror in which to view ministers. Twenty-five years ago, when I began a serious study of ministers in American fiction, Clifton Davis, then seminary librarian at Bangor Theological Seminary, helped me ferret out the relevant work of previous scholars. I am grateful to William Imes and Glenn Miller for conversations during which they gave me encouragement and shared insights. Malcolm Warford read an early draft of chapter 8 and said, "You can do better than that!" I hope I have. Susan Davies read early versions of several chapters and offered me the same fine criticism she gives her students. Over the course of a decade, scores of Bangor Seminary students suffered patiently (most of the time) as I was learning how to use novels to identify changing images of ministers in American culture.

I am indebted to the librarians at Mantor Library, University of Maine, Farmington, especially Janet Brackett, Sarah Otley, and Moira Wolohan. No matter how obscure the source I requested, they always found it. I am also grateful to dozens of used and rare book dealers, who didn't get around to culling their nineteenth-century fiction and who let me go through musty, dusty boxes of books they thought they would never sell.

Truman Fudge shared his enthusiasm for this project when I was just beginning it and led me to several novels that supported my thesis when it was barely clear to me. During ten years of lunch conversations, Allen Flint, friend and esteemed American studies scholar, fanned my enthusiasm for Hawthorne and all of nineteenth-century Americana. I regret that an untimely death prevents him from receiving my gratitude over one more lunch. When we have our first lunch in the next world, I'll buy. I am also conscious of my indebtedness to Craig Lewis, M.D., who disagrees openly with much of what I think and cares enough to tell me why. Scott Planting has been my pastor for thirty years; countless conversations with him have provided opportunities to test my perceptions of the changing role of ministers in American culture.

Several anonymous readers read the manuscript at various stages in its development and offered criticism that saved me from significant errors and oversights. Cynthia Garver who served as copy editor not only corrected countless mistakes and omissions, she also made helpful substantive suggestions. Readers who are searching for a source but cannot recall where it appears in the text will appreciate Jean Oplinger's excellent index. Wendy

Lochner, my long-suffering editor at Columbia University Press, provided just the right balance of support and critique during the five long years it took me to transform a manuscript into a book. I am deeply grateful for her wisdom and persistence.

My deepest gratitude goes to Sherry, my wife, who gave up hours and days of companionship so I could finish "the book." To her I say, "Finally, it's done. And I know you deserve more thanks than there are years to give it."

DISPLACING THE DIVINE

INTRODUCTION
Fiction as a Mirror of Culture

Images are not arguments, rarely even lead to proof, but the mind craves them.

—Henry Adams, *The Education of Henry Adams*

In the pages that follow, I show that Protestant ministers who appear as characters in American (U.S.) fiction over the past two hundred years, especially fiction published between the 1790s and the 1920s, mirror a discrediting and displacement, first of ministers and then of their God in American society.[1] I call this process of social and cultural change "displacing the divine." Fiction provides a historical record of the declining regard for ministers and their God. Changing portrayals of ministers in fiction mirror changing perceptions of ministers and their God in society. Fiction reflects culture.

The Social Sources of Ministers in Fiction

Fiction can function as a mirror of culture because it is more than the product of individual creativity; it is also shaped by the social and cultural experience of those who write it. Ministers in fiction are molded by perceptions that authors have of ministers in society or, to be more specific: the "cultural images" that define their perceptions of ministers. Cultural images that give shape to perception are a potent social phenomenon. A branch of sociology, usually referred to as the "sociology of knowledge," provides a theoretical foundation that supports this assertion. According to this school of thought, "reality" as we perceive it in the objective world is socially constructed. In *The Social Construction of Reality*, Peter Berger and

Thomas Luckmann offer one of the most helpful discussions of the social origins of our perceptions of reality. As the title suggests, Berger and Luckmann believe our perceptions of reality are socially constructed. We are born into an objective social world, but our perceptions of that world are deeply influenced by significant others (e.g., parents). Those significant others give a distinctive shape to what we perceive as they mediate their reality to us. Their distinctive reality reflects their social location (e.g., the middle class) and their idiosyncrasies (e.g., their individual attitudes as middle-class people).[2]

Once specific cultural images are established as our reality, we take them for granted. I can illustrate how they function by sharing a personal experience. Some years ago as we traveled together to a meeting, a friend described how exasperated he was by the behavior of his daughter. Suddenly he interrupted himself with, "I suppose she's acting just like a teenager!" When I agreed, he found some relief in the fact that I also thought of his daughter's teenaged behavior as normal. Her behavior still bothered him, but it felt less worrisome. She was simply a teenager, and everybody knows what teenagers are like! Looking back on the conversation, I am struck by how easily we both accepted the existence and shape of a cultural image or social category we referred to as "teenager." It seemed so matter of fact that neither of us felt the need to define it.[3]

Our perceptions of parents, teenagers, old people, and others who are closest to us are products of what Berger and Luckmann call "primary" socialization.[4] Primary socialization is global; it is not restricted to a single group or place. For example, it encourages the belief that people of a particular age behave, or should behave, in certain, characteristic ways. The "commonsense" convictions my friend and I shared as we discussed his teenaged daughter reflect our common socialization. As middle-class Americans, we expect teenagers to be exasperating. We have internalized this cultural image. The fact that we reinforce the cultural image in casual conversations like the one I just described is in itself significant: the conversation "can *afford to be casual* precisely because it refers to routines of a taken-for-granted world."[5] Except for times when we are self-consciously critical, we keep reinforcing our admittedly biased images, often following a kind of circular logic. We note seriously only teenagers who match our cultural image of teenagers. When we encounter a teenager who is *not* exasperating, we define his or her behavior as exceptional! Either the individual is not a typical teenager, or his or her behavior at the moment is not typical.[6] This process of circular reinforcement is more closed-minded in some of us than it is in others. As this book unfolds, I contend that new cultural images do emerge, especially during times of significant social change, and that these emerging images press us to revise our perceptions of reality. How available each of us is to make revisions depends on how normatively we experience the social and psychological factors that shape us. Those of us who are members of social groups that are more accepting and supportive of critical thinking, for example, and those of us whose psychological makeup is less rigid are more likely to revise our perceived reality and our cultural images.[7]

Defined perceptions of cultural figures like clergy are acquired during what Berger and Luckmann call "secondary" socialization.[8] Secondary socialization usually occurs later than primary socialization, as we mature and participate more as individuals in the larger society.[9] The process of secondary socialization is similar to primary socialization: we internalize mediated perceptions and generalize from them. But the internal images we form during secondary socialization are associated with more-specific contexts and functions. For example, our images of clergy are associated with specific events like worship services that happen in a church or synagogue or mosque and with functions like preaching that we identify specifically with clergy. We may gain our initial impressions of what clergy are like from specific individuals, but our cultural image of clergy is soon no longer limited only to them. Functions we identify initially with a particular minister or ministers soon become "minister functions" in our perceived reality: we realize another minister could provide them. We have internalized a cultural image of ministers as social figures. Once cultural images produced by our secondary socialization are defined clearly, we reinforce and defend them with the same tenacity that we use to maintain cultural images formed during primary socialization.

The overall process of socialization that produces cultural images is similar for all of us, but the cultural realities internalized vary considerably from group to group and culture to culture. Though the childhood friends I refer to in the preface (who insisted that I match *their* cultural image of ministers) might resist the suggestion, not everyone holds the same cultural image of ministers. Different social groups in different places and different times accept different, even contradictory, cultural images of ministers. Just recently at a party, I found myself conversing with a university professor who at first identified me as an academic colleague. He didn't realize I am also a minister. At one point in our conversation, he said, "I think ministers are leftovers from a former age. They don't play any significant role in society today." Before I could respond, someone interrupted our conversation. Later in the evening, he sought me out and apologized. Someone had told him that I am not only a professor but also a clergyperson. "Please don't take what I said personally. I wasn't referring to *you* when we talked earlier," he assured me. I was relieved to know that I am an exception to his summary dismissal of clergy! As we continued to speak, he said pointedly, "There are ministers and there are ministers." When he defined what he meant by this statement, he was surprised to discover that I perceive some of the same differences among ministers as he does. And, as we talked further, we discovered that both of us believe it is more difficult for ministers to play a significant role in society today than it was a few decades ago. We are each old enough to recall the 1950s and recognize that even then we expected ministers to play a more significant role in society. As we talked further, we discussed how differently ministers tend to be perceived among those with whom each of us interacts most frequently: for him, the university and academia; for me, the theological seminary and the church.[10]

The variations in perceptions of ministers that become apparent in exchanges like the one I just recounted suggest that cultural images of ministers reflect the times, places, and other social conditions of the groups that mold them. The varied social, ethnic, and economic experiences of different groups prescribe different roles for ministers and mold distinctive images of those who occupy these roles. The varied demands placed on clergy in different times encourage different images of ministers. As times change, new images are born; some old images, challenged by strong new images, are pushed aside. Some cultural images persist for many years; others for only a short time. The common assumption that we all picture "the minister" the same way does not hold up under critical examination. Ministers are perceived differently within the subcultures that compose our society. At any given moment in American history, cultural images of clergy are diverse and in flux.

Most of us can describe cultural images according to which members of our own social group perceive ministers. We find it more difficult to discern how ministers appear to members of groups with whom we have little contact or how they appeared to people who lived in times past. During my years of active teaching, whenever I supervised ministers learning to practice, I struggled to help them recognize that the image they have of themselves as ministers may be different from the image of the minister that prevails in the church and community where they serve. Even inexperienced theological students assume their image of ministers is correct. Many of them resist the idea that the cultural images they will inherit when they become pastors are as potent and durable as the image they intend to promote.

For many years, I searched for resources that would help my students recognize how varied cultural images actually are. After exploring a variety of sources, including history and biography, I concluded that ministers in fiction are the most reliable mirrors of present and past cultural images. Fiction writers' concern to *portray* commends fiction as a preferred source of cultural images. The genre of fiction demands that authors, even those with a religious or moral agenda, function as artists.[11] Artists portray; they present by representing. They characterize what they wish to communicate. They often incorporate the feelings a character evokes in them into their portrayal of that character. Unlike historians and biographers, fiction writers usually do *not* try to remain dispassionate or objective about their subjects. As a result, when we read a novel or a short story in which a minister appears as a significant character, we are not simply observers of the minister's behavior and its effects on others; often the writer takes us "inside" the minister. We are invited to think the minister's thoughts, to feel the minister's feelings, and to experience the thoughts and feelings of others with whom the minister interacts. In fiction, we can experience vicariously how people in other times and places image ministers. Cultural images come to life in fiction.

Is fiction then true to life—as true to life as history or biography? It can be. In fact, I believe fiction can be true to life even when it is not completely true to historical facts. In a provocative study of Nathaniel Hawthorne, J. Golden Taylor describes how an artful novelist transforms historical facts into a compelling vision of truth to life: "By heightening, concentrating, and symbolizing action, art creates an impact on the whole emotional and intellectual nature of the reader." The writer brings his or her personal *and* cultural experience to the historical material and transforms that material to reflect cultural truth as he or she sees it: "The truth to life conceived by the artist transcends and may contradict or ignore the truth to fact of the literal-minded scholar or historian." But these contradictions or oversights do not necessarily reduce the accuracy or value of the author's insight: "The truth to life is really preconceived by the novelist and may very well represent some facet of general historic truth about a culture and personify and dramatize it so effectively that the novelist's *particular insight may do much to inculcate some phase of historic truth better than some histories*." Thus truth to life in fiction can reveal cultural images more accurately than either history or biography because "the novelist who captures such profound and compelling truths is drawing on the very essence of history and supplements it rather than opposes it."[12]

Fictional characters mirror socially defined cultural images filtered through the personal perceptions of an author.[13] When authors create fictional ministers, they draw on a cultural image and give it their own distinctive shape. Does the author distort the image during the process of creation? Probably. Fictional characters probably do reflect their creators' biased perceptions of the real world.[14] But this inherent bias may be less of an obstacle than it seems to be initially because the reflected bias is at least as sociocultural as it is individual. The social and cultural experiences that impress authors shape the characters they create. An author's characters mirror cultural images that are native to either the subculture with which the author identifies or the subculture the author has in mind as he or she works (or both). Fictional characters have roots that stretch far beyond an individual author's unique imagination. Fiction mirrors culture. Fictional clergy mirror cultural images of ministers.

The social roots of fiction also strengthen its historicity. The social character of writing argues for a systematic association between images of clergy that are accepted at different times and places and those who appear concurrently as characters in American fiction. Each writer's characters are shaped by cultural images the writer believes his or her potential audience accepts, as well as by cultural images that the writer accepts. Though some authors may not be fully conscious of cultural images that have shaped them, most are quite aware of the cultural images their readers accept. Writers who want to be accepted—and most writers do, at least to some degree—need to be aware of the tastes and prejudices of their anticipated audience. They need to know what is and is not likely to be accepted by those who read their work. In fact, my study of popular fiction suggests that many writers of popular fiction mold characters explicitly to engage anticipated readers. If they could speak directly to readers, they would probably say something like "You and I know ministers like this minister, don't we" or "in these circumstances or in this time, you and I know ministers who are (or were) like this minister."[15] Clergy characters that resonate with cultural images through which readers already perceive real-life clergy are most likely to seem immediately plausible to readers. The concern to create characters that seem plausible to their readers encourages authors to fashion fictional characters according to cultural images drawn from real life.[16]

This close connection between fiction and social context explains why fictional variety mirrors social and cultural variety. Ministers who appear as characters in works of fiction written by authors who live, or identify with those who live, in different times and places reflect the variety of cultural images within which people perceive ministers in these same times and places. Character traits that fiction writers incorporate into characters they invent can be traced to cultural images accepted by particular social groups to which authors belong or with which they can identify. One can discern these specific social and cultural roots in even the most-unusual characters from the most-creative authors.[17]

The more novels one reads by authors rooted in a particular time and place and social group, the more clearly one sees the cultural images within which ministers are perceived then and there. Though individual authors give their own distinctive shape to the characters they create, underlying cultural images become apparent as one notes traits that are common among the characters based on a specific image. Images of clergy that are characteristic of particular times and places become clear in the accumulation of portrayals from authors who have similar cultural roots, identities, and perspectives. As one reads novel after novel rooted in a particular subculture, common elements begin to stand out. Eventually, a cultural image takes shape. Ideally, one should read all the works by all the writers who lived in a particular place and time, but, actually, such a comprehensive approach is not necessary. One can discover the essential characteristics of a cultural image by reading a sufficient number of representative works.[18]

Ministers in the Mirror of American Fiction

Most ministers who appear in American novels published from the 1790s through the 1920s reflect what I call "popular images" of clergy.[19] Popular images seem like common sense to most people in a particular time and place; they embody what members of a culture or subculture take for granted. Fictional clergy based on popular images reveal popular norms—what most people believe typical ministers are or were like. Popular images reflect the social conventions of particular places and times. For example, "muscular ministers" who appear in so many postbellum novels are patterned according to a widely accepted image of ministers in the American South and West immediately before and after the Civil War. They are quite different from the Congregational clergy who appear earlier in New England novels, like Lydia Maria Child's *The Rebels* (1825). Child characterizes Boston-area Congregational clergy immediately before the American Revolution as easygoing, well-educated, wise, and influential community leaders. These ministers, in turn, differ sharply from the clergy in Child's novel *Hobomok* (1824), written only one year before *The Rebels* but set 150 years earlier in the mid-seventeenth century. In *Hobomok*, Child portrays second-generation Bay colony Calvinist clergy as narrow, bigoted, and oppressive. The contrasting characterizations show how well Child knows both her history and her audience. Mid-seventeenth-century Puritan and pre-Revolutionary–established Massachusetts Bay clergy were quite different.[20]

Clergy cast according to popular images follow formulas authors know are familiar *and* acceptable to their anticipated readers. Even characters that seem exceptional honor accepted images—because they are cast clearly as exceptions. In her novel *Hope Leslie* (1826), which, like Child's *Hobomok*, is set in seventeenth-century New England, Catharine Maria Sedgwick portrays the Puritan divine John Eliot atypically—as a kind, tolerant, and humane clergyperson. But this characterization contradicts neither Sedgwick's nor her nineteenth-century readers' image of seventeenth-century Puritan clergy as bigots because Brother Eliot (like the historical character on whom he is based) is a missionary pastor to the Native Americans. He can appear as a warm and tolerant Puritan minister in this special role and still be a convincing character to her nineteenth-century readers. Most of them will see Eliot as an exception that proves the rule.

Another group of clergy who appear as characters in novels reflect images of ministers that are normative for members of one or more religious groups. I call these images "church images." I use the term "church" rather than "religious" to emphasize the fact that these images have a social base: they reflect the cultural norms of a religious group. I employ "church" as a broad sociocultural category to include organized congregations and denominations (Community Church, Bible Church, American Baptist Churches, Presbyterian Church, Lutheran Church, etc.), goal-oriented or cause-oriented groups that cross denominational lines (the "social gospel" in the nineteenth century; those pursuing social justice, church growth, and so on, more recently), and associations of those who identify with a specific theology or religious experience (evangelicals, fundamentalists, charismatics, etc.).

Norms are often very well defined within church groups. In most established denominations, candidates for the ministry are required to demonstrate specific theological and biblical knowledge and to attain certain levels of competence in areas of practice like preaching and pastoral care. Some churches even prescribe essential beliefs their ministers must accept. To become ordained clergy in these denominations, ministers must affirm that they believe the doctrines contained in the church's written standards. When they are being examined for ordination, most prospective clergy are also quizzed about the quality of their personal life and prayer life. The process is designed to maintain and reinforce accepted measures of piety and morality, as well as normative measures of theology and competence.

Beyond these formal procedures, there are subtler but equally powerful group norms that reflect church-based cultural images of the minister. Members of specific churches expect their minister to maintain a way of life that mirrors their image of "the minister." These expectations often encompass a minister's personal and professional lives. The way a minister functions at church suppers and other social occasions can be as important a measure of "orthodoxy" as the way he or she preaches or celebrates the Eucharist. The minister is not supposed to swear (at least not seriously or openly); he or she can drink coffee or tea but not alcohol; and, if the minister is a woman, she should never wear clothing that could be considered "provocative." The cultural image may even include prescribed behaviors for clergy spouses and clergy children.

Fictional ministers based on church images usually reflect the normative beliefs and behaviors associated with a particular church group. Fictional clergy cast according to a church image are meant to represent the "true" character of the group. They may even be designed intentionally to promote or discredit specific beliefs and practices. In *The Circuit Rider* (1874), for example, Edward R. Eggleston, a former circuit rider himself, portrays Morton Goodwin and Kike Lumsden as heroic Methodist ministers living on the Ohio frontier before the Civil War. One of Eggleston's purposes in writing the novel (as he explains in the preface) was to demonstrate the superior ability of Methodist clergy to minister to people living on the frontier. Methodist clergy who appear in *The Circuit Rider* consistently outperform clergy from other denominations, including a very pedantic Presbyterian. In a novel published only a few years earlier, *Inside: A Chronicle of Secession* (1866), the Presbyterian author William Mumford Baker argues an opposite viewpoint. The extensive scholarship that is required of Presbyterian clergy protects Mr. Arthur, the founding pastor of a Presbyterian congregation in a Southern town during the Civil War, from theological expediency. Mr. Baker, the less-educated Methodist minister, compromises (in the author's view) his pulpit to justify slavery and promote the cause of the South. He twists scripture repeatedly to make it support his proslavery position.

Several decades later, Winston Churchill designed Father John Hodder, the Episcopal priest in *The Inside of the Cup* (1914), as an argument for what contemporaries call the "social gospel." During the early years of the twentieth century, Churchill served as an active lay leader and advocate of the social gospel in the Episcopal Church. When his fictional cleric Father Hodder confronts powerful members of his vestry, including the chief warden, with the suffering their business practices bring to the poor who live in tenements they own, they tell him to "stick to religion." Hodder refuses to narrow his ministry—and pays a heavy price for that refusal. Only the support of his bishop prevents his antagonists from forcing him to resign. But once the crisis is past, events that follow vindicate both Hodder's liberal beliefs and the social gospel image of the ministry he reflects.[21]

Sometimes fictional ministers based on church images seem contrived—more like models than characters. When an author's concern to establish an argument overwhelms his or her creative work, the resulting character may be too good to be true: faithful and devoted, but not human. Sympathetic readers, however, are usually not put off by such artistic criticism—because fictional clergy who reflect an image that seems to detractors too good to be true still seem like real ministers to them. They see reality through the eyes of their faith.

Fictional clergy based on a third kind of cultural image challenge the norms of both popular and church cultures. They mirror what I call "radical images." Radical images offer provocative alternatives to accepted popular and church images. They reflect unconventional, sometimes even irreverent, perspectives. Radical images of ministers challenge the accuracy and adequacy of more widely accepted perceptions of ministers.[22] They reach below the surface of cultural convention to the roots (radix) of human experience and (often uncomfortably) hold up aspects of human experience that more conventional images may mask. This ability to represent radical perceptions is especially true of cultural images that appear in art fiction or fiction that is considered "literature."[23] Art fiction, like all art, may reflect something more or other than an author recognizes during the act of creation. While it obviously reflects what the author perceives and wishes to represent, it may also reflect something beyond or different from what the author intends. Radical images reflected in art fiction can be surprisingly provocative and revealing.[24]

Fictional clergy who reflect radical cultural images often combine attributes ministers are expected to have with attributes they are not expected to have. They both do and do not act like ministers are "supposed to act." Thus Arthur Dimmesdale, who appears in Hawthorne's 1850 novel *The Scarlet Letter*, both matches and challenges mid-nineteenth-century cultural images. He matches the contemporary popular perception of a bad clergyman when he commits adultery and suffers severely, but he does not match any contemporary popular image when Hawthorne implies that Dimmesdale's dysfunction is a *consequence* of his Calvinist theology. Hawthorne's intentionally disturbing portrayal invites the reader to believe there is an inherent connection between the nature of Dimmesdale's faith and his demise. The implied connection confronts many of Hawthorne's contemporaries with a challenging character. The fact that so many critics are not able to pass Dimmesdale off simply as eccentric suggests that Hawthorne's portrayal reflects an emerging cultural image. In Arthur Dimmesdale, Nathaniel Hawthorne challenges his contemporaries to re-image ministers.

Radical images like the dysfunctional believer reflected in Arthur Dimmesdale often encourage revisions in popular and church images of clergy. The radical cultural image that Hawthorne mirrors in his fictional clergy from the 1840s and 1850s emerged in popular culture after the Civil War in the form of the compulsive believer. Both Parson Hiram Kelsey, who appears in Mary Noilles Murfee's *The Prophet of the Great Smoky Mountains* (1885), and Andrew Joslin, the Cumberlands preacher in Emerson Hough's *The Way Out* (1918), reflect the new popular image.[25] Joslin, especially, is not just disturbed; he is completely out of control. The revised popular perceptions of clergy that Hawthorne's characterizations anticipated are profound. By the late-nineteenth and early-twentieth century, "bad" ministers in popular culture included not only those who were morally bad but also those who were profoundly dysfunctional. They suggest that misbelieving can be as damaging as misbehaving.

Radical images often mirror impending social and cultural shifts. Writers may base a fictional minister on a radical image because the image reflects a divergent perception of clergy they want to affirm—perhaps even to promote. The quaint thinking and believing Theron Ware, the central character in Harold Frederic's *The Damnation of Theron Ware* (1896), is no match for the sophistication of Celia Madden and the modernism of Father Forbes—the Renaissance woman and urbane Catholic priest who appear in the novel. The Rev. Mr. Ware's struggles to impress them become increasingly ridiculous as the story unfolds. The fact that he is unaware of his ridiculous appearance makes him a pathetic character. Frederic's characterization of Ware as an anachronism reflects his own belief that the demands of the time have outstripped the capabilities of most ministers. He portrays Theron Ware as a cultural antique. The radical image Ware mirrors suggests that ministers like him are obsolete. In fact, Harold Frederic creates Theron Ware as a character in part to suggest that ministers like Ware *are* obsolete. In Frederic's novel, it is clear that he believes ministers who continue to function as nineteenth-century rural parsons are irrelevant anachronisms in the modern world. Ware the character is Frederic's creation, and there is a bit of polemic in Frederic's portrayal. But the image that the fictional Rev. Mr. Ware reflects is cultural. Frederic picks it up and uses it to create a character because it matches his bias.[26]

The progressive transformations that cultural images undergo confirm that they are both historical and social products. Images vary with time, as well as with place and group. Different groups, different places, and different times nurture different popular, church, and radical images. Major social events like the American Revolution, the disestablishment of churches, urbanization and the rise of factories, the opening and settling of the frontier, the massive influx of immigrants, the Civil War, the advent of feminism and women's suffrage, and the emergence of modernism bring major cultural changes. They nurture different social contexts that encourage and sometimes demand new perceptions of cultural figures like clergy. New cultural images of clergy form to match the changed perceptions of clergy. This process of transformation may happen quickly or it may take decades, but when it is played out, both contemporary and past images of ministers are revised. Ministers now and ministers then are recast according to new cultural conventions. Different social contexts bring forth different cultural images—in life and then in literature.[27]

Cultural images of ministers in American fiction represent a cumulative cultural heritage. Images through which we perceive ministers now are products of the present, but they are also products of the past. Social change during some historical periods fosters massive and abiding cultural change. I believe the nineteenth century was one of those times. In the early-nineteenth century, American ministers and the faith they represented exercised a cultural dominance in public life. By the early-twentieth century, ministers had lost their dominant position in public life, and so had the faith they represented. Fiction reflects the change. Cultural images of ministers reflected in American fiction between the 1790s and the 1920s reveal a progressive discrediting of Protestant clergy in American society. That discrediting, which is the central concern of this book, is already apparent in American fiction between the 1790s and the 1850s, and its culmination is reflected in American fiction between the 1860s and the 1920s.

Changing perceptions of ministers that emerged between the 1790s and the 1920s shaped varied and sometimes opposing subcultures in American society that still exist today.[28] Cultural images of ministers in nineteenth- and early-twentieth-century American fiction mirror these subcultures. Some cultural images of clergy reflected in this fiction seem contemporary to us because some of them *still are* contemporary. Some characteristics of fictional ministers from this former time seem current to us because the cultural images through which we perceive ministers now include elements from our culture's past. As we make our way through American fiction written in this former time, we discover a cultural legacy: the ways they perceived ministers then continue to shape the ways we perceive ministers now. We can see the changing shape of American Protestantism in the faces of ministers in American fiction.[29]

PART I
Exposing the Divine
1790s–1850s

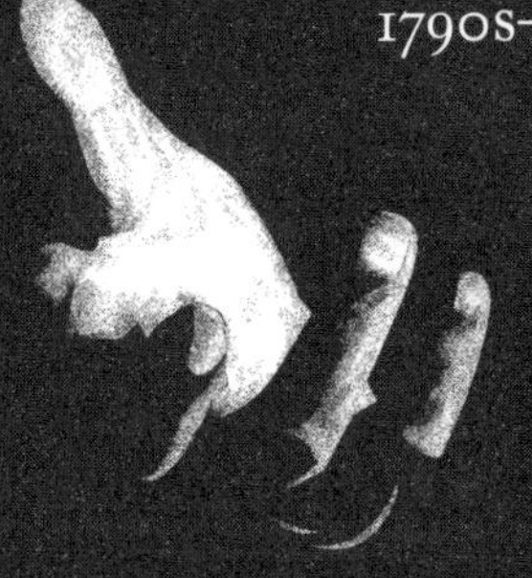
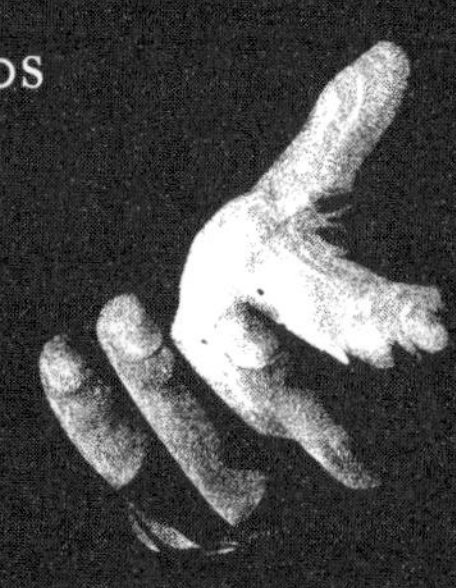

For doth not Scripture intimate, that He holdeth all of us in the hollow of His hand?—a Hollow, truly!

—Herman Melville, *Pierre*

[As a minister he was] not fairly thrown into the field of life. . . . The gayety passed him by; the politics pass him by. Nobody wants him; nobody holds him by the button but some desperate, dilapidated philanthropist. People say, while turning a corner, "How do you do, Doctor?" Which is very much as if they said, "How do you do, Abstraction?"

—Rev. Orville Dewey to Rev. William Ware, *Autobiography and Letters of Orville Dewey*

1

FALTERING FATHERS AND DEVIOUS DIVINES

Popular Images

Misfits in America

Ministers served in America for nearly two hundred years before distinctly American clergy emerged. Until the middle of the nineteenth century, most Protestant clergy in America followed Old World ways as they ministered. Even after the Industrial Revolution transformed the quiet villages of the American East into factory towns, and tens of thousands of Americans rushed west, when it was obvious everywhere that Old World models did not suit pastors for ministry in the New World, many ministers still kept to them. Because the old ways were norms. Ministers believed in them.

The Revolutionary War strained the American colonies' political, economic, and cultural ties to the Old World. Victory in the "American Rebellion" (as an English friend terms it) encouraged Americans to challenge Old World legacies. After the war, many turned inward to America, captivated by the promises of their New World. Fewer and fewer Americans felt obligated to honor Old World thinking and Old World ways. Literature from the decades after the Revolution suggests that many Americans used their newfound freedom to deride Old World culture and Old World institutions. Cultural images of the time mocked those who embodied Old World ways, including American clergy who continued to pattern their ministry according to Old World cultural images. As Americans forged their own identity, the "old-fashioned" Old World minister became an object of derision in American literature and American life.[1]

The clergyman who is a misfit in the New World because he follows Old World patterns of ministry is a common character in several American novels published just after the Revolutionary War, including H.H. Brackenridge's *Modern Chivalry* (1792–97). *Modern Chivalry* chronicles the adventures of a fifty-three-year-old free-living bachelor, Captain John Farrago, and his even freer living Irish sidekick, Teague O'Regan. The minister enters the story when he, the captain, and Teague are overnight guests at the same inn. The captain and the minister fall into conversation after dinner and soon discover that they hold different views on almost all matters. The clergyman is described as "a good young man, but inclining to fanaticism, and being righteous overmuch." The captain, by contrast, is "somewhat skeptical [an understatement] in his notions of religion" (52).

The three men in Brackenridge's story—the naive minister, the worldly-wise adventurer, and the comic—mirror cultural images that Brackenridge could be certain were familiar to most of his readers. As the tale unfolds, the characters play out their expected roles. The captain and the minister grow weary of arguing and retire. Under cover of darkness, Teague sneaks into the bedchamber of a young woman living at the inn. When she wakes up and discovers him in her bed, she cries out loudly and awakens the entire household. The minister, who is sleeping in an adjoining room, rushes into the young woman's room in his nightshirt. The captain and the landlady quickly join him. The light brought by the last to arrive reveals Teague, the captain, and the minister standing with the young woman. Teague "whose natural parts were not bad, and presence of mind considerable" is quite up to the occasion:

> I was aslape in my own bed . . . when I heard the sound of this young crature's voice crying out like a shape in a pasture; and when . . . I come here, I found this praste, who was so wholy, and praching all night, upon the top of the bed, with his arms round this young crature's neck; and if I had not given him a twitch by the nose, and bid him lie over, dear honey, he would have ravished her virginity. (53)

In response to Teague's false accusation, the minister can only stare "with his mouth open"; he is "shocked . . . beyond the power of speech." The landlady is enraged: "It is a pretty story that a minister of the gospel should be the first to bring scandal upon the house." Her outburst brings the clergyman back to his senses. He loudly protests his innocence. Bedlam ensues, but the captain is able to calm the arguing parties with the suggestion that this attempted seduction is "no great affair. . . . The love of women is a natural sin, and the holiest men in all ages have been propense to this indulgence." And to prove his point, he proceeds to list biblical characters that succumbed to the same temptation of which the minister is accused! The minister tries again to establish his innocence. But recognizing that everyone is weary, he accepts the captain's suggestion that no real harm is likely to come from the matter and gives up the protest.

Events soon confirm the minister's worst fears, however. News of the bedroom scene comes to the attention of the consistory, the ecclesiastical body to which the minister is accountable. Realizing now that his very standing as a minister is on trial, the clergyman pleads with the captain to come to his defense. The captain then confronts Teague. He gives Teague credit for quick thinking when he was caught in the attempted seduction but goes on to describe the serious consequences that have come from throwing the blame on the minister. Teague appears before the consistory and invents yet another description of the bedroom incident. He tells the gathered ecclesiastics that the young woman actually misunderstood the minister's purpose that night in the tavern. The minister had really gone to her room "to save her soul from the devil." Teague's deceit succeeds; the gathered clergy accept his story; he still manages to keep blame away from himself, and the minister is now absolved as well (54–56).

The three men in the story act as most of Brackenridge's contemporary readers would have expected them to act. The captain and Teague are typical freewheeling adventurers who know how to survive in the unregulated society that characterized the New World. The minister, in contrast, is naive and helpless. He is not at all able to withstand the challenges of life in this world, especially in the new America. His skills, as the captain suggests, equip him only for a significant role in "the other world." In fact, he avoids disaster only because the worldly-wise captain and his Irish sidekick Teague rescue him.

The cultural image of ministers that Brackenridge portrays in *Modern Chivalry* reflects a theme that often appears in late-eighteenth- and early-nineteenth-century American fiction: the Old World, especially England, is like a garden; America, by contrast, is a wilderness. Society in the garden is orderly and regulated; society in the wilderness is unrestrained, often disorderly.[2] In the ordered garden society, everyone's place is assumed, established, protected. Society in the New World offers no such guarantees. Here only the fit and worldly-wise survive. No one's place, including the minister's, is guaranteed. Everyone must make his or her own place—and cultivated, "hothouse," Old World clergy are simply not up to the task.

The frequent characterization of Old World scholar ministers as inept in early American fiction suggests that, even before the Revolution, many Americans believed that ministers shaped according to Old World models of ministry were out of their element in the New World. Following a pattern recorded most notably in George Herbert's popular manual *The Country Parson* (ca. 1630), these learned clerics give preeminent attention to academic preparation. Superior scholarship is essential to their ministry: their professional authority rests on their knowledge of the "classics" in general and of theology in particular. Relentless study equips them to carry out what they view as the primary responsibility of ministers of God: to set forth "right" belief and to identify and correct wrong belief. Even when they appear in their most public performing role, as preachers, their preaching is valued according to its doctrinal correctness. They may or may not move their hearers, but they *must* be sound.[3]

In *Swallow Barn* (1832), John Pendleton Kennedy presents a Southern version of the Old World minister who is a misfit in the New. *Swallow Barn* is set in the Tidewater area of Virginia and describes plantation life before the Revolution and the opening of the Western frontier. Mr. Chub, the Presbyterian minister who appears several times in the novel, is a bookish, eccentric, and largely irrelevant clergyman. He gives most of his attention and time to his library. Mr. Chub, immersed in the ancient world his books reflect, is out of touch with the living world around him. His reading is confined "entirely to the learning of the ancients. . . . He has never read any politics of a later date than the time of the Emperor Constantine—not even a newspaper" (65, 66). When he is not engaged in scholarly activities, Chubb spends most of his time in tedious conversations with socially defenseless young women, who are the only residents of Swallow Barn willing to tolerate him.

Inept Old World ministers like Mr. Chub are often parodied in American novels during the first half of the nineteenth century. Mr. Grant, who appears in James Fenimore Cooper's *The Pioneers* (1823), and Mr. Worden, who appears in Cooper's *Satanstoe* (1845), struggle to overcome old models and to discover ways of ministry adequate to the needs and conditions of life in the New World. Mr. Grant shows some admirable qualities. He is a genuinely dedicated minister who willingly accepts poverty as a missionary pastor. He has learned much by careful study of "the great book of human nature" (115). But these strengths do not compensate for Mr. Grant's misguided assumption that his imported ways of ministry are entirely sufficient for ministry in the New World. That overconfidence earns him a deserved rebuff during an exchange with Natty Bumppo, the archetypal Native American in Cooper's novels:

> "This [world] is but time [Mr. Grant tells Natty Bumppo] . . . but I would have you prepare for eternity. It is incumbent on you to attend places of public worship, as I am pleased to see that you have done this evening. Would it not be heedless in you to start on a day's toil of hard hunting, and leave your ramrod and flint behind?"
>
> "It must be a young hand in the woods," interrupted Natty, with another laugh, "that didn't know how to dress a rod out of an ash sapling or find a fire-stone in the mountains. No, no, I never expected to live forever; but I see times be altering in these mountains from what they was thirty years ago, or, for that matter, ten years. . . . I never knowed preaching come into a settlement but it made game scarce, and raised the price of gunpowder; and that's a thing that's not easily made as a ramrod or an Indian flint."
>
> The divine, perceiving that he had given his opponent an argument by his own unfortunate selection of a comparison, very prudently relinquished the controversy; although he was fully determined to resume it at a more happy moment. (*The Pioneers*, 123, 124)

Mr. Grant's difficulty is much more basic than an "unfortunate selection of a comparison." He lacks the essential knowledge and skills required to minister effectively in the New World. And he never gains the insight or skills that would enable him to be more effective because he assumes that his Old World theological thinking and style of ministry are superior to the "primitive" culture of those who live in America. In the New World, Mr. Grant's supposed superiority is neither self-evident nor, as he discovers in the exchange with Natty, easy to demonstrate. Those who share his European cultural roots and prejudice continue to give him a place of honor, but he gains no honored place and very little respect from those to whom the "wilderness" is home. As the novel progresses, even the European Americans begin to wonder whether this representative of the Old World can be effective in the New.[4]

Mr. Worden in *Satanstoe* is a less-rigid, sometimes even earthy, character, who mixes easily with ordinary people; he even bets at horse races and attends cockfights. But that relaxed personal style does not carry over into matters of ministerial practice or dress; in these matters, Mr. Worden is not at all adaptable. For example, he insists on wearing clerical garb in every situation. The younger Mr. Littlepage, the narrator in *Satanstoe*, describes how those who leave the streets of New York and Albany to travel in the forest put on clothing suited to the woods. Whenever they enter the forest, the men wear buckskin breeches, gaiters, and moccasins. Cocked hats are laid aside in favor of forest caps. The women wear beaver hats and shorter skirts that enable them to walk more easily in the woods. Everyone adapts—except Mr. Worden:

> As for the divine, he was so great a stickler for appearances, he would have worn the gown and surplice, even on a mission to the Indians, which, by the way, was ostensibly his present business. . . .
>
> "The first thing is to teach men to respect holy things, my dear sir, and a clergy man in his gown and surplice, commands threefold the respect of one without them." . . .
>
> It was in consequence of these opinions, that the divine travelled in his clerical hat, clerical coat, black breeches, and band, even when in pursuit of the souls of red men, among the wilds of North America! (286)

While Mr. Worden's misfit is often humorous, the inability to adapt one's style of ministry to address life in the New World leads to more serious consequences for Parson Amen in *The Oak Openings* (1848). Initially, Parson Amen seems to be just another one of the opinionated clergymen who are so common in Cooper's novels. He insists, for example, that the Native Americans are the lost tribes of Israel and refuses to consider any evidence that contradicts that perspective. But Parson Amen is not just another inflexible minister. His beliefs are firm, not rigid; his primary commitment is not to defend a set of holy ideas but to act as a person of faith, regardless of personal cost. Cooper suggests that Parson Amen is able to escape the bigoted moralism that misfits so many American clergy for ministry in the New World because he is not formally educated to follow the Old World ministerial model. Amen's primary concern is not doctrinal correctness but the witness his life bears to those with whom he lives.

The setting of *The Oak Openings* is the hazardous Michigan forest during the War of 1812. Surrounded by Indians in an ambush and facing certain death, Amen stands out as a person of uncompromising faith. When one of his companions urges him to bear arms against the attackers, he responds: "Think nothing of your arms, Brother Flint. . . . My means of defence come from on high; my armor is faith; and my only weapon, prayer. I shall not hesitate to use the last on this, as on all other occasions":

> Accustomed to preach and pray to these people in their own dialect, the worthy parson made a strong appeal to their charities. . . . [He] made a very happy exposition of those sublime dogmas of Christianity, which teach us to "bless those that curse us," and "to pray for those who despitefully use us." Peter [an Indian chief who already was acquainted with Parson Amen], for the first time in his life, was now struck by the moral beauty of such a sentiment, which seldom fails, when duly presented, of producing an effect on even the dullest minds. (395)

Though they are moved by his preaching, Peter and the other chiefs cannot separate Amen from the people he represents. They condemn him to death. Before the sentence is carried out, they agree to grant him "a few minutes for prayer to [his] God." At the end of this prayer, the parson

> prayed for his enemies. The language used was his mother tongue [English], but Peter comprehended most of that which was said. He heard his own people prayed for; he heard his own name mentioned, as the condemned man asked the mercy of the Manitou in his behalf. Never before was the soul of this extraordinary savage so shaken. . . . Here was an exemplification in practice of that divine spirit of love and benevolence which had struck him, already, as so very wonderful. There could be no mistake. There was the kneeling captive, and his words, clear, distinct, and imploring, ascended through the cover of the bushes to the throne of God. (405, 406)

When the parson finishes his prayer, the executioner carries out the sentence with the single blow of a tomahawk. But instead of mutilating this "enemy," as was customary, they carefully bury the parson's body. They are deeply moved by the living witness of a godly man.

Parson Amen is an exceptional cleric in Cooper's novels. Most of the ministers that appear in his fiction are bungling misfits in the New World.[5] They uphold specific beliefs and practices of ministry not because they are effective but because they are "correct."

Harsh Puritans and Fanatical Calvinists

The same attitudes that inspired early-nineteenth-century Americans to examine their Old World heritage encouraged them to look critically at their American past—especially at their New England forebears. The independent self-confidence that characterized this new generation of Americans was dramatically different from the controlled and controlling attitudes of the Puritans who settled New England two hundred years earlier. Nineteenth-century historians like George Bancroft reflected the liberal theology, as well as the liberal politics, of the time when they re-imaged the historical Puritans not only as courageous settlers but also as bigoted and harsh believers. Many younger novelists embodied a similar recasting in their fiction. The bigoted orthodox Calvinist pastor who appears in fiction by James Paulding, Catharine Maria Sedgwick, James Fenimore Cooper, Lydia Maria Child, and others is not a historical recollection; he is a seventeenth-century character constructed intentionally to embody a nineteenth-century cultural image.

The Rev. Roger Conant whose narrow outlook dominates the pages of Lydia Maria (Francis) Child's first novel, *Hobomok*, is a prime example. Child was a precocious twenty-two-year-old, who had been a radical feminist for nearly a decade when she completed the novel.[6] Mary Conant, the central character of the novel (in spite of its title) is at once a reflection of Child's personal experience and a heroine in the tradition of Sir Walter Scott—whose novels Child read as an adolescent. Hobomok is a wise and good Indian, much like those Lydia Francis met during her teenage years when she lived in Maine. He is similar to the Native American heroes who appear in the Leatherstocking tales of James Fenimore Cooper. Charles Brown, Mary's lover, is an Anglican who embodies the depth and benefits of the Old World high culture that narrow Puritans like Mary's father reject. Mary's mother, who dies when Mary is a teenager, offers Mary the only care and understanding she receives as a child. Even when her oppressive father subjects Mary's mother to emotional abuse, she continues to function as his dutiful wife. The simple, uncomplicated nature of the characters in *Hobomok* reflects Child's youth and inexperience as a writer. But their relative simplicity also makes them unusually clear reflections of the cultural images on which they are based.

The plot of Child's novel resembles an old-fashioned melodrama. Mary is deeply in love with Charles Brown. Roger, her father, does his utmost to thwart Charles and Mary's relationship; he sees Charles as the personification of the corrupt Old World culture and religion which he and other Puritans have come to the New World to escape. Mary's sole emotional support at home comes from her sickly mother, who sympathizes with Mary's love for Charles but cannot offer open support because she is unwilling to oppose Mary's father. Convinced that Mary's father will never agree to their marriage, Charles leaves on a journey. Soon after he departs, Mary's mother dies. A few months later, the news arrives that Charles's ship and all aboard have been lost at sea. Overwhelmed with grief by the loss of both her mother and her lover, Mary flees into the forest with Hobomok and becomes his wife.

Roger's oppressive theology leads him to conclude that Mary's departure and marriage to Hobomok resulted from a lapse in his own faith. He interprets her leaving as God's punishment for wondering, as he watched Mary grieve for her lost lover, whether he should have allowed her to marry Charles. Events take an unexpected turn when the report of Charles's death turns out to be false. Hobomok is the first to discover that Charles is alive when he meets Charles on a forest path. Though Hobomok is tempted to kill Charles, he recognizes that Charles is Mary's true love. Hobomok emerges as the most selfless character in the novel when he spares Charles, divorces Mary, and disappears forever into the forest so that she may rejoin her true love. As the story ends, Roger sets aside his narrow Calvinism just long enough to perform the marriage ceremony for Charles and his daughter.

The Rev. Roger Conant is an unusually transparent reflection of the nineteenth-century cultural image of the fanatical Calvinist. Roger is controlled by an inflexible set of beliefs that narrow and ultimately distort his perception of both God and the world around him. He rejects the natural world and all sensual experience. He refuses to recognize any benefits from higher culture and turns his back on his own English cultural heritage. He views religious ceremonies that include any sensual or artistic elements as corrupted and corrupting. Roger Conant's narrow dogmatism is pervasive. He perceives all aspects of the natural and cultural worlds as frivolous, distracting, and corrupting. He has no tolerance for any beliefs that differ from his own.

Perhaps the most outrageous portrayal of the bigoted Calvinist in an American novel is James Fenimore Cooper's Meek Wolfe, who appears in *The Wept of Wish-Ton-Wish* (1829). Meek Wolfe's name offers a clue to his character: while this minister may initially appear to be meek, he is really a wolf. The novel is set in early colonial Connecticut, during the time of King Philip's War, a brutal struggle that began in June 1675 and brought horrendous suffering to Native Americans and European colonists alike. The Rev. Meek Wolfe plays a key role in the novel. He inherits religious authority in the settlement after the withdrawal of Mark Heathcote, a wise and gentle patriarch. When the settlement comes under attack, Conanchet, one of the attackers, takes the Heathcote family as prisoners. Their desperate plight moderates when Conanchet recognizes Mark Heathcote and recalls the kindly treatment he received from Mark years before. In gratitude for their kindness, Conanchet releases Mark and his family.

Meek Wolfe, however, refuses to recognize Conanchet's generosity. Wolfe views all Native Americans as ungodly people and sees himself as commissioned by God to eliminate them. When the Indians attack as the settlers gather for worship, Wolfe's true character emerges. The minister moves from his pulpit to stand at the front of the army and leads his parishioners into battle: "In one hand he bore a Bible, which he raised on high as the sacred standard of his followers, and in the other he brandished a short broadsword in a manner that proved there might be danger in encountering its blade. The volume was open, and at brief intervals the divine read in a high and excited voice such passages as accidentally met his eye" (251). This chilling picture of Pastor Wolfe, sword in hand, urging his parishioners onward into battle as he yells out Bible verses, is unforgettable.

What produces the kind of bigotry represented by the fictional Roger Conant and Meek Wolfe? Why do the Puritans who leave the Old World to escape religious persecution so quickly become persecutors themselves? Portrayals of Puritan clergy in early American fiction suggest two possible explanations for the Puritans' bigotry: the Puritans' limited understanding of religious freedom, and the extreme suffering that marks their early experience as colonists in America.

A careful reading of the historical sources reveals that the Puritans who settled New England did not believe in *individual* religious freedom. They came to America seeking the freedom to worship God in *their* way, but they believed their way was the way mandated by the Bible. The Puritans never advocated absolute religious freedom. They recalled the state-imposed religion of the Church of England as evil, but they did not view state-imposed religion per se as evil. They came to the New World to escape "the union of the state with the wrong church."[7] They saw *their* church and *their* theology as absolutely correct—and they viewed all those outside their church who did not share their rigid beliefs as wrong, bad, and at times even dangerous. Once they gained political authority, the Puritans saw nothing wrong with using that authority to restrain those who did not share the Puritan religious perspective.

But even the Puritans' limited understanding of religious freedom does not justify their extreme bigotry. Is it simply "the nature of man," asks one of the characters in John Neal's 1828 novel *Rachel Dyer*, for "the persecuted of today [to] become the persecutors of tomorrow?" (35). Or was there something distinctive in the early Puritan's experience in the New World that hardened them and transformed them into severe humans and harsh believers? Lydia Child hints at that possibility in *Hobomok*. When an old acquaintance visits the Rev. Roger Conant, he is amazed at the difference between the man he now sees and the Roger Conant he had known many years before:

> He gave me a cordial welcome; but after the numerous greetings had passed, as I slowly walked by his side, I thought his cheerful countenance had assumed an unusual expression of harshness. He had indeed met with much to depress his native buoyancy of heart. . . . Frustrated in his plans, thwarted by his rivals, misanthropy and gloom sunk deep down into the soul of this disappointed man. (8)

The psychological slant in Child's explanation may appeal to modern readers, but it is unusual among her contemporaries. It likely reflects her personal difficulties with her own father more than her observation of the Puritan experience.[8] Nineteenth-century novelists more often located the source of the harshness that marked the Puritan character in their common sufferings. The harshness in their collective character was shaped by the harshness of their environment. Catharine Maria Sedgwick describes the shaping process in her 1826 novel *Hope Leslie*: "The terrific obstacles they faced, and the hardships they endured, gave their characters a seriousness and solemnity, heightened, it may be, by the severity of their religious faith" (15). The Puritans suffered profoundly during the first decades they lived in the New World. That suffering exacted a price. As the years and generations passed, the Puritans became a stern, severe, and hardened people. In their case, the expense of fortitude was intolerance.[9] The demands of life in the New World transformed Puritans like Meek Wolfe and Roger Conant into harsh and intolerant believers.

Characterizing the Puritans' bigotry as a corruption of their true character served two purposes: it protected the cultural image of the Puritans as folk heroes and explained their fanaticism. The first generation to settle New England, the Founding Fathers, remained heroic believers—in Hawthorne's words, "those blessed fathers of the land, who rank in our veneration next to the evangelists of Holy Writ."[10] Bigotry was a failing of succeeding generations: "The first settlers brought with them genial influences, the refining culture, of a high state of civilization. The next generation were sterner and harsher men."[11] The harsh, bigoted, Puritan minister who appears in so many nineteenth-century novels is almost always a second- or third-generation Puritan. He is a fallen Calvinist who embodies the decline of Puritanism. As a spoiled believer, the second- or third-generation

Puritan minister became a vehicle that nineteenth-century novelists could use to criticize what they viewed as the inherently narrow and fanatical nature of Calvinism. They could image Puritan ministers of succeeding generations as bigots to point up what they saw as the corrupting nature of Calvinism without attacking the popular, widely accepted image of the Founding Fathers as American folk heroes.

The way nineteenth-century novelists portray victims of bigoted Calvinist clerics also honors the myth of decline. In his historical study of nineteenth-century novelists, *Hawthorne and the Historical Romance of New England*, Michael Davitt Bell describes the formula thinking that early-American writers reflect as they characterize good and bad believers, villains and rescuers, heroes and heroines. Second- and later-generation Puritan clergy like Meek Wolfe (*The Wept of Wish-Ton-Wish*), Roger Conant (*Hobomok*), and Thomas Moxon (Josiah G. Holland's *The Bay-Path*) are bad bigots; young, innocent, pious women like Naomi (Eliza Buckminster Lee's *Naomi*), Mary Conant (*Hobomok*), and Mary Pynchon (*The Bay-Path*) are victims who suffer under the ministers' narrow rule. Anglican lay people like Charles Brown (*Hobomok*) and clergy like William Blaxton (John Lothrop Motley's *Merry-Mount*, 1849) are invariably portrayed as good; so are exceptional Calvinist ministers like George Burroughs (*Rachel Dyer*) and John Eliot (*Hope Leslie*).

Burroughs, the minister in *Rachel Dyer*, goes to the defense of women he believes are unjustly accused of witchcraft. He is then accused of being a witch himself and pays with his life for his tolerance. In *Hope Leslie*, Sedgwick describes the unusual characteristics that make John Eliot different from other Puritan clergy. As Magawisca, an unjustly accused Indian woman is led from prison to stand trial before the magistrates, a "man of middle age walked beside her, whose deep set and thoughtful eye, pale brow, ascetic complexion, and spare person, indicated a life of self-denial, and of physical and mental labour, while an expression of love, compassion, and benevolence seemed like the seal of his Creator affixed to declare him a minister to his creatures" (282). When someone asks who Eliot is, a bystander responds, "That gentleman, sir, is the 'apostle of New-England,' though it much offendeth his modesty to be so called" (282). Neal and Sedgwick are careful to define George Burroughs and John Eliot as untypical Calvinists. When Eliot appears later in *Naomi*, Lee describes him as unique among Calvinists because he possesses "a tenderness of heart opposed to the dogmas of his creed" (282).[12] Burroughs and Eliot are exceptions that prove the rule.

By the middle of the nineteenth century, the myth of decline was well established in American culture, and the narrow Calvinist divine who embodies that myth is the dominant representative of Calvinism in American fiction. From midcentury on, nearly all Calvinist ministers who appear in American novels, regardless of the time in which the novel is set, are characterized as bigots or fanatics, or both. Some of the fanatics are downright frightening. In an act reminiscent of the crucifixion, Dudley Rainsford, the Calvinist minister in James Kirke Paulding's *Westward Ho!* (1832) offers his fiancée Virginia as a blood sacrifice to appease the Almighty! Ministers in Paulding's earlier novel *Koningsmarke, the Long Finne* (1823) and his later novel *The Puritan and His Daughter* (1849) are not as gruesome as Rainsford, but they are equally bigoted. So is Mr. Parris, the Calvinist pastor in John DeForest's *Witching Times* (1857). Even such a popular mid-nineteenth-century novelist as Mrs. Emma D. E. N. Southworth reflects the conventional perception of Calvinists. Adam Hawk, an orthodox Calvinist who appears in her *Virginia and Magdalene* (1852), revels in his vision of damned souls in the hellfire. By midcentury, the re-imaging of Calvinists is complete; "Calvinist" and "bigot" and "fanatic" are contained within the same cultural image.

Scoundrels in Collars

During the first half of the nineteenth century, ministers who are scoundrels were as common in American novels as ministers with faulty theology. A scoundrel minister plays a prominent role in one of the earliest post-Revolution novels, Hannah Webster Foster's *The Coquette* (1797). When he first appears in the story, the Rev. J. Boyer seems to be a person of impeccable character. But his true self emerges as the novel progresses. Mr. Boyer is actually a self-righteous moralist who uses people—and then casts them aside when they no longer serve his needs.

The Coquette consists of an exchange of letters among the major characters: Eliza Wharton; members of her family; her two suitors, Pastor Boyer and Major Peter Sanford; and their friends. In the early letters, Mr. Boyer seems to be the suitor who will make the better husband for Miss Wharton. Major Sanford's letters to a friend reveal that his intentions are not at all honorable; he simply wants to seduce Eliza. Eliza's family and friends are well aware of the major's reputation and his likely motive in pursing her. They urge her to reject his advances and to accept the minister's proposal.

But Eliza is not convinced that becoming a minister's wife leads to the ideal state her friends and family envision:

> I recoil at the thought of immediately forming a connection which must confine me to the duties of domestic life, and make me dependent for happiness, perhaps too, for substance, upon a class of people, who will claim the right of scrutinizing every part of my conduct, and by censuring those foibles, which I am conscious of not having the prudence to avoid, may render me completely miserable. (29)

Eliza decides to take her chances with the major rather than become a pastor's wife and embark on a life that she is certain will make her "completely miserable."

Eliza's rejection brings out Mr. Boyer's true character. In a public pronouncement, he declares that her unwillingness to accept life as a minister's wife reveals moral weakness. He accuses her of choosing Major Sanford because she has "an aversion to the sober, rational, frugal mode of living to which my profession leads." He then proceeds to scold her: "There is a levity in your manners, which is inconsistent with the solidity and decorum becoming a lady who has arrived to years of discretion. There is also an unwarrantable extravagance betrayed in your dress. . . . Too large a portion of your time is devoted to the adorning of your person." This criticism is not "from resentment" but, rather, "from benevolence. I mention your foibles, not to reproach you with them, but that you may consider their nature and effects, and renounce them" (83–85).

When Eliza ignores his advice, the tragic end the minister forecasts comes to pass. Major Sanford abuses her and abandons her. She dies alone, a ruined woman. But Eliza's death is neither the only nor the most significant moral of this story (though the tragedy that comes to Eliza after she elects to become the major's mistress no doubt made the novel acceptable for publication in 1797). The minister is the real villain in the novel. His public condemnation makes Eliza's downfall inevitable. He judges her and condemns her publicly. When she is cast out by Major Sanford, Mr. Boyer refuses to come to her aid. He feels no obligation to help her, nor, in his view, should anyone else. She who rejected him as her husband deserves the fate that befalls her. His supercilious moral posture seals her fate. The callous, self-righteous Mr. Boyer is really a scoundrel in a collar. His attitude toward women and his behavior with Eliza are as questionable as the major's. Both men view Eliza functionally. They want to use her: the major to gratify his sexual desires; the minister to gratify his social needs. Eliza's views reciprocate those of the men; she views *both* coquette and minister's wife as victim roles. Mr. Boyer responds viciously when she refuses to submit to him: he characterizes her publicly as a fallen woman and in so doing ensures that she will perish as a coquette. He takes great pains to explain his actions in such a way that they maintain his image as a good man. But his attitude and behavior demonstrate that he is really a scoundrel.

The proliferation of opportunists posing as clergy in American fiction reflects the massive social and economic changes that disrupted and transformed American society during the early decades of the nineteenth century. From the arrival of the first European settlers until nearly the end of the eighteenth century, the family, the local community, and the churched regulated the daily lives of most Americans. All three were vertically ordered institutions with primary authority vested in an institutional head: the father, the selectman, and the minister. Social relationships were marked by deference to these weighty characters; their authority was rarely challenged. This largely vertical social structure persisted as long as most people lived in stable communities where everyone could be known and where face-to-face relationships dominated.[13] Industrial growth and urbanization during the early decades of the nineteenth century undercut the old social structure. Manufacturing challenged agriculture as the major source of employment; rural villages grew into factory towns. In the opening pages of her novel *Fall River* (1833), Catharine Read Williams describes the effects of this social disruption in one typical community. In 1812, Fall River was a small settlement that contained "[fewer] than one hundred inhabitants." The land in and around the village was used primarily to support agriculture, and most of it belonged to three families. By 1833, just twenty-one years later, there were thirteen factories in Fall River, with "at least forty thousand spindles in operation." The little village had become a small city: "The number of inhabitants at the present date [1833] is said to exceed five thousand" (8).

The change that transformed Fall River transformed hundreds of places like it between 1820 and 1850. In each of them, the stable social setting where everyone was known and held accountable by familiarity was replaced by a mobile social world composed mostly of strangers. The anonymity the new urbanized towns provided undermined the old system of social accountability that regulated the behavior of public officials and other community leaders in the small villages and rural countryside that preceded them. Traditional institutions that were effective agents of social control in small communities faltered in the factory towns. Most of the daily life of most people was now beyond the scrutiny of fathers, ministers, and selectmen.

The massive growth of American cities in the early decades of the nineteenth century rendered them even more impersonal than the new factory towns. Those who emigrated from the countryside to large cities to escape rural poverty found even less opportunity in cities. That deprivation only worsened as the years passed. In Philadelphia, for example, between 1800 and 1860, the share of the city's wealth controlled by the most affluent 1 percent grew from less than one-quarter to one-half; during the same years, the share owned by the poorest 75 percent declined from about one-third to about one-thirtieth.[14]

This weakening of institutions that maintained established social order and moral boundaries gave unscrupulous persons more opportunities to take advantage of the vulnerable. In a social world composed mostly of strangers, it became more difficult to distinguish those who pretended to be ministers from those who were genuine. Contemporary fiction presents clerical confidence men as masters of deception. These scoundrels in collars pretend to be concerned about their victims, but their real aim is to take advantage of them. "Advice manuals" describe the methods of con men and warn those new to the city about the hazard they pose. They caution the unsuspecting that the confidence man's goal is not just to rob them or seduce them but, rather, to gain "total mastery" over them. Confidence men employ "influence," a mysterious force similar to the "magnetism" used by mesmerizers. Once in control, con men corrupt their victim's character. The victim is then at the con man's mercy; his or her downfall is certain.[15] Sophy, who appears in Southworth's *The Deserted Wife* (1855), describes her futile struggle to resist the mesmerizing Mr. Withers. As she slips under the evil minister's spell, she cries out "helplessly": "Oh, *what* is this? What is closing around me like irresistible destiny? Why cannot I awake, arouse from this? I know I'm free; *why* can't I use my freedom? What a spell, what a mystery, what a horror! Oh! My Heavenly Father!" (94).[16]

Williams's *Fall River* describes a minister's abuse of a young, single factory worker. The novel is presented as a "true story." When it opens, Sarah Cornell, a "factory girl," has just discovered she is pregnant. She visits a local doctor to seek assistance. He discovers she is unmarried and presses her to disclose the identity of the child's father. The young woman refuses to offer any details other than the fact that he is a Methodist minister. The doctor pieces together the accumulating evidence and realizes the seducer is the Rev. E. K. Avery, the local Methodist minister. He asks Miss Cornell if she has seen Avery since she discovered her pregnancy. She responds that he met her briefly on the meetinghouse steps and urged her to take thirty drops of oil of tansy, assuring her that it would "obliterate the effects of their connection." The physician is appalled; that amount would have killed her! Again he presses Miss Cornell to seek justice from Mr. Avery, and again she refuses. Against his better judgment, the doctor honors his vow of confidentiality and tells no one what he has discovered (20, 21).

In only a few weeks, the doctor's worst fears transpire: a local farmer finds Sarah Cornell's frozen body in a ditch. A "hasty and irregular jury" conducts a perfunctory inquest. They issue a verdict of suicide. However, when some women who volunteer to prepare her body for burial remove Sarah Cornell's clothes, they discover clear evidence that she was assaulted and likely beaten to death. This new information encourages a more thorough investigation. The evidence from that inquiry implicates Mr. Avery. He is charged with assault and murder and is brought to trial in both the civil and ecclesiastical courts. The parade of witnesses who testify at the long civil trial compromise the characters of both the victim and the minister. Though the testimony of nearly every witness indicates that Mr. Avery is responsible for Sarah Cornell's death, the jury in the civil court finds him not guilty. The townspeople are outraged by the verdict. But they take no action against the minister because they believe that the ecclesiastical court will act more responsibly than the civil court and will remove Mr. Avery from the ministry. They don't. The church court judges him "perfectly innocent and freed from all suspicion, and continues him in the service of his office" (61).

Williams's novel reflects concerns and attitudes that are characteristic of upper-middle-class, educated woman and men during the early decades of the nineteenth century. Williams regrets and fears the economic and social changes that are transforming rural villages into factory towns. These transforming changes lead to social and moral breakdown. Those who occupy positions of authority in factory towns like Fall River lack both the will and the integrity needed to keep moral order. Social relationships that are regulated only by appearance encourage an inferior class of ministers. These new preachers lack not only the gifts they need to fill the responsibilities of ministry but also the kind of maturity, class, scholarship, and self-control that ministers need to carry out their office. The author describes one such minister she observed preaching at a camp meeting: "He was exhorting the people to repentance with great vehemence and gesticulation. The bad English he used provoked many a smile from his hearers, while another class of his hearers seemed to listen with profound attention" (155). Williams argues that this kind of minister is more likely to abuse than help those who respond to his appeals. She obviously views "sectarian" clergy and revivalists *as a class* as low-quality and often-unscrupulous preachers.[17]

Catharine Williams is not the only contemporary small-town novelist who views sectarian ministers with a jaundiced eye. In the anonymously published novel *Retroprogression* (1839), every sectarian minister who appears is a person of questionable character; only those connected with the formerly established churches are portrayed as ministers with integrity. Questionable behavior is the norm among sectarian ministers who cater to the new working class. Even sectarian clergy who are not cast as scoundrels are depicted as inept—like the Methodist minister Hector Wigler meets in *The Yankee Traveller* (1817). He is not morally bad; he is simply incompetent. The anonymous author describes him as a preacher with "a bawling sort of eloquence" whose specialty is "groaning."[18]

Most scoundrel ministers simply use their clerical identity to take advantage of the innocent. *The Life and Adventures of Obadiah Benjamin Franklin Bloomfield, M.D.* (1818) begins with Bloomfield's feigned conversion. The shallow reality of Bloomfield's "conversion" quickly becomes apparent. He gives up the practice of law to become a minister but refuses to make any proper preparation for the ministry. Instead, he "learns the art of popular preaching from Mr. Method, an unlearned but successful revivalist."[19] His wife then discovers that

> it was her person not her mind that he thirsted after. . . . Soon cloyed with the possession of that, he . . . had the cruelty to keep her maid under her very nose. . . . It even afforded him peculiar delight to scoff at religion in her presence, and denounce the Holy Bible, pronouncing it the handy-work of certain interested imposters and fanatics. . . . He seduced her only sister—the wife of his most intimate friend, and killed that friend in a duel! (10, 11)

The Rev. Deodat Pigeon who appears in the anonymous *The Confessions of a Magdalene* (1831) is even more despicable than Bloomfield. He drugs the innocent Experience Borgia and then seduces her. He murders her child after it is born—and, like A. K. Avery, is acquitted of the crime by a jury of his peers. In Sedgwick's *Redwood* (1824), Reuben Harrington, a Shaker minister, kidnaps a young woman and then, like Pigeon and Avery, abuses her.[20] By the 1840s, even clergy from the formerly established churches are no longer portrayed in fiction as categorically superior. Superior education and social class are not sufficient to guarantee a minister's integrity. Mr. Bullneck, the Congregational minister who appears in Aesop's *The Hypocrite* (1844), is "a man of no ordinary acquirements as a scholar," yet even he is described as "wicked beyond a parallel" (38).

Antebellum fiction suggests that scoundrel ministers were at least as prevalent in rapidly growing American cities as they were in factory towns. A group of sensational and sometimes openly erotic novels detail the horrors of big city life.[21] George Thompson (1823–ca. 1873) was one of the most prolific writers of pulp fiction "documenting" city life from the 1830s to the 1860s.[22] Thompson offers only a feeble pretense of either literary or moral purpose in his novels. In a typical Thompson novel, only one character is clearly defined as a moral or ethical person, and this character is usually marginalized or rendered impotent by the degradation that surrounds him or her.[23]

As far as I am aware, *all* the ministers who appear in Thompson's fiction are scoundrels in collars. The Rev. Balaam Flanders, the Methodist minister in *City Crimes* (1849), is typical. Readers first glimpse his immorality through the eyes of a twelve-year-old girl. Mr. Flanders frequently calls on the girl's mother during the day when her father is at his business. The young woman becomes suspicious of the true purpose of the pastor's visits when she notices that her mother sometimes emerges from their "long and private conferences" with "disordered apparel and disarranged hair." Determined to confirm her suspicions, during the pastor's next visit she goes quietly to an adjoining room and watches through a keyhole as the pastor and her mother make love. Though initially she is too timid to confront either the pastor or her mother, she becomes bolder as she matures. As the pastor's behavior toward her becomes more and more lecherous, the young woman plots her revenge. She continues to attend Mr. Flanders's Bible classes for young people, even though he keeps her afterward and fondles her breasts. She leads him on, pretending she is unable to resist his amorous behavior. When her parents reveal they will be out of town on the coming New Year's Eve, the young woman plots the culmination of her revenge. She casually mentions the fact to Mr. Flanders—certain that he will call on her. A scene of frustrated seduction unfolds when he does. She permits the minister to sit next to her on the sofa. She lets him proceed with her body "just far enough to set his passions ablaze" and then rebuffs him. He pleads with her: "Dear girl . . . , why need you be so cruel as to deny me the pleasure of love? Consider, I am your minister, and cannot sin: it will therefore be no sin for you to favor me" (116). She appears to give in to his appeal and then rebuffs him again. She taunts him: from across the room, she exposes her shoulders and then her breasts. The tormented man falls on his knees and begs her to favor him. She replies that he is a despicable man and that she would prefer even the vilest lover to him—and then dismisses him into the night. When her father and mother return, she tells her father about Mr. Flanders's attempted seduction and about his sexual relationship with her mother. Her father then entraps the minister with her mother the next time he calls and exposes him.

Dr. Sinclair, the Episcopal priest in *City Crimes*, is an even more pathetic character than the reverend rake Mr. Flanders. Both Josephine Franklin, who facilitates Dr. Sinclair's downfall, and her mother are loose, immoral women. Josephine's affair with Dr. Sinclair begins when he meets her at a masquerade. She is disguised as a "Royal Middy," and he pretends to be the ambassador from Spain. When they are alone in conversation, the disguised minister propositions her. Josephine says that she is willing to accept. The minister asks her to remove her disguise. She says she will happily comply if he removes his as well. When they drop their masks, Josephine is amazed to discover that the ambassador is none other than "Dr Sinclair, the pious and eloquent rector of St. Paul's." Dr. Sinclair is even more startled to recognize the royal middy is one of his parishioners! But he rationalizes the discovery and proceeds with the seduction. Later as they part, Josephine agrees to keep their relationship a secret. The two of them begin a long affair.

Little does Dr. Sinclair know that Josephine had long regarded him with "eyes of desire;—*hers* was the conquest . . . and *he* was the victim" (172). As the months pass, the priest's immorality with Josephine takes its toll on him. He seems increasingly "ill at ease" to his parishioners. His preaching is not up to "his usual fluent and fervid eloquence. . . . In person, too, he was changed; his eyes were red, as if with weeping; his cheeks were pale and haggard, and the rosy hue of health was gone" (212). After one long evening together, Dr. Sinclair leaves Josephine's home quite drunk. On his way home, he challenges a watchman, who fells him with his nightstick and hauls him off to jail where he spends the night. In the morning, the discomfited priest is able to convince the magistrate to release him only by revealing that he is the rector of St. Paul's. Shortly after this incident, Dr. Sinclair is called to minister to a dying woman. Her deathbed confession reveals that Josephine and her mother actually perpetrated the murder of Josephine's father. The remorse he now suffers over his relationship with Josephine drives him even more to drink. When his condition becomes public knowledge, he is removed from his pulpit. Deprived of his means to earn a living, he is soon reduced to poverty. One evening as he wanders the streets, he is murdered.

Dr. Sinclair is a much more developed character than the usual Thompson cleric. When he first appears, he seems to be just another reverend rake, but as his affair with Josephine progresses, he becomes more pathetic. His infatuation with her becomes an obsession that leads him deeper and deeper into moral decline. His faith (which Thompson never actually describes) does not enable him to overcome his weaknesses. Thompson's characterization exhibits a psychological complexity that will be even more highly developed in Nathaniel Hawthorne's fictional ministers.[24]

George Lippard, a contemporary of George Thompson, also published a number of novels that detail the misdeeds of urban clergy. Like Thompson's, Lippard's novels were extremely popular. Over sixty thousand copies of *The Quaker City* were sold when it appeared in 1844; ten thousand additional copies were sold each year for the next decade.[25] Lippard's career as a social reformer was as impressive as his career as a writer—and lends credibility to his protest that he wrote sometimes-scandalous exposes of urban life to motivate others to address these abuses with social and economic reforms. During his lifetime, Lippard founded a reform newspaper and a radical labor organization, which within four years had 150 branches in twenty-four states. Lippard was also a committed feminist, who advocated economic independence for women.[26] In three novels published between 1844 and 1850—*The Quaker City* (1844), *The Memoirs of a Preacher* (1849), and *The Empire City* (1850)—Lippard offers penetrating criticism of contemporary abusive clerics. Actually, Lippard's critiques are designed to expose what he regards as an abusive social system and a corrupt religious establishment. He argues that organized religion as a whole is abusive, not just some of its leaders.

There is a literary depth and complexity in Lippard's work that raises it above the pulp fiction produced by many of his contemporaries. *The Quaker City*, for example, leads the reader through successive levels of complexity that illustrate the degrading entanglements of life in Philadelphia where the novel is set. The minister at the center of the story is the Rev. Dr. F. Altamont T. Pyne, or F. A. T. Pyne, as he is commonly known. Lippard describes Pyne as "one of those independent gentlemen who saving souls on their own particular hook, acquire degrees from some unknown college, and hold forth in some dark alley, two stories up stairs, where they preach brimstone, turpentine and Millerism, in large installments, according to the taste of their hearers" (201). From his first appearance, F. A. T. Pyne is obviously a scoundrel in a collar or, to use Lippard's words, "a fine specimen of a well-preserved dealer in popular credulity" (202). Lippard mocks both the theology and the cadence of contemporary evangelical preaching in the sermons he puts into the mouth of this pastor of the Church of True Believers and Free Repenters:

> We hold it to be a consoling belief, that of all the millions o' human bein's ever created by the Lord, three-fourths of them are roasting in the broad lake o' fire and brimstone, this very minnit! Our gospel is a gospel of fire and brimstone and abuse o' the pope o' Rome, mingled in equal quantities—about half o' one and half 'tother—that's what our Gospel is! (262)

Attacking Roman Catholics is a specialty for Pyne and his colleague, the Rev. Syllabub Scissors, editor of the *Patent-Gospel Expositor*. During a worship service at the Church of True Believers, Scissors tells a long and ludicrous story about a ship's crewmembers and passengers who visit the Vatican. Some of the visitors are supporters of the Church of True Believers. These visitors give gospel tracts critical of Catholics to the pope and cardinals. After this presumptuous gesture, nothing more is heard of them. They mysteriously disappear. "They went into the Vatican," Scissors tells the enthralled congregation, "but *they never came out again!*" Next door to the Vatican is a sausage factory. Soon after their disappearance, fragments of one of the tracts published by the Church of True Believers carried by the visitors to the Vatican appeared in sausages sent home by an American who purchased sausages from the factory: "Brothers and sisters, I will leave you to draw your own conclusions!" (265).

Though it often contains moments of intensity like this one, all of Scissors's and Pyne's fervent preaching is a masquerade. They are really scoundrels. After church services conclude, when church members think Pyne gives himself entirely to prayer and visiting the sick, he actually retreats to his secret apartment in the infamous Monks Hall. There he winks "rather viciously at the small Bible resting on the mantel-piece" as he counts the day's take "in the shape of solid gold and bank notes." He indulges in a little opium. Later in the evening, he turns from drugs to sex. He attempts to seduce Mabel, a young woman whom he and his wife have raised as their own daughter (she actually is not his daughter). In true con man fashion, he gives her a potion designed to overcome her resistance to his seduction. While Pyne waits for Mabel to fade from consciousness, he remembers he is to preach the anniversary sermon of the Gospellers on Christmas night, and he develops the sermon in his mind as he gazes lustfully at Mabel, who is slowly losing control over her body. The juxtaposition of minister and lecher is rendered even more blatant by the language Lippard chooses to describe the scene: "Dr. Pyne kissed the red lips of the girl with priest-fervor." The planned seduction fails only because the lecherous minister is interrupted by Devil-Bug, who is Mabel's true father.

Regardless of status or denomination, all of Lippard's clergy are scoundrels and rakes. Herman Barnhurst, the Episcopal priest in *The Empire City*, serves a prestigious New York parish. In his sermons, he berates the morals of the "infidels" and urges his parishioners to support missionaries to the unchristians of the world. But this public face Barnhurst presents is only a facade. Like the real-life Bishop Onderdonk of New York, who was convicted of adultery by a church court in 1845 and defrocked, Barnhurst secretly seduces women, including one young woman he discards to a bordello when he is finished with her.[27] Edmund Jervis, a Millerite who is the central character in Lippard's *The Memoirs of a Preacher*, is no better. Jervis is a lecher who drugs, seduces, and abandons a variety of women within and beyond his congregation. When he grows weary of his wife, Jervis justifies a divorce (and ruins her reputation) by spreading a false rumor that she is unfaithful. Dr. Bulgin, the Calvinist preacher in *The Empire City*, uses his great skill as a speaker to fool men as well as women. He describes the Christian religion as something to drug the masses and suggests that the church exists primarily to provide a good living and other opportunities for ministers who are smart enough to take advantage of it.

In these novels, George Lippard argues that not only their individual failures but also the nature of life as a whole in the city and the widespread belief that ministers are above temptation are to blame for the widespread corruption he portrays in his fictional clergy. In *The Memoirs of a Preacher*, Edmund Jervis pleads for sympathy as he faces the brother of a woman he has wronged:

> I am what I am. And what I am, the religion of society has made me. That religion fashions "the popular preacher." It takes the dreamy boy, whose passions are just passing into development. It plunges him into temptation. It elevates him for a few sounding words, uttered in a pulpit . . . into a mock God-head. It rouses all that is base and sensual in his heart. It brings him into contact with the wife, the daughter, the sister, and at the very moment when their minds, excited by Religion, (or what passes for Religion) behold him, not a man—like the husband, the father or the brother—but a God, clad with the powers of Heaven and hell. Is it strange that this Man thus elevated above his fellows should yield to temptation! (119, 120)

Both Lippard and Thompson argue that an idealized image of the minister places temptations before weak ministers that they cannot resist.[28]

The minister's status in American society became increasingly precarious as the firm social structure inherited from colonial times weakened. By the 1850s, a stable social order that guaranteed authority and social accountability for clergy no longer existed in many, if not most, places in the East, and it rarely characterized life on the frontier. Scoundrel ministers and con men who assumed the identity of a minister to pursue their unscrupulous purposes proliferated in the towns and cities. Their actions cast aspersions on all clergy. Conning clerics along with misfits and harsh Puritans who proliferate in popular fiction from the 1790s to the 1850s mirror the weakening image and influence of American ministers. By midcentury, merely holding the office of minister no longer guaranteed respect, much less authority. In the new America, ministers were not only less protected; their authority was increasingly precarious.

II

CLERICS IN CONTENTION

Church Images

In 1830 when Samuel Miller of Princeton Theological Seminary said he wished that novels could be banned, he probably spoke for the majority of America's clergy at the time. Miller's concern about the portrayal of ministers in American fiction was legitimate—as the novels discussed in chapter 1 attest. During the first half of the nineteenth century, novelists generally were not kind to ministers. But they were not entirely, or even mostly, to blame for the tainted images of clergy that come through in their characters. The characters that novelists invented reflect cultural images. The minister's fall described in American novels published between the 1790s and the 1850s is not fictional; it reflects a real decline in the minister's position in American society.

A variety of economic, social, and religious phenomena worked together in the first half of the century to curtail the local minister's authority.[1] Perhaps most important were the social and economic changes I allude to in the closing pages of chapter 1. In preindustrial villages, ministers associated with established churches were most often lifetime incumbents whose reputation and authority grew with each passing year. A study of Yale College graduates who entered the ministry between 1702 and 1775 reveals that 79 percent remained in one parish their entire lives, the majority for more than thirty years. Only 7 percent served more than two parishes. They were, in the words of one observer, the "ne'er to do wells."[2] This pattern persisted, though with some erosion, from 1775 to 1795; during those years, 57 percent served just one church. During the next decade, the pattern reversed completely: only 24 percent of Yale graduates between 1795 and 1805 who became ministers remained in one parish; 28 percent served four or more parishes. By the second decade of the century, the depth of the reversal was even more apparent among graduates of Andover Seminary in Massachusetts: fewer than 10 percent of those who graduated between 1815 and 1835 spent their entire ministry in one pulpit.[3]

These statistics point to a social and economic transformation that radically altered the minister's position in society. In fewer than fifty years, this social revolution changed the minister from a local official into a transient professional. Instead of being lifetime residents who occupied a place of social, intellectual, and religious authority in the life of one community, most ministers were now mobile professionals who served several congregations. The minister's primary connection was to a denomination, not a locale. The typical minister was now a church official and only a temporary resident of the community where he happened to be serving.

The official disestablishment of churches in the former colonies between 1777 and 1834 paralleled and reinforced this transformation of the minister's role. When the Declaration of Independence was signed in 1776, nine of the American colonies had established churches: Congregational in New England, and Episcopal in New York and the Old South. By law, these established churches and their clergy enjoyed privileged theological and social status. Ministers of the established churches held both a civil and an ecclesiastical office. Established churches and their clergy received tax support. Other churches (e.g., Baptists and Methodists) and their clergy enjoyed none of the privileges given to established churches. They and their clergy were viewed as dissenters and nonconformists. By 1834, the legal advantages that went with establishment were no longer available to any minister in the United States. In that year, by an act of its legislature, Massachusetts became the last state to officially disestablish its church. As the memory of ministers as civil office holders died away, ministers from the formerly established churches were left not only with the same legal standing as the former dissenters but also with the same reduced social status.

Theological shifts during the decades that followed independence also eroded the minister's authority. The predominant theology and ecclesiology of the established churches was patriarchal and authoritarian. Especially within Calvinist churches, God was commonly characterized as an unapproachable and undeniable authority. As earthly representatives of the unapproachable God, ministers were often accepted as equally undeniable authorities. That guaranteed authority became less secure with the rise of liberal and evangelical theologies. The ascendant liberal theology made God more humane and less fearsome. An evangelical image of God as one who seeks out and wants to save all sinners challenged the image of God as an unsympathetic and distant cosmic ruler. As liberal and evangelical theologies gained acceptance, God became less frightening and less threatening. The harsh God lost ground to the benevolent God.[4]

Changes in church affiliation during the first half of the nineteenth century mirrored the shift away from authoritarian theology. In 1800, only one in fifteen Americans belonged to a church; by 1850, one in every seven Americans was a church member, a significant increase. The denominational preferences of those who joined churches between 1800 and 1850 mirrored the shifts in theological preference: churches that embraced either liberal or evangelical theology accounted for *all* the increase. By 1850, Methodists boasted over 1.5 million members, Baptists over 1 million. As these churches grew, Congregationalists slipped by comparison—to only 207,608 members in 1850.[5] The socially and intellectually elite Unitarians (officially a denomination in 1825) also grew, but only to 13,350 members—mostly at the expense of the Congregationalists. Authoritarian theology associated with the formerly established churches no longer dominated the ecclesiastical landscape. Fewer Americans viewed the minister as an unassailable authority.

Many clergy were understandably not happy with the lower status and more-confined role awarded to ministers in mid-nineteenth-century America. Ministers acculturated within the formerly established churches experienced the most discomfort. In 1852, writing from Washington, D.C., to his friend and fellow clergyman William Ware, the Rev. Orville Dewey no doubt spoke for many of his middle- and upper-class clerical colleagues as he described the impotence he felt as a minister: "The gayety passes him by; the politics pass him by. Nobody wants him; nobody holds him by the button but some desperate, dilapidated philanthropist. People say, while turning a corner, 'How do you do, Doctor?' Which is very much as if they said, 'How do you do, Abstraction?'"[6]

Not all clergy responded so passively to the diminished significance Orville Dewey found so painful. Some were more aggressive. A few like Professor Samuel Miller lashed out at popular novelists who disparaged clergy. They argued that novelists offer jaded portrayals of ministers. Ministers in novels are not accurate reflections of real-life clergy. The novel is not a socially responsible medium. Novels corrupt those who read them; reading novels wastes time that should be put to more productive use. Some clerical critics even went as far as to suggest that novels have the same effect on the mind and character as alcohol and tobacco![7] This strident criticism persisted throughout the nineteenth century—with declining effect. Especially after the Civil War, clerics who berated the image of ministers in popular fiction often came across as pathetic protestors. The Rev. Mr. Sewell who appears in several novels by William Dean Howells embodies this perception of clerics as ineffective critics. Sewell is a ridiculous and at times even irresponsible character, whose opinions often have no foundation in fact. Sewell makes what more astute characters recognize as exaggerated observations, like "novels befool and debauch almost every intelligence in some degree" (*The Rise of Silas Lapham* [1885], 339). Sewell's opinions, like those of his real-life counterparts, impress only the culturally naive.

But the strident protests that real and fictional clerics like Miller and Sewell offered were neither the only nor the most-effective response to the demeaning image of ministers presented in popular novels. Beginning in the 1820s, authors who identified with a variety of churches and theological perspectives began to offer a response in kind. They created fictional ministers who reflected church images.

Fictional clergy who mirrored church images offered a concrete challenge to fictional ministers who reflected popular images. They embodied an alternative reality. Fictional ministers based on church images disputed popular belief that fictional clergy who reflected popular images were typical of all or even most real-life ministers. All ministers are not the same, the church protesters asserted; at least ministers from "our" church are different. Other ministers may not be what ministers should be or once were, but ours are. Other ministers may not deserve respect and authority, but ours do.[8]

Liberal Challengers

Most of the early novels that mirrored church images of clergy came from authors who were theological liberals.[9] Evangelicals in general were not as well educated as liberals, and they did not recognize the apologetic possibilities of fiction until after the Civil War. Liberals were more often upper- and middle-class individuals who enjoyed the advantages of education; their acculturation led more often to a sense of intellectual freedom. Theologically liberal authors tended to be more comfortable with literature in general and novels in particular. Both they and their readers perceived fiction as a more-accessible medium.

The changing image of God and godliness in American society during the early decades of the nineteenth century also worked to the liberals' advantage. As God was re-imaged as active and caring rather than as distant and judgmental, godliness underwent a similar re-imaging. Faithfulness was no longer measured primarily by adherence to specific doctrinal standards. Dynamic measures began to stand alongside cognitive measures. The behavior of its adherents became the preeminent measure of the value of a theology. Like the God they represented, ministers now had to demonstrate that they were godly by the way they lived.

Fictional clerics designed to show the superiority of liberal beliefs and the effects to which they lead appeared as early as the 1790s. Liberal ministers in these novels are always astute thinkers and caring persons; Calvinist and evangelical clergy who appear in the same novels are always blunderers or fanatics. The clergy in Royall Tyler's *The Bay Boy* (1792–97) are typical examples. An incident that reveals their different character takes place in a parish named Shingletrees. The local pastor, referred to only as "the Rev. Mr. B.," is assumed by all to be a strict Calvinist. However, one Sunday Mr. B. preaches a sermon in which he proposes that someone who simply does the works of righteousness, "charity, loving kindness, humility and chastity with all other Christian graces, might be a better Christian than he [Mr. B.] imagined himself to be" (68). The Calvinist clergy in the neighborhood are shocked to discover such liberal thinking in one they supposed to be orthodox. They ask one of their number, who is a good friend of Mr. B., to meet with him and point up his "errors." The conversation with Mr. B. goes poorly for the appointed friend. He stumbles repeatedly when he attempts to correct Mr. B.'s errors. In desperation, he suggests that the concerned colleagues might be convinced that Mr. B. is still an orthodox Calvinist if he names his next male child "Calvin." At this point, the dialogue becomes pure comedy. Mr. B. replies:

> I certainly should have no objection to any name you should propose but there is one obstacle to this *given* name. . . . My eldest boy has got a little snarling cur dog named Calvin. Now if we have two Calvins in the house the boy and the brute will be at a loss as to which we want when we call "Calvin, Calvin." If, however, you wish to have the babe bear the name of some eminent Christian, I am willing to call him Servetus which name always reminds one of the charitable Calvin. (70, 71; italics in the original)[10]

Most early fiction that promotes liberal church images is more sober. Henry Ware Jr.'s *The Recollections of Jotham Anderson* (1828) is typical. Ware's novel provides a detailed comparison of the behavioral effects of liberal theology with the behavioral effects of Calvinist theology. The central character, Jotham Anderson, is raised as a Calvinist in a pious household. In her dying moments, Jotham's mother gives him a lock of her hair and pleads that he never swerve from her orthodox Calvinist "teachings about God." Soon after his mother's death, Jotham is sent to another village to further his education. He is totally unprepared for the response he receives when he fails to represent himself clearly as an orthodox Calvinist. Jotham is unaware of the fine lines that orthodox Calvinists employ to distinguish themselves from the more liberal Arminians.[11] When the local minister and church elders ask if Jotham's family and congregation back home are orthodox or Arminian believers, he doesn't know. The examiners either do not recognize or are unwilling to excuse Jotham's lack of theological sophistication. Jotham's natural warmth and tolerance count for little with them. All that matters is his lack of exclusive commitment to orthodox Calvinist beliefs. Once they label Jotham as unorthodox, they shun him. Only a few theological rebels will be his friends.

After he has engaged the reader's sympathy by contrasting Jotham's endearing qualities with the cold mistreatment he suffers from the orthodox Calvinists, Henry Ware uses Jotham's reflections on the Calvinists' theology and behavior to thoroughly discredit them. "My blood chilled," Jotham says to a friend, "when I heard the arbitrary decree of election announced, and, connected with it, the joy of the righteous in the sufferings of the wicked" (36). Such callousness violates Jotham's sensitivity. As he matures and prepares for the ministry, Jotham struggles to maintain the promise he made to his dying mother. The contrast between the liberals' warm and tolerant theology and the orthodox Calvinists' cold and rigid belief system finally overwhelms him. He becomes a liberal believer and minister.

Liberal theology not only frees Jotham to find a satisfying faith himself but also equips him to help others struggling with the millstone of orthodoxy. Mr. Garston, one of his parishioners, explains why the doctrine of predestination led him to turn completely away from the Christian faith. Garston asks, "how can I suppose that immortal beings are formed by their Creator in a bondage so degrading and hopeless, as your system teaches—from which only a small proportion of them can ever be rescued, and they only by the sufferings and death of the Creator himself in human form?" Jotham draws on liberal theology to help Mr. Garston reconsider his apostasy:

> "I endeavoured to show him, that the objections he felt to the Christian system were, in fact, objections only to a certain mode of interpreting

> that system." . . . "For myself," said I, "I freely declare that I think it a very erroneous interpretation. I have hardly less dislike to it, than you have yourself. I think it an incredible system. But I still receive the instructions of Jesus with the greatest delight and comfort."

The new perspective helps Mr. Garston recover his faith. He reads the scripture now "with sober judgment of mature life; not interpreting it, as before, by the standard of Westminster, but by the light of a careful and sound comparison of itself with itself. . . . From this time he was an altered man. . . . His mind was at peace. He was happy" (113–18).

This fictional conversation portrays what Henry Ware obviously believes are the dastardly effects of Calvinism. And it gives him the opportunity to describe both the nature and the benefits of a more-liberal approach to theology. According to that liberal alternative, sound theology is not an enforced orthodoxy, defined for all time by some historical doctrinal statement ("the standard of Westminster"). The results of each believer's own thoughtful analysis ("a sound comparison of itself with itself"), the warmth of a believer's faith, and the quality of life to which that faith inspires those who believe it are the standards that determine whether a theology is sound. The accepted measures are rational, experiential, and behavioral; they are empirical, not doctrinal. What surely identifies someone as a Christian is not dogmatic believing but "Christian" behavior. In fact, Christian behavior is now more essential than Christian believing. An individual who demonstrates Christian character by good works deserves respect and admiration even if he or she fails the test of theological orthodoxy. Mr. Young, the pastor who stands at the center of the anonymously published novel *The Soldier's Orphan* (1812), offers one of the earliest statements of this revisionist theology:

> Whether we have any religion or not, is a question, and doubtless a momentous one, between us and our Creator; but whether we live orderly or not; whether we benefit or injure society by our conduct, are human concerns, which fall under the cognizance of the community in which we live. This distinction ought never to be overlooked. . . . The great variety of dogmas that have been adopted show the little dependence to be placed upon any. (31–33)

During the nineteenth century, well-defined empirically evident behavioral norms displaced doctrinal norms as the most common measures of faithfulness for many American Christians.[12] Faithful Christians in fiction that reflects the new perspective are self-sacrificing individuals who are content with their lot in life. They do their duty. And if suffering comes their way, they endure it without complaining—looking for lessons they can learn from adversity. Such good Christian behavior is exemplified by characters in two early novels by Sarah A. Savage: *The Factory Girl* (1814) and *Filial Affection* (1820). Unlike Henry Ware, Savage makes no attempt to cultivate the reader's sympathy for her characters before revealing their liberal beliefs. The liberal theology of Dr. Unwin, the minister at the center of *Filial Affection*, is evident in the opening pages of the book. He presents his young granddaughter Phebe with only "pleasant" images of God and shields her from all negative or harsh pictures of God: "For knowing the influence of early impressions, he was particularly desirous that her first ideas on that subject should be connected with pleasant emotions. Nothing of gloom or terror had ever mingled with his religion" (8).

Dr. Unwin maintains this positive attitude toward God even though the exterior circumstances of his life are far from easy: "His matrimonial connection was unfortunate" (8). He spends his entire ministry as the pastor of an obscure parish where he receives only a small salary. He suffers repeatedly from physical illness. But Dr. Unwin never complains about his circumstances; quite the contrary, he finds a positive meaning in each of his adversities. During one particularly difficult sickness, he observes: "The physical malady under which I am now laboring is designed, perhaps, to cure some moral disease" (42). Self-sacrifice, acceptance of whatever life brings, and doing one's duty are qualities of character that identify someone as a Christian.

Dr. Unwin's granddaughter Phebe learns well from her ministerial model. As her grandfather ages, it becomes clear to Phebe that it is her duty to care for him. Phebe willingly sacrifices her own desires, including marriage, to fulfill her calling. (The scene where she rejects a very eligible suitor is quite touching.) Like her minister grandfather, Phebe accepts her lot in life without complaint, maintaining a pleasant demeanor and discovering moral benefits in the midst of self-denial:

> She found in the performance of the sacred duties of her station a full portion of felicity which is compatible with the probationary state. Her sweet countenance, while supporting her now infirm grandfather during his walks, fixing his easy chair, or reading to him aloud, demonstrated to every beholder that happiness is not confined to external situation. (160)

Both Phebe and her grandfather accept their stations in life without complaining, both willingly sacrifice personal desires to duty, both maintain a pleasant demeanor, and both look for and find spiritual benefits from their self-denial.

While the attributes Savage gives her characters suggest ideal behavior for all people, Christian novelists most often promote them as standards for women and clergy. In fact, the identity and roles prescribed for women in both popular culture and liberal religious fiction especially during the first half of the nineteenth century are strikingly similar to those being defined for clergy during the same period. In *Sensational Designs*, a study of nineteenth-century fiction and the popular culture it reflects, Jane Tompkins describes how the self-denying behavior of women gained religious significance in the nineteenth century. Tompkins describes a popular culture that admires subservient women who deny themselves to become "vehicles of God's will."[13] A large number of religious manuals published especially for women during the middle years of the century corroborate Tompkins's findings. Novels and diaries that described how women could fulfill their self-sacrificing vocation were often best sellers among women readers.[14] Susan Warner's *The Wide, Wide World* (1850), for example, which spells out in painstaking detail the moral qualities and self-denying behaviors that make a woman an exemplary person, was the best-selling book of 1850. In two years, *The Wide, Wide World* went through fourteen editions.[15] Mrs. E. Prentiss's *Stepping Heavenward* (1869) is typical of the large number of instructional diaries and manuals written for women. A "Publishers' Note" printed in the front of the 1880 edition of Prentiss's book reports that by then it had sold 75,000 copies in the United States alone.[16]

Ministers now displaced from the civil power structure, their ecclesiastical position popularly defined by a less-demanding theology, found themselves left with a "station" or status similar to that of women. They no longer commanded authority by virtue of a public office. Like women of the time, their ability to effect depended on their ability to impress. The sympathetic association of women authors and liberal clergy that Ann Douglas describes in *The Feminization of American Culture* would have been unlikely if this social and cultural affinity had not emerged. While some clergy were unwilling to acknowledge the minister's reduced status and authority, as the century progressed the minister's lower status became an inescapable fact. Few American ministers could *command* respect as their Puritan forebears did; like women, they had to persuade.

This weakening authority of clergy was already apparent to Sarah Savage in 1820—and she casts Phebe and her grandfather Dr. Unwin accordingly. Phebe can learn appropriate behavior as a Christian woman from her clergyman grandfather because their prescribed statuses and roles are similar.

While Dr. Unwin's liberal theology might have seemed radical to many of his contemporaries, few of them would have been offended by his personal behavior. For many Americans, the model minister was now perceived as a moral and pious person, who, like a good woman, seeks to influence others by moral example.[17]

The Rev. Arthur Kavanagh in Henry Wadsworth Longfellow's novel *Kavanagh* (1849) is a much stronger person who copes more creatively with ministers' reduced authority than Sarah Savage's clergy do. As a young man, Kavanagh exhibits such unusual intellectual gifts that his upper-class Roman Catholic family sends him to a Jesuit college in Canada to further his education. Kavanagh's inquiring mind soon takes him far beyond the theological boundaries prescribed for Roman Catholic students; he leaves behind the "many dusky dogmas [and] many antique superstitions" of his Catholic heritage. "By slow degrees," Kavanagh becomes a liberal Protestant and prepares for the ministry (76).

When he completes his preparation, the congregation at Fairmeadow (Maine?) invites Kavanagh to assume the pulpit of their church. They have grown weary of the rigid Calvinistic theology of his predecessor, Mr. Pendexter. With Kavanagh standing in the wings, Pendexter ends his twenty-five-year ministry at Fairmeadow with a sermon that expresses his complete frustration with the people of this parish. He concludes the homily

> by telling the congregation in general that they [are] so confirmed in their bad habits, that no reformation was to be expected in them under his ministry, and to produce one would require a greater exercise of Divine power than it did to create the world; for in creating the world there had been no opposition, whereas, in their reformation, their own obstinacy and evil propensities, and self-seeking, and worldly-mindedness, were all to be overcome! (44)

After the sermon, "Some were exasperated, others mortified, and others filled with pity" (44).

Unlike the pastor who preceded him, hardly any urgency marks either Kavanagh's personal life or his ministry. His sermons are quite different from those of his predecessor; they encourage good behavior rather than rigid belief, the ways of gentle Unitarianism rather than rigid Calvinism. Kavanagh has plenty of time for socializing with friends. He marries a lovely young woman regarded as the ideal wife for a gentleman. Confident that the parish can carry on without him, Kavanagh and his bride sail to Europe for what is to be a one-year honeymoon—and stay three years!

The only stress that marks Kavanagh's ministry comes out of encounters with local sectarians and rigid Calvinists. Like the author who created him (and who likely based him, at least in part, on his liberal minister brother), Kavanagh finds Calvinists and sectarians equally offensive.[18] One evening as they stroll, he and his friend Mr. Churchill hear the sounds of a camp meeting in the night air. The familiar voice of a church elder rises above the rest. Churchill and Kavanagh wonder together about this "strange fanaticism" that engages even members of their own congregation. Moments later as they walk along the river, a distraught young woman from the parish becomes a tragic victim of the despair Kavanagh believes the sectarians encourage. Beyond their reach, she drowns herself in the river. As they stand helplessly by and watch her pass beneath the water, Kavanagh and Churchill hear the words of a hymn being sung at the camp meeting:

O, there will be mourning, mourning, mourning, mourning—
O, there will be mourning at the judgment-seat of Christ! (103)

This sad and poignant scene in *Kavanagh* captures what liberal novelists often portray as the unfortunate but all-too-typical result of misguided belief during the 1840s and 1850s. In *Margaret* (1845), the Rev. Sylvester Judd paints a similar picture of camp meeting religion. Judd contrasts Margaret's simple faith and sensual enjoyment of the natural world with the inhibitions and excesses of the sectarians. In *Records of the Bubbleton Parish* (1854), E. W. Reynolds compares harsh Calvinists with gentle and caring Unitarians. In Julia Caroline Ripley Dorr's novel *Lanmere* (1856), a young mother's morbid Calvinism leads her to abuse her children, until she sees a better way through the ministry of a compassionate Unitarian pastor.

Like their counterparts in real life, liberal ministers in fiction often express dismay at the behavior of Calvinists and sectarians; occasionally, they even ridicule them, but they never attack them directly. Their most common response to what they see as the excesses of orthodoxy and sectarianism is to reaffirm the gentle and compassionate character of liberalism. Liberal beliefs produce morally superior behavior. To be and do good is a sufficient argument. The most-enlightened liberal ministers in fiction join word with example to embody this argument.

Faithful Calvinists

During the early decades of the nineteenth century, the novel must have seemed like an unsuitable medium to most conservative Christian writers. Popular writers consistently portray Calvinist clergy, especially Puritan clergy, who appear in their novels as narrow, fanatical, and bigoted characters. This overwhelmingly negative portrayal likely discouraged Calvinists from considering fiction as a suitable vehicle to promote their theological perspectives. Many conservatives found history and theological essays better suited to their purpose. While Arminian Christians and other liberals used fiction to present the faith of the Puritans as an outmoded and repressive theological straitjacket, conservatives wrote essays and histories that defended the Puritan forebears as still "the best models of piety and conduct for the 1800s."[19] They viewed liberals of the day not as theological reformers but as theological saboteurs undermining the foundational faith of their great-grandparents.

This defensive attitude persisted among conservatives at least until the late 1840s. By then, several significant social and theological shifts began to make fiction seem more promising to theologically conservative writers. During the 1820s, 1830s, and 1840s, influential American writers like James Fenimore Cooper established the novel as a more reputable literary medium.[20] The theological perspective of some conservative Calvinists began to moderate in the 1830s and 1840s, when work published by conservative Christian novelists like Susan and Anna Warner and Harriet Beecher Stowe demonstrated that fiction could be turned into a moral force. These changes within both the church and the larger social climate helped make fiction more palatable to conservative readers.

Not surprisingly, clergy who appear as positive characters in the few novels published by Calvinist authors before the 1840s are cast as heroic defenders of the historic, orthodox Calvinist faith. The Rev. George Tracy who stands at the center of the earliest orthodox Calvinist novel of which I am aware, *Triumph of Religion* (1825), is typical. His steadfast faith converts most of those he encounters, including the heroine, Sophia Forbes, whom he loves. Tracy is a strong, unwavering Calvinist whose rugged orthodoxy overwhelms all who challenge him. Clergy in two novels from the 1830s, the anonymous *A Blossom in the Desert* (1836) and Robert C. Waterson's *Arthur Lee and Tom Palmer* (1839), are similar to the Rev. Mr. Tracy. In *A Blossom in the Desert*, the preacher who goes forth to establish a Sunday school on the frontier bests not only faithless opponents but also Irish Catholic detractors. The minister who dominates *Arthur Lee and Tom Palmer* converts a rebellious seaman by demonstrating the superior strength of orthodox faith.

On the whole, these and other efforts of early conservative writers failed to gain a large audience. In retrospect, they seem quite crude, especially when placed alongside the more refined novels of Joseph Alden that appeared in the 1840s. The wider appreciation and support of Alden's books suggest that conservative authors were becoming more sophisticated and that "appropriate" novels were acceptable to conservative readers. The subtitle of his 1846 novel *Elizabeth Benton; or, Religion in Connection with Fashionable Life* may indicate why Alden's work finds a sympathetic audience among conservative readers. He does not simply promote traditional Calvinism as superior in this novel; he establishes that superiority with images and arguments designed to appeal to the more moderate religious and social attitudes of the emerging middle class. He is sensitive to their genteel social ways.

The minister in Alden's 1847 novel *Alice Gordon* is the most interesting of Alden's clergy. Alice, orphaned by her father's death and without any funds to provide for her care, seems destined for the orphanage. She turns hopefully to her church, but it has no extra funds. Individual members, however, respond to her situation. Mr. Wright, a member of the congregation, invites her to join his family. She is educated "affectionally," not intellectually, by Mr. Beals, the pastor—no doubt deemed the fitting kind of education for a girl at the time.

The plot becomes complicated when Mr. Newell, a man relatively unknown to the pastor and congregation, becomes Alice's suitor. Newell is initially attracted to her out of altruistic motives: he recognizes her intellectual ability and is concerned that she have the privileges of a fine education. He speaks to Alice's guardian, who agrees to accept the funds Newell will provide anonymously to pay for Alice's education. To ensure that his motives in arranging for her education will not be suspect, Mr. Newell agrees to stop seeing Alice. But his plan fails when a chance meeting that occurs between him and Alice is observed by Mrs. Apthorp, the local gossip. Newell immediately seeks to redeem himself and Alice by proposing marriage. But Mr. Beals, the protector-pastor, questions Newell's suitability; Newell does not appear to be an orthodox believer. Despite Beal's objection, Mr. Newell and Alice Gordon are married. The story comes to a climax as Newell prays and reads the Bible on their wedding night. The pastor's steady witness has brought about the suitor's conversion. Mr. Newell has become a faithful Christian.

This surprisingly sentimental novel from the pen of an openly Calvinist author is designed to present conservative Christianity in a socially, as well as theologically, appealing light. Mr. Wright, the church member who takes Alice into his family, renders the generous caring the author wishes her readers to believe grows naturally out of orthodox faith. Mr. Beals, the pastor who guides Alice's education and theological development, protects her from a suitor whose theology and piety are suspect.

Alice Gordon is a prototype of the moralistic novels that dominate conservative fiction at midcentury. These novels hold up the importance of acts of charity, like Mr. Wright's care for Alice. They warn those who might be tempted to put their faith in worldly goods that possessions do not offer security. They suggest that faithful believing and the good works that grow out of that believing are ultimately rewarded. They show how God works through the events and circumstances of life to bring errant people to heel and to bless those who are faithful. Thus, the difficult life experiences of the errant sailor in Waterson's novel bring about his conversion; and Alice, the orphan in Alden's story, begins penniless but finds her faith rewarded and is blessed with marriage to a strong, caring, affluent, and faithful man.

By the late 1840s and 1850s, many of the characters, especially women and ministers, who appear in conservative religious novels are surprisingly similar to their liberal counterparts. Conservatives and liberals remain on opposite ends of the theological spectrum. But the emphasis on moral behavior that now dominates conservative novels is similar to the behavior that liberal authors advocate through their characters. The morality and piety that commend Alice Gordon and her pastor as people of faith, for example, are nearly identical to the morality and piety that commend Phebe and her pastor-grandfather in *Filial Affection* by liberal author Sarah Savage. While theological orthodoxy remained the acid test for ministers in conservative novels through midcentury, charitable behavior and piety grew steadily in importance.[21]

The new rationalism that spread among educated people in the nineteenth century encouraged what is for many conservatives a painstaking scrutiny of traditional theology and doctrine. In the 1850s, Harriet Beecher Stowe began to produce fiction that explores the difficult theological dilemmas challenging conservative clergy in her generation. Much of Stowe's fiction grew directly out of her own personal struggle to remain faithful to the traditional Calvinism she inherited. Stowe's theological pilgrimage resembles that of many others: she began as a strict Calvinist and in her later years became a more moderate believer. Stowe's reluctant questioning of the theology of her youth reflects the religious displacement that afflicted many others who lived during the middle and last half of the nineteenth century. Like the obviously autobiographical Dolly Cushing, the central character in her 1878 novel *Poganuc People*, Stowe found some nurture in the Episcopal Church.[22] But that association does not resolve some of the most troublesome questions that plagued her. The sensitive characterization of Dr. Cushing in *Poganuc People*, for example (no doubt based on Stowe's father, Lyman Beecher), shows how fondly Stowe recalled the well-ordered Calvinist worldview in which she trusted as a child. Stowe's midlife belief crisis resembles that of many of her contemporaries who also were raised as strict Calvinists: as an adult she could neither fully embrace Calvinism nor completely abandon it.[23]

Stowe's fiction published during the 1850s seems to me to be a much more accurate reflection of the Calvinism she longed to retain than the novels written after the Civil War. When Dr. Hopkins, the heroic Calvinist who is the central character in her 1859 novel *The Minister's Wooing*, encounters challenges to his beliefs, he refuses to compromise on *any* point. Basic points of doctrine are not debatable. Essential beliefs are theological certainties that must be affirmed and defended, regardless of personal cost. When Hopkins's parishioner Mary Scudder thinks her unconverted lover James is lost at sea, the Calvinist theology that Dr. Hopkins maintains offers little hope of salvation for James. Hopkins meets Mary's frantic questions simply by advising her to stop questioning and trust God. When the trials of life tempt one to doubt, one must remember that the ways of God are ultimately beyond human comprehension. A doctrine that appears from a human perspective to be cruel cannot really be so because God, by definition, is benevolent.[24]

The total submission to God's will that Samuel Hopkins and Mary Scudder exemplify resembles the compliant social role that many real-life women and both conservative and liberal ministers imagined for themselves at midcentury. Wide theological differences still separated liberal from conservative believers in the 1850s, but the social roles they envisioned for themselves are quite similar. The conservative ideal of self-submission is behaviorally similar to the liberal ideal of self-denial. The central thrust of orthodox Calvinism discourages self-assertion. Believers know that their salvation is entirely in the hands of God. Individuals can do nothing to alter God's decisions or to assure their election. In such a situation, a believer demonstrates faith by submitting to God's will.

The efficacy of this total submission is portrayed most convincingly by Mary Scudder and the Rev. Dr. Samuel Hopkins, who stand at the center of *The Minister's Wooing*. Hopkins is a powerful advocate for orthodox

Calvinism. A true believer is a totally self-sacrificing believer. The central act of faith is *unconditional* submission to the will of God. Dr. Hopkins shows a heroic lack of self-concern throughout his life and his ministry. When he becomes convinced that owning slaves is against God's will, for example, he preaches against slavery openly and repeatedly, despite the protests of prominent members of his congregation who are slave owners. Even when opposition builds and his parishioners begin to attend a neighboring congregation, Hopkins is unwavering. In one moving exchange, when a parishioner questions whether slaves wish to be free, Hopkins suggests that the parishioner ask them—and then abide by their responses. Hopkins's submission to the will of God knows no limits. He is even willing to be damned for all eternity if that somehow serves the purpose of God!

Mary Scudder's faith is of similar quality. When her beloved appears to be lost at sea, Mary resigns herself to his loss and his likely damnation as well. She accepts her lot in life without complaint, convinced that it is God's will for her. Following a pattern of self-sacrifice similar to the one Phebe follows in *Filial Affection* when she devotes her life to caring for her pastor-grandfather, Mary Scudder prepares to marry and devote the rest of her life to caring for the much older Dr. Hopkins.

What finally commends these Calvinists (and, they hope, the superiority of their doctrine) is the sacrificial behavior to which their convictions lead. Through characters and a story set in a time when the Congregational Church was still legally established in New England, Stowe addresses the powerlessness that many disestablished nineteenth-century Christians felt by arguing that moral force, not structural power, is the strength of Calvinist faith. Dr. Hopkins never appeals to the structural power that goes with his socially established office to advance his beliefs. The moral force of his life is power enough.

Samuel Hopkins probably represents Stowe's attempt to address the perceived contradiction between narrow Calvinism and generous behavior. Though Hopkins holds fast to a narrow and sometimes brutally inflexible Calvinist theology, he is a kind, caring, gentle, understanding person. At times, his gentle behavior seems to contradict his rigid theology. How can this be? Stowe proposes that Hopkins and all believers be judged by their actions, not their theology. The theological resolution in *The Minister's Wooing* hinges on character, not logic. God and godly humans surpass logic. They exceed logical expectations. A demanding God and humans inspired by God turn out to be more benevolent than we expect them to be. The conclusion of the novel suggests that a believer's absolute commitment opens the way for God to work for his or her benefit—often in unanticipated and mysterious ways.[25] Mary's beloved, James Marvyn, returns; he is not lost at sea after all. Though Mary feels bound to honor her promise to marry and care for Dr. Hopkins, he releases her to marry James—finding great personal peace in doing so. And James reveals that he experienced conversion during his ordeal at sea. He becomes a leading member of Hopkins's congregation.

The symbolic juxtaposition of a clergyman and a faithful woman as central characters in Stowe's novel is no accident; each character type reinforces the other. Neither minister nor woman now has any structural power in the contemporary social order. Each witnesses with only moral force: the devoted, sacrificing woman and the minister who submits totally to God's will. Hopkins doesn't need nor does he exercise the structural power the established church gives him; his faith and moral force are sufficient. Samuel Hopkins and Mary Scudder both submit and are rewarded; he is honored, and she is cared for.

> Although the figure of Mary reflects a popular antebellum stereotype, it is carefully anchored to Puritan precedent and is used in such a way as to convert the novel into an exemplum of humanization in the Edwardsian tradition. Mary is not so much Hopkins's theological antagonist as the embodiment of what is spiritually vital in Hopkinsianism. She is the Muse who inspires him to write his [theological] Treatise; her influence is the main reason her husband eventually becomes a pillar of Hopkins's church. Mary, in other words, is used as an instrument for revising and reaffirming a still-viable tradition.[26]

In the last analysis, the path of faith presented in Stowe's novel is not at all radical; it matches the social experience and expectations of many, if not most, of her readers. Her characters faithfully reflect the similar social roles most often assigned to women and ministers in the years leading up to the Civil War. In real life, as well as in novels, the only power many believe is available to them is what Jane Tompkins calls "sentimental power."[27] Women and ministers exhibit superior submission; they "win" by sacrificing themselves: "They enact a philosophy, as much political as religious, in which the pure and powerless die to save the powerful and corrupt, and thereby show themselves more powerful than those they save."[28] Such an attitude, though heroic in the eyes of some, is replete with hazards. It can encourage those who embrace it to become heroic victims. As Ann Douglas suggests, "Sentimentalism provides a way to protest a power to which one has already in part capitulated. . . . The minister and the lady . . . were in the position of contestants in a fixed fight: they had agreed to put on a convincing show and to lose. The fakery involved was finally crippling for all concerned."[29]

Precarious Pastors

Not every mid-nineteenth-century pastor in fiction or real life finds submission to be a winning way. The "crippling fakery" is painfully evident in ministers who struggle valiantly and still lose when they try to carry out a faithful ministry within the more limited social role now assigned to clergy. A group of novels written by authors with firsthand experience of parish life, many of them wives of ministers, portray faithful servants who are both disempowered and frustrated. The disempowering they suffered was by no means entirely of their own doing.

The official disestablishment of churches that diminished the status and restricted the role of American ministers was not only, or even mostly, an ecclesiastical phenomenon; it reflected a massive redistribution of civil, social, economic, and religious power. The transformation from an agrarian to a manufacturing economy gave birth to a new class of entrepreneurs, who soon dominated the social, political, economic, and religious institutions in burgeoning cities and factory towns. As the new manufacturing economy emerged, it brought profound changes to many local communities. In the space of a few years, everything was different. The Rev. Mr. Kavanagh, the central character in Longfellow's *Kavanagh*, is startled by the changes he finds when he returns to Fairmeadow after three years in Europe: "In the morning, Kavanagh sallied forth to find the Fairmeadow of his memory, but found it not. The simple village had become a very precocious town. New shops, with new names over the doors; new streets, with new forms and faces in them; the whole town seemed to have been taken and occupied by a besieging army of strangers" (117). In the space of only three years, Fairmeadow changed from a village where the stranger is a novelty into a town where most people are strangers to one another—and to the minister as well.

Villages like Fairmeadow were no longer self-contained, relatively independent economies. Daily life was now shaped as much by influences beyond the village as by those who lived within the local community. Even ministers and churches were subject to market forces in the new economy. When the national economy was strong, the market was favorable, and local entrepreneurs were skilled, towns thrived. Depressions, falling markets, poor business decisions, or a fire that destroys the local mill could bring an entire town to ruin. After an absence of several years, the narrator of *Our*

Parish (1854) returns to what he remembers was a thriving Brooksboro and discovers a town in desperate straits. The railroad has bypassed Brooksboro. The local mill has burned; "vast masses of machinery lay piled on the ground" where it once stood. The remaining walls of the mill stand out "against the blue sky of summer in bold relief, blacked and begrimed." The former owners' houses are all deserted. As the narrator walks the streets, he sees nothing but "devastation" in every direction. The only person he recognizes is the village doctor, "getting old very fast." He is stunned by the silence. The village seems "entirely dead. There is no interest, no life, anywhere." The fate of the village becomes the fate of its churches. The once-thriving parish church is reduced to a faithful few who gather on Sundays in the meetinghouse. They are served only occasionally by a "travelling clergyman. . . . No one had yet accepted a 'call' there, and it looked now quite unlikely that for some time any one would" (450–52).

Many local congregations and clergy, especially those affiliated with the formerly established churches, were unprepared for the challenges of ministry in the new industrial America. Congregations located in economically disadvantaged communities like the fictional Brooksboro struggled simply to survive. But economic trials were not necessarily the most troublesome. Ministers who served churches located in growing cities and factory towns now faced congregations composed of people with different and often-conflicting expectations of churches and ministers. In the years before the disastrous fire that destroys Brooksboro's mill and its local economy, Mr. Humphreys, pastor of the parish church, becomes a victim of the conflicting expectations of those who now make up the congregation. He is simply not good enough for the newly arrived mill owners, who see themselves "a little in advance of the honest and simple people of our parish" (356):

> And pretty soon this new circle began to assert its own peculiar influence and authority. The leading families . . . took it upon themselves to pass their judgments freely on all around them. . . . People who had lived for years there, happy in the simple enjoyments our little church so bountifully dispensed, now for the first time in their lives found that the singing was "just no singing at all." Mr. Humphreys, too, preached plainly and practically; and his warnings, and exhortations, and frequent appeals were truly earnest in the cause he had espoused for his life. But these strangers pretended to be not altogether *satisfied* with him. He was a little past their *fashions*. They hinted ominously of the possibility of better ministers being in the field. Then they whispered of

> calculations that had been made among them for the erection of a new church that should be located nearer to their part of town. (358)

Like most of his colleagues, nothing in Mr. Humphreys's education or background prepared him for the full-scale conflict he now faces. The very idea of contending for his pulpit violates his sensibilities. The dissidents soon have their way. He resigns.

If the conflict had been over theology, Mr. Humphreys could have contended with it well. Fictional pastors like Mr. Humphreys are well prepared to defend their theology, but not their style or methods of ministry. They respond confidently to parishioners who challenge their orthodoxy, but they are at a loss when faced with critics who find their preaching out of fashion or who question whether they are effective as ministers. Taught that they hold authority by virtue of their office, pastors trained in the tradition of Mr. Humphreys are startled to discover that their authority depends on their performance. Most not only have a distaste for competition; they are incapacitated by contention. The only response many can muster is to reaffirm their orthodoxy and work harder to prove that they are faithful. These efforts rarely succeed; orthodoxy and dedication are not the issues that most concern their critics.

Mr. Holbrook, the pastor in Elizabeth Stuart Phelps's *A Peep at Number Five* (1852), is typical of those unprepared for ministry in the new industrial America. During the first months after his graduation from seminary, he serves as the supply preacher of a small church in the Green Mountains of Vermont. His fine preaching and earnest approach to ministry soon win the hearts of the parishioners. They form a committee who call on him and invite him to settle as their pastor, promising to pay him the modest sum of $400 annually. The local committee has scarcely departed before the three strangers knock at his door. During the weeks before the committee's call, Mr. Holbrook had noticed these three strangers among the local worshippers. Mr. Kennedy, their spokesperson, is somewhat familiar to Mr. Holbrook. He is the son of a local family who has become a successful businessman in the city. He provides well for his aging parents and contributes liberally on their behalf to the support of the small, country church where he grew up. Mr. Kennedy explains that he and the other two men are leaders in the Downs Street Church, a large city church. They describe how much Mr. Holbrook's preaching has impressed them and invite him to become a candidate for the pulpit at their church. The salary there will be $1,400. The young minister struggles through the night to decide between the two calls. By morning, his decision is clear: "the call to the city appeared one of duty; it had come in a remarkable manner; he felt that there was a Providence in it" (29). The candidating sermon at Downs Street Church is successful. Within six months, the young minister and Lucy, his new wife, are off to the city to begin their ministry.

But the work at Downs Street Church challenges the new minister in unexpected ways. The members have unreasonably high expectations of his preaching; they expect *every* sermon to be dazzling. In fact, they expect their minister to outperform all other ministers in the city. While Mr. Holbrook is an excellent preacher, he is also a conscientious pastor. The sheer volume of pastoral work that confronts him in this large congregation often interferes with his sermon preparation. He finds that he cannot do the required pastoral work and prepare three sermons of exceptional quality each week. Lucy tries to relieve some of the pressure on her husband by doing some visitation on his behalf. In spite of the couple's dedicated efforts, dissatisfaction increases in the congregation. The climax comes when a group of church leaders call one evening to express their disappointment with the results of Mr. Holbrook's ministry. They are concerned about the lack of "applications to our Examining Committee lately." As a remedy, they propose a series of revival meetings. They point to good results from revivals in neighboring parishes: "They are having . . . crowded houses, and everybody gets wide awake whenever they try such meetings." What does the pastor think of this proposal?

Mr. Holbrook responds by reaffirming his traditional view of ministry: "The value of protracted meetings in my view, depends very much upon the evidence of success attending the *ordinary* means of promoting the interests of religion." The committee is obviously displeased. During a long discussion, they propose "measures" they think will increase attendance and membership— none of which appeal to Mr. Holbrook. Finally one of them, Mr. Sampson, cannot contain his exasperation: "I do not care how it is done, whether by protracted meetings, or inquiry-meetings, or morning prayer-meetings, but [we need] some measures—"

> "That's it," broke in Mr. Lovering, "*some* measures which will put us all to work, and make a talk. There is a great deal in making a *talk* especially in a city. Why, if you put a notice in the paper that a preacher has a remarkable nose, everybody will run the next Sunday to see it, and then he has a fine chance, you know, to give them good Bible-doctrine, and ten to one, they will go away better than they came." (174–75; italics in the original)

Deacon Silas, recognizing the poor taste of Mr. Lovering's outburst, proposes another plan to the pastor: "to hold a series of daily prayer-meetings."

 To everyone's relief, the minister agrees. Silas then uses the good will he hopes he has earned to steer the conversation back toward the real purpose of their visit: "I suppose . . . that *you* think, brother Lovering, it would be profitable to suspend doctrinal preaching for awhile, and have a course of hortatory sermons?" The choice of words is revealing. The real argument is now in the open: hortatory sermons are "profitable." They get results—they draw a crowd; doctrinal sermons do not. The focus of disagreement is completely clear: preaching that is faithful to the established doctrines of the church versus preaching that draws a crowd and that yields "dollars and cents."

After the visiting committee leaves, Mr. Holbrook spends a restless night. In the morning, he shares the conversation of the previous evening with his wife. Lucy reassures him and reaffirms her confidence in his approach to ministry. But later in the day when she visits Mrs. Roberts, a parishioner, Lucy hears the same complaints that the committee made the evening before. The months that follow are filled with turmoil. Though some of his detractors leave, the congregation is divided. In the midst of the controversy, Mr. Holbrook receives a call to serve another church at a much larger salary. He decides not to accept it. He persists as pastor of the Downs Street Church. He even has some success that appears to vindicate his style of preaching. But the disagreement over his approach to ministry is never really resolved.

Several novels from the 1850s describe similar conflicts between ministers with traditional, doctrinal approaches to ministry and church members who represent the attitudes of the new business culture.[30] In each instance, the lay leaders' concern is whether their minister's approach, especially his preaching, makes their church competitive or "profitable," while the minister is more concerned that his preaching teach the true faith, as he understands it.

In the new industrializing America, parishioners increasingly demand that ministers prove their worth according to standards drawn more from the marketplace than from either scripture or tradition. The devoted pastor and preacher who gains authority year after year as he serves the same parish (often for a lifetime) soon exists only as a memory. The new standards are more troublesome for pastors with average ability like Mr. Humphreys and the Rev. Henry Edwards, who serves the fictional parish of Weston in Elizabeth Stuart Phelps's first novel, *The Sunnyside* (1851). Leaders in Weston evaluate Mr. Edwards entirely on the basis of his ability to attract new members to their church. When the congregation's growth fails to meet their expectations, they question his overall capability as a pastor. Their dissatisfaction weighs heavily on Edwards. He tries earnestly to live up to the congregation's expectations but fails to gain "results" (converts). As criticism of his ministry increases, Edwards's self-esteem deteriorates. Though he and his family struggle to live within the meager income the parish provides (compounded by the fact that salary payments are often late), he is reluctant to ask for an increase. He sees himself as undeserving, a mediocre minister who won't "advance." Unable to envision himself in another parish, he spends his life in Weston. Though the church there prospers at times, especially after his daughter Kate marries a clergyman who joins in the ministry with him, Henry Edwards dies believing that he is a failure as a minister.

Social change not only encourages congregations to be more demanding of their ministers, it encourages ministers to judge themselves according to their success in the church marketplace. In Martha Stone Hubbell's novel *The Shady Side* (1853), the Rev. Edward Vernon struggles to fulfill both traditional and contemporary expectations. Against his own better judgment, he leaves a satisfying ministry in a rural church to accept a call to a large church in Millville, a manufacturing town. But here the congregation expects him to draw large crowds "like the Methodists." When his ministry fails to meet their expectations, they secure his dismissal. Mrs. Elton, a member of the congregation, explains the dismissal to some visitors: "He was very talented, but unequal and moody. He didn't grow as we expected" (229). Millville expects much of its pastors but pays them little. Vernon leaves his post there, discouraged and deeply in debt. When he receives a call from Olney, a small congregation similar to the first church he served, out of desperation he accepts. His ministry in Olney is even more difficult than his prior ministries. The work there soon breaks his health. He dies in Olney, a disillusioned and defeated minister.

When the minister is weak and his antagonists are strong, the minister's vulnerability often leads to his undoing. Such an abusive scene occurs in Samuel Hayes Eliot's anonymously published *The Parish-Side* (1854). This book, written from the point of view of a layperson ("clerk of the parish of Edgefield," the title page announces), is obviously a rebuttal to novels like those by Phelps and Hubbell written from the minister's perspective. Eliot's novel proposes that the difficulties ministers experience don't stem from social change but more often arise from their own unwillingness to live by the faith they preach about. Toward the end of the novel, Mr. Brown, the minister, has confessed to Esquire Peters, the village lawyer, that he and his family cannot live on his salary of $400 a year; he has run up some debts. He asks for an increase of $100 so he can repay his debts. Esquire Peters replies that the minister's unwillingness to live modestly is the source of his financial difficulties:

> "But you don't live on the 'four hundred.' You have made a debt."
> "True, but I am now rigidly economizing, and contrive to live on the salary."
> "You can't as well economize on more, as on less."
> "How so?"
> "Because the temptation to spend money is greater. You may set it down as a truth, that if you receive a salary of five hundred dollars a year, instead of four hundred, that you will be under the temptation, and will yield to it, to buy just so many more articles of living, and spend just so many more dollars of salary, as there are dollars added."

The lawyer then goes on to argue that ministers who receive more money simply buy more books and a better horse and a finer carriage and take more expensive vacations. The minister seems puzzled by the lawyer's argument that an increase in salary will simply make his situation worse! He already owes four hundred dollars; how can he repay his debts if his salary remains at only four hundred dollars? The lawyer advises him to sell his horse and carriage, his cow, his books, his home furnishings! When Mr. Brown protests that he could not then do his ministry, and that his family could not live without the cow and furnishings, Esquire Peters responds that the minister's dependence on these material goods shows that he lacks faith: "You bought these goods on credit, now part with them, and my word for it, our people will within three weeks give them all back to you! *That's the way, sir, to raise your salary!* Put yourself in the hands of your people" (240). After some inner struggle, Mr. Brown agrees to follow the course of action the lawyer suggests. While the narrator reports that Mr. Brown "felt immediately relieved of his depression," he neglects to tell the reader whether Mr. Brown's resolve leads to the results Esquire Peters predicts. He does say that he wishes "every minister in the country could have heard the conversation."

The Rev. Ernest Helfenstein in Elizabeth Oakes Smith's novel *Bertha and Lily* (1854) is one of the few precarious pastors who is able to stand up to his critics. Ernest differs in both temperament and personality from other pastors who appear in antebellum parochial novels. Though he is well aware of the reduced authority of ministers after disestablishment, Ernest refuses to play the part of the compliant pastor.

During one of his sermons, Ernest challenges the people of his parish to act out their faith by bringing children from the almshouse into their own houses and including them as members of their own families. Ernest then follows his own exhortation and brings two children, Willy and Kate, into his home. The following Sunday, he declares publicly that they are members of his household when he has them sit in the pastor's pew! Helfenstein's action creates an uproar in Beech Glen. Julia, the woman who seems most likely to become Ernest's wife, warns, "Why Ernest, you will lose your parish; your people will not have their pastor become the keeper of a Foundling Hospital" (80). Deacon Hopkins calls to warn the pastor that the selectmen consider his action as "doing great mischief." The next day, the selectmen themselves confront the pastor. They warn that the town will soon "be filled with children without fathers" if he persists in his action. Young women will feel it doesn't matter whether they bear children out of wedlock "so long as these children [from the almshouse] are treated as well or better than children lawfully born" (103). The town fathers demand that Helfenstein return the children to the almshouse and in the future keep his sermons focused on "religious matters." Their warnings do not deter Ernest. The selectmen are equally undeterred: "We engaged you to preach to an orthodox, respectable people, Parson Helfenstein, and we'll take care of the town business ourselves, and first we'll take these children back to the Alms House" (131). But Ernest refuses to give the children up. The selectmen respond by challenging him to sign papers of legal adoption. So he does, and the selectmen leave, clearly defeated.

Ernest Helfenstein is a reluctant, but not uncertain, contender. He knows that his actual authority is precarious, but when confronted with views he believes are contrary to the scripture, he responds with *personal* strength. Those who oppose Ernest use many of the same arguments and strategies that bring pastors down in the other parochial novels published during the 1850s, but they do not prevail. Ernest may not have the official authority they have, but he is as strong, if not stronger, in character as they are.

Ernest also may triumph where his fictional colleagues do not because he is the creation of an author who is both a Universalist and a feminist. Like many of the other authors who write about parish life in the 1840s and 1850s, Elizabeth Oakes Smith was a pastor's spouse and had firsthand experience of parish life. But the submissive patterns of faith and ministry that fetter many orthodox Calvinist clergy do not fetter Smith or her characters—female and male.

Bertha, one of the title characters in *Bertha and Lily*, and Pastor Helfenstein embody what Smith sees as the strengths of women and Universalism. Bertha openly complains that male orthodox Calvinist preachers in general are tedious and ineffective: "The sermons of our clergy [are] dull as they must necessarily be . . . where the mind is bent solely to establish and elucidate old dogmas; I find it impossible to sit them out" (32). She proposes that women be admitted to the pulpit to liven up the services! Her arguments fail to convince the local church officers, but the officers' opposition fails to silence Bertha. When one of the local deacons points to St. Paul's statement that women should keep silence in church gatherings to justify their refusal to let her speak in the services, she responds by questioning St. Paul's inspiration in the matter: "In so far as St. Paul uttered what is partial in its import, he is so much less inspired." She further confounds the deacon with the suggestion that St. Paul is more likely inspired when he argues there is no distinction between "male and female" in the eyes of God (55–56). Bertha then builds a meetinghouse of her own and offers lectures that draw more listeners each week than attend the parish church services!

Bertha's unorthodox interpretations of scripture and her lively approach to worship challenge her pastor, as well. In a clear reversal not only of accepted lay and pastor roles but also of accepted female and male roles, Ernest begins to pattern his ministry on hers. He decides to provoke his congregation out of their lethargy: "My predecessor in Beech Glen has . . . so swathed, balsamed and glued [the congregation] into orthodoxy, that they are perfectly mummified therein," Ernest complains: "I wish people came to pray, to worship, not to cavil, sleep or be respectable. This respectability is becoming very tiresome. . . . I mean next Sunday to tell my people to sin—that they may have the zest of repentance, for their dullness is contagious" (57, 72–73).

Ernest Helfenstein survives the challenges to his ministry, and, like his mentor, Bertha, he becomes a stronger person and a stronger minister as a result of them. When challenged to "make up his mind to reject salary, or to reject truth," he continues to speak the truth as he sees it, fully aware that his words and deeds may lead the church to withhold his salary. None of the threats against Ernest materialize. He does not lose his pulpit, as his fiancée, Julia, fears he will. The local church leaders do not withhold his salary nor do they dismiss him, probably because they recognize that neither action will defeat him.

Ernest Helfenstein stands at the end of one era and the beginning of another in the history of the American minister. As the pastor of a Congregational Church, he has roots in a formerly established church. But his sense of personal freedom and his belief that he has the right to honor his own convictions, even if doing so leads him to defy traditional doctrine and break out of traditional definitions of the minister's role, point to the future. In many respects, Ernest's personality and style of ministry anticipate the Methodist, Baptist, and sectarian clergy who play a more dominant role in American society after the Civil War. As Sidney Mead suggests, the independent thinking and acting minister who became a powerful figure especially after the Civil War is a natural development in America.[31] Doctrinally rigid and refined scholarly pastors who embody an Old World model of ministry do continue to appear in popular novels published during the 1870s and 1880s, but they are most often portrayed as reactionaries or as pastors who are *not* equal to the challenges of ministry in postbellum industrial and frontier America.

The cultural image of the self-denying minister, like that of the submissive woman, loses appeal after the Civil War. While some clergy (and women) in real life, as well as in fiction, continue to affirm the theological and moral validity of these images, many others do not. They view self-denial and submission not only as weak but also as sentimental foolishness. They recognize accurately that subservience demeans both those who employ it and encourages those who would abuse them. Ernest and Bertha, the minister and the woman in *Bertha and Lily*, stand in opposition to such sentimental foolishness. They reflect cultural images of strong ministers and strong women that will blossom fully after the Civil War. They provide early glimpses of ministers and women who gain respect because they stand on their own and think for themselves.

III

VULNERABLE DIVINES

Radical Images

Victims of Their Believing

From his first appearance, it is clear that the Rev. Arthur Dimmesdale, the minister who stands at the center of *The Scarlet Letter*, will become an infamous character in American literature. In 1851, just after *The Scarlet Letter* appeared, Arthur Cleveland Coxe writing in the *Church Review* dismissed Hawthorne's recently published book as simply "the nauseous amour of a Puritan pastor."[1] Despite this critic's obvious discomfort (and he was clearly not the only contemporary reader offended by Hawthorne's portrayal of a Puritan pastor), *The Scarlet Letter* attracted more public interest than anything else Hawthorne published. More than 150 years later, it is still Hawthorne's best-known novel.[2]

The Rev. Mr. Dimmesdale was not the first "nauseous" Calvinist to appear in American fiction. At least two dozen American novels that depict Calvinist clergy as rigid and sometimes destructive characters preceded *The Scarlet Letter.* In chapters 1 and 2, I describe some of the cultural images these prior characterizations reflect. Though it is difficult to find specific evidence, it seems likely that Hawthorne was aware of at least some of Arthur Dimmesdale's fictional predecessors (Cooper's Meek Wolfe, for example) as he created his own Calvinist ministers. But Hawthorne's clergy are not copies; there is only a surface resemblance between Hawthorne's ministers and the Calvinists who appear in earlier American novels.

Nathaniel Hawthorne immersed himself in the history of American Calvinism, especially that of the New England Puritans, for more than a decade before he wrote *The Scarlet Letter*. He likely read at least sixty works of American history, including the most significant studies of the early New England Calvinists.[3] Hawthorne's attention to American Calvinism reflected more than a casual interest. The content of his reading and his writing before 1851 shows his concern about the abiding influence of Puritan Calvinism in American culture. Hawthorne's concern about this cultural legacy was both personal and professional. One of his forebears, Colonel John Hathorne, served as a judge during the Salem witch trials. Hawthorne seemed embarrassed and at times even troubled by the role his predecessor played in this sorry episode in American history.

Hawthorne's years of study gave him a profound understanding of Calvinist theology, as well as the social and psychological dynamics of Calvinism. He is clearly the nineteenth century's most discerning critic of the Puritan Calvinist legacy in American culture.[4] Most fictionalized accounts of the early Puritans published by other American authors during that century, especially those that appeared before *The Scarlet Letter*, focus on Calvinists' "bad" behavior. They rarely probe the roots of that behavior: *how* or *why* what Calvinists do to others and to themselves grows out of what they believe. Hawthorne broke new ground in his fiction when he proposed that the Puritan Calvinists are victims of a self-imposed, narrow perception that distorts their experience and turns many of them into disturbed believers.

Hawthorne viewed not only Calvinism but all religion from the perspective of a critic. He stood apart and observed the results of believing. His fictional portrayals of Calvinist clergy, for example, display a profound knowledge of Calvinist doctrines. But the ambivalence Hawthorne reflects in these portrayals shows that he did not accept these doctrines personally.[5] The critical attitude toward religion that Hawthorne exhibited as an adult may have been set early in his life. Though it seems likely that Hawthorne participated in church life as a child, there is no evidence that he was pressured to commit himself wholeheartedly to one particular set of beliefs. Quite the opposite: nearly all of those in his extended family in Salem were members of liberal Congregational churches that became Unitarian during the 1820s. This liberal shaping could be expected to produce just the stance Hawthorne's writing reflects: the perspective of an interested observer looking critically at the way faith functions. The mature Hawthorne always stands on the side. He watches how different kinds of believing shape their adherents.[6]

The clergy who appear in Hawthorne's fiction live out the effects of different approaches to believing. They include a far greater variety of ministers than the disturbed Calvinists for whom Hawthorne is most remembered. Viewed together, they suggest that Hawthorne perceived both hazards and benefits in most religious perspectives. For example, the liberal Anglican priest in "The May-Pole of Merry Mount" (1836) is open-minded and tolerant in ways that his Puritan critics are not, but he also encourages a debilitating permissiveness among the worshippers who congregate at the May-Pole. The Unitarian minister who appears toward the end of "The Minister's Black Veil" (1836) tries to free Father Hooper from a horribly misguided sense of sin, but he is so concerned to correct Hooper's theology that he utterly fails to bring any comfort to his dying colleague. Parson Thumpcushion in "Passages from a Relinquished Work" (1834) brings great enthusiasm to his preaching, but he is sometimes so carried away that he breaks the pulpit furniture in the churches where he leads worship.

Hawthorne's writing identifies him as a theological liberal. But he is not a doctrinal liberal. Hawthorne does not advocate *any* religious perspective, liberal or otherwise, as always beneficial or harmful. He accepts the liberal emphasis on conduct rather than doctrine: he agrees with the liberal view that the value of particular beliefs is most evident in the behavior those beliefs encourage. But he goes beyond the common liberal standard to argue that the worth of religious beliefs must also be judged according to the effect they have on *each* person who accepts them. And in Hawthorne's writing, that effect varies not only from person to person but often within the same person in different circumstances. In a monograph titled *Hawthorne's Ambivalence Toward Puritanism*, J. Golden Taylor shows that not only do Hawthorne's stories offer positive and negative portrayals of American Calvinists but also he often portrays the same historical Calvinist positively in one story and negatively in another. Different circumstances reveal the benefits or shortcomings of the same theological commitment. In "Main-Street" (1849) and "Endicott and the Red Cross" (1838), stories in which Hawthorne is severely critical of the Puritans, he nonetheless admits that their rigid theology nurtures a disciplined way of life that enables them to survive the challenges they face in the unfamiliar New World. In a sketch written in 1830, Hawthorne portrays Ann Hutchinson as someone who offers a valid criticism of the Puritans' rigid control of civil and religious life and of their limited view of inspiration. But he then goes on to suggest that Hutchinson is egotistical and disruptive and that the Puritans are justified when they exclude her from their community.[7] The Puritans' bigotry leads even their children to persecute the young Quaker, Ephraim, in

Hawthorne's story "The Gentle Boy" (1832). But the gentle boy's Quaker mother is so overwhelmingly devoted to her faith that she neglects and finally abandons Ephraim. In the end, his adoptive parents—who are Puritans—offer more responsible care for Ephraim than his Quaker parents do. In Hawthorne's fiction, the value of a theological conviction cannot be judged apart from the overall effect it has in someone's life.

Hawthorne's preoccupation with the New England Puritans and their legacy in his early writing reflects his great concern about the damaging effects Calvinism seems to have in the lives of some of its adherents.[8] Hawthorne's concern is more than historical; it has roots in his conviction that the Puritan cultural legacy was still active in his own time. Hawthorne produced historical fiction to serve a contemporary agenda. He recognized the lingering influence of the Puritan legacy in the attitudes and religious experience of many of his contemporaries. The characters in his fiction are more representative than historical. There seems little doubt that he created them to represent the effects of different kinds of believing. He chose actual historical persons and historical situations and transformed them into fictional characters in fictional situations to show the psychological and social consequences of holding different beliefs.[9] History casts shadows that concerned Hawthorne. He perceived some of the same destructive tendencies at work among people living in his own time that he observed among the Calvinists in early New England.

Hawthorne's writing benefits from the growing recognition during the nineteenth century that believing is a multidimensional reality, not simply a theological phenomenon. People's believing may or may not reflect God's working in their lives, but it *always* reflects *their human* experience of God. God may mold what someone believes; Hawthorne offers no clear opinion on this possibility in his published work. But in Hawthorne's fiction, there is no such thing as "pure" believing—believing that is not mediated through someone's individual human experience. Each person's beliefs are shaped by and through his or her psychosocial perception of reality. Individuals and groups who are psychologically disturbed may promote and sometimes even demand disturbed believing. Those who do not recognize the psychological and social dynamics of believing are vulnerable to "mis" believing. The Calvinists in early New England become the primary vehicle that Hawthorne uses to describe this possibility.

The Puritans' obsession with human corruption, especially their preoccupation with their own sinfulness, is the major concern in much of Hawthorne's early fiction. In several of his tales and especially in *The Scarlet Letter*, Hawthorne re-creates what Q.D. Leavis terms the "sense of sin" that shaped the social and spiritual history of early New England. But in Hawthorne, by a wonderful feat of transmutation, this sense of sin has no religious significance; "it is a psychological state that is explored."[10] In Hawthorne's fiction, a distorted sense of sin encourages dysfunctional believing. His most memorable clergy are designed intentionally to exhibit the baleful consequences of a preoccupation with one's own sinfulness, a cancerous kind of believing to which Hawthorne thinks humans in every age are vulnerable. These fictional ministers reflect and help clarify an emerging radical image: the minister who becomes a victim of his own believing.

The Adamant Richard Digby

> In the old times of religious gloom and intolerance lived Richard Digby, the gloomiest and most intolerant of a stern brotherhood. His plan of salvation was so narrow, that, like a plank in a tempestuous sea, it could avail no sinner but himself, who bestrode it triumphantly and hurled anathemas against the wretches whom he saw struggling with the billows of eternal death.[11]

The Rev. Richard Digby, "The Man of Adamant," represents the self-destructive potential of narrow Puritan Calvinism, embodied in a single character and lived out to its logical and extreme conclusion. Digby seems designed to show what can happen when believers think scripture, *as they perceive it*, is the sole source of truth. He is a social and religious alien—a man without either a country or a church.

Hawthorne subtitled Digby's story "An Apologue." An apologue is a tale that combines allegory and parable. The characters, objects, and actions in the story have symbolic meanings. And the story as a whole is created to convey a single, useful lesson—in this instance, the peril of isolated believing. Richard Digby insists on his own way of salvation; he trusts no intermediary—no human, no experience, nothing within the natural order of creation. He seeks total isolation to ensure that no one will disrupt his narrow plan of salvation. He withdraws from society and church, even from the natural world. As he leaves civilization behind, he pauses "to shake off the dust of his feet against the village where he had dwelt, and to invoke a curse upon the meeting-house." Within "his hallowed seclusion . . . [Digby] talked to himself . . . ; he read his Bible to himself . . . ; and, as the gloom of the forest hid the blessed sky, I had almost added, that, at morning, noon, and eventide, he prayed to himself. So congenial was this mode of life to his disposition, that he often laughed to himself, but was displeased when an echo tossed him back the long, loud roar."

As he wanders through the forest, Digby happens on a well-concealed and gloomy cave. He decides to make it his home. It seems ideally suited to him. And it is, in ways that he does not anticipate. The slow dripping of water from the ceiling initiates a process by which everything that is swept into the cave is turned into stone—as hard as adamant. These surroundings resemble a process that is at work within Digby. Before he left civilization he was diagnosed with a "distemper," an incurable disease depositing calculous particles in his heart, destined ultimately to turn "his fleshly heart to stone."

Richard Digby's refusal to look beyond his own narrow vision ensures that he will become a victim of his own misbelieving. A spring of fresh water lays only a few paces beyond the mouth of the cave. But Digby refuses to venture outside to drink from it. He takes only "now and then a drop of moisture from the roof, which, had it fallen any where but on his tongue, would have been congealed into a pebble"—surely "unwholesome liquor," Hawthorne notes, "for a man predisposed to stoniness of heart." At the end of the third day in this "sepulchral cave," Digby sits near the opening, reading his Bible—"reading it amiss," Hawthorne observes, because the light from the setting sun cannot "penetrate the dismal depth of shadow around about him, nor fall upon the sacred page." Suddenly, a faint shaft of light strikes the page Digby is reading, causing him to raise his eyes. The source of light is a young woman who stands before him. He recognizes her as Mary Goffe who had been converted by his preaching years before, during the time he was a pastor in England. He frowns sternly and tells her to be off. But she refuses to leave. She informs him that she has made a long journey to be with him "because I heard that a grievous distemper had seized upon thy heart; and a great Physician hath given me the skill to cure it." Again Richard orders her to leave and turns back to his Bible. Now it has grown so dark that he makes "continual mistakes" as he reads, converting all that is "gracious and merciful, to denunciations of vengeance and unutterable woe, on every created being but himself." But Mary Goffe refuses to be deterred. She walks to the nearby spring and scoops up some water in a small cup. As she kneels and offers it to Richard, she weeps, her tears falling into the cup. "Drink of this hallowed water," she pleads. "Then, make room for me by thy side, and let us read together one page of that blessed volume . . . and kneel down with me and pray! Do this and thy stony heart shall become softer than a babe's." But Richard will not relent. He strikes the cup of water from her hand, "rejecting the only medicine that could have cured his stony heart." "Tempt me no more, accursed woman," he warns and then asks, "What hast thou to do with my Bible?—what with my prayers?—what with my Heaven?" And with these words, his heart ceases to beat, and Richard Digby, wearing a forbidding frown, turns to stone.

Hawthorne's haunting story is made even more so by the symbols he chooses. The cave Digby chooses augers his end. He sees it as a place of inspiration, like the cave on Mt. Horeb where Elijah hears the voice of God; but Hawthorne suggests it is more like Abraham's sepulchral cave at Machpelah—the cave that served as Abraham's tomb. Mary Goffe appears to Digby on the third day—in the Christian New Testament the day of resurrection. She bears the same name as Jesus' mother and as his close friend, Mary Magdalene—the first a symbol of grace, the second a model of repentance that leads to new life. Mary Goffe's image is like that of an angel: "the sunbeams bathed her white garment, which thus seemed to possess a radiance of its own." She comes to Richard as the agent of Godly healing: "I heard that a grievous distemper had seized upon thy heart; and a great Physician hath given me the skill to cure it." ("Physician" is capitalized in the original.) When Richard refuses to accept her aid, Mary's face becomes like "a sorrowing angel." The cup of water Mary gives to Richard is sacramental—a mingling of the human and divine. Hawthorne calls it a cup of "hallowed water" and notes that "a few tears mingled with the draught, and perhaps gave it all its efficacy." But nothing that Mary (or anyone else) offers can help Digby. The tale moves relentlessly to its tragic conclusion. The Rev. Richard Digby's plan of salvation is too narrow; it excludes even this angelic messenger who could have cured his fatal disease. As Mary weeps over his unwillingness to accept the healing grace she brings, Digby turns to stone, becoming one with the tomb he has chosen. He is damned, "like some ironic Lot turned to stone for *not* looking back."[12]

Hawthorne's story provides an amazingly accurate representation of a narrow strain in American Puritanism. The most likely historical source is the church of the Rev. John Davenport, pastor in New Haven during the 1640s, a congregation Michael J. Colacurcio describes as "the single most exclusive church known to seventeenth-century Puritanism and at the same time, in most interpretations, the very essence, epitome, and *reductio* of the distinctive New England way."[13] Davenport's doctrinal narrowness was a matter of constant concern even to other conservative Calvinist divines. He maintained the narrowest possible gate into the church by steadfastly refusing to baptize children unless their parents could testify to some discernable Christian experience of their own. Davenport was unwilling even to attend the discussions where his fellow clergy consider widening the entrance into the church. Actually in his New England ministry, Davenport maintained a long-established pattern; before he emigrated, he refused to participate in theological discussions with his fellow clergy—like Digby, refusing to recognize that someone else might have inspiration that could guide or even correct his own believing. And, in case the circumstantial parallels between the fictional Digby and the real-life Davenport might not make the historical connection clear, Hawthorne gave Mary Goffe the same surname as Stephen (or Steven) Goffe, one of the ministerial emissaries who came from England to Holland to plead with the Rev. John Davenport. Like his fictional counterpart, Davenport was relentlessly adamant. Even age did not soothe his savage conservatism. In the 1660s when he was called to the pulpit of Boston's First Church, Davenport's persistent intransigence split that congregation, a split that Perry Miller suggests "nearly destroyed New England."[14] Hawthorne recalls Davenport's stubbornness in Richard Digby—a haunting reminder that in a closed and obsessive personality narrow and rigid believing can be fatal.

The Veiled Mr. Hooper

It's a typical bright Sunday in Milford.[15] The church bell rings, summoning the people of the village to worship: children "in the conscious dignity of their Sunday clothes"; feeble old men and proper old women; "spruce" bachelors and pretty young maidens. The assembling people of the parish wait on the meetinghouse porch for Mr. Hooper, the village parson, to arrive. But today when their pastor emerges from his door and makes his way toward the meetinghouse, he adds more than an expected solemnity to the gathering congregation. His appearance startles everyone: a veil of black crepe hangs from his forehead, covering most of his face.

Though his parishioners are "wonder-struck" at the sight of Mr. Hooper, he follows his customary Sunday routine. As he enters the meetinghouse, he greets those on the steps with his usual kindness. He makes his way slowly down the aisle of the church, bowing respectfully as he passes the oldest member of the parish. In a familiar voice, he announces the psalm, reads the scripture, prays, and preaches. But the new black veil over Mr. Hooper's face casts a shadow on everything he does: it shakes "with his measured breath" as he recites the psalm, it throws "its obscurity" between him and the Bible as he reads the lessons, it lays "heavily on his uplifted countenance" as he prays, and it adds a "subtle power" to his preaching. At the close of the service, the worshippers hurry away from the meetinghouse. The village squire even forgets to issue his customary invitation to Mr. Hooper to join him at

Sunday dinner. Left alone on the steps of the meetinghouse, the veiled parson walks slowly to his parsonage. As he pauses at the door and looks back at the few parishioners remaining in the street, they notice a sad smile "flickering" from his mouth—the only portion of his face that is not obscured by the black veil.

Elizabeth, the woman to whom Mr. Hooper is engaged, is understandably mystified when he wears the veil even in her presence. She asks him to lay it aside and then to tell her why he has chosen to wear it. He refuses to take it off. It is a "type and symbol" he feels bound to wear always: "Even you, Elizabeth, can never come behind it!" She wonders, has he done some terrible thing? Nothing more terrible than other humans, he tells her. Then take away the veil, she pleads, lest people imagine it hides some scandal. Again Mr. Hooper refuses. None of Elizabeth's arguments persuade him. In final desperation, she bursts out, "Lift the veil but once, and look me in the face." "Never! It cannot be!" he replies. "Then, farewell!" she says and hurries away.

As the years pass, the black-veiled Parson Hooper becomes a surprisingly effective minister. People struggling with an awareness of their sin sense that he understands their plight and are converted. People on their deathbeds refuse to die until he is present to pray with them. Though rumors persist that Mr. Hooper's veil hides some terrible guilt, the quality of his ministry gains him more and more respect among the New England churches. In his latter years, he is honored with the title of "Father" Hooper. But he never removes the veil. Even on his deathbed, attended by Elizabeth who had refused to become his wife and by the Rev. Mr. Clark, a colleague, Mr. Hooper's resolve holds firm. As what are certain to be his last living moments approach, Mr. Clark suggests that the dying Father Hooper has now completed a life of faithful witness; certainly he is entitled to die with an unveiled face. But when Mr. Clark reaches out to remove the veil from Hooper's face, with a vigor that startles those gathered at his deathbed, Mr. Hooper grasps the veil and holds it tightly over his face. "On earth, never!" he cries out. And then he gasps his last breath and falls back on his pillow, "a veiled corpse, with a faint smile lingering on his lips."

What is the meaning of this black veil that Mr. Hooper suddenly dons and then refuses to remove for the rest of his life? Is Mr. Hooper simply hiding his face to cover guilt suffered as the result of some terrible act? At least one critic believes Hawthorne's Hooper mirrors the infamous "Handkerchief Moody," a minister from York, Maine, who accidentally killed a friend and was so mortified by what he had done that he spent the rest of his life with a veil over his face.[16] But even a casual reading of Hawthorne's story suggests that what afflicts Mr. Hooper is more than guilt from one terrible deed. Hawthorne may have taken the idea for Mr. Hooper from Parson Moody, but the fully developed Mr. Hooper is an entirely different character from his historical antecedent. Mr. Hooper wears the veil to symbolize a concern that stretches far beyond whatever personal guilt he may feel. The veil unquestionably brings an all-encompassing change to Hooper. It affects both his outlook (gives "a darkened aspect to all living and inanimate things") and his character (enhances the already "gentle gloom of Mr. Hooper's temperament"). Though some of Mr. Hooper's parishioners wonder openly whether the veil symbolizes a conscience troubled by "some great crime, too horrible to be entirely concealed," his veil actually represents the exact opposite of their suspicion. It is his visible protest against the notion that he and perhaps only a few other humans have committed an awful, unforgivable sin. Mr. Hooper dons a veil to testify not to a distinctive but to a *common* reality. As he says to Elizabeth during their painful, final interview, "if I cover [my face] for secret sin, what mortal might not do the same?" What troubles Mr. Hooper is his entire congregation's, *everyone's*, ignorance (and denial) of their profound sinfulness. *Everyone* is sinful. The common smiles of civility are simply a futile attempt to veil the reality of common, inescapable sinfulness.

The point of Mr. Hooper's veil becomes apparent when he stands within the historical context that Hawthorne likely had in mind as he wrote "The Minister's Black Veil." Mr. Hooper is an "awakened Puritan" living among well-mannered and respectable but not spiritually aware parishioners in New England during the 1730s and 1740s. Their commonsense religiosity and respectability challenged the fearsome God of Calvinist Puritanism. Those who followed this practical Puritanism, which was openly advocated by contemporary moral philosophers like Benjamin Franklin, believed that determined and self-disciplined humans could live a good life by their own strength. The Great Awakening led by Jonathan Edwards protested this watered-down Calvinism. Edwards preached classic Calvinism: *all* humans are depraved, utterly dependent on God's grace for *any* goodness. *All* people are sinners alienated from God and from each other. There are no exceptions. The smiles that people put on their faces when they greet one another are simply a vain attempt to mask their common guilt.

The names Hawthorne chose for some of his characters suggest the historical setting he likely had in mind in "The Minister's Black Veil." Squire Saunders, who is so taken aback by Mr. Hooper's veil that he forgets to invite the pastor to Sunday dinner, carries the same last name as Poor Richard Saunders, the practical Puritan who is the protagonist in Benjamin Franklin's famous "Almanack."[17] Governor Jonathan Belcher who invites Mr. Hooper to preach an election sermon was an orthodox Calvinist who served as governor of both New Hampshire and Massachusetts beginning in 1730. Belcher later became governor of New Jersey and was influential in the founding of the College of New Jersey, another seat of orthodoxy designed by its founders to promote orthodox Calvinism. The Rev. Mr. Clark who tries (and fails) to persuade the dying Mr. Hooper to remove his veil is a likely reflection of another later, nineteenth-century Mr. Clark who served as the ministerial associate of no less a Unitarian (and Arminian) than the Rev. Charles Chauncy.[18]

The historical references implied in the names Hawthorne gave these minor characters highlight the contrast between Mr. Hooper and the members of his parish. Mr. Hooper is an impeccable Puritan living among cultural churchgoers. The people of Milford parish have lost the overwhelming sense of sin that dominated the faith of their forebears. As he ministers among them, Mr. Hooper's constantly veiled face is a symbol of the orthodox Calvinism he affirms. Mr. Hooper does *not* see himself as exceptional. There is no single, terrible sin in Mr. Hooper's past. His sinfulness is common, human sinfulness—the sinfulness that everyone shares—and from which no one by his or her own effort can escape. To look directly into another's eyes or to see one's own image in a mirror is to confront the grave reality of this human condition. The impeccably orthodox Mr. Hooper stands solidly against the popular (Arminian) belief that humans become acceptable to God when they recognize and repent of their "sins." All human attempts at righteousness are bound to fail. Those who try to please God may look good and they may act respectably, but their goodness is only a veneer. Behind every melancholy smile is a sinful human.

"The Minister's Black Veil" is more than a somber recognition of the strength of orthodox Calvinism, however. Mr. Hooper embodies Hawthorne's critical ambivalence toward religion: he appears to be designed to display the weakness, as well as the strength, of orthodox Calvinism. Mr. Hooper offers a powerful apology for orthodox Calvinism. But he seems unable to make his point and move on. Mr. Hooper is stuck: "From his initial donning of the black veil straight through to his final deathbed speech, his insight bears only repetition. It may deepen, but it does not lead on to anything else. Indeed it seems to trap him."[19] What begins as a witness ends up as an obsession. Mr. Hooper is fixated on the black veil, and that fixation becomes his undoing. In the beginning, the veil separates Mr. Hooper from human community; in the end, it comes between him and God. The darkening crepe locks Mr. Hooper inside of himself, and once he enters that dark prison, he is unable to see the light of the gospel. Even in the moments of his approaching death, the veil still "lay upon his face, as if to deepen the gloom of his darksome chamber, and shade him from the sunshine of eternity." The sunshine of eternity never penetrates the crepe that closets Mr. Hooper. And the protest that excludes him from dinners with the squire and unveiled marriage with Elizabeth cuts him off from the only community possible in this world: community with sinners.[20] Like that of Richard Digby in "The Man of Adamant" and Arthur Dimmesdale in *The Scarlet Letter*, this isolation proves to be Parson Hooper's undoing. Shut up inside of himself, his soul withers and he becomes a victim of his own believing.

The Vulnerable Mr. Dimmesdale

While Richard Digby and Father Hooper and their stories are not well known, Hester Prynne and Arthur Dimmesdale and their story are familiar to many Americans. Her brave acceptance of the Puritan community's punishment when she bears an out-of-wedlock child, her defiant wearing of the scarlet letter "A," his silence and the slow deterioration of his health and character when he cannot bring himself to confess publicly that he is her child's father have become canonical images in American fiction.

Like many others in my generation, I became acquainted with Arthur Dimmesdale as a high school student when I first read *The Scarlet Letter*. Like most of the others in my high school American literature class, I learned the story but gained only a superficial understanding of the characters. I did perceive Hester as the strongest character in the story and Arthur as the weakest. I even had some sense of the dilemma Hawthorne's characterizations pose: the free-spirited Hester, who appears to have little regard for the laws of church and society, seems to have far more integrity than her theologically correct and publicly idolized minister-lover. Of course, they both sin, our teacher emphasized, and must suffer for their sin. This suggestion that their adultery and the suffering it leads to is the overwhelming moral of the story was no doubt meant to ward off any inclination we students might have had to diminish their sin or, worse, to accept Hester as a role model. But her fervent moralistic explanation failed to thwart either our curiosity or our admiration; at least some of us knew there is more to Hester and to Arthur than our teacher was willing to admit.

Looking back from the vantage point of fifty years, I now recognize that both my teacher and we, her students, had accurate insights. *The Scarlet*

Letter is about sin and suffering. And Hester *is* the hero of *The Scarlet Letter*, the only (though not completely) admirable character in the story.

The major actors in Hawthorne's romance—Hester Prynne, Arthur Dimmesdale, Hester's husband Roger Chillingworth, and the Puritan church community—interweave like counterpoints in a marvelously crafted fugue. They happen together: each one's character emerges in the counterpoints the others provide. Hester is the foil Hawthorne uses to clarify the nature and consequences of Arthur's and his Puritan church's beliefs. Arthur's vulnerability becomes painfully apparent as Roger victimizes him, and the church unwittingly compounds that victimization. Hawthorne reverses many of the outcomes contemporary readers would have expected. Arthur who is a completely orthodox believer is neither protected nor healed by his faith; quite the opposite: Arthur is progressively undone by both his own believing and the believing of his church. Hester, whose beliefs are totally unorthodox and who is an unrepentant sinner in the eyes of the community, becomes a stronger and stronger person as the story progresses; she even regains the respect of the church and community. Roger, the physician, who uses his medical knowledge and his status as a doctor to torture and destroy Arthur, his patient, is neither exposed nor punished for his evil actions.

The adroit ambiguity Hawthorne employs both makes his characters complex and compromises their culpability. Hester arrives in Boston two years before her husband Roger, and during that separation from him she and Arthur become lovers and conceive a child. Hester refuses to reveal her child's father, and the Puritan authorities imprison her. When she persists in that refusal, they sentence her to wear a scarlet "A" at all times, and they reveal that sentence to the public by forcing her to stand in the public marketplace on the scaffold of the pillory. Hester is startled when she sees Roger in the crowd that gathers to witness her public humiliation. Realizing that Hester recognizes him, Roger makes a gesture that she is not to acknowledge him. Later when he arranges time alone with her by assuming the role of her physician, he forces Hester to promise that she will never reveal their true relationship. This exchange between Roger and Hester establishes him as the demonic villain in Hawthorne's story, but the fact that he is Hester's husband to some degree justifies the revenge he will take on Hester and Arthur, her lover.

The Rev. Arthur Dimmesdale is an even more ambiguous character than Roger Chillingworth. On the one hand, Arthur is an impeccably orthodox Calvinist minister; on the other, he is a spineless man and a morally compromised pastor. Arthur not only commits adultery with a parishioner; when she bears their child, he protects himself by refusing to confess his own part in her dishonor. Hawthorne compromises Arthur's culpability by implying that Arthur may not be entirely to blame for his silence; his moral weakness appears to be confounded by psychological dysfunction. Roger takes advantage of Arthur's psychological vulnerability. Arthur's faith should give him courage and protect him against the evil influences Roger represents, but it does not. His moral compromise and his psychological weakness combine to undermine his faith and compromise his character. Thus Arthur is simultaneously a vulnerable person, a weak character, and a victim of the image his own congregation insists he fulfill. Hawthorne reveals these conflicting character traits in Arthur's relationships with Roger, Hester, and his congregation.

The struggling minister attracts the demonic doctor. At first, Roger Chillingworth seems to be aware only of the symptoms, not the cause, of Arthur's suffering. But closer contact brings a sense that there is something more than a pastor-parishioner relationship between Hester and Arthur. In the disguise of a person needing spiritual guidance, he seeks out the innocent pastor. Arthur is both flattered and fascinated that a man of science should seek advice from him—and hopeful that Roger will be able to relieve his mental and physical suffering. They hold long conversations. Roger gathers information he will use to torment Arthur. Under the guise of needing better access to his patient, Roger suggests that they take rooms in the same house. This arrangement makes Arthur accessible to Roger at all times and permits the doctor to assess freely the debilitating effects of his treatment.

Roger recognizes that a passionate and guilty man lurks beneath Arthur's appearance of piety—and that the minister's passionate nature erupted and led him to do "a wild thing" with his own wife, Hester (137). Roger takes revenge. Under Roger's "care," Arthur Dimmesdale's condition worsens. Others may be aware that Roger's diabolical plot is the cause of this worsening condition, but not the victim. Hester recognizes that, whatever efficacy there may have been in Arthur's feelings of remorse, "a deadlier venom had been infused into it by the hand that proffered relief" (166). Others in the church and community recognize that some evil influence is at work in their minister, but they are unwilling to intervene to help him. They decide "that the Reverend Arthur Dimmesdale, like many other personages of especial sanctity, in all ages of the Christian world, was haunted either by Satan himself, or Satan's emissary, in the guise of old Roger Chillingworth. This diabolical agent had the Divine permission, for a season, to burrow into the clergyman's intimacy, and plot against his soul" (128). As his church and the God they envision look on, Arthur Dimmesdale is destroyed by the collusion of his physician with his sick soul.

Arthur's experience with Roger reveals his psychological captivity; his experience with Hester reveals his theological and social captivity. Hawthorne uses a long conversation between Hester and Arthur that stretches over chapters 17 and 18 at the center of the book to describe how Arthur is imprisoned by his beliefs. Hester is concerned about the increasing influence Roger exerts over Arthur. She arranges to meet Arthur in the forest as he returns from a visit to the Rev. John Eliot, the "Apostle" to the Indians. They come upon each other on a forest path; it is the first time they have been alone with each other in seven years. They walk and talk for a while; then, in a tender moment, they stop and look into each other's eyes. Arthur asks Hester if she has found peace. She says nothing but only smiles "drearily, looking down upon her bosom" at the scarlet letter. Then she asks Arthur the same question. "None!" he blurts out, "nothing but despair!" and then goes on to lament the turmoil of his soul. Hester seeks to counteract Arthur's obvious misery by pointing out that the people of his church revere and honor him for the good works he does among them. Surely their respect and admiration bring him comfort? None, he responds; he is only made more miserable when he sees their esteem because he knows that he does not deserve it. But "you have deeply and sorely repented," she protests: "Your sin is left behind you, in the days long past. Your present life is not less holy, in very truth, than it seems in people's eyes. Is there no reality in the penitence thus sealed and witnessed by good works?" Arthur finds none. "There is no substance in it! It is cold and dead, and can do nothing for me! Of penance I have had enough! Of penitence there has been none. . . . Happy are you, Hester that wear the scarlet letter openly upon your bosom! Mine burns in secret!" (191–92).

Hester is appalled by Arthur's condition. "Advise me what to do," he pleads. Hester responds by suggesting that Arthur can escape his tormentors simply by distancing himself from them—by moving away. The two of them could vanish together into the forest. Neither Roger nor the people of the parish would be able to find them. The blowing wind in the forest floor would cover their tracks. "But only under the fallen leaves," Arthur says dejectedly, not during the height of summer. Hester tries again. She invites Arthur to flee with her over the "broad pathway of the sea!" They traveled that pathway when they came from the Old World to the New; they could sail back across it to their native land. In the freer social climate of England, Arthur would be beyond the reach of both Roger and the Puritan "iron men and their opinions" who now keep him "in bondage." But Arthur is not able to pursue this option, either; it is "as if he were called upon to realize a dream." He feels compelled to stay. He cannot quit his post. Hester pleads with him to reconsider. His present assignment is not the only ministry in the world! He could find another ministry somewhere else where he would be out from under the torment and despair he suffers here. But Arthur cannot envision himself in any of her suggestions. He is completely immobilized.

The contrast between Hester and Arthur could hardly be greater. Why is Arthur so completely paralyzed and Hester so free? What determines the difference between them? The answer, Hawthorne suggests, can be found in the contrasting beliefs that shape them and in the contrasting mindsets their different social roles encourage. In an earlier chapter, Hawthorne describes Hester's unique way of thinking: he says she assumes "a freedom of speculation, then common enough on the other side of the Atlantic, but which our forefathers, had they known of it, *would have held to be a deadlier crime than that stigmatized by the scarlet letter*" (164; italics mine). The statement is surprisingly strong: giving oneself the right to think freely is a more serious crime for the Puritans than adultery! What is more, Hester's position as a social outcast actually encourages her natural inclination to challenge the normative boundaries of the Puritan society.

Arthur's natural tendencies and his social experience are completely different from Hester's. Except for some titillating intellectual conversations with Roger Chillingworth, Arthur has never been moved to question Puritan beliefs or practices. Moreover, his social role as a minister reinforces his already rigid believing. As a Puritan minister, he is not only required to uphold Puritan theological and social norms but also to exemplify those norms—the very norms that now so disastrously confine him. He "had never gone through an experience calculated to lead him beyond the scope of generally received laws. . . . At the head of the social system, as the clergymen of that day stood, he was only the more trammeled by its regulations, its principles, and even its prejudices. As a priest, the framework of his order inevitably hemmed him in" (200). Arthur is totally confined within the beliefs he has embraced. He has neither the permission nor the capacity to critique them.

The contrast between Hester and Arthur could hardly be greater. Hester's beliefs, reinforced by her social experience, give her a freedom the minister cannot even envision. She has a "latitude of speculation" that is "altogether foreign" to him. The scarlet letter excludes Hester from society. But it does not do "its office"; it does not move her to repentance in the way the Puritan authorities envision it will. Her offense and her continued refusal to act the role of the penitent places Hester in what the Puritans perceive as "a moral wilderness." But instead of exhibiting moral decline, her daily life becomes more and more virtuous. She gives freely "of her little substance to every demand of poverty." She visits the sick with little regard for her own safety when pestilence grips the town. She weathers the taunts of children and refuses to return the verbal abuse of adults. Her nature shows "itself warm and rich; a well-spring of human tenderness." Hester the outcast becomes a living challenge to the social and religious system that excludes her. "Such helpfulness was found in her,—so much power to do, and power to sympathize,—that many people refused to interpret the scarlet A by its original signification. They said that it meant Able" (161). During the seven years that separate her forest meeting with Arthur from her initial condemnation, Hester's virtuous living forces her detractors to revise their first estimate of her character. When she meets Arthur in the forest, she has become an able and admirable person in the eyes of the community that earlier condemned her. In her ministry in the community, Hester functions as a good pastor would.

As Hester blossoms, Arthur declines. But he is not simply a weak man who lacks the courage to confess. He perceives the constraints of the religious and social system within which he lives as a minister very accurately. The office he holds places him at the head of that system. As a minister, he is expected to feel like a sinner but not to act like one. Arthur knows there is no effective penance for ministers who *act* sinfully. If he confesses to his transgression with Hester, there will be no forgiveness from the community; he will lose his ministry. If he owns up to what he has done, he will be punished but not forgiven. To maintain his social position and his authority, Arthur knows that he must stay within the cultural image the community and church associate with his office. He gains some personal authority when the church perceives his persistent suffering as a God-given means of strengthening him spiritually. But he knows that this personal authority would be short-lived if his parishioners were to discover his real sinfulness. His authority as a minister depends on maintaining the image associated with his office. So he keeps silent—and grows sicker in heart, mind, and body. Like a festering wound, the burden of his awful secret, aggravated by the demonic ministrations of Roger Chillingworth, finally overwhelms and destroys him.

As the head of the conterminous Puritan ecclesiastical and social systems, the Rev. Arthur Dimmesdale embodies the destructive moral idealism that pervades his church and community. The church community of *The Scarlet Letter* is the corporate villain of the story. Functionally, it is a community of judgment, not forgiveness. Instead of reaching out to sinners and enabling their forgiveness, the community judges them, condemns them, and excludes them. Arthur and Hester share the common status of outcasts. She carries the stigma of being an outcast visibly as she wears the scarlet letter; he masks his condemned status from public view—though he cannot hide from it within himself.[21] Both perceive accurately that this church cannot offer healing forgiveness. It is a moral community more than a community of faith; it protects its moral self-image by condemning transgressors. Hester and Arthur are victims of their church's shortsighted faith.

In true liberal fashion, Hawthorne focuses on behavior as the critical measure of faith. He challenges the widely assumed cause-and-effect relationship between orthodox beliefs and moral superiority in his characterizations of Hester and Arthur. Hester, who does not affirm the Puritans' beliefs, is actually a superior performer. Even her Puritan critics recognize her moral performance as "admirable." Hawthorne solidifies his challenge of the cause-and-effect relationship between right belief and moral behavior when he describes Hester's beliefs critically. In the forest scene, he identifies her as a person who "had wandered without rule or guidance, in a moral wilderness" (199). But Hester's deficient beliefs do not result in deficient behavior. Quite the opposite: even her severest critics are forced to recognize that her caring morality is exemplary.

The reversal that is posited in Hester is completed in Arthur. The orthodox beliefs that are supposed to redeem Arthur do not. In fact, Hawthorne suggests, as long as Arthur remains within this Puritan community, they cannot. Faith as acted out in this community contributes to his decline. So the reversal of contemporary expectations is complete: Hester's defiance of the beliefs and strict behavioral norms of the church and community makes her an outcast. But her position as an outcast actually enables her "salvation." Hester Prynne is not an orthodox believer; but ultimately, neither is she a victim. Arthur Dimmesdale is both an orthodox believer and a victim of that believing. There is no salvation for Arthur Dimmesdale. He withers and dies—a victim of his own and his church's misbelieving.

More than 150 years after *The Scarlet Letter* appeared, it is clear that Dimmesdale and the Puritans portrayed in the novel, like Richard Digby and Parson Hooper in Hawthorne's earlier stories, are psychologically dysfunctional. They suffer ill effects from believing, not simply because they are Calvinists but because they are morbid Calvinists. Their faith is warped by their dysfunctional psychology. The comparative experience of Hester and Arthur shows that supposedly better beliefs do not necessarily result in better believing. In *The Scarlet Letter*, Hester's beliefs are not portrayed as superior to the Puritan Calvinists' beliefs; in fact, Hawthorne suggests that at least some of Hester's beliefs are inferior to some of theirs. But on the whole, Hester is a healthier person than they are. Hester's relatively better psychological health enables her to escape from the tangle of dysfunction that ensnares Arthur and the Puritans who condemn her. Hawthorne's characterizations suggest that orthodox believers are not necessarily better off because they are orthodox believers. Calvinism as a theological system presents clear hazards to people like Richard Digby, Father Hooper, and Arthur Dimmesdale. Their psychological makeup renders them especially vulnerable to the hazards a misconstrued Calvinism poses. Morbid people are likely to become morbid believers; they distort whatever theology they embrace, and that distorted theology contributes to their dysfunction. Some theological systems have the potential to be especially damaging. Misguided Calvinism can be lethal to vulnerable believers.

Perpetrators of Oppression

Hawthorne's fictional ministers are such complex and elusive characters that it is difficult to discern what Hawthorne believed by studying the clergy he invented. It is much easier to discover what Hawthorne did *not* believe by reading his fiction than to discern what he did believe. Most of his fictional ministers seemed to be designed intentionally to act out what Hawthorne saw as flawed beliefs. I think this analytical approach reflects Hawthorne's personal attitude toward religion. He characteristically viewed religion from the perspective of an interested but critical observer. Hawthorne may have avoided deep religious commitments himself because he saw how destructive those commitments could become in others.

Herman Melville's clergy are both similar to and different from Nathaniel Hawthorne's ministers. The clergy in Melville's novels are typically minor characters who are less complex than most of Hawthorne's ministers, but they are at least, if not more, oppressive. The minor roles Melville's clerics play in his books and their lack of complexity actually serve to enhance their oppressiveness. Melville is a much more transparent person than Hawthorne. Even when Melville's writing is obscure, his personal attitudes toward religion are apparent in his fiction. Melville's God often seems like a cosmic tyrant. Most of the clergy Melville creates function as agents of an oppressive God and an oppressive religious establishment. Melville often seems haunted by his religious experience. Throughout most of his adult life, he struggled with and against his perceptions of God. Melville never seemed able either to accept or to escape the God he perceived. Most of Melville's fictional missionaries, chaplains, and ministers reflect his lifelong irresolvable "quarrel with God." They reveal a man who was often angry with God and those who represent God.[22]

The gloomy perspective that dominated Melville's religious outlook and his writing may have roots in his childhood—a childhood that, at first, resembled and then became vastly different from Hawthorne's. Hawthorne spent nearly all his childhood years in Salem, Massachusetts, as a member of an established and respected family. His family's church affiliation reflected their social standing. His parents and their extended families were affiliated with liberal Congregational churches that became Unitarian in the 1820s. He attended Bowdoin College, an educational institution that then catered almost exclusively to New England's elite young men. Franklin Pierce, a future U.S. president, whom Hawthorne met at Bowdoin, became one of his lifelong friends. Hawthorne's socialization and his early religious experience combined to encourage the social confidence and independent, liberal religious perspectives he exhibited as an adult.

Until he was eleven years old, Herman Melville's childhood seemed destined to follow a pattern similar to Hawthorne's. His mother Maria Gansevoort and his father Allan Melvill (as the name was spelled before Herman's mother added an "e" sometime during the year after Allan's death) had roots in distinguished families. During Herman's early years, Allan Melvill prospered as a New York merchant, continuing a trade he learned from Herman's grandfather, the successful Boston merchant, Thomas Melvill. The family celebrated grandfather Melvill not only as a successful merchant but also as one of the instigators of the Boston Tea Party. Maria Gansevoort, Herman's mother, bore the name of a distinguished Dutch family who emigrated from Holland to Albany, New York, in the mid-seventeenth century. During those years, the Gansevoorts prospered as brewers and intermarried with the best Dutch families in Albany. As a young child, Herman learned that his maternal grandfather, General Peter Gansevoort, was the "Hero of Fort Stanwix." General Gansevoort's successful defense of Fort Stanwix saved Albany, and perhaps all of New York, during the Revolution.

But neither inherited fortune nor social standing was sufficient to protect Allan Melvill from economic disaster. It is unclear whether Herman and his family were victims of Allan's poor business judgment or simply casualties of one of the many downturns that characterized the volatile American economy during the early decades of the nineteenth century. Whatever may have been the cause of their misfortune, late in the day on October 9, 1830, Herman and his father gathered up the few personal items that remained in their Manhattan house and hurried off to board the night boat to Albany. His mother and older brother, Gansevoort, had left quietly a day earlier, taking the family's furniture from New York City to Albany. As Herman and his father prepared to leave their Manhattan home for the last time, Herman may not have fully understood why their departure was so urgent: that Allen Melvill was three months behind in the rent and they were leaving quickly to evade creditors who could have had Herman's father arrested and thrown into debtors' prison. A vicious storm delayed the riverboat's departure until morning and no doubt increased Allen Melvill's anxiety. But as the boat finally pulled away from the pier the next morning, carrying him and Herman away from New York City toward Albany, Allen knew their escape was successful.

The bleak night was a harbinger of the years to come. Herman's father never recovered from his business failure. Unable to raise the capital needed to begin another business, he was reduced to working as a clerk in a clothing store. In fewer than two years, he was dead. During Herman's remaining years at home, the family never regained economic security. Often they had to depend on the good will of relatives for funds; sometimes they even had to move in with them. The family tried to support Herman's schooling; he attended the Albany Academy for a time. But the need for Herman to work to help support the household interrupted and finally thwarted his formal education. During his teenage years, Melville held a variety of jobs—including clerking in a store, farming, and teaching school. None of them seemed to offer a promising future. At the age of nineteen, like other young men with nothing to look forward to, Herman Melville went to sea. On June 5, 1839, when he left pier 14 on the East River, hired as a "boy" on the *St. Lawrence*, a small, three-masted, square-rigged merchant ship bound for Liverpool, Herman was only two years older than Nathaniel Hawthorne was when he left Salem to become a student at Bowdoin College. Melville spent most of the next five years as a seaman. In later life, he described the years he spent at sea as his alternative higher education.[23]

The struggles that mark Melville's early years left him with a nagging sense of vulnerability. The worldview most often apparent in Melville's writing suggests an author who feels he and most other humans are both vulnerable and precarious. That sense of his plight in the world may stem, in part, from the dominant religious perspective that surrounded him during his teenage years. Even before Allen Melvill's death, Maria Melvill's inherited Calvinism, not Allan Melvill's Unitarianism, became the formal religion of the Melvill household. If Herman did attend worship services during his adolescence, he likely heard, as one of his biographers suggests, "austere, earnest, pessimistic orthodoxy" expounded by the Rev. Mr. Ludlow and the Rev. Mr. Vermilye, pastors who served the North Church (now

First Church) in Albany that Melville's mother attended after his father's death. While Herman may have absorbed some sober theology from the sermons of these Calvinist divines, he never quite embraced it. His mature writing, especially the novels *Moby-Dick* and *Pierre*, suggests that Melville resented orthodox Calvinism—and his own inability either to accept it or deny it.[24]

Only a hint of this gloominess breaks through in Melville's first novels. The discouraged young son who went to sea in 1839 returned a dashing adventurer who regaled his family with tales of exotic escapades in the South Seas. They were captivated by Herman's stories and urged him to write them as a book. At age twenty-five, with no certain future in place and with little desire to return to the difficult life of a seaman, he did. The book that emerged he called *Typee: A Peep at Polynesian Life*. Melville presented the book as an authentic account of his travels and experiences among the inhabitants of the Marquesas Islands. But in *Typee*, story is more important to Melville than fact; the "true" account is actually more fiction than fact. It follows a pattern Melville would repeat in many of his novels. In *Typee*, he interweaves his own experiences with information he gleaned from other sources.

In the winter of 1845 Melville took his completed manuscript to Harper Brothers publishing house. He had good reason to believe Harpers would publish his book; they had recently published Richard Henry Dana's *Two Years Before the Mast*. The assigned copyreader, Frederick Saunders, who reviewed Melville's work for the Harpers, was impressed with the manuscript and recommended publication, observing that *Typee* "if not as good as Robinson Crusoe seems to me to be not far behind it." But Harpers decided not to publish *Typee* because, in their judgment, "it was impossible that it could be true and therefore was without real value." Melville was devastated by the rejection of his book, in part because he knew the Harper Brothers' assessment was valid. *Typee was* at least as much the product of his imagination as the record of what he actually witnessed. But the setback was only temporary; Melville's fortunes soon took a better turn. President James K. Polk's secretary of State, James Buchanan, rewarded Herman's brother Gansevoort for his support during the president's election campaign with an appointment to the U.S. legation in London. When Gansevoort departed for England, he carried Herman's manuscript with him. Soon after his arrival in London, Gansevoort presented the manuscript to John Murray, an English publisher. Though Murray, too, had doubts about *Typee*'s authenticity, he had sufficient confidence in its salability to set them aside. In December, he agreed to publish the book. It appeared in 1846.[25]

Typee transformed Herman Melville into a folk hero. It also made him a controversial author. *Typee* not only contains titillating material; it contains strong criticism of westerners in general and of Americans and Christians in particular—especially in the original, English edition. In *Typee*, Melville presents the Marquesan Islanders—among whom he says he lived for four months (it was actually only three weeks)—and other native islanders as neither culturally nor religiously inferior to Europeans and Americans (124–25, 171). What is worse, in the novel, Melville argues that western missionaries sent to bring the gospel to the "primitive" peoples do not simply fail to live up to the tenets of the Christian faith, they actually take advantage of those they are sent to convert. Melville's descriptions of the disruptive effects western civilizing and evangelizing efforts have on the islanders and his images of the missionaries' unethical behaviors are graphic:

> Among a multitude of similar exhibitions that I saw, I shall never forget a robust, red-faced, and very lady-like personage, a missionary's spouse, who day after day for two months together took her regular airings in a little go-cart drawn by two of the islanders, one an old grey-headed man, and the other a rogueish stripling, both being, with the exception of the fig-leaf, as naked as when they were born. (196–97)

Contemporary readers understandably found passages like this one inflammatory. (The American publisher John Wiley insisted that the most offensive be expunged before he would publish an American edition of *Typee*).[26] Though attacks on the missionary enterprise were not unknown in the literature of the day,[27] Melville's criticism was especially damaging. He represented himself as one who actually observed the ill effects of missionaries' unethical behaviors.

Typee unleashed a backlash of criticism. Reviewers in the evangelical press attacked Melville's views of the missionary enterprise, and they offered an even more damaging criticism: they questioned his credibility. They accused Melville of fabricating his stories (and later criticism reveals that they were largely correct).[28] But fortune was again on Melville's side. Just at the height of the outcry, a rescuer appeared. Richard Tobias Greene, or "Toby," who was Melville's traveling companion during the adventures he describes in *Typee*, suddenly surfaced in Buffalo, New York. In an interview published in the *Buffalo Commercial Advertiser*, Toby defended Melville's credibility. The characters and events Melville describes in *Typee are* factual, he told the newspaper: "I am the true and veritable 'Toby,' yet living, and I am happy to testify to the entire accuracy of the work so long as I was with Melville."[29]

Melville was vindicated—but he was not content. He continued to present critical images of westerners and Christians in his writing. His objection was not simply to missionaries in particular but to the church in general. He portrays almost all of the church leaders who appear in his novels either as individuals who use their position to advance their own interests or as lackeys of an oppressive social establishment and its religious institutions.[30] In Melville's books, most clergy function as agents of social and religious oppression. A navy chaplain who appears in *White-Jacket*, for example, is out of touch and unsympathetic to the common seamen. And because he serves at the pleasure of the officers aboard ship, the chaplain enables the officers' control—and sometimes their abuse—of ordinary sailors. The "lord-spiritual, with the exception of the purser, was in the highest favour with the commodore." The chaplain's sermons are "ill-calculated to benefit the crew" (156): they are designed to please the captain and the other officers, not to benefit the ordinary sailors.

Ministers gain respect in Melville's writing only when they have theological integrity like Father Mapple in *Moby-Dick* or when they are able to break free of obligation to the social and religious establishment. One of these rare positive portrayals appears in *Redburn*. In a brief passage, Melville recalls the Church of England clergy he saw ministering at the floating chapels on the docks during his first visit to Liverpool: "Never have I heard religious discourses better adapted to an audience of men, who, like sailors, are chiefly, if not only, to be moved by the plainest of precepts. . . . [These priests who took] familiar themes for their discourses, which were leveled right at the wants of their auditors. . . . And several times on the docks, I have seen a robed clergyman addressing a large audience of women collected from the notorious lanes and alleys in the neighborhood." Melville speculates that these priests are successful precisely because they have left "converted and comfortable congregations" to minister in "the infected centers and hearts of vice" (176). Their disassociation from the establishment makes them effective. These Anglican (and non-American) clerics who appear in *Redburn* are exceptions that prove the rule.

In *Moby-Dick* and *Pierre*, Melville escalates his criticism of ministers to the level of an argument with God. In these two novels, human experience points to a cosmic order where everything and everyone is at the mercy of a tyrannical God. The scene at the New Bedford Whaleman's Chapel, described in chapters 7 and 8 of *Moby-Dick*, and Father Mapple's sermon in chapter 9 picture this cosmic tyrant. Ishmael, who narrates the novel, struggles through the driving sleet of a winter storm to visit the chapel on a Sunday morning. Once inside, he finds a small congregation of seamen and seamen's wives and widows who sit alone or in small groups. An eerie silence dominates the church, broken only by the howling wind of the storm. The worshippers seem to isolate themselves from each other purposely "as if each silent grief were insular and incommunicable" (34). The "silent islands" of men and women are absorbed in thought as they scan the memorial tablets attached to the walls on either side of the pulpit. Each tablet is dedicated to the memory of a sailor lost at sea: one to

> John Talbot
> Who, at the age of eighteen, was lost overboard
> Near the Isle of Desolation, off Patagonia.

Another recalls six sailors in a boat from

> THE SHIP ELIZA
> Who were towed out of sight by a Whale.

Another memorializes Captain Ezekiel Hardy:

> Who in the bows of his boat was killed by a
> Sperm Whale on the coast of Japan. (35, 36)

Though he has no way of knowing whether any of the relatives of those memorialized in the tablets are present in the congregation, Ishmael takes their absorption and the "unceasing grief" he sees in their faces as signs that the tablets cause "old wounds to bleed afresh" (36).

Father Mapple, the resident chaplain to the sailors, enters suddenly, wearing a great cloth seaman's jacket, his hat and coat covered with sleet. He removes his coat and hat and walks toward the high raised pulpit. Access to the pulpit consists of a ladder, much like a ship's ladder. Father Mapple ascends the ladder with the sure steps of a man ascending to the maintop of his vessel. The ascent is no play-acting: the worshippers know that this preacher, now old in years, served in his youth as a sailor and harpooner. The members of the congregation recognize in him one who knows both the ways of the Almighty and the precarious nature of the sailor's life at sea. Once in the pulpit, Father Mapple turns and raises the ladder—an act that seems to place him in a shiplike fortress where he is entirely at the bidding and mercy of God. Ishmael describes how the physical appearance of the pulpit augments the preacher and his message. Its front is like a ship's bow with the Bible resting on a projecting piece of scrollwork, "fashioned after a ship's fiddle-headed beak. What could be more full of meaning? [Melville conjectures]—for the pulpit is ever this earth's foremost part; all the rest comes in its rear; the pulpit leads the world. From thence it is the storm of God's quick wrath is first descried, and the bow must bear the earliest brunt" (40).

After the congregation sings a hymn, Father Mapple announces his text. His sermon will be based on the book of Jonah, the final verse of chapter 1: "And God had prepared a great fish to swallow up Jonah." The preacher's theme is Jonah's sinful disobedience and his futile effort to escape God's will for him. Jonah's unsuccessful attempt to flee shows there is no escaping the Cosmic Pursuer. God relentlessly pursues anyone who disobeys him, the preacher warns. Jonah tries to escape God by boarding a ship bound for Tarshish, a city that seems to him to be placed at the furthest edge of the earth. But the journey has only begun when a ferocious storm threatens to destroy the ship. Jonah confesses to the terrified sailors that his effort to flee from God is the cause of the gale that seems certain to annihilate them all. He must accept his fate at the hands of God; there is no escape. Jonah tells the sailors to cast him overboard—and when they do, the storm ceases. However, Jonah's compliance does not result in his death but in his salvation. When he tells the sailors to throw him to what he thinks is certain doom, Jonah accepts "his dreadful punishment as just." Accepting his punishment as deserved "is true and faithful repentance; not clamorous for pardon, but grateful for punishment" (46, 47). Accepting God's punishment as gracious is the key to salvation.

Father Mapple's sermon presages the novel that follows. It likely also reveals Melville's own perception of God. Some of his personal observations around the time he was writing the novel suggest that this tyrannical God who rules the cosmos in *Moby-Dick* is also his God. In a June 1851 letter to Nathaniel Hawthorne, Melville writes, "The reason the mass of men fear God, and *at bottom dislike Him*, is because they rather distrust His Heart, and fancy Him all brain like a watch."[31] This heartless perception of God is played out in *Moby-Dick*.[32]

Melville's argument with God culminates in *Pierre*, his next novel. The two ministers in *Pierre* reflect the two most common cultural images of clergy that Melville presents in his earlier novels. The opportunistic Rev. Mr. Falsgrave is a pathetic human, as well as an oppressive minister; the minister and pamphleteer Plotinus Plinlimmon represents God as a cosmic tyrant. Pierre Glendinning, from whom the novel takes its title, is a privileged, idealistic, simple-thinking, and simple-believing young man who is unequipped for life in the real world. When the story begins, Pierre has just become engaged to Lucy Tartan. Lucy, who is described as a "wondrous, . . . fair of face, blue-eyed, and golden-haired, the bright blonde . . . arrayed in color harmonious with the heavens," appears to be an ideal match for Pierre (33). The beautiful couple seem destined to enjoy an idyllic life together. But the dream never becomes a reality. Pierre receives a letter that reveals his father, who died when Pierre was twelve years old, had an extramarital affair and fathered an illegitimate daughter named Isabel. Once he discovers Isabel, Pierre feels morally obligated to take responsibility for his now-impoverished half-sister. And he mistakenly believes his mother and his pastor, the Rev. Mr. Falsgrave, will feel the same sympathy and concern for Isabel that he does. He is taken aback when they do not. As he listens to them castigate another transgressor, Pierre realizes he should have anticipated their insensitivity toward Isabel. Ned, a local man of the parish, has strayed much as Pierre's father did. The stifled anger Pierre's mother feels toward his dead father erupts in her vicious response to news of Ned's transgression. She describes him as "worse than a murderer." She condemns Ned, his lover Delly, and even their child. Her railing tells Pierre how she thinks he should feel toward both his dead father and his newly discovered half-sister: "Has he not sacrificed one woman completely, and given infamy to another—to both of them—for their portion? If his own legitimate boy should now hate him, I could hardly blame him" (100).

Even the opportunistic Rev. Mr. Falsgrave is taken aback by Mrs. Glendinning's severity. "The sins of the father shall be visited upon the children to the third generation," he says, questioningly. "Does she really mean to imply that the community is to condemn and exclude even the innocent child?" That is what she means: "If we forget the parentage of the child, and every way receive the child as we would any other, feel for it in all respects the same, and attach no sign of ignominy to it—how then is the Bible dispensation to be fulfilled? Do we not then put ourselves in the way of its fulfillment, and is that wholly free from impiety?" (100). Mrs. Glendinning's heartless theology of retribution is too much for the minister; his face colors. That reaction, however, doesn't deter her at all. "Pardon me," continues the lady, courteously, "but if there is any one blemish in the character of the Reverend Mr. Falsgrave, it is that the benevolence of his heart, too much warps in him the holy rigor of our Church's doctrines. For my part, as I loathe the man, I loathe the woman, and never desire to behold the child" (100, 101).

Mr. Falsgrave is neither as hard nor as vengeful as Pierre's mother. But in the end, he is not able to stand up to her and support Pierre. Mrs. Glendenning is the benefactor of the parish, the "generous foundress and the untiring patroness" of the church Mr. Falsgrave serves. That financial dependence is also obvious to Pierre. But he seems unaware of the likely consequences of the minister's growing personal interest in his mother. Mr. Falsgrave waits on Mrs. Glendinning, not only in the role of a pastor visiting an important parishioner but also as a suitor. Marriage to her would bring personal and ecclesiastical advantage. If he marries Mrs. Glendinning, her dead husband's fortune will become his.

Pierre's innocence ensures his downfall. With reckless disregard of the consequences, Pierre openly embraces Isabel. He confounds the affront to his mother by embracing Ned's mistress Delly as well. Neither Pierre's pastor nor his mother supports his charity. Quite the opposite: they conspire to do him in. Though he cringes a bit at Mrs. Glendenning's unforgiving moralism, the minister compromises his own integrity. Like the missionaries in *Typee*, the Rev. Mr. Falsgrave uses his office to take advantage of an innocent victim. He joins with Pierre's mother in a successful plot to disinherit Pierre.

Pierre's personal loss does not deter him from reaching out to Isabel. He assumes responsibility not only for Isabel but also for Delly. He invites them to forsake Saddle Meadows for New York City where he hopes to find a better life. But life in the city is no better for Pierre than it was in Saddle Meadows; his downfall continues. In New York, his naive perception of his own nature causes him to falter as much as his naive view of other people. From their first meeting, Pierre not only feels concern for Isabel's welfare but also is physically attracted to her. In New York City, that attraction proves irresistible. Pierre and his half-sister become lovers—at least in fantasy, if not in fact. Such is the pattern of Pierre's life: each attempt to do what is right leads him further into ruin. Pierre's innocent outlook, his naïveté, and his idealistic faith combine to destroy him. He is unable to distinguish between the good that is possible for him to achieve and Good as an unachievable ideal. Pierre always reaches for the ideal Good—and overlooks opportunities to realize the possible good he might have accomplished.

Pierre's ultimate failure has roots in something more profound than his own idealism: the cosmos is stacked against him. Melville uses Plotinus Plinlimmon, the other clergy character in the novel, to show how God's ordering of the cosmos makes it impossible for naive believers like Pierre to succeed. As Pierre journeys away from Saddle Meadows, he finds a theological pamphlet by Plinlimmon in the seat of the carriage in which he is traveling. The theological essay published in this pamphlet serves the same purpose in *Pierre* that Father Mapple's sermon serves in *Moby-Dick:* it sets forth the nature of the cosmos in which the characters must live. Plinlimmon's work appears under an obscure subtitle, "Chronometricals and Horologicals," but its message illuminates Pierre's dilemma. The pamphlet explains why it is impossible for humans to live godly lives in this world. Plinlimmon uses the analogy of ship's time and local time to explain why humans find it impossible to live godly lives on earth. Chronometrical time is God's time. God's time is like the Greenwich time to which all ship's clocks are set and which they maintain wherever they happen to be located. Thus a ship's clock in China will read Greenwich time, even though the time where the ship happens to be located is different from Greenwich time. Humans, Plinlimmon says, are "chronometrical souls" created to run according to God's heavenly order. To be acceptable to their creator, humans must live by God's time (order). But this requirement is an impossible task: to be godly on Earth would require humans to impose heavenly time (God's order) on Earth. Such an effort is bound to meet with horrendous opposition. When someone tries to be godly (as Pierre has), he will "array all earthly time-keepers against him, and thereby work himself woe and death." Plinlimmon suggests that Jesus' human experience is unique and that uniqueness clarifies the human dilemma. On Earth, Jesus does live perfectly according to God's order. But that ability stems from Jesus' unique character; Jesus succeeds only because he *is* God. Ordinary humans are not God, and they cannot live perfectly—even though by design they are supposed to and God requires them to. Their efforts to be godly make humans dysfunctional on Earth. These efforts are "apt to involve those inferior beings eventually in strange, *unique* follies and sins" (213). The pamphlet explains why Pierre's efforts to be godly always result in disaster: it is impossible for ordinary humans to be godly. Pierre is the hapless victim of a flawed cosmos. The preacher-pamphleteer is the bearer of bad news. Significantly, the pamphlet is torn; the conclusion is missing.

Exposing the Divine

The cosmic tyrant who rules the natural order in *Moby-Dick* resembles the rigid and callous God who rules human experience in *The Scarlet Letter.* The caricatured Calvinist God who dominates Hawthorne's and Melville's fiction makes unreasonable demands of his creatures and then becomes inaccessible when they falter.[33] The Revs. Digby, Hooper, Dimmesdale, Mapple, Falsgrave, and Plinlimmon feel the overwhelming burden of God's requirements but have little or no experience of God's grace. Without grace, the requirements of God become unreasonable; believers either are oppressed or become oppressors (or both). The orthodox Calvinist theology that Hawthorne and Melville inherited always considered the ways of God inscrutable and beyond reason. But huge gaps separate inscrutable from inaccessible and beyond reason from unreasonable.

Those gaps distinguish the clergy that Hawthorne and Melville create from those created by orthodox Calvinist writers like Joseph Alden and Harriet Beecher Stowe. Both Hawthorne and Melville would find Stowe's God, as portrayed in *The Minister's Wooing*, not only inscrutable but also unreasonable. When Mary Scudder's unconverted lover James Marvyn is presumed lost at sea, both she and her pastor, Dr. Hopkins, presume James is also lost for eternity. He has never gone through a conversion experience; therefore, they assume God has not chosen him as one of the elect. Scudder and Hopkins mourn James's loss; *but they do not question God's ways.* Hopkins's willingness to accept whatever God wills for him is startling—especially his readiness to be damned for all eternity, if necessary, for the glory of God. The idea that such a requirement might be unreasonable never occurs to him. When James returns, Scudder and Hopkins are relieved that he was not lost after all, but they still accept the fact that God's justice would have been served *even if James had drowned and been damned.*

The demands of believing that deepen Hopkins's faith in Stowe's novel make ministers either crazy or oppressive in Hawthorne's and Melville's fiction. To Calvinists like the fictional Hopkins, God's demands may *seem* unreasonable, but God is never perceived as unreasonable. God's ways are beyond reason; humans cannot grasp them. When someone finds believing difficult, the problem is always his or hers, never God's. Failure to understand God's ways is always a human failure. God is not flawed; the would-be believer's ability to understand God is flawed. So Calvinists like Samuel Hopkins and Mary Scudder believe beyond and even in spite of what seems reasonable to them. Their faith reaches beyond logic. God is not inaccessible to their experience: they pray, and their faith tells them that God hears their prayers. The demands of God's justice are absolute, but God somehow reaches beyond that justice to bring salvation to those with faith. In the providence of God portrayed in Stowe's novel, the faithful do receive salvation.[34]

Calvinism without this kind of faith is pure misery. Richard Digby's, Parson Hooper's, and Arthur Dimmesdale's *faith* fails them. They have belief but not faith: they live under Calvinist theology but have no access to God. Without the access faith provides, they become unreasonable and represent God as unreasonable. Without any experience of faith, the Calvinist perception of predestination where humans are predestined to be saved or damned and helpless to alter their fate seems not only unjust but also capricious. In Father Mapple's sermon and Pierre Glendinning's life, God is both inaccessible and heartless.

The always-composed Hawthorne finds the questioning of orthodox faith and the God it perceives challenging and potentially hazardous. The often-uncomposed Melville finds doubt more troubling. Melville *suffers*, not only from lost faith but also under residual belief. Hawthorne's ministers embody the hazards he sees; Melville's ministers act out the anger and tragedy he experiences. Though quite different, the fictional clergy both of them create represent the dilemma of partial disbelieving. Both authors seem to want to reject Calvinism but can't quite do it. Hawthorne sees how abusive orthodox theology can become in those who lack lively faith, but he fears that a society where people do not image God as omnipotent may become chaotic. Melville accepts God's omnipotence but can't believe in God's absolute goodness. The result is a cosmic tyrant. The orthodox Calvinist God he perceives exacts but doesn't support.

Hawthorne and Melville may not be able to dispense entirely with orthodox theology and its image of God because they cannot imagine an alternative. Both are functional agnostics, but neither is sure he can or wants to purge the old God from his memory. As with many of their contemporaries, the loss they experience is freeing in some ways, but it is not a happy loss. As A. N. Wilson suggests in his study of faith and doubt in the nineteenth century, Victorians like Hawthorne and Melville are relieved to be out from under the Calvinist God, but, at the same time, they mourn their lost belief and sometimes wish the old God were back.[35] They live between relief and nostalgia.

These radical images that reflect clergy as vulnerable believers anticipate a growing crisis of faith among Americans—a crisis that the coming Civil War will exacerbate. Hawthorne's fear that civilized society *requires* belief in the controlling providence of God was and is deeply ingrained in the American experience. It surfaced profoundly fifteen years after *The Scarlet Letter* in Abraham Lincoln's second inaugural address. On that dark and cold day in 1865, Lincoln drew on his own lingering sense of God's providence in the cosmos to find some redemptive meaning in the bloody war between the North and the South. "No man had a stronger or firmer faith in Providence," William Henry Herndon, Lincoln's friend and law partner once remarked, but that conviction did not mean "that he believed in a personal God. [He] had no faith in the Christian sense of that term." God was for Lincoln as God was for Hawthorne and Melville: "remote, austere, all-powerful, uncommunicative." In his biography focused on Lincoln's religion, Allen C. Guelzo characterizes Lincoln's belief as "Calvinized Deism." God is neither Son nor Spirit. God ways are unfathomable; God is an inaccessible cosmic ruler.[36]

Lincoln was not alone in his sense of God's displacement from the lives of individuals. Whatever grand effect believers like Lincoln might hope for from the hand of God in history, that metaphor had already ceased to represent the assurance of *personal* solace for others besides the president. In several poems written during the early 1860s, Lincoln's contemporary Emily Dickinson describes her frustration with a remote and elusive God. During the rest of her life, Dickinson found little comfort in the old faith—either for herself or for others. A poem she wrote four years before she died reflects her lament of a displaced divine:

> Those—dying then,
> Knew where they went—
> They went to God's right Hand—
> That Hand is amputated now
> And God cannot be found—[37]

Dickinson's words image an anguish similar to the despair Pierre Glendinning suffers when he decides that God's grace is powerless (or unavailable) to help him, "for doth not Scripture intimate, that He holdeth all of us in the hollow of His hand?—a Hollow, truly!" (200).

An undercurrent of doubt that becomes more and more pervasive as the century progresses lurks beneath Hawthorne's and Melville's challenging images of the Protestant minister. Imaging ministers as vulnerable humans casts doubt not only on their authority but also on the sufficiency of God who is supposed to stand behind them. Faith no longer ensures that believers will not fall victim to their own vulnerabilities. Hawthorne's portrayals suggest that even the most orthodox divines can be crazy, sometimes quite crazy—and, what is worse, that what they believe can contribute to their craziness.[38] Melville's portrayals imply that orthodox preachers are often unethical. They are oppressors—and so is the God they represent. The emphasis varies between Hawthorne and Melville. Ministers may be disturbed and eccentric or unethical and oppressive. Their shortcomings may lead them to harm mostly themselves or lead them to abuse those who happened to be around them. In either case, they are not ministers who deserve authority. And in the eyes of a growing number of reluctant doubters, neither is the God they represent. Wherever these emerging images and the uncertainty they encourage gain acceptance, ministers' authority becomes precarious—and so does the faith they represent.

PART II

Discrediting the Divine

1860s–1920s

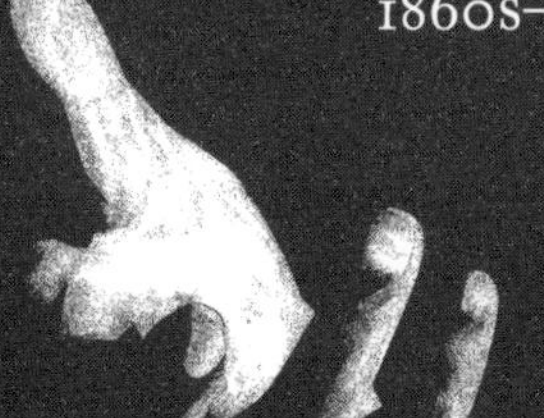

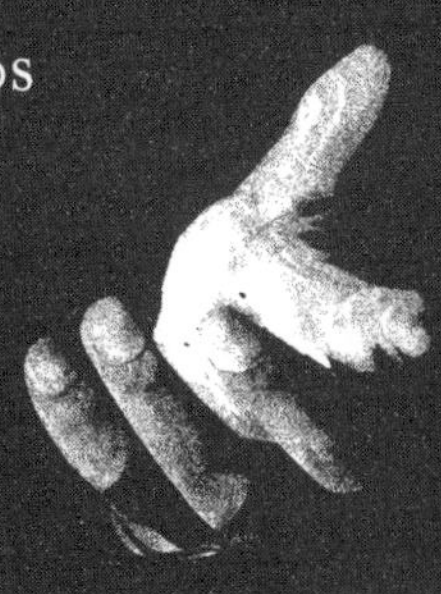

Of all the conditions of his youth which afterwards puzzled the grown-up man, this disappearance of religion puzzled him most.... He went through all the forms; but neither to him nor to his brothers or sisters was religion real.

—Henry Adams, *The Education of Henry Adams*

"It's all in a single word, Mr. Ware," she proceeded, in low tones. "I speak for others as well as myself, mind you—we find that you are a bore."

—Celia Madden describing the Rev. Theron Ware
in Harold Frederic, *The Damnation of Theron Ware*

IV

COMPULSIVES AND ACCOMMODATORS

Popular Images (1)

Compelled Believers

In 1864, when she was only twenty years old, Elizabeth Stuart Phelps began to keep a diary that four years later became the basis for *The Gates Ajar*, one of the most popular novels of the post–Civil War era.[1] Phelps began the journal in an attempt to overcome the despair she felt when the young man she had hoped to marry was killed in the Civil War. Many years later in her autobiography, Phelps says she made the transformation from journal to novel to give courage and hope to others who suffered losses similar to hers: especially to "the bereaved wife, mother, sister, and widowed girl . . . whom the war trampled down . . . who thought little but loved much, and, loving, had lost all."[2]

Mary Cabot who narrates *The Gates Ajar* is only a thinly veiled Elizabeth Stuart Phelps; her struggle to keep her faith in God and her frustration with the often cold and unhelpful ministers who surround her resembles Phelps's own experience.[3] When the book opens, Cabot is secluded in her house, unable to set aside the grief and hopelessness that have oppressed her since she first learned her brother Royal was "shot dead" on a Civil War battlefield. Except for one neighbor, no one penetrates her self-imposed isolation. That caller turns out to be an insensitive intruder, who urges her to get hold of herself and come out to a church gathering. But Mary cannot move beyond her sorrow, and she senses (quite rightly) that neither the pastor nor any of the members of her parish will be helpful to her. When she excludes herself from the communion table on Sunday, Mr. Quirk, the parish deacon, decides it is his duty to visit Mary. She anticipates correctly that this callous man will only question and pressure her to accept her lot as the judgment of a just God.

The ministrations of Mary's pastor, named appropriately Dr. Bland, offer no more comfort than those of Deacon Quirk. The first Sunday Mary is able to attend worship services again, she is momentarily hopeful when Dr. Bland announces he will preach on the text "For our conversation is in heaven." But she finds little that is helpful in the sermon. Dr. Bland offers only dispassionate, abstract theological observations. In heaven, we should look forward to an endless opportunity to "study the character of God." In preparation, we should emulate the man "who, on being asked if he expected to see the dead wife of his youth in heaven, replied, 'I expect to be so overwhelmed by the glory of the presence of God, that it may be thousands of years before I shall think of my wife.'" At this point in the minister's presentation, Mary notes that "poor Mrs. Bland looked exceedingly uncomfortable" (69, 70).

Mary finds no comfort or hope from anyone until her Aunt Winifred arrives for a visit. Winifred shares Mary's experience of grief; she has just lost her husband, a missionary minister on the western frontier. Winifred's perceptions of God and of heaven, which, she indicates, her minister-husband shared, are quite different from Deacon Quirk's and Dr. Bland's. In the heaven Winifred envisions, the dead are not solely preoccupied with God, nor are they cut off from the living. Those who have passed on to the next world continue their concern and affection for the living; they are even available to continue relationships with those living on earth. Winifred is not only comforting to Mary, she is convincing. She offers scriptural support for her views, and Mary finds Winifred's use of scripture more compelling than the theological arguments of either Deacon Quirk or her pastor.

As the weeks pass, Winifred's words ease Mary's pain and renew her faith. Winifred also challenges Dr. Bland. Though the minister finds her to be a formidable opponent, her arguments have little effect on his believing—until tragedy enters his own life. One day while she is tending the stove, Mrs. Bland's clothing catches fire; she is seriously burned and, after suffering horribly, dies a few days later. In the midst of his own grief, much to his surprise, Dr. Bland gains little solace from the theological arguments he has used to persuade others. No "Greek and Hebrew 'original,' no polished dogma, no link in his stereotyped logic, not one of his eloquent sermons on the future state, came to his relief. . . . Brought face to face . . . with the blank heaven of his belief, he stood up from before his dead, and groped about it, and cried out against it in the bitterness of his soul." In misery after his own belief fails him, Dr. Bland comes to see Winifred: "'You said once some pleasant things about heaven?' he said at last, half appealingly, stopping in front of her, hesitating; like a man and a minister, hardly ready to come with all the learning of his schools and commentators and sit at the feet of a woman" (217–19). As Winifred offers Dr. Bland words of comfort similar to the words of hope she offered Mary, he, too, finds solace.

In *The Gates Ajar*, Elizabeth Stuart Phelps proposes a warm, person-centered theological vision to complement Calvinist doctrine. She argues that spiritualist perceptions of a joyous afterlife and open communication with the departed are quite compatible with traditional Christian beliefs. The departed are not only not lost, they are accessible. This message of hope strikes home in post–Civil War America, where so many have experienced a loss similar to hers. Thousands of readers write to Phelps to express their appreciation for her work.

Phelps's roots in the Phelps and Stuart families, and in the orthodox environment of Andover Seminary, probably helped give her arguments credibility in the eyes of many of her readers. Phelps's connection to Harriet Beecher Stowe, another well-known Andover figure, also probably helped commend her work. In many ways, *The Gates Ajar* recalls Stowe's *The Minister's Wooing*, though the revisions to traditional theology in Phelps's book are more blatant and far-reaching than those Stowe proposes in hers. The similarities between the two books are striking. At the center of each novel is a woman named Mary who has lost someone she loves. Each Mary's experience resembles that of her real-life creator. Both Stowe and Phelps wrote their novels to protest the failure of traditional Calvinist theology (and its clerical representatives) to assuage the grief they experience following the tragic loss of someone they love. The orthodox Calvinist ministers in each novel are unable to move beyond their rigid theological constructs to bring solace to those who face personal tragedy. Hopkins's and Bland's perception of God is entirely intellectual—right thinking based on scholarship. That cerebral theology controls their believing and governs their ministry. When parishioners like Mrs. Marvyn and Mary Cabot suffer grief, their orthodox Calvinist pastors see only potentially catastrophic doubting. The pastors' sole agenda is to bring their parishioners back to right theological thinking.[4]

The constrained, one-sided clergy in *The Minister's Wooing* and *The Gates Ajar* reflect a powerful and enduring postbellum cultural image. I call them "compelled believers." Compelled believers are *driven* by the beliefs to which they are committed. They allow themselves no theological flexibility. In the 1860s, both religious figures like Harriet Beecher Stowe and the young Elizabeth Stuart Phelps, who remained loyal to the Calvinism they inherited, and more irreverent writers like Donald G. Mitchell and Oliver Wendell Holmes created fictional clergy who reflect what they saw as the dangers of coldly intellectual and inflexible Edwardsian Calvinism.[5] In a strategy most likely designed to make their characters more acceptable to those who might be offended by their critical portrayals, they often set their compelled believer clerics in a former time, usually the eighteenth or early nineteenth century—with the clear implication that one-sided ministers like them, *not* Calvinism entirely, should be left in the past.

Compelled believers are so constrained by their theology that they are unwilling to question or adapt it in any way. Their theology constrains even their humanity. Dr. Moses Stern in Harriet Beecher Stowe's *Oldtown Folks* (1869) is typical. As his first and last names suggest, Stern is a hard and inflexible legalist. The narrator of the story recalls the fear that Stern engenders in those who hear him. Whenever Dr. Stern

> appeared in the pulpit everybody trembled before him. . . . An austere, inflexible, grand indifference to all things earthly seemed to give him the prestige and dignity of a supernatural being. His Calvinism was of so severe and ultra a type, and his statements were so little qualified either by pity of human infirmity, or fear of human censure, or desire of human approbation, that he reminded one of some ancient prophet, freighted with a mission of woe and wrath, which he must always speak, whether people would hear or whether they would forbear. (379)

Stern's sermons live up to his reputation. When Emily Rossiter, a fourteen-year-old young woman, attends worship just days after her favorite, but likely unconverted, brother Theodore has died, Dr. Stern preaches a sermon titled "The heavenly hosts will praise God for punishing the finally impenitent forever." The sermon lives up to its title; it leaves no doubt concerning the fate of the unconverted, as well as the appropriate attitude of believers toward God's dealings with those who are damned: "And all who are conscious that they cannot say 'Amen, Alleluia' [to the everlasting punishment of the unconverted] may know that they are yet sinners, and essentially different from saints, and altogether unprepared to go with them to heaven and join with them in praising God for the vindictive justice he displays in dooming all unholy creatures to a never-ending torment" (387, 388).

After hearing Dr. Stern's sermon, "Emily suffered so much in the struggle, that her aunt became alarmed for her health" (388).

Like the fictional Dr. Hopkins who precedes him, Dr. Stern is not a harsh man by nature—nor is there any reason to believe that the way he functions is evidence of some unresolved psychological issue: "Like many other teachers of severe, uncompromising theories [Dr. Stern] was an artless, simple-hearted, gentle-mannered man." Dr. Stern's character is not the result of some psychological deficiency. Orthodox Calvinist theology, formed by single-minded devotion and relentless study, compels Dr. Stern's believing: "He was a close student, and wore two holes in the floor opposite his table in the spot where year after year, his feet were placed in study." No temporal concern could distract him. Even "when his whole summer's crop of hay was threatened with the bursting of a thunder-shower, and . . . he was importuned to lend a hand to save it, he resolutely declined, saying, that if he once began to allow himself to be called on in any emergency for temporal affairs, he should become forgetful of his great mission" (380).

Dr. Johns, the central character in Donald Grant Mitchell's *Dr. Johns: Being a Narrative of Certain Events in the Life of an Orthodox Minister of Connecticut* (1866), is a similarly compelled believer. Dr. Johns is "by nature a quiet, almost a timid man; but over the old white desk and crimson cushion, with the choir of singers in his front and the Bible under his hand, he grew into wonderful boldness" (36). The theology to which Dr. Johns feels bound completely dominates his personal life, as well as his ministry. In a sermon preached shortly after his beloved, but doubting and likely unregenerate, wife dies, he refuses to moderate his beliefs:

> We do know in our hearts that many whom we have loved fondly—infants, fathers, mothers, wives, may be—shall never, never sit with the elect in Paradise. . . . Shall we be tortured with the knowledge that some poor babe we looked upon only for an hour is wearing out ages of suffering? "No," you may say, "for we shall be possessed in that day of such sense of the ineffable justice of God, and of His judgments, that all shall seem right." (81, 82)

Ministers like Dr. Stern and Dr. Johns are respected not simply for their orthodox faith but because they are often the most-informed and best-educated members of the communities where they serve.[6] Their strong words and actions stem from strong and well-informed convictions. But as the years pass, the quality of rigidly orthodox clerics deteriorates in real life as well as in fiction. Contemporary sources indicate that both the personal and the intellectual quality of those seeking ordination declined at least from the mid-nineteenth century onward—and perhaps beginning even earlier than that. Many candidates for the ministry were less impressive than their fathers and grandfathers were.[6] (One, likely mythological, student at Andover Seminary in the 1850s is so ill informed that he listed Benedict Arnold as one of the great Protestant reformers!)[7] Beginning in the 1860s, and especially in the 1870s and 1880s, fictional characterizations of clergy as compelled believers reflect this deteriorating quality. Compelled believers are portrayed not only as rigid believers but also as uninformed and narrow thinkers. Many are also psychologically unbalanced individuals. Increasingly, they are not simply strong characters compelled by their convictions. More and more of them are vulnerable, driven, and, at times, even obsessed persons.

Bartholemy Stoker, who appears in Oliver Wendell Holmes's novel *The Guardian Angel* (1867), anticipates the transition. Holmes, whose life spans the century (1809–1894), was a brilliant, irreverent, sometimes caustic character who was not only a physician but also a popular lecturer and writer. Though his father, Abiel Holmes, was a respected and largely orthodox Congregational minister, even as a child, Holmes developed negative feelings toward both Calvinism and the Congregational Church. Young Holmes believed the congregation his father served during his childhood years was not only unappreciative but also abusive. While a student at Andover Academy, Holmes suffered abuse himself at the hands of a well-intentioned but overly severe Calvinist teacher at the academy. One physical beating Holmes received from this teacher was so brutal that years afterward he still felt emotionally scarred from it. The fictional clergy Holmes creates are shaped, in part, to reveal what he viewed as the damage authoritarian Calvinism causes.[8] Holmes's reputation as an outstanding physician and Harvard professor lent credence to his theological protest.

Holmes anticipated the declining respect for clergy in general and compelled believers in particular in his portrayal of the Rev. Bellamy Stoker in *The Guardian Angel.* Stoker is compelled at least as much by his weak character and his psychological deficiency as he is by his Calvinist theology. Called to minister alongside the aging parish pastor, Dr. Pemberton, Stoker uses feigned devotion to his calling both as an excuse for his lack of care for his chronically ill wife and to pay undue attention to young women in the parish.

Stoker's preaching is notorious "for the vividness of his descriptions of the future which was in store for the great bulk of his fellow-townsmen and fellow-worldsmen" (155). But it soon becomes apparent that Stoker's character is not as pure as his theology. Stoker is much more concerned with appearance than substance. The carpet in front of his mirror is worn threadbare from the hours the minister spends attending to his appearance, while the cloth on the knees of his pants shows no wear at all. Stoker's reputation as a preacher depends mostly on three hell-fire sermons, remembered by his hearers as much for their side effects as their content: "the *sweating* sermon, the *fainting* sermon and the *convulsion-fit* sermon" (155). But Stoker's limited homiletical ability and deficiency in prayer are by no means his greatest shortcomings. Stoker has a weakness for the "ewe lambs" in the parish. That weakness is painfully apparent to his wife as she watches the preferential treatment he gives to adolescent young women who visit him in his study. This differential treatment of ewe lambs is particularly noticeable in Stoker's relationship with the teenaged Myrtle Hazard. He arranges to spend inordinate amounts of time alone with her in the name of encouraging her spiritual formation. At first, Myrtle is innocent of his intentions, even after the purpose of his attention to her is obvious to others in the parish. Stoker's real intentions finally become clear to Myrtle one afternoon when he describes the blissful relationship she and he will enjoy in heaven—and hints that perhaps they should begin that blissful relationship now. Once she recognizes that her pastor is a closet lecher, Myrtle rebuffs him. Stoker is infuriated and unwilling to admit that his anger really stems from guilt. Determined that Myrtle shall pay for casting him aside, the next Sunday Stoker draws on his "savage medieval theology" to preach his "well-worn 'convulsion-fit' sermon." Much to the minister's chagrin, Myrtle is not among the suffering listeners in the congregation. She attends worship at the Episcopal Church.

Myrtle Hazard's rebuff is not the only retribution Stoker is to suffer. In what Holmes obviously intends as a caricature of the Calvinist doctrine of Providence, a few days after lightning strikes the church building, disaster strikes Stoker just after he preaches on the text "The wolf also shall dwell with the lamb, and the leopard shall lie down with the kid" (Isaiah 11:6). Its mounting likely weakened by the lightening strike, the huge sounding board that hangs above the pulpit breaks loose and falls, "crushing the Rev. Mr. Stoker under its ruins. . . . He was not fatally injured," the newspaper account notes, "but, sad to report, he received such a violent blow upon the spine of the back that palsy of the lower extremities is likely to ensue" (409). Stoker's palsy "of the lower extremities" represents poetic, if not providential, justice. So does the fact that with Stoker's forced confinement and the onset of his palsy, his wife immediately recovers from her illness.

In her blunt portrayal of the theologically rigid and compulsive John Ward, Margaret Deland offers an even more thorough critique of compelled believing than Holmes does in *The Guardian Angel*. Deland's open criticism of what she perceived as repressive Calvinism made *John Ward, Preacher* one of the most controversial and best-selling novels of 1888.[9] The single-minded, unwavering John Ward carries the doctrines of predestination, election, and eternal damnation "to their logical conclusion." As a human being, Ward is a gentle, kind man, like many of the compelled believers who precede him in American fiction, but he is not at all the intellectual giant they are. Ward is a simplistic believer. He "could not hold a belief subject to mutations of time or circumstances. Once acknowledged by his soul, its growth was ended; it hardened into a creed, in which he rested in complete satisfaction. It was not that he did not desire more light; it was simply that he could not conceive that there might be more light" (41).

John Ward's approach to believing differs as much in kind from that of Helen Jeffrey, who becomes his wife, as Arthur Dimmesdale's differs from Hester Prynne's. John is not only compelled by his beliefs, he is enslaved by them; like Hester Prynne, Helen Ward is neither ruled nor compelled by hers. Though John knows that scripture advises against being "yoked together with unbelievers," he rationalizes his desire to marry Helen with the thought that marrying her will enable her salvation. To marry Helen becomes "a sacred right and duty . . . that he might take her away from the atmosphere of religious indifference in which she lived, and guide her to light and life. . . . 'I will save her soul!' he said to himself" (43). But in Helen's mind, fulfilling the obligations of a pastor's wife does not include accepting the beliefs he and his congregation espouse. For a while, she is able to put John off. But her refusal to believe orthodox doctrines increasingly troubles John. More and more, he presses her to accept them. He insists that he can prove them to her, if only she will let him. But she refuses, explaining that "dogma [in her view] can never be an antidote for doubt" and "argument never can result in conviction to either of us, for belief is a matter of temperament" (99).

A tragic incident in John's parish provokes an impasse between John and Helen. Fire breaks out in the home of Tom Davis, a resident of the village who is notorious for his lack of believing and his addiction to alcohol. When the drunken Tom thinks mistakenly that his young son is trapped in the fire, without any regard for his own safety, he runs back into the burning building to look for his son—and perishes in the fire. Though John Ward and the elders in his church admire Tom's bravery, they still conclude that his unconverted state at the time of his death condemns him to hell for all eternity. Helen is shocked by the comments of a church elder, who has just visited the grieving widow. "Yes, I saw her," the elder responds. "I'm just coming from there now. It is an awful judgment on that man: no chance for repentance, overtook by hell, as I told Mrs. Davis, in a moment! But the Lord must be praised for his justice: that ought to comfort her" (169). Helen is mortified. "How dared you say such a thing? How dared you libel the goodness of God? Tom Davis is not in hell. A man who died to save another's life? . . . How could you have had the heart to make her think God was so cruel?" (169, 170).

Helen's public outburst against orthodox Calvinist theology creates a dilemma for John. Members of the church session demand that he reproach his wife for her misbelief and bring about her conversion. When John confronts Helen, she is stunned by his refusal to at least honor her beliefs and affirm her as his wife. "What does it matter?" she pleads with him. "We love each other, so never mind what we believe. Believe anything you want, darling. I don't care! Only love me, John. And if my ideas offend your people, let us leave Lockhaven" (304). But John is unable to stand up to his elders. In a desperate act designed to force her conversion, he banishes Helen from the parsonage. He tells her that she must leave and not return until she converts. John's extreme action does force Helen to recognize how compelling John's faith is. "He makes me suffer . . . that I might be saved. And, indeed, I don't see how he can do anything else," she tells her uncle, Dr. Howe, an Episcopal priest with whom she finds some respite and sympathetic understanding (389). Though she loves John deeply, Helen cannot comply with John's demands. She cannot affirm the doctrines John insists she must accept to remain with him. When John makes no effort to reach out to Helen, Dr. Howe goes to talk with him. He finds John unwilling to accommodate in any way. If Helen returns without converting, John says he will simply send her away again.

John and Helen's extended separation finally ends tragically. The tension between John's compelled believing and his demanding church session on the one hand and his love for Helen on the other proves too much for him. He becomes seriously ill. Even when his condition worsens, he refuses to see Helen. John Ward dies a faithful and broken-hearted man. His compelled believing fails to convert Helen; in the end, it serves only to alienate Helen completely from the Christian faith and church (459).

In his study of the culture of the late-nineteenth century, Paul Carter suggests that *John Ward, Preacher* reflects accurately the depth of the religious disputes that marked the time: "That two normal, non-fanatical people in love could come to shipwreck over a matter of mere religious dogma may seem highly implausible" to modern readers. But such is the nature of John and Helen's dilemma. He is a compelled believer, and she is a modern rationalist. Their inability to come to terms with each other shows that "the emotional stakes of the religious debate in the Gilded Age were just as high as the scientists and the preachers said they were."[10] John and Helen are unable to penetrate, much less accept, each other's worlds. His rigid dogmatism mystifies her; her questioning rationalism baffles him. The fearsome Calvinist divines who precede John Ward in American fiction are giants by comparison. They are fearless believers. John Ward is a frightened believer. He is intimidated by his wife, his elders, and his theology.[11]

Parson Reuben Ward, who appears in Mary E. Wilkins Freeman's novella *The Love of Parson Lord* (1900), is another compelled believer who struggles unsuccessfully to resolve the tension between compelled believing and human love. The word "Love" in the novella's title is the name of Parson Lord's younger daughter. Love's mother dies soon after Love is born. Parson Lord then entrusts his daughter's care to Cousin Daphne Weatherhead, "a rigorous widow," who trains her "according to all letters of law and faith" (4). As a child, Love sees little of her father. Parson Lord is consumed by his beliefs and his ministry. Freeman recalls him as a person "so closely welded to his faith and devotion that he seemed to gain therefrom a strange stiffness, almost ossification, of spirit." She says that Lord's parishioners "regarded him with awe which had in it something of terror" (5).[12]

Parson Lord's two brothers serve as foreign missionaries. He had resolved to become a missionary himself, but poor health prevented him from fulfilling the vow. Then when he married, he determined to commit his first son to the mission field. But Lord's wife bears only daughters: Love, and an earlier sister, who dies at the age of seven. Now only Love remains, and the parson promises her to the mission field. He removes all influences from his daughter's life that might compromise her dedication to her intended vocation: no toys, no playmates, no fancy clothes.

When Love is twelve, Cousin Daphne dies and Love assumes responsibility for running her father's household. As Love grows toward maturity, her father's vision of her as a missionary is challenged by a kind neighbor. Sunday after Sunday as Love sits in the minister's pew, she catches the sympathetic eye of old Aunt Betsey Ware living at the squire's home. Aunt Betsey decides to fill the emptiness she perceives in Love's life. She asks Love to join her occasionally for tea. Then one day Love returns from an errand to find a new and very beautiful doll sitting in a chair at the parsonage. The surprised Love assumes the doll was placed in the chair by Aunt Betsey. She is even more surprised when her father agrees to let her keep the doll. Other gifts of clothing and shoes follow—which the little girl wears when she has tea with Aunt Betsey. The years pass, and Love grows into a beautiful young woman. She catches the eye of the squire's son Richard. The two young people fall in love, and Richard asks Love's father to consent to their marriage. Parson Lord refuses. Richard then says they will marry without his consent. Though he publishes the banns of marriage beginning the following Sunday, the parson refuses to marry them—even when the squire confronts him and demands that he recognize that the young woman's happiness should prevail over the compulsive vow he made on her behalf before she was old enough to appreciate its meaning. The parson ignores the pleas of all. In desperation, the squire uses his civil authority to marry his son to Love.

In the spring after Love's marriage, Parson Lord suddenly becomes ill and dies. After the funeral as she is going through his effects, Love finds her father's journal. When she reads it, she discovers that the beautiful doll and all the gifts she thought had been given to her by Aunt Betsey actually came from her father. His diary records a series of sad entries that testify to his failure to resolve the conflict between his compelled believing and his human affection for his daughter. Love realizes that during her father's life his compelled believing almost completely overwhelmed his human affections. Only after his death does she realize that she was the love of her father's life.

Compulsive Believers

The popularity of stories like *John Ward, Preacher* and *The Love of Parson Lord* signals a declining sympathy for compelled believers in American society. Beginning in the 1880s, ministers who were compulsive believers replaced the compelled believers who loomed so large in American fiction immediately after the Civil War. These compulsive clerics are not only less educated than older divines like Stern, Johns, Ward, and Lord, they are psychologically dysfunctional. They are intellectually deficient and psychologically unbalanced. They are unsophisticated, unbalanced compulsive believers.[13]

Parson Hiram Kelsey, the preacher in Mary Noilles Murfee's *The Prophet of the Great Smoky Mountains* (1885), reflects the new image. Kelsey has little formal education. What reading he does is confined to the Bible. Kelsey is both a rigid Calvinist and a biblical literalist. He is driven by those religious commitments and by a compelling commitment to justice. Kelsey comes to his calling as a preacher by a tragic error. When he was young and newly married, both his wife Emily and their baby become seriously ill. The doctor visits them while Kelsey is not at home and leaves medicine for Emily. Kelsey returns and finds the medicine intended for Emily, but he can't read the doctor's writing and mistakenly gives her medicine to the baby. The medicine is too much for the child, who dies soon after Kelsey gives it to her. Emily recovers from her illness but is so overcome with grief after the death of her child that she flings herself off a cliff. Overwhelmed by this double loss, Kelsey turns to religion hoping to find some meaning or purpose for his life in the tragedies he assumes God has dealt to him: "I'd never hev thunk o' takin' up with religion . . . ef I hed been let ter live along like other men be, or ef me an' mine could die like other folks be let ter die! But it 'peared ter me ez religion war 'bout all ez war lef', arter I hed gin the baby the stuff the valley doctor hed lef' fur Em'ly" (78).

The seeming injustice in his own life drives Kelsey to an impassioned concern for justice in his ministry. When Gid Fletcher, the local blacksmith, turns in the unfairly accused and fleeing Rick Tyler to gain a reward of $200, Parson Kelsey confronts Fletcher with the dishonor of his deed. The blacksmith protests that the reward money he gained is "lawful" money for him to receive:

> "Lawful!" exclaimed the parson, with a tense, jeering laugh. "Judas war a law-abidin' citizen. He mos' lawfully betrayed *his* Frien' ter the law. Them thirty pieces o' silver! Sech currency ain't out o' circulation yit!"
>
> Quick as a flash the blacksmith's heavy hand struck the prophet in the face. The next moment his sudden anger was merged in fear. He stood, unarmed, at the mercy of an assaulted and outraged man, with a loaded rifle in his hands, and all the lightnings of heaven quivering in his angry eyes.
>
> Gil Fletcher had hardly time to draw the breath he thought his last, when the prophet slowly turned the other cheek.
>
> "In the name of the Master," he said, with all the dignity of his calling. (67–68)

As the blacksmith mounts his horse and rides slowly away, he feels the magnitude of his mistake with the preacher: "The parson's rifle-ball would be preferable to the gross slur" that he has just incurred. In a place where honor is, perhaps, even more esteemed than piety, he realizes that his reputation is ruined. "What a text!" he thinks. "What an illustration of iniquity [he will provide] for the sermons, foretelling wrath and vengence" (68).

Unfortunately, Hiram Kelsey's faith never becomes as certain as his commitment to justice. Kelsey struggles constantly with his believing. At times his faith completely deserts him, and he despairs; he feels himself to be "the only unbeliever in a Christian world." Then, just as suddenly, "his flickering faith would flare up, and he would reproach God who had suffered its lapse." As Kelsey explains it, "The Lord lifts me up . . . ter dash me on the groun'!" This bipolar interior turmoil plagues Kelsey the preacher. He preaches "wild sermons" and prays "frantic prayers."

Parson Kelsey's inability to resolve his interior struggles finally does him in. He loses his faith altogether and gives up preaching after making a humiliating public confession of his lost belief to his congregation. Without the anchor of faith, Kelsey becomes even more driven. Finally, he runs afoul of the law. His activities on behalf of an unjustly accused fugitive land him in jail. Kelsey never recovers his faith. He has some admirable qualities, but he is unable to restrain the compulsions that drive him.

Andrew Joslin, the Cumberlands preacher in Emerson Hough's *The Way Out* (1918), is an even more driven man than Hiram Kelsey. The two resemble each other in stature as well as character. Joslin looks to be fifty; in reality, he is past seventy. He is tall with a large frame, bushy hair, and a dense beard that gives him a look of "singular fierceness." A man with a "somber, dour nature," his main mission in life is "to proclaim the wrath of God." In the book's opening scene, Joslin returns unexpectedly to his cabin on the Sabbath. He finds his twenty-eight-year-old son, David, and his ninety-year-old mother looking a bit sheepish. They obviously have been doing something other than keeping the Sabbath. Andrew demands to know why David isn't attending services somewhere. When David responds defensively that there are none available close by, Andrew shifts the focus of the interrogation to Calvin's *Institutes*.[14] Has David read the copy he gave him? David explains that just recently he sat up all night trying to read the book with the aid of Preacher Cuthbertson, a neighboring minister. But they both fell asleep, and when Cuthbertson awoke anxiously he shook David awake: "David, David, I've been thinkin' over them Institutes so hard . . . I believe they've injured my mind!'" (6, 7).

The wide smile on David's face as he finishes kindles his father's anger, which heightens into fury when he reaches into the loft and discovers David's fiddle and realizes David was playing on it just before he arrived home. Andrew rips the strings from the instrument and hurls it into the flames in the fireplace: "That's whar it belongs . . . ! In hell fire is whar all them things belongs, an' the critters that fosters 'em" (9). After a long tirade berating David and his grandmother for their sinful activity on the Sabbath, Andrew banishes his son from the house. He tells David never to come back. After David leaves, Andrew's mother notices a red pool forming under the chair where Andrew is sitting. Absalom Grant, a member of a family with whom the Joslins have an ongoing feud, had come up behind him and stabbed him in the back. Andrew's mother dresses his wound and makes his supper. But later in the evening Andrew realizes the wound is fatal. Unwilling to suffer a slow death, he hangs himself.

Adrian Plummer, the Christian Church minister at the center of Homer Croy's *West of the Water Tower* (1923), is neither physically violent nor psychologically troubled like Hiram Kelsey and Andrew Joslin. Plummer is a classless and simplistic believer whose lack of sophistication and education render him socially and intellectually inept. Seen through the eyes of his able and ambitious son Guy, Adrian is not only a compulsive believer but also an embarrassment. The novel opens with Guy Plummer's high school commencement. The graduation ceremonies take place on a hot, stuffy evening in Junction City, Missouri, at his father's church. Guy, who won the Missouri state championship in debate earlier in the school year, is to give the student oration. He hopes his speech will "sweep the people off their feet"—especially Bee Chew, daughter of Charles G. Chew, "the ablest lawyer and the richest man in town, and the prettiest girl in the senior class." In recognition of his position as pastor of the church where the commencement is being held, Guy's father is asked to give the invocation. As his father prays, hands raised in supplication, Guy lifts his head and opens his eyes enough to see "the uncouth posture of his father" that exposes "a blackened place under the imitation gold button" on his father's shirt sleeve. Guy is embarrassed to be associated with the preacher: "Never would his father pay any attention to his clothes. . . . Plummer's life was too full of matters of soul to spend time on the intricacies of dress" (8, 9).

At the commencement, Adrian Plummer is forced to share the platform with Charles G. Chew, who is not only the richest man in Junction City but also the town atheist. Chew epitomizes the threatening forces of modernism that Adrian Plummer despises—and fears. Chew is comfortable, intelligent, and gracious. The community regards him as a man of integrity: "It was known that if he did not believe in the integrity of a client and in the honesty of a case, he would refuse it. It marked him out sharply" (7). The fact that Charles Chew is an atheist does not seem to compromise his reputation—much to Adrian Plummer's chagrin. Chew's excellent standing and success make the classless preacher even more conscious of his own insignificance and modest status in the eyes of the community. Plummer harbors a deep resentment against Chew. The community's respect for Chew makes Plummer even more determined to discredit him.

Plummer's determination becomes a self-destructive obsession. When the pulpit committee from a large church in a nearby city visits Junction City to consider him as a candidate for pastor of their church, Plummer's fixation on Chew leads to an outburst that defeats what appears to be his only chance to move on as a pastor. Before the Sunday morning worship service as Plummer and the visiting committee walk together toward the First Christian Church, they pass Charles Chew's house. In front of the house is a hay wagon full of laughing young people, about to leave for a picnic in the country. Just as they come abreast of the wagon, Chew himself emerges, carrying a picnic basket and "surrounded by a laughing group of hero worshipers." Plummer trembles with rage. "Don't you know what day of the week this is?" he demands. The loaded question leads to a heated exchange between Plummer and Chew. Plummer quickly loses control of himself, and soon he is shouting into Chew's face. The three men on the visiting committee look knowingly at one another: this minister is "not the one they wanted for their polite church" (156, 157).

Adrian Plummer's behavior during several other similar incidents becomes an increasing embarrassment to his congregation, as well as his family. Eventually, he loses his pastorate and with it his ability to make a living. He and his family endure even greater poverty than they have known during his years as a minister. In the midst of his suffering, he comes to some awareness of the havoc his compulsive believing brings on him and those he loves. He is even able to feel some admiration for Charles Chew during the lawyer's last days, especially when Chew tells him that he respected his beliefs even though he could not share them. But all his losses do not lead Plummer to real self-understanding. He remains a pathetic character—a compulsive believer, who is a victim of his believing and the destructive behavior to which it leads.

Compulsive believers like Adrian Plummer lack the extensive education and social accountability that regulate their forebears in faith. The compelled believing of the older New England divines was informed by their broad education and regulated by the relatively stable communities in which they served. This intellectual and social framework that surrounded their believing provided a cognitive and behavioral accountability.[15] Church and community set and maintained norms that ministers were expected to honor. Late-nineteenth- and early-twentieth-century preachers who served in rural mountain communities or in small towns in the Middle West or in emerging communities on the frontier often lacked the benefits of this social and ecclesiastical accountability. Many were self-appointed clerics. Their admission to ministry depended entirely on the experience of a "call" and was not governed by broad educational requirements or other standards set by an established church organization. At best, they were accountable only to loosely organized congregations, often composed of those who were no more able or stable than they were. When these compelled believers became compulsive believers, no counterbalancing forces were available to moderate the effects of their chaotic and sometimes destructive believing.[16]

Accommodating Believers

As uncomfortable as nineteenth-century writers like Harriet Beecher Stowe and Oliver Wendell Holmes were with overly rigid (in their view) Edwardsian Calvinism, many of them were even less at ease with liberal alternatives. Calvinism for believers like Stowe implies not simply an impartial God but also an active cosmic ruler who maintains the universe and whatever may lie beyond it as a *moral* order. Theologians like Edwards, Bellamy, and Hopkins may have perceived God as unduly severe, but the liberals' neglect of what Henry James Sr. called "the old virile religion" places humans in an even greater peril.[17] In January 1865, fully aware of the horrors of the Civil War, Stowe describes how essential belief in this virile God of justice was to her: "The great affliction that has come upon our country is so evidently the purifying chastening of a Father, rather than the avenging anger of a Destroyer, that all hearts may submit themselves in a solemn and holy calm still to bear the burning that shall make us clean from dross and bring us forth to a higher national life."[18] As horrible as the war is, it nonetheless reflects the governance of a cosmic ruler. For Mrs. Stowe, the discrediting of Calvinism "is more than just a private agony for those it afflicts; it is also a public calamity. With that loss, the old bonds are broken, the old order denied." Without the cosmic ruler in place, "things fall apart."[19]

Stowe's friend Oliver Wendell Holmes may not have shared her strong conviction that Calvinist faith is essential, but he, too, found the liberal alternative inadequate. In *Elsie Venner* (1860), after he describes the moderate but orthodox Calvinist pastor who presides over the first of two meetinghouses that face each other across the town square, Holmes turns his attention to the Unitarian pastor, the Rev. Chauncey Fairweather: "The meetinghouse on the other and opposite summit was of a more modern style. . . . Mr. Fairweather's sermons are modern—and innocuous. 'The beauty of virtue' got to be an old story at last. 'The moral dignity of human nature' ceased to excite a thrill of satisfaction after some hundred repetitions. It [the liberal minister's preaching] grew to be a dull business" (46, 47).

The equally easygoing Episcopalians in Holmes's novels are only slightly more esteemed than the Unitarians. In *The Guardian Angel*, Holmes locates the Episcopal Church (symbolically) on the edge of town—suggesting that it is beyond the conflicts that consume the Trinitarians and Unitarians: "The Rev. Ambrose Eveleth, Rector of Saint Bartholomew's . . . was one of a class numerous in the Anglican Church, a cultivated man, with pure tastes, with simple habits, a good reader, a neat writer, a safe thinker, with a snub and well-fenced mental pasturage, which his sermons kept moderately close without exhausting demand upon the soil" (189).

Harriet Beecher Stowe offers an even more searching critique of liberal preachers in her fiction than Holmes does in his. The innocuous Mr. Lothrop who appears in *Oldtown Folks* reflects her perception of the decline they represent. This "third generation of Massachusetts clergy"

> were mostly scholarly, quiet men, of calm and philosophic temperament, who, having from infancy walked in all the traditions of virtuous and pious education, and passed from grade to grade of their progress in irreproachable quiet and decorum, came to regard the spiritual struggles and conflicts, the wrestlings and tears, the fastings and temptations of their ancestors with a secret skepticism,—and to dwell on moralities, virtues, and decorums, rather than on those soul-stirring, spiritual mysteries which still stood forth unquestioned and uncontradicted in their confessions of faith. (5)

The cultured and theologically liberal Mr. Lothrop chooses an equally cultured and liberal wife. "Lady Lothrop," as she is known locally, is a Boston-bred widow "of large property, from one of the most aristocratic families of Boston." The substantial resources she brings to their marriage supplement the pastor's modest salary and ensure that she and Mr. Lothrop will always live comfortably. While Lady Lothrop agrees to act the role of the parson's wife, and does so well, Parson Lothrop, in return, honors her Episcopal heritage and her regular use of the Book of Common Prayer. Mrs. Lothrop participates weekly in the parish church he serves, but she also continues to observe the festivals and fasts of the Church of England.

His association with Lady Lothrop gives a certain elegance to Mr. Lothrop, but he is not very effective as a pastor. His soft theology handicaps his ministry. Though he is determined, for example, to follow in the footsteps of John Eliot, the "Apostle to the Indians," he lacks Eliot's passion and orthodox convictions: "He did not, like his great predecessor, lecture them [the Native Americans] on the original depravity of the heart, the need of a radical and thorough regeneration by the Holy Spirit of God, or the power of Jesus as a Saviour from sin, but he talked to them of the evil of drunkenness and lying and idleness, and exhorted them to be temperate and industrious." When the Native Americans do not heed his words, he suggests the fault is entirely theirs. They are "children of the forest," he explains, a race "destined to extinction with the progress of civilization" (6). His approach is obviously ineffective, but Pastor Lothrop clings stubbornly to it. He seems oblivious to his deficiencies.

Mr. Lothrop's preaching is no more engaging than his ministry to the Native Americans. His sermons are "well-written specimens of the purest and most elegant Addisonian English"; no one can find anything objectionable in them. Looking back on them, the narrator in Stowe's novel notes that they "were sensible, rational, and religious, as far as they went" (which in his view is not far enough). Local people wonder why so "elegant a scholar" is willing to "employ his abilities in so obscure a town and for so inconsiderable a salary." Mr. Lothrop admits that the salary is small, but he also notes that it is "as secure as the Bank of England [a reference brought to mind, no doubt, by his wife's assets], and retirement and quiet give me leisure for study" (6).

In her fiction, Stowe portrays "proto-Unitarian" clerics like Lothrop as a decline, not an option. According to Alice Crozier, her biographer, Stowe believed these weak liberals were a regrettable consequence of Edwardsian theology. The wrathful, unapproachable God the Edwardsians presented actually served to make "the moral argument against Calvinism" plausible. But Stowe did not see liberal alternative clerics like Lothrop as a viable alternative. Ministers like Jonathan Edwards and Samuel Hopkins (both actual and fictional) and the fictional Moses Stern were most of all people of sound faith. They accepted the teachings of scripture and Calvinist theology as compelling statements that *describe the nature of reality*. Calvin's theology was as convincing to them as the cosmology of Copernicus and Newton. His teachings, based on what they accepted as the revealed Word of God, gave believers an accurate perception of their place in the cosmos.

But the Edwardsians' ominous picture of God made their otherwise satisfying theology difficult to defend. In fact, Stowe thought the Edwardsian characterization of God so offensive that it became an obstacle. Many nineteenth-century would-be believers could not move beyond it to appreciate the essential attributes of Calvinist theology that Edwards and his disciples inherited. If the Edwardsians had not imposed this harsh re-imaging, "loyal Calvinists like her [Stowe's] father and brothers . . . might have provided those revisions of the old confession which were necessary to a newer day."[20]

But difficult as Edwards's vision is for Stowe, the contemporary alternative, "namely the Unitarians, is so appalling as to make him [Edwards] and his followers heroes and saints by comparison."[21] Stowe reflects her concern to preserve the essential tenets of Calvinism in a letter written March 7, 1879, to her son Charley, then just beginning what would become an extremely conflicted ministry as pastor of a church in Maine. She advises Charley *not* to accommodate the old theology, whether to please himself or members of his congregation: "When a young man of original mind begins to preach truth as he sees it & *to adapt* truth to the wants of the men he meets—he immediately steps out of the formulas & in that way excites the fears of good men, who are accustomed to the sound of certain formulas. This was your grandfather's experience—it was your uncle Henrys—& I apprehend it will be yours." She tells Charley to proceed carefully when he is tempted to set old truths aside: "I hope you will never say or do any thing to express a young mans self esteem & that might look like want of reverence for the hardy old Christian soldiers who have been bearing the burden of the day in Maine—Never preach *against* old formulas—quietly substitute truth for error."[22]

Prudent Believers

In her 1879 letter offering advice to her son, Harriet Beecher Stowe advises Charley to be "prudent" in his new ministry. She counsels him to proceed carefully: "Your constitutional danger is from sudden unadvised movements." Though the temptation to become a Unitarian is understandable to her, she advises Charley to resist it: "That you agree with conservative Unitarians is because conservative Unitarians are becoming every year more orthodox." But to leave his Calvinist roots behind and become a Unitarian seems like a fatal compromise to her: "Your uncle [Henry Ward Beecher] is precisely the model I would hold up to you, of how a manly and honest man should guide himself in the ministry in an age when God is shedding new light on religion thro the development of his own natural laws in Science—What he could not conscientiously preach he let alone." Ministers like Charley's Uncle Henry "differed in many points with the reserved orthodoxy of their day—but they made no noise about it—they preached what they *sincerely did believe* & left what they were in doubt about to the further teachings of God's holy spirit."[23]

The last sentence is the heart of Stowe's advice. Be a prudent believer; preach sincerely what you do believe, and, where you doubt, wait for God to give you insight. Be open to new thoughts, but also be wise. In an age rampant with new and conflicting ideas that challenged traditional theology, Stowe's suggestion represents a balanced approach. Likely it also reflects the intellectual culture of her household. In letters he sent home during a visit to Germany, Calvin Stowe shared the excitement he felt as he conversed with Continental scholars and read their work.[24] But he managed to balance that excitement with respect for the Calvinist theology in which he was nurtured. Had he followed the radical course that tempted his son Charley, he would certainly have lost his post at Andover Seminary.

The Rev. Mr. Avery who appears in *Oldtown Folks* and Dr. Cushing who appears in her *Poganuc People* (1878) act out the balanced, prudent believing that Stowe urges on her son Charley. The Calvinism of Mr. Avery is "sharp and well defined," but it is not "gloomy and fateful" like Dr. Stern's. He has "a passion for saving souls." He is a "firm believer in hell," but he also believes "that nobody need go there" and that "nobody should go there if he could help it." His preaching matches the historical time in which he lived: the years immediately after the War for Independence. It implies "liberty of growth—the liberty to think and to judge freely upon all subjects." It is preaching "on the move" that is "slowly shaping out and elaborating those new forms of doctrinal statement that inevitably grow out of new forms of society" (*Oldtown Folks*, 443, 444, 446).

Mr. Avery's humanity balances the severity of the theology he inherited: "Mr. Avery was a man who always corrected theory by common sense" (461). Working people say that when he hoes "more than usual in his potato-field" the Sunday sermons are better. The narrator of the story recalls how impressed he was as a boy with the minister's skill as an angler. He went fishing with "*abandon*. Eye, voice, hand, thought, feeling, all were concentrated on trout. . . . So perfectly absorbed was he that we would be obliged to jog his memory, and, in fact, often to drag him away by main force, when the hour for the evening lecture arrived." But once he mounted the pulpit, Mr. Avery became "as completely absorbed in his work of saving sinners as he had before been in his temporal fishery" (449).

In *Poganuc People*, the fourth and final of Stowe's New England novels, written ten years after *Oldtown Folks*, Stowe recalls her father Lyman Beecher in the fictional pastor, Dr. Cushing.[25] Dr. Cushing is a more controlled Calvinist than Mr. Avery, but his believing is tempered by a similar sensitivity and humanity. Dolly, Dr. Cushing's young daughter, is disappointed when he is unwilling to celebrate Christmas with decorations, gifts, and singing carols like her Episcopal friends do. But Dolly remembers one Christmas when her father "rose up early . . . and proceeded to buy a sugar dog at the store of Lucius Jenks," and when Dolly came down to breakfast, he called her to him and presented it, saying as he kissed her, "Papa gives you this, not because it is Christmas, but because he loves his little Dolly."

Stowe mirrors the openness she believes can moderate orthodox Calvinism to suit a new age in these fictional Calvinist clergy from her New England novels. Mr. Avery and Dr. Cushing retain the strengths of the old orthodox Calvinist faith, but they are not as narrow, closed-minded, or rigid as Edwards and his disciples are. They are prudent believers who do not permit their theology to overwhelm either their humanity or their common sense.

Stowe's friend Oliver Wendell Holmes feels none of the obligation to defend Calvinist doctrines that she does, but he still recognizes the inherent strength of a Calvinist worldview. The Rev. Pierrepont Honeywood, the Calvinist divine who appears in Holmes's *Elsie Venner*, is as balanced and prudent a believer as Stowe's Dr. Cushing. Holmes describes him as an open Calvinist believer who "held to the old faith of the Puritans, and occasionally delivered a discourse which was considered by the hard-headed theologians of his parish to have settled the whole matter fully and finally." But Holmes then goes on to observe that Dr. Honeywood "exercised his human faculties in the harness of his ancient faith with such freedom that the straps of it got so loose they did not interfere greatly with the circulations of the warm blood through that system" (45). When the senior deacon of the parish tells Dr. Honeywood that some of the people need to be "reminded of the great fundamental doctrine of the worthlessness of all human effort,"[26] the minister listens gravely "with an inward smile." After the deacon leaves, Dr. Honeywood does try to honor his advice. He considers preaching an old sermon on "Human Nature" but quickly falls to correcting expressions that now seem "too harsh" and inserting explanations and qualifying comments. His rewriting is interrupted by Letty, his granddaughter, who comes bounding into his study. As his eyes fall away from the discourse on human perversion and turn to his smiling grandchild, "it flashed across him that [contrary to the theology in the sermon] there was nothing so very monstrous . . . about the specimen of congenital perversion that he was looking at." The juxtaposition of his old sermon with this delightful young woman causes the minister to wonder about the universality of Original Sin: "Was it to be supposed that this healthy young girl, with life throbbing all over her, could not, without a miracle, be good according to the invalid pattern and formula?" (172–74).

Letty announces that Sophy Robinson, an old woman, formerly a servant in the Venner household, wishes to see the minister. What Dr. Honeywood learns from his long conversation with Mrs. Robinson increases his doubt about the universal application the Calvinist doctrine. In the preface to *Elsie Venner*, Holmes says that the novel is intended to call the doctrine of Original Sin into question, and he likely designed Dr. Honeywood's reflections after Mrs. Robinson's visit to advance his argument. After Mrs. Robinson departs, Dr. Honeywood finds his old sermon even less satisfactory. He lays it aside and begins a new one based on the text, "Shall not the Judge of all the earth do right?" The sermon he now writes, destined to become famous in the parish, is quite different from the one he puts aside. The new sermon is titled "On the Obligations of an Infinite Creator to a Finite Creature." As he preaches it, the people are astonished to hear their "dignified . . . old Patriarch . . . put his foot into several heresies, for which men had been burned," especially when they said that "he thought a man with a crooked spine would never be called to account for not walking erect. He thought if the crook was in his brain, instead of in his back, he could not fairly be blamed to any consequence of this natural defect, whatever the lawyers or divines might call it" (182).

Dr. Honeywood embodies Holmes's belief that traditional Calvinist doctrines need to be balanced by emerging "scientific" knowledge. In a long conversation that consumes an entire chapter, "Why Doctors Differ," the minister and the local physician probe the strengths and vulnerabilities of each other's worlds of knowledge. Dr. Honeywood is never defensive during the conversation, even when the doctor's statements are pointed. Toward the end of their conversation, when the physician asks his pastor if he can speak bluntly, the minister encourages him. And the physician *is* blunt: "We [physicians] are constantly seeing weakness where you see depravity. . . . We used to be as hard on sickness as you were on sin. We know better now. . . . We know that disease has something back of it which the body isn't to blame for, at least in most cases, and which very often it is trying to get rid of. Just so with sin" (238, 239). When the minister offers his own views, he is equally as frank as the physician. In response to the doctor's suggestion that the behavior of humans is simply the result of external influences that shape them, he warns: "Prove to a man that his will is governed by something outside himself, and you have lost all hold on his moral and religious nature. There is nothing bad men want to believe so much as that they are governed by necessity" (234, 238, 239).

Throughout these sometimes-difficult exchanges, it is obvious that these two men with very different viewpoints on matters of great significance have deep respect for each other. Dr. Honeywood defends his beliefs passionately throughout the conversation with Dr. Kittredge. At the same time, he looks for insights in the physician's arguments even when they challenge some of his core beliefs. That open and prudent outlook obviously makes him a model believer in Holmes's eyes and gives the minister a degree of wisdom that the orthodox but narrow Deacon Shearer seems to lack. Dr. Honeywood recoils when the deacon dismisses Dr. Kittredge as an "infidel." He perceives the physician quite differently—as an "honest, kind, charitable, self-denying man" who is "always reverential, with a cheerful trust in the great Father of all mankind." Considering the two men side by side, if the text "By their fruits ye shall know them" is valid, the physician seems "the better Christian of the two." In fact, the minister thinks to himself, "he shouldn't be surprised if he met the Doctor in heaven yet, inquiring anxiously after old Deacon Shearer" (240, 241).

Mr. Stanyard, the minister who is the central character in Gideon Hiram Hollister's *Kinley Hollow* (1882), reflects the same theology and composure as Dr. Honeywood: he affirms an orthodox but open theology and refuses to capitulate to the reactionary deacon who attacks him. Stanyard maintains his composure even when the intolerant deacon in the story becomes vicious and tries to defame the minister's character.

Mr. Whittaker, the Presbyterian minister who appears in Edward Eggleston's *Roxy* (1878), is a similarly prudent believer and wise pastor. He not only upholds the faith but also restrains the worst and calls forth the best in those who are under his care. When young Nancy discovers that Mark Bonamy, a local preacher, has betrayed her and vows vengeance, Mr. Whittaker intervenes. He helps Nancy recover emotional and theological balance. He also helps the remorseful and suicidal Mark find hope, even though he has compromised his faith and betrayed those who love him.

Probably the most popular and certainly the most endearing prudent believer in late-nineteenth- and early-twentieth-century popular fiction is Margaret Deland's Dr. Lavendar. Dr. Lavendar first appears in Deland's *Philip and His Wife* (1894), which was published six years after her *John Ward, Preacher*, and he reappears in at least six novels Deland published over a span of more than thirty years. Dr. Lavendar is quite different from John Ward. Dr. Lavendar recalls Dr. Howe, the moderate Episcopal priest who opposes Ward's narrow believing and provides haven for Ward's wife Helen when the compelled pastor banishes her from the parsonage. Dr. Lavendar's occasional references to God imply that he is an orthodox believer, but he never becomes consumed by his theology like John Ward does.

Dr. Lavendar's strongest attributes are his wisdom, his common sense, and his conservative morality. His actions in a story called "The Note" that appears in *Dr. Lavendar's People* (1903) are typical. When the story opens, Algeron Keen and Mary Gordon have become lovers. They keep their relationship secret because they know that Mary's father and brother, along with most of the rest of those who live in Old Chester, consider Algeron to be a young man of little promise and an unsuitable match for Mary. When Mary believes she is pregnant, she and Algeron go to Dr. Lavendar for help. Though he opposes their premarital affair, he recognizes their love for each other and marries them. He then goes to see John and Alex Gordon, her father and brother, and asks them to rise above their anger and accept Mary with her new husband into the family. They refuse to heed Dr. Lavendar and, instead, disinherit Mary and banish her and her husband from the family home. The marriage soon becomes public knowledge in Old Chester, along with the rumor that the two lovers have committed "the unpardonable sin." But when one of the town gossips accosts Dr. Lavendar and asks him whether the rumor is true, he responds with characteristic grace. He refuses either to reveal what he knows or to condemn Mary and Algeron. He tells the busybody, "Just be ready to forgive other folks and you needn't be afraid of the unpardonable sin for yourself" (70).

Dr. Lavendar maintains high standards of religion and morality, but he adapts them wisely to account for human foibles. In "At the Stuffed-Animal House," the final story in *Dr. Lavendar's People*, the disabled Annie Hutchinson kills her sister who is sick with cancer to free her sister from the horrible pain she suffers. Dr. Lavendar tells Annie that was not right to kill her sister—but he also instructs her never to tell anyone what she did. And he also keeps silence in the matter.

Most of the ministers in Margaret Deland's later stories reflect the same genial view of providence that Dr. Lavendar does. In *The Promises of Alice* (1919), the Rev. William Alden marries a woman he believes will become the ideal minister's wife, only to discover that she is intent on the two of them becoming missionaries to China. When Mrs. Alden discovers her husband's true feelings about missionary activity ("I don't like to interfere with other people's religions"), she decides that their first and only child will go to China in their place. When the girl, Alice, is too young to realize what she is doing, she yields to her mother's wishes. The promise becomes an increasing burden to Alice. When she becomes a young woman, she realizes that becoming a missionary to China is not at all what she wants. She wants to stay home and marry Neely, a local young man with great potential. Alice is relieved when her mother's rich and irreverent bachelor brother from California refuses to provide the money for Alice's education as a missionary ("If your girl will undertake to convert the Christian Chinee [*sic*] back to the faith of his fathers, I'll hold up both hands—and then put them in my pockets for her"). But Alice's respite is short-lived: Miss Mary Alden, her father's distant cousin, is so moved by her mother's tears of disappointment that she agrees to pay for Alice's missionary training. Just as Alice's unwanted vocation seems inescapable, her mother dies. Pastor Alden is at once saddened and relieved. He and the family decide Alice's duty is now to her father; she must stay home and keep house for him. The matter of Alice's future seems settled until the practical cousin Mary comes forth with what seems to her the ideal solution for everyone. She proposes that she and Mr. Alden marry. She can oversee his household, and Alice can go to China. But Alice never does go to China, and she does finally become Neely's wife. The Rev. Mr. Alden is appropriately restrained, pious, and wise during all the convoluted episodes that involve his daughter. In the end, he has the opportunity to marry the commonsense cousin he obviously should have married when he graduated from seminary. Providence does smile on those who do their duty faithfully.

Margaret Deland's books that feature Dr. Lavendar enjoyed great popularity from the 1880s through the 1920s. Dr. Lavendar and Old Chester seemed wonderful to so many of her readers that Deland often received letters from readers who wanted to know where Old Chester is located. They wanted to visit the village and meet Dr. Lavendar. Deland's fictional minister obviously matched their image of what a minister should be like. Actually, Deland did create Edward Lavendar to exemplify the human characteristics she believed an ideal minister would have. He embodied qualities she admired most in her own pastor, Phillips Brooks; in Dr. William Campbell, her minister uncle; and in Lorin Deland, her husband—to whom many of the books in which Dr. Lavendar appears are dedicated.[27]

Ministers like Deland's Dr. Lavendar and Stowe's Mr. Avery are far different from the compelled believers who appear in the novels cited at the beginning of this chapter. Compelled believers like Stowe's Moses Stern are emboldened by strong and urgent theological convictions. They see themselves and are perceived by others as ambassadors of the ruler of the universe. They speak with urgency about heaven and hell and a God who determines the ultimate fate of everyone. They press their message relentlessly on everyone who comes near them. Those who take them seriously find them compelling. And even some of those who avoid them are haunted by the possibility that what they say might be so.

As the fear of God fades, ministers become more human. Prudent believers like Dr. Lavendar and Mr. Avery engender respect, but not fear. They are wise and caring, and at times brave humans, but they are not heroic believers. Their human qualities commend them, not their theological convictions. They gain respect because they are moral figures, not because they represent a dreaded keeper of the cosmos. They still loom, but not nearly as large as their grandfathers. A preacher who is admired for his skills as an angler is a far cry from one who calls forth the judgments of the Almighty.

V

CON MEN IN COLLARS AND HEROES OF THE CLOTH

Popular Images (2)

The frontier fiction that became increasingly popular during the last third of the nineteenth century reflects a freewheeling and often irreverent culture that is quite different from the more staid and regulated culture of East Coast America. A typical story appears in *Tall Tales of the Southwest: An Anthology of Southwestern Humor, 1830–1860*. As the story begins, a group of revivalists board a riverboat named the *Franklin* and begin to hold services day and night. Their preaching, loud singing, and praying soon annoy some of the other passengers, who complain to Mr. Simmons, the *Franklin*'s captain. The captain listens sympathetically to the objectors but instructs them not to disrupt the revival services. The captain's warning, however, does not suggest that he thinks religious groups should receive preferential treatment. When the revivalists object to the activities of card players on the boat, the captain refuses to let the revivalists interfere with the gamblers:

> Gentlemen [Captain Simmons tells the revivalists], amuse yourselves as you like: preach and pray to your hearts' content—none shall interfere with your pious purposes; some like that sort of thing, I have no objection to it. These men prefer to amuse themselves with cards; let them—they pay their passage as well as you gentlemen, and have as much right to their amusements as you have to yours, and they shall not be disturbed. Preach, play cards, dance cotillions—do what you like, I am agreeable; only understand that all games, preaching among the rest, must cease at ten o'clock.[1]

This incident on the *Franklin* points up deep cultural differences that distinguished the newly settled American West from the much longer settled American East. In the West, neither newcomers nor old-timers were ranked automatically according to some stable, community-wide social and moral hierarchy. Frontier society was an open society, a social marketplace where everyone, ministers included, had to be ready to prove they are who and what they say they are.

Phony Preachers

Nineteenth-century Westerners were particularly hard on pretenders, especially pretentious preachers. A number of stories from the frontier describe how counterfeit preachers who pretend they are morally superior are brought down when a clever con man exposes their duplicity. Sut Lovingood, the baldly irreverent hero of George Washington Harris's novel *Sut Lovingood* (1867) turns the tables on one preacher who is both morally pretentious and duplicitous. The tale begins when Sut happens upon a revival meeting and decides to join the congregation. His less than pious purpose for becoming one of the worshippers is quickly apparent. He strikes up a conversation with an attractive young woman in the congregation and convinces her to go off with him into the bushes. Their tryst is interrupted when the local preacher discovers them and subjects both of them to a tongue-lashing. A few days after the revival, the young woman's father (who is unaware of her tryst with Sut) invites the preacher to dinner. Afraid that her father will beat her if he learns of her adventure with Sut, the young woman promises to cook the preacher an exceptionally fine dinner if he promises not to reveal her transgression to her father. The preacher promises to hold his tongue, but when his stomach is full he reneges. He tells the young woman's father about her amorous behavior with Sut. The angry father then subjects his daughter to a vicious whipping.

When news of the preacher's duplicity reaches Sut, he vows to expose the minister's hypocritical morality. His opportunity comes when the minister preaches a hellfire sermon, describing how serpents crawl about the bodies of sinners in hell. The minister is so captivated by his own preaching that he fails to notice a bag of serpents that Sut places at the bottom of his pants leg. The preacher continues his sermon unaware of the serpents crawling up his clothing. Only when a snake pokes his head out of the preacher's shirt collar does he realizes that serpents are all over his body.

Reduced to frenzy, he rips off his clothing and runs naked through the crowd of now-screaming women who have gathered at the revival.

Sut Lovingood never pretends to be anything more than an unabashed opportunist. The preacher, in contrast, presents himself as a moral superior. But his behavior at the young woman's home shows that his morality is as much a matter of convenience as Sut's. The preacher is not beyond going back on his word when doing so works to his advantage. Within the mindset of Western frontier culture, the pretentious minister is a phony and deserves to be exposed and brought down. And when Sut, the con man, exposes the duplicitous preacher, and he stands naked (literally) in front of his own congregation, George Washington Harris could be certain that most of his readers would applaud Sut for a job well done.

Preachers are not the only religious types who had to survive close scrutiny on the frontier. Some tall tales from the West portray believers in general as naive people who are a danger both to themselves and to any others they happen to convert. The con man who becomes a counterfeit preacher and takes advantage of unsophisticated believers may be a less than upright character himself, but when he exposes them as gullible, he becomes a hero. During one of his adventures, Captain Simon Suggs, the crafty con man who appears in Johnson Jones Hooper's *Some Adventures of Captain Simon Suggs* (1846), becomes just such a folk hero when he exposes the naïveté of those gathered at a local camp meeting. The con begins with Suggs's overdone "conversion":

> The Captain remained groveling in the dust during the usual time, and gave vent to even more than the requisite number of sobs and groans, and heart-piercing cries. At length, when the proper time had arrived, he bounded up, and with a face radiant with joy, commenced a series of vaultings and tumblings, which "laid in the shade" all previous performances of the sort at that camp meeting. (124)

After this impressive "performance," the newly converted Suggs tells the gathered congregation that he feels called to preach. He would go to school to learn how, but he has no money. The congregation responds by taking up a generous offering to advance Suggs's theological education. However, a few of them are uneasy about simply giving the money to the new convert. The congregation assigns one of their members to travel with Suggs and carry the collection to ensure that the offering goes toward Suggs's education for the ministry. After Suggs and the man holding the purse journey only a short distance, Suggs tells the purse holder he would like to hold the money for a few moments because he feels the need to pray over it. The guardian of the purse is happy to pause for prayer but uncomfortable when Suggs tells him he wants to take the money and pray over it in private. Suggs convinces the purse holder to let go of the money by assuring him he will go only a short distance away to pray. When he has the purse in hand, Suggs makes his way through the brush to find a horse he tied there earlier—and rides off with the offering safely in his saddlebag.[2]

Simon Suggs who cons the revivalists is without a doubt a questionable character, but Johnson Jones Hooper's portrayal implies that Suggs also performs a valuable service to the community. The fact that Suggs fools the revivalists demonstrates that their religion has not made them astute. If the revivalists were keen, they would see (as Suggs does) that other preachers are already taking advantage of them. Though he is clearly a fraud, Suggs is doing the revivalists (and any who might be taken in by them) a favor by exposing their gullibility.

Both Sut Lovingood and Simon Suggs are brazen opportunists, but so is the preacher Sut brings down. In fact, Harris's tale suggests that the two-faced preacher who hides behind a mask of pious morality is at least as bad a character as the conniving Sut. Sut is a clearly recognizable con artist, but the preacher is even more dangerous: he is a less-apparent con man who hides behind a mask of morality and bilks his congregation again and again. When Sut exposes the preacher's true character, he does the church a favor.

Con men of all kinds, including those who present themselves as preachers, are common on the frontier during the nineteenth century. The proliferation of opportunists in the West so impressed Eastern author Herman Melville during his pre–Civil War journey to the Middle West that he made *every* character a con man in *The Confidence Man* (1857), the novel he based on his experience of the frontier. Passengers on the Riverboat *Fidele*, where the story takes place, cannot trust anyone, including the Methodist minister, to be what they represent themselves to be. Mark Twain's *The Adventures of Huckleberry Finn* (1884), published almost thirty years after Melville's *Confidence Man*, recalls the same antebellum river culture. Twain's novel includes two masters of deception, the King and the Duke. Both assume a variety of counterfeit identities. The King's include posing as a preacher: "I've done considerable in the doctoring way in my time. Layin' on o' hands is my best holt—for cancer and paralysis, and sich things; and I k'n tell a fortune pretty good when I've got somebody along to find out the facts for me. Preachin's my line, too, and workin' camp-meetin's, and missionaryin' around" (116).

To survive on the frontier, one needs to be able to recognize who is a phony and who is not. The tall tale speaks to this necessity. The tall tale thrives in a land where everyone is new. Those who "know the territory" get the point of the story. The fact that they do demonstrates that they are insiders. Newcomers need to pay close attention to the locals' tall tales. As James M. Cox suggests in his study of Mark Twain's humor, the tall tale "is not a lie which conceals, but a lie which *exposes* the truth. In a world of lies, the tall tale is the only true lie because it does not mask as the truth but moves the listener to ask what the truth is." Truth becomes apparent from "the skeptical state of mind which the tale evokes in the listener, forcing him to maintain a questioning alertness in the face of experience."[3] To be safe in this world, one needs to challenge everyone, including preachers, to prove that they are who and what they pretend to be. The gullible, even when they are pious, are most at risk. Anyone, even a minister who seems beyond reproach, could be counterfeit.[4]

Muscular Ministers

Though they were very different from most Eastern clerics, there was nothing fake about the muscular ministers who are reflected in late-nineteenth- and early-twentieth-century novels from the South and West. These strong characters are as clever and resourceful as the phony preachers I just described, but, unlike the conning clerics, their integrity is above reproach. They are as upright as they are strong; their spiritual conviction matches and augments their physical strength.

Hilliard Watts, the Baptist "Bishop" of post–Civil War Cottontown and the central character in John Trotwood Moore's novel *The Bishop of Cottontown* (1906), is a classic muscular minister. Watts is a person of simple faith. His body is as strong as his belief; he can fight as well as he can pray. He has a good mind, shaped and governed by a Bible-based theology. He is as much a man of the world as a man of the cloth; his parishioners admire both his spiritual wisdom and his ability to pick a good racehorse. Watts's character is also tempered by personal suffering: when he was married only a year, both his young wife and her baby died during childbirth. His own trials give Watts the ability to enter into the suffering of others.

Cottontown where Watts serves as pastor still endures the aftereffects of Reconstruction. The local mill that is owned by Northerners and managed by locals who have sold their souls to the absent owners provides the only employment in town. The bishop is the only source of comfort to those who live in Cottontown; they have no hope of escaping from the poverty that grips them. He goes "every day, from house to house, helping the sick, cheering the well, and better than all things else, putting into the hearts of the disheartened that priceless gift of coming again. . . . In the rush and struggle of the strenuous world around them, this humble old man was the only being to whom they could go for spiritual help" (317).

Watts's willingness to use his physical strength to protect his flock marks him as a muscular minister. This muscular character of his faith shows forth when he comes to the defense of a child who is so sick she is unable to report for work at the mill. The child's mother tells the bishop that her little girl first went to work in the mill at age seven because "We was starvin' an' had to do something." Within a week, she had two fingers crushed. Now, two years later, she is completely debilitated, sick with fever. The bishop says he will sit with the sick child for an hour so her mother can finish the washing. The child falls asleep as the bishop sits quietly reading his newspaper. Loud, heavy steps soon fill the hallway, and the door bursts open, startling both of them. Jud Carpenter, the mill foreman, known locally as the "whipper-in," enters the room and demands to know what ails the child. "Mill-icious fever," the bishop replies, emphasizing the first syllable. The foreman is not impressed:

> "They ain't half as sick as they make out an' I've come to see about it. That spinner is idle over yonder an' I guess I'll jes' be carryin' her back."
>
> "Jud Carpenter," said the old man rising—"I am a man of God. . . . I'm getting' old, but I have been a man in my day, an' I've still got strength enough left with God's he'p to stop you. You shan't tech that child." (321–22)

The bishop's audacity makes Carpenter furious. He lands a vicious blow on the bishop's face. The old man turns slowly: "Strike the other cheek, you coward, as my Master sed you would." The angry foreman lands an equally cruel blow on the bishop's other cheek. He says with a sneer:

> "What else kin I do for you at the request of yo' Master?"
>
> "As He never said anything further on the subject . . . I take it He intended me to use the same means He employed when He run the thieves an' bullies of His day out of the temple of God."

The bishop's "old-time strength" returns in a "wave of righteous indignation, and, like the gust of the whirlwind striking the spars of a rotting ship" he is at the foreman. The whipper-in hits the floor with such force that he feels like every bone in his body is broken. Ten minutes later, he opens his eyes to discover the bishop bathing his bruised face with cold water. He realizes how ridiculous he must look.

> "Wal, I reckin you've 'bout converted me this time."
> "Jud Carpenter," [says] the Bishop, his face white with shame, "for God's sake don't tell anybody I done that—." (321–24)

After the foreman leaves, the feverish child eats the gingerbread man the bishop brought her. Two days later, she dies.

The Rev. Gordon Harrington, the central character in George R. Varney's *Out of the Depths* (1909), is a bit more reserved than Hilliard Watts but just as able to stand up to antagonists. Harrington confronts unanticipated challenges when he is called away from his ministry in a quiet Eastern village to become the pastor of a church in a Western city. Corruption is rampant in the city. Saloons and prostitutes proliferate in the working-class district. They bleed workers of their meager wages, which brings even more misery to already-impoverished families. When Harrington preaches sermons that describe the corruption and its effects, he shocks the congregation of his middle-class church. His open criticism threatens Jim Tracy, a local hoodlum and saloon owner and, unbeknownst to the minister, some of his church's leaders who secretly profit by the saloon trade. The profiteers warn the minister to hold his tongue, but he refuses. They try to impugn his character by telling him a prostitute is sick, convincing him to visit her, and making sure he is observed by others when he does. Their plot fails. Their situation worsens when drunkenness leads to the death of a local workingman, whose ill wife dies soon after. The tragedy is compounded when the couple's orphaned son saves a baby about to be trampled by runaway horses pulling a beer wagon—and then is unable to escape himself. In his dying moments, the boy says he is glad to die because he has nothing left to live for. Death will at least reunite him with his mother.

The impact of the tragic incident converts the notorious saloon owner, Jim Tracy. With Harrington's encouragement, Tracy tears down his saloon and begins to build a social center for workingmen in its place. These developments suggest that Harrington is winning against the local forces of evil. But a covert enemy, one of the deacons in Harrington's church, is involved with a crime syndicate that profits from the local corruption. When the deacon realizes he will not be able to stop Harrington's reform efforts, he has Harrington and Miss Gillespie, a reformed prostitute, kidnapped.

 During their captivity, when Clogston, one of the captors, reaches Miss Gillespie's tent, obviously intent on violating her, he suddenly finds Harrington towering over him. A single surprise blow knocks the captive down and saves Miss Gillespie's virture. Kidnappers and rescuers alike are awed by Harrington's strength and physical prowess as he brings about his and Miss Gillespie's escape from their captors. With the criminals safely in custody, Detective Burns is "filled with wonder and admiration" as Harrington describes what he did to secure his and Miss Gillespie's freedom: "Not many preachers could deliver such a blow as that, or get out of a scrape like that. If you lose your job as a preacher, come to me and I will give you a place on my force" (343–44).

One of the earliest muscular ministers in American fiction is a woman. Jerusha Bangs, the central character in Elizabeth Stuart Phelps's short story, "A Woman's Pulpit" (1870/1879) combines many of the strengths and none of the pitfalls of the muscular minister.[5] "A Woman's Pulpit" begins with an exchange of letters between Jerusha and the Rev. Z. Z. Zangrow, the secretary of the Home Missionary Society serving the state of New Vealshire (*Veal*shire is probably a play on *Ham*pshire). In her first letter, Jerusha offers to serve as pastor of one of the small congregations in Zangrow's district, "place and time entirely at your disposal." She informs the secretary that she is not a college graduate but nonetheless "the possessor of a fair education." She offers the names of two references who will attest to her competence, a clergyperson and a seminary professor. She signs the letter "J. W. Bangs."

Mr. Zangrow sends a favorable response to "My Dear Sir." The lack of collegiate education is not an "insurmountable" obstacle. He has a post available among the "Gray Hills." It pays six dollars a week, plus housing. Will that be satisfactory? Jerusha responds, "Terms are satisfactory," and "I neglected to mention in my last that I am a woman." She signs the letter "Jerusha W. Bangs." The letter elicits only a brief note from the secretary: "Dear Madam,—You have played me an admirable joke. Regret that I have no time to return it." She writes back: "Dear Sir,—I was never more in earnest in my life." Two days later, Mr. Zangrow writes back: "Dear Madam,—I am sorry to hear it" (179).

In her next letter, Jerusha challenges the secretary to meet with her for fifteen minutes—and, if he does so, promises to convince him to send her to one of the churches in New Vealshire. In three days, Jerusha is on a train bound for Storm, New Vealshire. She arrives in the midst of a snowstorm, to be met by three women and Mr. Dobbins. The latter guides her to an old buggy sleigh and says, "I'll put ye in." Dobbins is a very short man. In fact, Bangs observes, "I could have 'put' Mr. Dobbins into anything twice as comfortably as I could support the reversal of the process" (186). The overly solicitous Mr. Dobbins is the foil Phelps uses to advance her argument that a woman can meet the challenges of ministry just as well as a man can—and sometimes better. The next morning, Jerusha rises early, prepared to preach her first sermon, only to be greeted by Mr. Dobbins with the news that the service has been cancelled:

> "Ye see there's such a heft of snow, and no paths broke, and seein' it was a gal as was goin' to preach, me and the other deacon we thought she'd get her feet wet, or suthin', and so we 'greed we wouldn't ring the bell!"
>
> "Will your paths be broken out by night?"
>
> "Wal, yes. In spots; yes; middlin' well."
>
> "Will my audience be afraid of wetting their feet, after the paths are broken?"
>
> "Bless you, no!" said Mr. Dobbins, staring, "they're used to 't."
>
> "Then you will please to appoint an evening service, and ring your bell at half past six precisely. I shall be here, and shall preach, if there is no one but the sexton to hear me. And next Sabbath you will oblige me by proceeding with the regular service, whatever the weather, and without the least anxiety for my feet." (190–91)

After Bangs's sermon, Mr. Dobbins expresses the sentiments of all: "Folks is all upsot about ye. That there was an eloquent discourse, marm. Why, they don't see but ye know jest as much as if ye was n't a woman!" (193). Bangs's words and actions as a pastor in Storm successfully transform this initial surprise into a firm conviction. As the weeks pass, she is steadfast in her intent to be taken seriously: "I would gain the respect of my parishioners, whether—well, yes—whether I gained their souls or not" (191). As the story unfolds, she gains both.

Probably the best-known muscular minister in American fiction is Harold Bell Wright's Dan Matthews. Wright left the ministry soon after the turn of the century to become a full-time writer. Within only a few years, he became one of the most popular authors in early-twentieth-century America. By the early 1930s, sales of his books exceeded nine million copies; *The Calling of Dan Matthews* alone sold over one million copies.[6] In an interview given in 1934, Wright recalled what motivated his decision to become a writer: "Pittsburg [Kansas where Wright served as pastor] was a coal mining town where the churches gave the laboring man a cold welcome but the saloons gave him a warm one. I wanted to make the church a little less divine and a lot more human. So I wrote 'That Printer of Udell's' to broadcast the idea."[7]

Both Wright's belief in the power of a muscular ministry and his personal agenda with the church are clear in his characterization of Dan Matthews. Dan's integrity is as impressive as his body. He reflects "the healthy life of the woods and hills" where he grew up. He carries his father's "powerful frame" and "the gentle mind and spirit of his mother" (33, 34). When he alights from the train to begin his ministry in the town of Corinth, the crowd gathered to greet him sense that somehow this pastor is different from the other ministers they have known. The church ladies gasp when they see him, their eyes "full of admiration." This preacher—"with his father's great body, powerful limbs and shaggy red-brown hair; and his mother's . . . spirit ruling him" makes them feel he is "clean through and through" (46).

The difference the new minister embodies is shortly apparent. On the day he arrives, Jud Hardy, a surly character from neighboring Windy Cove, comes to Corinth for the fair. By late morning, Hardy is already quite drunk. He places himself in the doorway of the post office, stepping aside with pretentious gallantry to let the women pass and daring any man to pass through the door in front of him. Denny, a young lad with a crippled foot that requires all of his attention when he walks, fails to take note of Jud's warning. When Denny crosses Jud's path, Jud curses him and then, with a blow of his fist, knocks Denny down on the pavement. The crowd gasps. "Why does someone not do something!" a woman moans.

Someone does. "With one clean, swinging blow," the newly arrived pastor lifts Jud "off the ground to fall several feet away from his senseless victim." But the fight is not out of the bully. He is quickly on his feet, reaching into his pocket for a hidden gun. The crowd who know him all too well scream out a warning: "But the mountain bred Dan needed no warning. With a leap, cat-like quickness, he was again upon the other. There was a short struggle, a sharp report. A wrenching twist, a smashing blow, and Jud was down once more, this time senseless. The weapon lay in the dust. The bullet had gone wide" (52).

Dan Matthews's unique character and physical strength set him apart in the minds of his parishioners. But he soon discovers troubling inconsistencies between the teachings of the Christian faith and the behavior of some of the most influential lay leaders in his congregation. When he points out specific discrepancies to them directly, they are offended. Dan's blunt words reach beyond the constraints ministers are expected to honor. A minister is expected to preach about wrongdoing, but he is not expected to address the shortcomings of church members directly. The hypocrisy of leaders in his congregation becomes especially difficult for Dan to countenance when he develops a close relationship with Hope Farwell, a local nurse who is severely critical of the duplicity she sees in leading members of Dan's congregation.

Events that transpire during the following winter increase Dan's disenchantment with the church. When Deborah, the lame Denny's caregiver, is unable to meet the payments on their home, Judge Strong, the leading elder in Memorial Church, shows no mercy. He forecloses on the property. The significance of this merciless action is compounded when Mike McGowan, Deborah's brother, returns unexpectedly. Dan encounters the angry Mike outside Deborah's house. Mike tells the minister that he paid off the mortgage on Deborah's property years before. Judge Strong, thinking that her brother would never return, neglected to inform Deborah of the settlement. He has been collecting payments to which he is not entitled ever since.

A visit to the bank verifies Mike's story. Dan confronts the church elder with his dishonesty. The elder agrees to make restitution. But when Dan presses him to confess his transgression publicly, Judge Strong refuses. Dan confronts another elder with Strong's refusal. He says the church should forgive Judge Strong and that his transgression must never come to light—to protect the church's reputation. This proposed collusion is too much for Dan Matthews; he determines not only to go through with the resignation he has been contemplating but also to leave the ministry entirely. He now believes that he can accomplish more good as an honest businessman than he can as a minister in the church.

Once Dan is released from his pastoral obligations, he feels free to take justice into his own hands with Judge Strong. He confronts the judge in the latter's home: "In the name of the people you have tricked and robbed under the cover of business, in the name of the people you have slandered and ruined under cover of the church, I'm going to give you what such a contemptible rascal as you are, deserves." Though the judge is a big man, in the prime of life, he is like "a child in the hands of the young giant, who thrashed him until he lay half-senseless, moaning and groaning in pain, on the ground" (354). Though he has left his pastorate with Memorial Church, as he thrashes Judge Strong it is obvious that Dan sees himself doing a godly act—punishing evil as a minister of God.

Though this line of thinking still appeals to some believers, it is fraught with hazards. Those hazards are undeniably apparent in Thomas Dixon Jr.'s novel *The Leopard's Spots* (1905). *The Leopard's Spots* is set in the postbellum South and describes what Dixon apparently sees as the damaging effects of

 Reconstruction in Southern society. The Rev. John Durham is the muscular minister who appears in the novel. He is obviously designed to give a religious legitimacy to Dixon's baldly racist views. When Dixon introduces Durham, he describes him as one who is above any political or cultural bias: He "never touched on politics. . . . When he ascended the pulpit he was the Messenger of Eternity. He spoke of God, of truth, of righteousness, of judgment, the same yesterday, to-day and forever. . . . He was narrow and dogmatic in his interpretation of the Bible. . . . He never stooped to controversy. He simply announced the truth" (39).

Actually, Pastor Durham's views are shaped much more by culture than by the scripture. Just a few pages after Dixon describes Durham's scriptural purity, the minister encounters a woman from the North who is intent on beginning a school to educate recently emancipated African Americans. Her proposal obviously angers the pastor. "Your mission is not to proclaim the gospel of Jesus Christ," he tells her. "Your mission is to teach crack-brained theories of social and political equality to four millions of ignorant Negroes. . . . Your work is to separate and alienate the Negroes from their former masters, who only can be their real friends and guardians. Your work is to sow the dragon's teeth of an impossible social order that will bring forth its harvest of blood for our children" (46). Pastor Durham's words display the novel's bias: *The Leopard's Spots* presents a cultural and racial contest between Southern whites and their former slaves. African Americans in the novel are cast as childlike people who are incapable of caring for themselves and therefore need to be under the care *and control* of their former masters. Northerners and local sympathizers who pretend to be concerned for the welfare of African Americans are cast as questionable characters who take advantage of naive blacks to further their own interests. Southern leaders are cast as righteous defenders of society. Charles Gaston, the hero of the novel, becomes governor after local white leaders led by another muscular minister, the Rev. Duncan McDonald, pastor of the First Presbyterian Church and who also was "a brave young officer in the Confederate army," frighten black voters away from the polls. Gaston's action enables white voters to successfully take back control of local government from the Northern scalawags who usurped it during Reconstruction.

Gaston also comes to the rescue when an angry and out-of-control Durham tries to kill a young scalawag who tries to compromise Mrs. Durham's honor. Allen McLeod, a young Northerner the preacher and his wife take in after his mother dies, is the stereotypical scalawag. He repays Pastor Durham's charitable act by making sexual advances to Mrs. Durham when the pastor is away from home—and then slandering her when she rebuffs his advances. The preacher is incensed by McLeod's subterfuge and moves quickly to a violent defense of his wife's honor. Only the efforts of Charles Gaston restrain the angry pastor from delivering a fatal blow.[8]

Pastor Durham is a stereotypical postbellum, Southern-style muscular minister. His willingness to kill the scalawag McLeod to protect his wife's honor also defends the cultural foundation on which that sense of honor stands. Charles Gaston's restraining act keeps Durham from becoming a murderer, but it also leaves the symbolic value of Durham's action intact. His intervention gives a quasi-religious legitimacy to the old antebellum white supremacist order he and Durham represent—a legitimacy that is fraught with hazards. When culture overwhelms religion, religion may lose its ability to critique the social order it reflects.

Gallant Parsons

The gallant parsons who appear in several novels set in the East stem from the same cultural strain as muscular ministers. Gallant parsons are usually more-restrained and more-refined heroes of the cloth than muscular ministers. They sometimes rise to righteous indignation, but they never lose control of themselves. The Rev. Stephen Castle, who appears in Caroline Atwater Mason's novel *A Minister of the World* (1895), is typical. He is described as "a tall, athletic fellow . . . [whose] face wore the stamp of thought and study, and indeed there was upon it a suggestion of spiritual purity and earnestness, which united with the boyish freedom of his movements and his thoroughgoing manliness, to make a peculiarly winning personality, even to one who saw him only for a moment (13, 14).

Castle arrives in Thornton, his first parish, with his widowed mother, who "followed him wherever he went." His background suits him well for ministry in Thornton, a small and obscure village. He prepared for the ministry "in the humbler and more rural schools of New England" so he feels no "deprivation or sacrifice" when he accepts the call to Thornton (14). But the idyllic ministry in Thornton is brief. The minister's performance at a wedding impresses one of the guests, Stephanie Loring, a visitor from New York City. She extends her visit, and the two of them spend many hours together. When she departs for Newport, where she will spend the rest of the summer, she looks directly into Stephen's eyes and promises, "I shall see you again." Then she adds, "This is not where you belong, but I must not say any more. You will understand" (53). After Stephanie leaves Thornton, the local people notice a change in Stephen. They recognize that he is no longer content. He seems preoccupied. And he is: Stephanie and her parting words are constantly on his mind. The villagers' fears are confirmed on a November Sunday when two strange gentlemen attend the morning service. Their visit is followed a month later by Stephen Castle's announcement that he is resigning the pulpit of the Thornton church to accept a call to become the pastor of the Church of All Good Spirits in New York City.

Stephen's humble and somewhat moralistic mother is completely out of place in the new parish. In truth, Stephen is as uneasy about the lifestyle of his new parishioners as his mother is. The ways of business rule those who lead his new parish: in church, no less than at work. Mr. Loring, Stephanie's father, "the most influential member of the Church of All Good Spirits," is a clear example. He is "a man of wealth and culture" with "a decided interest in the affairs of the church, but in this and in all things . . . although not unscrupulous" he is "a master at manoeuvre, and, first and last and always, a business man" (72). In a revealing conversation with Stephen, Mr. Loring describes the business-like ministry that people anticipate Stephen will provide as pastor of the Church of All Good Spirits. The congregation does not expect Stephen to engage in pastoral work except in extreme cases—at times of illness and death. They do expect him to meet parishioners frequently "at dinners and receptions and all that." Most of all, "what our church wants is good preaching,—brains, in short, Mr. Castle; and that is what we have secured. We are entirely satisfied on that point" (74).

As the months pass, Stephen Castle feels more and more like an alien in his "ultra-fashionable" new parish. But after a soul-searching conversation with Stephanie, who reassures him that he has not made a mistake in moving to New York, Stephen pours himself into his new ministry. And, as his mother predicted, he becomes more and more like the people of the parish he now serves. Within a year, he is transformed. The leaders of All Good Spirits are very pleased, especially Mr. Loring. At a social occasion, he tells a friend how pleased he is with the new pastor's transformation:

> He was full of a lot of Puritanic notions [when he first arrived in New York]. . . . But . . . inside of a year he settled down to business in great shape, and I certainly never saw a man improve so rapidly in my life. He has traveled, you know; is up on art; hears good music, an opera now and then,—nothing beyond clerical propriety, of course,—preaches elegant sermons, and can hold his own socially with any clergyman in New York. (89)

In truth, Stephen is not as pleased with his transformation as his parishioners are. At the same party where Mr. Loring brags about him, he receives news that his beloved Aunt Eliza has died back in Thornton. Overcome by sadness, Stephen excuses himself. Arriving at home, he seeks refuge in his study. Among the envelopes that have come in the day's mail is one that contains a letter inviting him to preach the ordination sermon for a seminary graduate who has just been called to serve the church in Thornton. He immediately writes his acceptance.

Stephen's trip back to Thornton brings more than nostalgia. In this simple setting as he preaches again in his old church and the next day as he walks with his first love, Emily Merle, delivering flowers to the shut-ins of the parish, Stephen Castle regains his bearings. He now sees the transformation that enables him to fit the role of pastor at All Good Spirits has taken him away from authentic ministry. He decides to resign as pastor of the Church of All Good Spirits and to begin a ministry among the poor in the city. As he and Emily part, Stephen realizes that before long he will return and ask her to join him in his new ministry. Within a few months, she does—and Stephanie Loring becomes a major financial supporter of his ministry among the poor of New York.

The message implicit in Mason's novel is not simply that Stephen Castle's rural roots ill-suit him for ministry at the Church of All Good Spirits; the culture of All Good Spirits is incompatible with a Christian life. One cannot be a faithful minister and serve a church like the Church of All Good Spirits. To be a faithful minister in a world dominated by business and commercial interests, a minister must reject the ways of that world in favor of a ministry patterned on the simpler ways of Christian faith.

Donald Brown, the gallant Episcopal priest in Grace S. Richmond's novel *The Brown Study* (1915), comes to the same conclusion as Stephen Castle does. Brown, who is pastor of St. Timothy's, an upper-class city parish, when the novel opens, soon becomes disillusioned with this ministry. He leaves it and rents a small apartment located in a poor neighborhood and begins a ministry to those who live in the area. When church members in his former parish ask why he has left them for this new ministry, he explains he has done so for the good of his soul. "Do you know what was the matter with my heart when I came away?" he asks them, and then answers his own question: "I do. It was high living. It was sitting with my legs under the mahogany of my millionaire parishioners' tables" (120). He ministers now in this poor neighborhood because he finds real needs here and for the good of his soul. Even he with his upper-class roots cannot find a way to be an authentic Christian minister and serve an upper-class church.

A brief return to the posh surroundings of his old life tests Donald's dedication. At a formal dinner he again meets Helena Forrest, the woman he would likely have married had he remained rector of St. Timothy's. The host, Webb Atchison, places Helena on Brown's right at the dinner table, consciously employing her as a "weapon" to draw Donald back to his old life and parish. Later in the evening, they find themselves alone in their host's den. With her close by, Donald feels caught between love and vocation. With a "sudden fierceness" he asks, "Are you tempting me, too?" Obviously Helena is tempting him. She pleads with Donald to return to "this great parish—surely there is work for you here, wonderful work. Won't you do it—*with me?*" He cannot agree. He responds to her plea with one of his own, "Will you live—and—work with me—*there?*" among the poor. She cannot assent. "'Oh!' She drew back. 'How can you—Do you realize what you ask?'" (156, 157; italics in the original). They are at an impasse. But all is not lost. Helena is too engaged by this sacrificing minister to stay away. Several weeks after the dinner party, she and a friend come to hear Donald preach to the "factory girls." Helena is profoundly moved by the minister she sees. Within weeks, she decides to give up her affluent life and join with Donald in a ministry to the poor—and to contribute her substantial resources to help make that ministry possible.

Robert McPherson Black, a Scot, who at age thirty-five assumes the pastorate of a suburban town's "fine old, ivy-grown church generally known as the 'Stone Church,'" is probably the most gallant of the gallant parsons. Grace Richmond's 1919 novel *Red and Black* in which he appears reflects the bellicose and euphoric mood that grips the United States during and after World War I. Early in the novel it becomes apparent that Black is an open advocate of Christians doing their part to fight the war. At a men's dinner, an obviously pacifist church member challenges Black's "sympathy" with the war. Black responds: "Perhaps you might rather say I am in sympathy with those who have had the war thrust upon them. What else is there for them to do but to make war back—to end it?" The challenger retorts: "Christ was the Man of Peace—He told us to turn the other cheek—." Every eye in the room is on Black as he responds slowly and quietly: "My Christ . . . if He were on earth now, and the enemy were threatening Mary, His mother, or the other Mary, or the little children He had called to Him, would seize the sword in His own hand, to defend them" (70).

As the story proceeds, the gallant minister's deeds match his words. He enlists in the army as a chaplain—and returns a wounded hero. During the course of his ministry as a chaplain in France, he is wounded. While recovering from his wounds, he encounters Jane Ray, a skeptic in his parish back home, who is working as a nurse in the hospital where he is confined. As they become reacquainted, Donald is able to win her both to Christian faith and to be his wife. They are married shortly after his return from the war. At the wedding breakfast, Black's new brother-in-law reveals that Black has been awarded a medal for distinguished service as a fighting soldier. Over Black's protest, he describes how Black won his medal:

> [A machine gun] had lost its last gunner, trying to put out a machine-gun nest of the enemy's which was enfilading our men and mowing them down. This Bob Black of ours comes up, jumps in, and keeps things going all by himself till—the spit-fire over there was silenced. It may not have been the proper deed for the chaplain—I don't know—but I do know that he saved ten times more lives than he took—and I say—here's to him—and God bless him! (380)

On the battlefield, the gallant Robert Black becomes a muscular minister. As appealing as his heroism may appear, Black's transformation from chaplain into fighting hero may be another instance of culture overwhelming religion. His willingness to stand up and fight like a muscular minister may make him a man's man. It may also compromise him as a minister. Muscular ministers and gallant parsons are portrayed intentionally as ministers who are *real* men. But their willingness to employ physical violence and to accept that violence, even reluctantly, *as a morally justified act* is ethically questionable. When Hilliard Watts thrashes the "whipper-in," does he stand morally above the mill foreman, or does he descend to the mill foreman's level? Does the regret Watts feels afterward really justify the thrashing? Similarly, is the fact that Dan Matthews gives Judge Strong a beating *after* he formally leaves the pastoral ministry simply a literary device? Or, does Harold Bell Wright sense that some of his readers would find Dan less than believable *as a minister*, if he beat up the judge before he resigned his pastorate? In other words, is such a violent act out of character for a minister? The reader may feel that the "good guy" got the "bad guy" when Dan Matthews beats up Judge Strong, but there is no evidence that this act contributes in any way to Judge Strong's redemption. It is difficult to justify as an act of ministry.

Whether the fictional clergyman is portrayed as a muscular minister or a gallant parson, there is little connection in these novels between the hero minister's physical strength and his faith. This disconnection becomes blatant when the minister turns to violence. John Trotwood Moore and Grace Richmond offer ample evidence to support their contention that their fictional ministers are potent men but little or no evidence that demonstrates they are potent believers. Richmond's portrayal of Robert Black as a gallant chaplain who becomes a machine gunner on the battlefield poses the same ethical dilemma as Dan Matthews's thrashing of Judge Strong. Black, like Matthews, keeps his ministerial identity when he becomes a fighting man. But Black's new brother-in-law's justifying statement, "He saved ten times more lives than he took," seems even more expedient than Watts's guilt as he gazes at the bloodied face of the foreman. Killing an enemy to survive on the battlefield may be an awful alternative. But does the fact that someone is classified as an enemy—that is, as bad—make it morally right for one who is supposed to exemplify Christ-likeness to kill them? To characterize the Rev. Mr. Black's acts as a machine gunner *as acts worthy of a minister* raises deep ethical questions. Violent acts, whether individual or corporate, signal a failure in human relations. Ministers as humans are certainly subject to human failings. But Black's facile movement from chaplain to machine gunner suggests there may be some distance between his Christ and the Christ.

VI

ACTIVIST PREACHERS AND THEIR DETRACTORS

Popular Images (3)

The proliferation of cities interconnected by railroads and the development of large-scale manufacturing that followed the Civil War transformed American life and posed as many challenges for ministers in the closing decades of the nineteenth century as the frontier did in midcentury. Between 1860 and 1910, the population of the United States tripled, from thirty-one million to nearly ninety-two million. The increase in the number and proportion of Americans living in incorporated municipalities of more than twenty-five hundred was even more dramatic—from six million in 1860 to forty-five million in 1910, an increase of 750 percent. By 1910, nearly one-half of all Americans were urban dwellers, compared with fewer than one-fifth in 1860. Rapidly growing cities emerged in nearly every area of the country.

A massive, often-chaotic complexity characterized these late-nineteenth- and early-twentieth-century American cities. The pace of growth and the sheer number of new arrivals were overwhelming. Nearly twelve million new city dwellers appeared between 1900 and 1910, for example. Immigrants from abroad accounted for 41 percent of these new urbanites, 29.8 percent were Americans who migrated from farms to cities, 21.6 percent were children born to those already living in a city, and 7.6 percent lived in areas that cities annexed. Most of these former rural residents were not at all prepared for city living. The vast majority of the Americans who settled in cities and most of the immigrants from abroad had rural roots. Only about one-quarter had *any* prior experience of urban living. Few of the new urbanites moved to the city by choice; economic hardship and changes in agricultural technology forced them to leave rural, ancestral homes. City life was rarely better for most of these reluctant rural emigrants. Economic, cultural, and linguistic barriers confined them to neighborhoods where opportunities for employment were limited, social problems ran rampant, and social services were meager or nonexistent. Many discovered they had traded rural poverty for urban poverty.[1]

Both contemporary church sources and novels written between 1865 and 1920 suggest that most ministers underestimated the range and magnitude of these social and economic changes. Clergy recognized that the world in which they served was different, but they still envisioned their ministry in personal terms. Massive social problems surrounded them, but they believed these social ills were rooted in powerful and greedy individuals, not in an unjust social and economic *system*.[2] Most ministers in real life and in fiction accepted the existing order as a given and envisioned their ministry within it. Only a handful considered the possibility that the existing social and economic order should or could be altered or replaced with some different or better arrangement. Most contemporary pastors and preachers defined their ministry relationally: they envisioned themselves as individuals called to appeal to other individuals. They honestly believed that those who heard their appeal had not only the responsibility but also the ability to right the social and economic wrongs that characterized the new urban society.[3]

A few progressive clergy and lay leaders developed a "social gospel" to respond to the needs of those living in American cities at the end of the nineteenth century and the beginning of the twentieth century. They urged other church leaders to broaden the focus of church life beyond its traditional preoccupation with the next world to include an equal concern for the plight of those living in this world. The new social gospel challenged church members to apply Christian principles in their business and political life and to take responsibility to improve the quality of housing, health care, sanitation, education, recreation, and other services. This concern to address social issues emerged just after the Civil War within Episcopal and Congregational churches and spread to Lutherans and Methodists by the 1880s. A variety of interdenominational and nondenominational social service agencies were also at work among the urban poor and displaced workers by the 1870s. In the last two decades of the nineteenth century, these city missions, social service agencies, and settlement houses proliferated. Though never more than a minority of clergy and church members participated directly in the new social Christianity, those who did gained more attention and exerted more influence than their numbers warranted.

Clergy who appear in novels that reflect the social gospel are based on three contemporary cultural images: the social minister, the social activist, and the social evangelical. The largest number of social gospel novels feature social ministers. Pastors who become social ministers expand their personal ministry beyond their own congregations to reach out to the poor, unemployed, or others in need. Some fictional social ministers urge their congregations to develop social ministry programs that provide recreation, education, and health benefits and that offer assistance to the unemployed. A few more courageous social ministers use their pulpits to attack corrupt business and political figures. The subjects of their criticism often include members of their own congregations who exploit workers and who profit from either the liquor and vice trades or the substandard tenement housing they own.

Social activists find the role of the minister, even the expanded role of the social minister, too limiting. They believe that ministers must go beyond the traditional role defined for clergy to minister effectively in the new urban America. Some social activists take secular jobs, others become political or labor activists, a few even run for elected office. Social activists consider their new vocations a legitimate form of ministry, but they rarely gain sympathy or support for their new ministries from leaders in their congregations and other clergy. Most other church leaders who appear in social gospel novels view the social activists' radical approach to ministry as unorthodox and the theology that informs that approach as heretical. When repeated attempts to convince their detractors fail, most social activists become disillusioned with the church.

Social evangelicals look on social ministry as a means to witness to their faith in God. They see themselves primarily as evangelists who testify to the reality of God in order to facilitate the conversion of those who are not Christian believers. Fictional clergy who are social evangelicals are often portrayed as heroes whose faith is tested. Whatever they may be called on to suffer, they always maintain their faith and trust in God. That faith in God is often vindicated when their antagonists undergo a dramatic conversion.

Grier Nicoll identifies the majority of those who produce social gospel novels as professional writers.[4] The thirty-four professional authors on Nicoll's list include overtly Christian novelists, like Elizabeth Stuart Phelps and Winston Churchill, and others, like W. D. Howells and Edward Bellamy, whose statements about their beliefs suggest that they were not Christian believers. In addition to professional writers, Nicoll lists three journalists, two university professors, two social workers, two politicians, and one businessperson who produced at least one social gospel novel. Nicoll identifies only ten ordained ministers who use novels as a vehicle to promote the social gospel. Fictional clergy who appear in novels by minister authors (Charles Sheldon is probably the best known) are most often portrayed as social evangelicals. The primary message embodied in fictional ministers cast as social evangelicals is that God (or, more specifically, Christ) will act to support the socially concerned pastor who has faith. Both the cultural roots and the character of the social evangelical image suggest that this image is a church image, and therefore I discuss it in chapter 7, along with other church images from this period.

From the 1880s through the 1920s, authors whose fictional clergy mirror popular images of social gospel ministers are not as optimistic as those whose clergy reflect church images. Ministers patterned on popular images often face huge and sometimes insurmountable obstacles as they try to minister effectively in the new industrialized urban America. In novels that reflect popular culture, God rarely acts directly and the church is most often a source of frustration. Social ministers who mirror popular images usually encounter as much or more opposition from lay leaders in their congregations and ministers of other churches as they do from opponents in the community. These fictional clergy reflect a turn-of-the-century subculture that perceives theologically orthodox lay people and clergy as reactionaries who object as much to modern methods of ministry as they do to modern beliefs.

Social Ministers

Emanuel Bayard, the central character in Elizabeth Stuart Phelps's *A Singular Life* (1894), is one of the earliest and also one of the most powerful characterizations of a social minister in American fiction. Emanuel's unorthodox beliefs and view of ministry mark him as one destined to become a social minister even while he is a seminary student. His inability to accept some central tenets of Calvinist theology presages the frustration he will meet when more-orthodox clerical colleagues prevent his ordination.[5] The fact that Bayard leaves seminary with unresolved theological questions does not make him unique among candidates for the ministry; but, unlike other questioners, he is scrupulously honest and open about his doubts. He assumes (naively, it turns out) that those who must approve his ordination will regard his deep faith in God and unqualified commitment to the ministry as sufficient and respect him for being open about his reservations.

After graduation from seminary, Bayard begins work in the seacoast parish of Windover, Massachusetts. From their first acquaintance with him, it is clear to residents of Windover that Emanuel is an untypical minister. He not only visits active church members but also begins an unconventional ministry among those who live in Angel Alley, a disreputable neighborhood frequented by seamen. In fact, a fateful incident in Angel Alley, typical of many that will set Bayard apart from his clerical colleagues, makes him late for his examination by the ecclesiastical council that must approve his ordination.[6] Bayard comes upon a fight between a laborer and a fisherman, both of them quite drunk. A young boy, the fisherman's son, tries to intervene; he pleads with his father to stop fighting and come home. Instead, the boy's father begins to beat him. Bayard quickly sets aside his silk hat and valise, steps into the fray, and lands a well-placed blow that knocks the fisherman down. He then pins the fisherman to the ground and frees his son. The crowd warns Bayard not to let the fisherman loose: "He'll thresh the life outen ye! . . . He'll make short work on ye." But the minister, trained as a boxer in his student days, knows the fisherman won't retaliate. "He respects a good blow when he feels it," he says. And then to the crowd's surprise, he calls the fisherman by name, "Job Slip," and offers an unexpected compliment: "He would do as much himself if he saw a man killing his own child" (59).

Bayard's intervention increases the respect residents of Angel Alley already have for him. But the delay it causes does not endear him to the waiting ecclesiastical council. The chairman's explanation that "an act of Christian mercy" made Bayard late allays the council's annoyance only somewhat. After a brief intermission to permit Bayard an opportunity to dust off his clothes, the meeting begins. During the opening worship, Bayard has difficulty concentrating on the business at hand; his mind keeps wandering back to the scene on the street. But once the examination itself begins, the examiners' leading questions jolt him into the present. For years afterward, those who observe the proceedings on this day recall them as "three quivering hours" of the "most ingenious ecclesiastical inquisition which had been witnessed in that part of the State for many a year" (66). Bayard struggles with some of the initial questions but mostly acquits himself well—until the questioners turn to theology. Here his attempts to be forthright come across to the council as equivocations. Bayard's simple honesty is not the unequivocal assent that council members seek. By a majority of five they refuse to ordain Emanuel Bayard to the ministry.

With a heavy heart, Bayard leaves Windover. But the judgment of the council will not keep him from ministry there. A group of local people who are impressed with Bayard's approach to ministry ask him to begin a new work centered in Windover's Angel Alley. After some inner debate, Bayard agrees and soon is back ministering among the fishermen, drunkards, and prostitutes. Within a few weeks, those who compose a new congregation gather for their first service of worship. The service is interrupted almost as soon as it begins when someone brings word of an impending disaster. A vessel is caught on "ragged rock," a shoal just outside the harbor. The crew is certain to be lost. Bayard suspends the service and rushes to the scene. There he discovers the reason for the ship's plight: the ship veered off course because the crew are all drunk. Someone in the crowd gathered on the beach says they are all men of no account and not worth saving. Bayard does not agree. Two men are struggling in the raging water. Bayard quickly ties one end of a line around his waist and throws the other end to the crowd on the beach. He then wades into the crashing surf and swims toward the strugglers. He manages to save one man; the other is beaten against the rocks and drowns. On the beach, Bayard discovers the crewman he has rescued is Job Slip, one of the fighters he encountered on the way to his failed examination. Looking his rescuer in the eyes, the ashamed seaman says, "Mr. Bayard, sir, I wasn't wuth it." "Then *be* worth it!" the minister responds in a loud voice. Job Slip becomes worth it. He stays sober.

Not everyone in Angel Alley is pleased with Bayard's effectiveness as a minister. Initially, saloon operators and those who profit from the prostitutes simply scoff at his ministry, but they become more aggressive opponents when their business declines. They seek to discredit Bayard by associating him with scandal. When he befriends Lena, a local prostitute, and asks her to sing during services in the chapel, they accuse him of being her customer. Bayard refuses to withdraw the invitation. He heightens his attacks on those who profit from sin; in turn, they become more vicious in their attacks on him. Emanuel refuses to be intimidated. Those associated with the chapel become increasingly concerned for their minister's safety. In an act of desperation, Bayard's opponents set fire to his chapel. It burns to the ground. But even this disaster does not defeat him. He leads a successful effort that raises funds needed to build an even larger and more adequate building.

During her family's vacation visit to Windover the next summer, Helen Carruth, the daughter of one of Bayard's professors at Cesarea Seminary, becomes active in the work of Bayard's chapel. As they spend more and more time together, Emanuel and Helen recognize that their former love for each other is still very much alive. When they learn that Emanuel's enemies plan to attack him during the week before the chapel is to be dedicated, he and Helen decide to marry immediately. After the ceremony, they go away by themselves for several days, returning on the day of the dedication, confident that they have avoided the danger to Bayard's life. But as Helen and Emanuel walk together in the crowd leaving the new chapel after the service of dedication, someone throws a stone that strikes Emanuel in the head. He lingers in and out of consciousness for a week. On the seventh day he appears to rally but then dies quietly during the night with Helen by his side.[7]

When James Cameron, the social minister who stands at the center of Harold Bell Wright's first novel, *That Printer of Udell's* (1902), urges his congregation to begin a social ministry in Boyd City, he faces many of the same frustrations that Emanuel Bayard does in Windover. An incident that opens the novel personalizes the plight of displaced young men looking for work in cities like Boyd City, a town located somewhere in the Midwest. Dick Falkner, forced from the farm by technological changes that transformed agriculture across America after the Civil War, now unemployed, penniless, and weak from hunger, appears at the Thursday evening prayer meeting of a church in Boyd City. The text for the evening is "Inasmuch as ye have done it unto one of the least of these, my brethren, ye have done it unto me" (Matthew 25:40). At the end of the service, Dick waits by the door to speak with the preacher. "Sir, may I speak to you for a moment?" he asks. "If you'll be brief," the preacher replies; "I have an engagement soon." Dick asks the minister if he or some of the church members will help him find work. None of those remaining has a suggestion. "Been out of work long?" one of them asks. "Yes sir, and out of food, too." Then a woman asks,

> "Are you a Christian?"
> "No."
> "Do you drink?"
> "No ma'am."
> "Well, don't get discouraged; look to God; he can help you; and we'll all pray for you. Come and hear our Brother French preach; I am sure you will find the light. He is the best preacher in the city. Everybody says so. Good night." (31, 32)

Dick finds himself back on the street still hungry, still without a job. He looks up at the figure of Christ, "wrought in the costly stained glass window. 'One of the least of these,' he muttered hoarsely to himself" (32).

George Udell, a local printer who stands apart from the churches in Boyd City because he objects to their reactionary theology and lack of social concern, is the one who finally gives the starving Dick Falkner some food and some work. When Dick appears at Udell's print shop, Udell at first thinks he is drunk. But then he realizes that Dick's hands tremble from hunger not alcohol. Udell sends out to a local restaurant for a hot meal. When he calls Dick away from the press where he is setting type and invites him to eat, Dick's trembling hands drop the tray of type and he faints from hunger. As Dick falls forward, his outstretched fingers come to rest symbolically on Udell's feet.

By a "strange coincidence" the following Sunday at Jerusalem Church, the Rev. James Cameron preaches on "The Church of the Future." In the opening paragraphs of his sermon, Cameron describes how the church of the present fails to touch "the great problems of life: poverty, unemployment, the liquor trade." He pleads for a more "practical" Christianity and describes a future church that will be concerned for people's physical needs, as well as their souls. Though most of the local ministers and many of the leaders in his own congregation oppose the social ministry James Cameron proposes, he presses ahead with his plans to develop a church program that will provide services for the unemployed.

A tragic incident during the winter highlights the plight of the unemployed in Boyd City. One very cold night, a young man, penniless and unable to find shelter, dies of exposure on the church steps. When no one is able to establish his identity, George Udell provides for his funeral. Over the protests of Goodrich and other church leaders, Udell insists that the young man's grave be marked with a stone. He has the stone engraved with a pointed inscription: "I was a stranger and ye took me not in."

Udell's pointed message fails to impress local pastors and church leaders. But it does move local young people to action. With Pastor Cameron's encouragement, Dick Falkner proposes that Jerusalem Church establish a rehabilitation center for men out of work. The building will have "sleeping rooms, dining rooms, sitting room, kitchen, store room and a bath room" (123). In an effort to head off opposition he is certain will come from local church leaders, Falkner proposes specific procedures designed to distinguish between those who are seriously looking for work and those who are not—to be certain that irresponsible people will not take advantage of the center.

Under Dick Falkner's and Pastor Cameron's leadership, the social ministry thrives in Boyd City. Then tragedy strikes James Cameron as he ministers to Frank Goodrich, the estranged son of one of his most vocal critics. While living in another town, Frank becomes ill with smallpox. When he realizes he is going to die, he sends for the minister—without letting Cameron know the nature of his illness. Even after Cameron discovers Frank has smallpox, he decides to remain with him. After Frank dies, to be certain he will not expose others to the disease, Cameron remains at the remote cabin, hoping he will not come down with smallpox. But he does, and to prevent others from catching the disease, he insists that no one visit him. After Cameron dies, Dick Falkner is elected president of the mission he and Cameron spearheaded. In the years that follow, Falkner marries Amy Goodrich, and his reforming efforts are so impressive that he gains a statewide reputation and eventually is elected to Congress.

Though Harold Bell Wright's first novel may seem simplistic and contrived to many twenty-first-century readers, it must have been convincing to many who read it when it first appeared. *That Printer of Udell's* sold hundreds of thousands of copies, many more copies than any previous novel that features a social minister.[8] Some social gospel novelists who come after Wright exhibit more sophistication than he does, but with some variations most of them follow the same basic formula that he does. A minister hero has a vision of "practical Christianity." Entrenched lay leaders in his congregation and other ministers in the community oppose his vision, usually on doctrinal grounds and because it threatens their business interests. They defend their opposition by telling the minister that those who are poor or disadvantaged in some other way suffer because they are morally deficient. Aiding them will simply encourage their irresponsibility. A young woman, often the daughter of one of the minister's detractors, is sympathetic with the minister's vision. She goes against her father's wishes and supports the minister and his work. She usually becomes romantically involved with either the minister or one of the other protagonists.[9] The hero often relinquishes or is deposed from his ministerial post, but he usually continues his social ministry in spite of those who oppose him. Thomas Nelson Page's *John Marvel, Assistant* (1909) follows this basic formula, as does Winston Churchill's *The Inside of the Cup* (1914).

John Hodder and Alison Parr, the Episcopal priest and the strong woman at the center of Churchill's novel, are more defiant protestors than similar characters in Wright's and Page's novels. Hodder openly doubts the validity of orthodox doctrine and eventually accepts beliefs that are far more radical than those of most other social ministers who appear in American fiction. He not only holds firmly to his radical beliefs and survives even when leading members of his vestry accuse him of heresy, he persists in a social ministry his church leaders oppose and still manages to retain his pastorate. Parr is a powerful character in her own right. She unmasks her own father's effort to cover his unscrupulous business practices with a veneer of Christian charity. She offers a penetrating critique of traditional conservative theology that forces Hodder to reexamine his own theological convictions.

In the opening pages of the novel, John Hodder makes a strong first impression at St. John's Church, but as the months pass, he becomes increasingly uneasy with some aspects of his new parish. The grand mansions of the formerly fashionable Dalton Street neighborhood that surrounds the church building are now tenements filled with poor residents. Few of those who live in this neighborhood participate in St. John's Church. As the months pass, this disconnection between affluent church members who live in fine houses located some distance from the church building and the deprivation of those who live in its shadow troubles Hodder more and more. During the second year of his ministry, he shares his concern with the vestry and proposes that the church build a settlement house to provide services for the neighborhood poor. Hodder is grateful when vestry members support his proposal, but he is not comfortable with the way they view it. "I congratulate you upon the new plans, Mr. Hodder,—they're great," the wealthy trust company president, Mr. Plimpton, tells him at a formal dinner held in the home of the Fergusons, another affluent church family: "When we get the new settlement house we'll have a plant as up-to-date as any church in the country." "Up-to-date"—"plant"! Plimpton's terms resound in Hodder's mind. Suddenly he understands why Plimpton, Eldon Parr, and other leaders in his church support the settlement house. They view it as a means of bringing St. John's Church "up to [a] state of efficiency [similar to] Mr. Plimpton's trust company!" They do not see it as a ministry that will help those it serves to improve themselves (111).

The discomfort that begins at the Ferguson's dinner party becomes more pronounced when Hodder meets Alison Parr, the daughter of Eldon Parr, the chief warden of the vestry. On a Sunday when Alison attends worship at St. John's for the first time in several years, Eldon invites John to his home for lunch after the services. At the lunch table, Hodder discovers why Alison dissociates herself from her father and from St. John's Church and the Christian faith. He marvels when she boldly and ably challenges her father at the lunch table. Hodder is as taken by her appearance as he is by what she says. As he watches her speak, he notices that she is "very tall for a woman." She ties her hair in "a Grecian knot." She has about her "all the elements of the classic, even to the firm yet slender column of the neck" (121).

This "classic"-looking woman has substance: she is informed, astute, outspoken, and formidable. She mercilessly attacks the lifestyle of businessmen like her father who attempt to cover their economic opportunism with a veil of philanthropy. Eldon asks his daughter if St. John's proposed settlement house falls within her perception of contemporary philanthropy. Hodder finds her response quite unsettling:

> The social system by which you thrive, and which politically and financially you strive to maintain, is diametrically opposed to your creed, which is supposed to be the brotherhood of man. . . . Your true creed is the survival of the fittest. You grind these people down into what is really economic slavery and dependence, and then you insult and degrade them by inviting them to exercise and read books and sing hymns in your settlement house, and give their children crackers and milk and kindergartens and sunlight! (122, 123)

Alison Parr's words return again and again to haunt Hodder as he begins to visit the poor in the neighborhood that surrounds St. John's Church. He shudders at what he discovers. The plight of the Garvin family is typical. He meets Mrs. Garvin one afternoon as she enters the church to pray. When Hodder engages her in conversation, she tells him of a sick child. He insists on accompanying her to her home. The boy Dicky is seriously ill. He needs a doctor immediately. When his father returns and discovers Hodder is the minister from St. John's Church—which he refers to as "Eldon Parr's church"—he launches into a tirade. He will accept no doctor brought by a minister of St. John's. He would rather let his son die than accept help from the pastor of Parr's church! Hodder prods the angry father, and Mr. Garvin reveals the cause of his hatred: Parr swindled him and countless others in a stock deal. They lost everything at Parr's hand and now are forced to live in a squalid tenement that Parr owns. Voices in the hallway interrupt Mr. Garvin's outburst. The door to the apartment opens, and a man introduced simply as "Mr. Bentley" (a former parishioner at St. John's and another of Eldon Parr's victims) enters the room. The presence of this gentle, elderly man who spends his days ministering to the neighborhood poor has an immediate calming effect on everyone. Mr. Bentley instantly recognizes the gravity of the young boy's condition. He encourages the Garvins to accept help from the doctor Hodder wants to call. And they do.

Several more conversations with Horace Bentley and Alison Parr force John Hodder to rethink his theology, as well as his perception of the church. He realizes reluctantly that church leaders like Eldon Parr use orthodox doctrine to excuse their reactionary social attitudes. He decides he must reexamine his own theology. He buys and reads works of modern theology and biblical criticism—including several he refused to read when he was a seminary student. As Hodder studies and discusses the insights he gains with his new friends, both his theology and his approach to ministry begin to change. He spends more and more time calling among the people who live in the Dalton Street neighborhood. As he reflects on his reading in the light of his visits among the Dalton Street poor, he comes to terms with a world of reality that he and many of his colleagues "had feared" to examine: "He had insisted upon gazing at the universe through the coloured glasses of an outworn theology, instead of using his own eyes" (251). The core of the Christian faith is not to be found in a set of theological propositions; it is found in the living Christ through whom God "teaches us how to live" (260). God who was incarnate in the human Jesus is again incarnate in people like Mr. Bentley—many of whom are not orthodox-believing Christians. "The test of any doctrine is whether it can be translated into life, whether it makes any difference to the individual who accepts it," he tells Alison Parr: "The doctrines expressed in the Creeds must stand or fall by this test" (284). Those who *act* in Christ-like ways *are* Christ-like, quite apart from whether they *think* orthodox theological thoughts. And the opposite is also true: those who affirm orthodox theology but do not act in Christ-like ways are not Christ-like.

After a summer of reflection, Hodder brings all of his social and theological discoveries together publicly in a sermon he preaches on a fall Sunday. Members of the parish are sharply divided in their response. A few like Horace Bentley and Alison Parr are heartened by his words. But most of those who hear Hodder's sermon leave the service in anger. What he says threatens their entire way of life. Hodder's detractors follow a predictable course: they accuse him of preaching unorthodox theology. He disagrees. They ask him to resign. He refuses. They vote to stop paying his salary. The largest contributors decide to stay away from worship services and to withhold their contributions to the parish. They write to the bishop, detailing their charges and asking him to depose Hodder.

Within a short time, Hodder receives the expected summons from his bishop. As they sit together in the bishop's study, the bishop reads aloud one of the many accusatory letters he has received concerning Hodder. He asks Hodder to respond. Hodder corrects some misinformation in the letter and then goes on to describe his perception of the church as an agent of ministry and the obligation he feels to confront injustice, no matter what the cost. He describes the horror of the Dalton Street neighborhood that surrounds the church building and details how leading members of his congregation are responsible for the ruin of many who live there. He describes how he confronted the culprits and how they responded by attacking his theology and his way of ministry. He shares his wish to remain as pastor of St. John's, even though he receives no salary and the financial base of the church is in peril.

Hodder is surprised and heartened by his bishop's response. The bishop tells Hodder he has followed the events at St. John's carefully for many months. He talked just recently with Asa Waring, one of the few untainted members of Hodder's vestry. Only a few days ago, he received a request for an appointment from Horace Bentley. He shares Hodder's great respect for Mr. Bentley. Instead of receiving Bentley at the bishop's residence, he went to see Bentley at his home in Dalton Street and saw firsthand the conditions of life there and the ministry Mr. Bentley gives to those who live there. The bishop warns Hodder that those who oppose him may become vicious. He tells Hodder that he has the utmost respect and admiration for the ministry he now pursues. Not only will he not depose Hodder, he will stand behind him: "Whatever happens, you may count upon my confidence and support" (471).

The Inside of the Cup is more demanding and shows more sophistication than most social gospel novels. The theological discussions between John Hodder and Alison Parr and between Hodder and Horace Bentley reveal Winston Churchill's astute knowledge of both historical and contemporary theology. Churchill's portrayal of Hodder's bishop reflects his own experience as an Episcopal lay leader and his belief in the strength of Episcopal polity. Unlike many social ministers, Hodder is not forced from his pulpit when he becomes a radical believer and a socially active pastor. Hodder survives, but not simply by his own strength of character. Hodder's bishop believes in the integrity of his ministry and uses his ecclesiastical authority to prevent Hodder's detractors from ousting him. While his bishop's support assures that Hodder will not be deposed as pastor of St. John's, his future there is far from certain. Parishioners who furnish the bulk of the church's financial support have withdrawn. There is no clear indication that members who continue to attend will accept either the neighborhood poor who respond to Hodder's social ministry or the liberal thinkers like Horace Bentley and Alison Parr who affirm his new theology.

Churchill's novel raises significant issues, but it provides few concrete suggestions. Hodder finds faith again after he passes through a time of deep doubt, but the answers he proposes to many of the theological questions that plague him are vague and undeveloped. Alison Parr (who becomes his wife) does not simply object to certain aspects of orthodox Christian theology, she doubts the validity of most of it. By the end of the novel, she has come to believe in John Hodder but not in the God he represents. Even he is unable to respond to many of her theological challenges. No character in the novel offers *developed* alternatives to the orthodox beliefs John and Alison question. To be fair, this deficiency is not unique to Winston Churchill. Few turn-of-the-century fictional ministers are able to reform the church they criticize and the theology they abandon. John Hodder is typical. As Churchill's novel ends, his ministry among the poor remains mostly a personal effort. It seems unlikely that he will be able to convince most members of his congregation to support it or to accept those who benefit from it. In popular culture, social ministers are most often seen as lonely heroes who continue their social ministry even after they are rejected by the church they seek to reform.[10]

Entrenched Reactionaries

Church leaders who oppose social ministers in social gospel novels are more than just an aggravation; often they succeed in driving the social minister out of the church. Social ministers who succeed in creating an *enduring* social ministry are usually forced to establish the ministry as a separate program or mission. In Emery J. Haynes's 1887 novel *Dollars and Duty*, Paul Havens sees the control that Lemuel Norcross, the local mill owner, exercises over his father's ministry and decides to go directly to a mission parish when he becomes ordained. In Phelps's *A Singular Life*, Emanuel Bayard establishes a separate chapel in Angel Alley after the ecclesiastical council refuses to ordain him to ministry in the parish church in Windover. The chapel has no connection to the parish church in Windover. In Wright's *That Printer of Udell's*, when leading members of the congregation and *all* the neighboring ministers oppose his social ministry efforts, James Cameron establishes a separate program in a separate facility. Lawrence Freeman, the social minister in Bradley Gilman's *Ronald Carnaquay* (1903), resigns his pulpit when the congregation will not support his social ministry. He and his wife move to a modest apartment in the city where he establishes a separate ministry to people in the neighborhood. Freeman is able to support himself by writing and teaching. His financial independence enables his ministry. He is a free man, as his name suggests—free to pursue his social ministry because he is no longer obligated to please an unsympathetic congregation. In Page's *John Marvel, Assistant*, John Marvel ministers at a separate working-class chapel. Though Dr. Bartholomew Capon, the rector of the parish that supports the chapel Marvel serves, encourages his parishioners to run benefits to raise funds for the mission chapel, he states clearly that neither Marvel nor the poor Marvel serves are welcome in the main church of the parish.

The obstacles John Marvel and other social ministers face when they try to open their congregations to the poor have social and cultural as well as ecclesiastical roots.[11] Huge barriers divided the social classes in early-twentieth-century America. When clerics like John Hodder begin a social ministry, they discover that churches reflect and support these barriers. Social ministers are rarely able to break down the class barriers that separate the middle-class and upper-class congregations that employ them from the poor they want to serve. When they bring members of the underclass into the midst of their middle-class congregations, lay leaders like Eldon Parr turn barriers into barricades. And they use orthodox theology to justify their defense of the status quo.

Class barriers are often presented as insurmountable obstacles in social gospel novels. Entrenched reactionaries who defend these barriers are powerful opponents: social ministers who attempt to integrate the classes into their congregations are *always* defeated. The reactionaries who defeat them are entrenched, both socially and institutionally. They hold community-based social power and church-based ecclesiastical power. In Isaac G. Reed's *From Heaven to New York* (1894) when the Rev. Melville Goodheart tries to convince his congregation to include the poor who surround them, local church leaders force him to leave. In Magee Pratt's *The Orthodox Preacher and Nancy* (1901), the Rev. Magee Pratt suffers a similar fate, as does the Rev. Mr. Smiley in Elizabeth Neff's *Altars to Mammon* (1908). In George and Lillian Chester's *The Ball of Fire* (1914), the Rev. Smith Boyd is unable to convince his congregation to forgo construction of a long-planned "cathedral" church and spend the money on a social ministry instead. Boyd resigns when he realizes he will never persuade the congregation he serves to accept a ministry to the neighborhood as central to the ongoing life of the parish. *The Mixing* (1913) offers a fictionalized account of Charles Bouck White's efforts to mix the social classes of a New York village in the congregation he pastored there. White, a native of Middleburgh, New York, a small village west of Albany, went on to Harvard College after high school and a few years later entered the ministry. *The Mixing* offers graphic descriptions of local leaders who resist the village minister's integration efforts. (Local residents of Middleburgh were appalled when they recognized themselves as characters in White's novel.)[12] Like most fictional social ministers who attempt to integrate the poor into their congregations, White's fictional pastor is unsuccessful.

Even the most able and perceptive social ministers in fiction are unable to prevail against the entrenched reactionaries in the parishes they serve. The fictional Rev. Julius Peck in William Dean Howells's *Annie Kilburn* (1881) is much more astute than the real-life White. But even he is unable to convince local leaders to accommodate their middle-class congregations to accept the working poor. Howells's novel is set in the fictional New England factory village of Hatboro. Hatboro is composed almost entirely of two classes: an overclass of mill owners, professionals, and proprietors and an underclass of mill workers. Several women in the village are concerned about the workers' *cultural* deprivation. They propose a "Social Union" that will provide theatricals and other entertainments to which members of both classes will be invited. They convince Annie Kilburn, a liberal-thinking, unusually able, and articulate young woman to serve as their spokesperson. Annie presents their ideas to the Rev. Julius Peck, the liberal minister who serves the Congregational Church in Hatboro—fully expecting he will support their proposal. She is surprised when Peck questions the accuracy of their perceptions of working-class people: "These things are invented by well-to-do people who have no occupation, and think that others want pastimes as much as themselves. But what working people want is rest, and what they need are decent homes where they can take it" (59).

Annie is a bit unsettled but not deterred by Peck's reaction to the committee's proposal. She elaborates their plans in an attempt to dispel his concern. She tells him that she and her group envision a variety of offerings at Social Union occasions: plays, suppers, and dances. These will be inclusive, "public" affairs. Peck is still not convinced that working people will feel comfortable at the events: "But even in a public affair like this," he tells Annie, "the work-people would feel uncomfortable and out of place, wouldn't they, if they stayed to the supper and the dance? They might be exposed to greater suffering among those whose manners and breeding were different, and it might be embarrassing all around" (62).

Annie Kilburn and her friends ignore the minister's cautions and implement their plan—and it produces the results he predicts. Working people who participate in the initial social occasion feel awkward and behave in ways that violate the sensitivities of the upper-class sponsors. Members of the working class who attend the event don't recognize the specific faux pas they commit, but they do realize that some of their behaviors make the overclass participants uncomfortable. In the end, the attempted mixing is not satisfactory to members of either class.

Some entrenched reactionaries defend their interests even when those efforts set them against members of their own families. In Susan Glaspell's *The Visioning* (1911), Katherine Jones begins a personal effort to convince church leaders to support better working conditions for factory workers who provide the affluence that upper-class families like hers enjoy. One of those she confronts is her uncle, an Episcopal bishop. During a revealing conversation, she asks him whether he ever thinks of Christ. He is so astonished by this question from his niece that he drops his cigar. What does she mean? That Jesus was so often with the working people, with the suffering poor, she responds. When her uncle stands at the altar, "don't you hear them moaning and sobbing down underneath?" she asks (334). Of course he does. So do others like him—which is why the church supports so many charities. He has missed her point: charities are superficial. They "are like waving a scented handkerchief over the stock-yards. Or like handing out after-dinner mints to a mob of starving men." "We don't give them mints," her uncle responds; "We give them soup." She prods him: "Why don't you give them jobs?" Because, he instructs her, "There aren't 'jobs' enough to go around" (336). The repartee between them continues for some time, but in the end even his own granddaughter is unable to crack his class bias and engage his sympathy.

A similar disagreement between Olivia Jordan and her minister father in W.J. Dawson's *A Prophet in Babylon* (1908) is much more painful. Dr. Jordan is a particularly vicious reactionary who uses every means at his disposal to discredit the social activist minister John Gaunt and his "League of Service." When Olivia tells her father she intends to join this social service movement, he forbids it. But she is of age, a person in her own right, and, for the first time in her life, she says she will disobey him. The depth of Olivia's commitment and her challenge to his authority impress Dr. Jordan, but he remains completely closed-minded. Olivia reminds him that a similarly callous attitude contributed to the ruin of her brother, Robert. All of Olivia's appeals fail to move her father. When she joins the league, he banishes her from his house.

What is likely the most caustic portrayal of entrenched reactionaries appears in Jack London's futuristic novel, *The Iron Heel* (1907). Based on what is purported to be a surviving manuscript by a fictional social philosopher, the novel describes a world of increasing chaos and oppression that results when people fail to heed the warnings and apply the suggestions of socially progressive leaders, including visionary clergy. During a small gathering described early in the novel, Ernest Everhard, a working-class social activist, argues that the beliefs most church leaders advocate actually intensify the sufferings of the working class. One of those present, Bishop Morehouse, challenges him to prove his accusation. Everhard then takes the bishop on an eye-opening tour through some of the worst neighborhoods in the city where the bishop lives. As he views the city through Everhard's eyes, Bishop Morehouse undergoes a life-changing conversion.

When the enlightened bishop shares his new commitment to a social ministry with other church leaders, he is surprised by their response. They do not just defend their reactionary beliefs; they attempt to discredit the bishop. At a meeting of the I. P. H. (the full name of the group is never given), the bishop describes his conversion to radical Christianity. He tells of driving through poor neighborhoods of the city in his brougham and looking out for the first time at the suffering of those who live there. "What would the Master do?" he asks himself. He stops the carriage and engages in conversation with two prostitutes: "If Jesus was right, then these two unfortunates were my sisters." He takes them home to his mansion. "They are going to stay with me," he tells the audience. "I hope to fill every room in my palace with such sisters as they. . . . The palaces of the Church should be hospitals and nurseries for those who have fallen by the wayside and are perishing. . . . We must do as Christ did; that is the message of the church to-day. . . . And so I say to the rich among you, and to all the rich, that bitterly you oppress the Master's lambs. You have hardened your hearts." At this point in his address, two men rise and lead the bishop from the platform as the audience sits "breathless and shocked" (112–16).

The bishop's associates describe his address at the I. P. H. convention as an "outbreak." They attribute it to overwork and convince him to take a vacation. But when he returns, his first sermon reiterates the views he advocated at the convention. Bishop Morehouse's colleagues decide he needs more extensive treatment and place him in a private sanitarium for the mentally ill. The newspapers report that he is suffering from a "mental breakdown." After he is released from the sanitarium, Bishop Morehouse appears to be "recovered"; he preaches tame sermons that resemble the discourses he gave before his "conversion." But his apparent "recovery" is a pretense. One day the bishop disappears. His friends discover that he has sold all his possessions and deposited the funds covertly in several bank accounts. The proceeds the money will earn are earmarked to benefit the poor. Several weeks later, a truly sympathetic friend discovers Bishop Morehouse living in an urban neighborhood. He is dressed in working-class garb, residing in a single room, content to spend the rest of his days ministering to the poor among whom he now lives. But Bishop Morehouse never has the opportunity to fulfill his new vocation. Some of his detractors find him and have him committed permanently to an asylum. No one is permitted to see him. The newspaper accounts report there are only "slight hopes" for his recovery. Reflecting on the bishop's fate, the socialist Ernest Everhard observes: "Christ told the rich young man to sell all he had. The bishop obeyed Christ's injunction and got locked up in a madhouse. Times have changed since Christ's day. A rich man to-day who gives all he has to the poor is crazy. There is no discussion. Society has spoken" (203).

Several other novels published between 1880 and 1920 offer similarly caustic portrayals of typical clergy as callous reactionaries. In *Caesar's Column* (1891), Ignatius Donnelly describes the normal minister as one who tells the poor to "be patient, endure the ills of the world, because this world is only a sojourn to life in the next. . . . Rejoice in poverty, resign to evils, and lay up treasures in heaven" (190, 191).[13] Dr. Wilkinson, who serves an affluent congregation in Vida D. Scudder's novel *A Listener in Babel* (1903), is similarly coldhearted. He says that those who are poor deserve to be poor; poverty is simply the result of immorality. In *My Brother's Keeper* (1910), Charles Tenney Jackson depicts pastors as a whole as moralistic and self-righteous people who are insensitive to the social and economic obstacles that frustrate the poor and unemployed. Most social gospel writers share Donnelly's, Scudder's, and Jackson's perspective: typical ministers in their novels are depicted as entrenched reactionaries; social ministers are rare exceptions. The extraordinary sales many social gospel novels enjoyed during the late-nineteenth and early-twentieth centuries suggests that many educated middle-class American readers shared the novelists' critical views of what they saw as typical churches and their ministers.[14]

Social Activists

Sometimes the result of reactionaries' opposition to a social minister is the opposite of what they intend. Their opposition enables the minister's social ministry rather than snuffing it out. When they are forced out of the pastoral ministry, some ministers move on to what they view as even more significant social ministries. In William J. Dawson's futuristic novel *A Prophet in Babylon*, after reactionary leaders in John Gaunt's New York City congregation oppose his social ministry and force him from his pastorate, Gaunt begins a social movement that comes to be known as the "League of Service." Gaunt attracts so many followers and coworkers that the league is forced to meet in Madison Square Garden. His reform movement grows so powerful that it challenges the corrupt leaders of the City of New York.

Deposed clerics like John Gaunt leave pastoral ministry behind, often happily, and use their independence to devote themselves completely to social ministry. Freed from the pastoral responsibilities and controls of a congregation, these social activists engage in ministries that take them beyond, sometimes far beyond, what was possible when they served as pastors. Though they lose their standing as ordained clergy—and appear especially to their critics to have left the ministry—most social ministers who become social activists still view themselves as authentic ministers.

Emerson Courtright, the social activist in Herbert Quick's novel *The Broken Lance* (1907), never achieves results similar to those John Gaunt does, but in some ways he is an even more compelling reflection of this cultural image. When Quick's story opens, Emerson, who has just begun to teach in a rural school, is face to face with Morgan Yeager, a burly sixteen-year-old student accused of fighting. Emerson instructs his rebellious student to come to the front of the classroom. When Emerson demands that Morgan explain why he was fighting, the young man refuses because "it wouldn't do any good under the rules." Determined now to punish Morgan for his insolence, as well as for fighting, Emerson gives Morgan two minutes to remove his coat. As Emerson is about to force him to remove his coat, Morgan rips it open to reveal a shirt full of holes. In a tearful outburst he says has no mother at home to mend his clothes, no money to buy thread or socks for his feet; he wears mittens made from grain sacks. Emerson quietly tells the young man to return to his seat. At the end of the school day, when all of the other students have left, Emerson removes his own overcoat from the rack and gives it to Morgan.

When Morgan Yeager and Emerson Courtright meet a decade later, Emerson is the pastor of the prestigious First Church of Lattimore. After services one Sunday, Emerson comes upon a crowd gathered in the town park to listen to an agitator standing on a soapbox. Emerson is surprised to hear the speaker berate the sermon he has just preached as empty idealism, like "clouds without water." Most preachers have no real knowledge of poverty or of what keeps men and women trapped in it. They preach a "false gospel of patience." Emerson fails to recognize that the critic on the soapbox is his former student—just as Morgan Yeager does not realize the preacher he ridicules is his old teacher. Morgan's diatribe against clergy and the church finally tests Emerson's patience. He asks a nearby police officer to arrest the agitator. Emerson is shocked when the next morning's newspaper identifies the agitator arrested the day before as Morgan Yeager. Emerson goes to the jail immediately and convinces the police to release his former student.

Courtright and Yeager's renewed acquaintance soon becomes a relationship in which their roles are reversed. Yeager, who has become a radical socialist since Emerson last saw him, helps his former teacher learn what the world of poverty is really like. During a series of sermons, Emerson shares his new perceptions of the causes of poverty with his congregation. Naively, he anticipates they will respond positively to the vision he brings by giving up their abusive business practices and opening their church to the poor who surround it. He gains a glimpse of how they will really respond as he shares his new convictions with Amy, his wife. When he describes great philanthropists and pious church members as "modern robber-barons," she sits "in rigid unresponsiveness, her class pride mortally offended, every precept of her rearing and education violated" (157). Emerson fails to see the portent in Amy's silence. As the series of sermons unfolds, members of his congregation, unlike his wife, are not at all reticent. Leading members do not just criticize him, they stop attending services and they stop contributing. Finally, they resort to a familiar tactic: they slander Emerson. They accuse him of having an affair with Olive Dearwester, the lead soprano at First Church. Though he is not guilty of the charge, Emerson realizes he cannot escape the fallout; too many old-line members want to force him out and will keep the slander alive as long as he remains.

Though he receives a number of invitations to become a candidate, Emerson's outspokenness discourages other churches from calling him. He tries unsuccessfully to find other employment. His personal resources are soon depleted. Amy, who has never been without affluence, now pregnant with their first child, wonders how she will survive without luxury and servants. When Emerson decides to give himself completely to ministry among the poor regardless of the cost to them personally, Amy decides to leave him and return home to her family. Amy's people, the Bloodgoods, embrace her, and, after Emerson and Amy's child is born, they tell Emerson he is no longer welcome in their home. Unable to support himself from ministry, Emerson moves from place to place and job to job. He finally ends up in Chicago, living in a sparsely furnished room with no heat. Forced to live at the same level of poverty as those he serves, Emerson begins to find a fulfilling ministry. He resolves to experience life completely as the poorest workers do so he can discover how Christian faith can speak to that life. His determination leads Emerson to accept one of the worst jobs available: he becomes a "sticker," the one who stabs animals to death in a slaughterhouse. His former student Morgan Yeager is startled when he finds Emerson engaged in this "horrible vocation." "I had to do it," Emerson explains:

"If the society in which I live calls upon some man to do nothing but slaughter all day long—and maybe it's that very specializing in killing which makes it wrong—why, who am I to refuse the burden of sin, if sin it be, and stand aside for another to take the pollution?" (387).

Though Yeager is moved by Emerson's commitment, Emerson's declining health and the dangers to which he subjects himself in his work with the local labor union alarm him. He urges Emerson to consider another less-stressful job. Emerson refuses to alter his way of life. The dangers Morgan anticipates soon materialize. A conflict between workers at the slaughterhouse and its owners leads to a riot. Emerson is seriously injured when he tries to quell the disturbance. When Emerson recovers, he again ignores Morgan's advice and returns immediately to his work with the union. Discord between workers and owners intensifies, and soon there is a strike. Local authorities, afraid that a riot will occur, call out the troops. The soldiers arrive just as Emerson walks out into the street with some of the strikers to announce that he has mediated a settlement. He raises his hand in a sign of peace when the soldiers approach. Before he can speak, someone throws a piece of crockery into the air; it lands between the workers and the troops, smashing to pieces but harming no one. The careless act provokes an appalling response. The soldiers are under the command of John Bloodgood, Amy's brother. Bloodgood treats the thrown crockery as a hostile act that justifies a hostile response. As Emerson's friends watch in horror, his former brother-in-law orders the soldiers to raise their rifles and shoot Emerson Courtright to death. John Bloodgood then tramples Emerson's body with his horse.

The newspaper account of the tragedy describes Emerson Courtright as an "ex-preacher" who forsook his wife, "one of the sweetest of Christian women," to pursue "guilty love" with a "notorious woman." Though once a respected minister, he foolishly abandoned "old-fashioned preaching of old-fashioned conversion and churchly living" and ended up working in a slaughterhouse at the "most disgusting task possible." Emerson's funeral is held in a union hall; no one from his former church attends. Morgan Yeager pays tribute to his fallen friend before the gathered workers who compose Emerson's final parish. Emerson "brought forth the spiritual philosophy of Jesus, applied to the things of to-day," he tells them: "He showed me that Jesus was killed, not because of His theology, but for His politics" (542).

The Rev. Mr. Northmore, the social activist in Neff's *Altars to Mammon*, shares Emerson Courtright's commitment to social activism, but Northmore is neither a victim nor a martyr. The unscrupulous business owners who dominate Northmore's church oppose his liberal theological and social views, but he never permits them to treat him as a subordinate—even as he gives up his pastorate. When local leaders refuse to support Northmore's proposal that their church take the lead in providing better housing for local workers, Northmore resigns both from this church and from the ministry. He is then free to give himself completely to what he now sees as a more-significant ministry: that of a social activist businessman.

John Brown, the social activist minister in Richard J. Talbot's *The Chainbreakers* (1914), leaves the ministry not to enter business but to become a progressive politician. Brown campaigns for governor on a platform that advocates laws to give women the vote, prohibit child labor, provide benefits for widows and older citizens, and increase citizen access to recall and referendum. After a successful term as governor, he moves on to the national scene as the leader of a national "Party of Progress."

Excluded from the ordained ministry by an unsympathetic church, fictional ministers like Courtright, Northmore, and Brown have few, if any, regrets. Comparing their present life to their former life as ordained clergy convinces them that the reactionary leaders and reactionary theology who dominate the church stifle even the most effective clergy. The freedom they enjoy as social activists gives them greater opportunities for authentic ministry. Life as a socially concerned reformer, business leader, or politician offers more opportunities for spiritual authenticity and service than the life of an ordained minister.[15]

Utopian Idealists

Between the 1880s when novels that feature social ministers and social activists first appeared and the 1920s when their popularity began to fade, disillusionment with the church as well as the ministry became a progressively more common theme. Some novelists expressed their frustration with things as they were by offering utopian visions of churches and ministers completely unencumbered by the defects they perceived in churches of the present. Edward Bellamy presents his utopian vision in *Looking Backward* (1887). The narrator of Bellamy's novel, Mr. West, falls asleep in 1887 and wakes up to discover he is in the United States in the year 2000. At the breakfast table on the third day of his visit, when his host Dr. Leete asks if he would like to hear a sermon, Mr. West is surprised to discover that churches still exist: "So you still have Sundays and sermons! We had prophets who foretold that long before this time the world would have dispensed with both." Dr. Leete explains that churches and ministers function very differently in the world of 2000. Those who wish the services of a minister can request one and pay for the cost of the minister's service by using a credit card. Anyone who wants to hear a sermon can either go to a church building or listen at home. The Sunday paper lists preachers and their sermon titles. Transmissions of sound over telephone wires—the same technology that makes it possible for listeners to hear musical performances at home—also enables them to hear sermons at home. Since Mr. West doesn't know any of the preachers listed in the morning paper, he decides to follow Dr. Leete's recommendation and listen to a sermon by Mr. Barton, a minister who preaches "only by telephone," often to "audiences reaching 150,000." At the appointed time, the Leete family and Mr. West seat themselves in comfortable chairs in the music room and listen to the telephone preacher.

In his sermon Mr. Barton contrasts the affluence and altruism of the United States in the year 2000 with the poverty and competitiveness that marked the nineteenth century. The cause of this difference is neither "a moral new birth of humanity" nor "a wholesale destruction of the wicked. . . . It finds its simple and obvious explanation in the reaction of a changed environment upon human nature. . . . [A] form of society which was founded on the pseudo self-interest of selfishness, and appealed solely to the antisocial and brutal side of human nature, has been replaced by institutions based on the true self-interest of a rational unselfishness, and appealing to the social and generous instincts of men" (276, 278). The daily struggle to survive in this former world dominated by competitiveness brought the base element in human nature to the forefront even among Christians. The result was "a general decay of religious belief." When Mr. Barton turns from history to the present, he touts the benefits of socialism. With the transformation of society from capitalism to socialism during the twentieth century, there was soon no more poverty and therefore people no longer needed to take advantage of one another for survival. In the twentieth century, socialism accomplished the reform that churches and ministers failed to enable in the nineteenth century. With the advent of socialism, "We believe the race for the first time to have entered on the realization of God's ideal of it, and each generation must now be a step upward" (292).

In his utopian novel *God and the Groceryman* (1927), Harold Bell Wright offers a detailed plan for transforming present clergy and churches into more-effective and more-efficient ministers and churches in the future. A disillusioned Dan Matthews leaves the ordained ministry at the end of Wright's 1909 novel of the same name and reappears eighteen years later in *God and the Groceryman* as a highly successful and affluent businessman. Matthews compares his experiences as a businessman with his experiences as a minister and decides that the outmoded doctrine and practices associated with denominationalism are like outmoded business practices. They prevent pastors from being effective. Were ministers to apply up-to-date business principles in their ministry like those he uses in his own successful business, they would become equally successful. To prove his point, Matthews offers to use his own money to replace *all* the denominational churches and ministers in a medium-sized American city with modern, independent churches and pastors. These independent churches and their pastors will be free of the reactionary theology and competition that throttle denominational churches and pastors. Dan shares his proposal with a colleague, John Saxton, who agrees to direct its implementation. After considering a variety of possible sites, they settle on Westover, a small city in the Middle West. Saxton visits Westover and chooses Joe Paddock, a successful groceryman, as the local coordinator. Paddock shares Matthews and Saxton's belief that successful churches are like successful businesses: they need to be guided by practical ministers who are astute business leaders and preach a simple social gospel.

Under Saxton's guidance, Joe Paddock begins a systematic campaign to convince local business leaders to implement Matthews's plan. "The future of Christianity and, therefore, of your country, your homes, your children, is in the hands of capable Christian businessmen like you," he tells them. His views of the contemporary minister's predicament mirror those of his mentor, Dan Matthews:

> The modern, down-to-date clergyman, under the ruthless competition of this denominational system, has little time or strength for the Christian religion. He is ten per cent social visitor, tea drinker and diner-out; five per cent handy man and speaker for all kinds of boosting clubs; five per cent political henchman; twenty percent denominational advocate; five per cent protector and comforter of that portion of his membership who, because their deeds will not bear the light, must live under the cloak of the church; and fifty percent public entertainer. The remaining five per cent of him is teacher of the truths of Jesus, which alone, constitute one hundred per cent of Christianity. (165)

At a large gathering in Westover, Matthews shares his assessment of the source of the church's ineffectiveness and the remedy he suggests. He proposes to build three temples, each seating five thousand people to replace the forty-four denominational churches in Westover. The salaries of temple ministers will be paid by a foundation. The ministers of these temples will be free to "preach the teachings of Jesus only" because they will not be beholden to either a denomination or their congregations for support. The cost of building these new temples is $1 million—much lower than the cost of maintaining the churches currently serving Westover. The savings in operating costs will enable Westover to have adequate church facilities and provide nearly $40,000 each year for the relief of the poor.

Most of the current pastors in Westover oppose Matthews's plan. But he gains the trust and support of most of the town's civic and business leaders. The first temple is soon completed. The first gathering for worship includes the "leading citizens" of Westover. When worshippers enter the temple, they find a tasteful sanctuary that is comfortable without being showy. There is no pulpit furniture except for a central reading desk. Instead of pews, there are seats "as comfortable as the seats in the best motion-picture theaters." On the back of each seat is a receptacle to receive the offering of the person sitting in the seat behind it, along with a card the worshipper can fill out to request help or offer personal service. The minister who leads the worship doesn't wear a robe. He doesn't wear any "distinctive garb." He reads a few words of Jesus from the scripture and preaches a sermon that commands "the attention of the best minds in the audience" but that is also simple "like the sermons of the Master." After the service, there is "no effusive and perfunctory hand-shaking by an appointed committee." The congregation leaves "quietly, under the spell of the truths of Jesus' teaching" (343, 347, 349).

Though Wright's futuristic story sometimes seems contrived and many of his proposals seem idealistic, *God and the Groceryman* reflects convictions he shares with other early-twentieth-century popular writers and their appreciative readers. Fantasies like Bellamy's and Wright's reflect their dissatisfaction with the churches and ministers they see around them. Many social gospel novels argue that denominational churches and their pastors are obsolete and need to be replaced by efficient modern churches served by ministers who present and follow the moral teachings of Jesus.[16] Unfortunately, these fanaticized images are truly utopian. They speak of what should be, not of what could be. Fictional ministers who reflect utopian ideals are disconnected from ministers of the present. They seem idealized and manufactured.

The theological erosion that characterizes the nineteenth century and that these social gospel novels reflect may be partly to blame. It is significant to note that God is no longer a force to be reckoned with—in fact, God is rarely mentioned—in most social gospel novels. Ministers like Emanuel Bayard and Emerson Courtright may have their moments of inspiration, but they rarely, if ever, perceive God as an omnipotent force or present power they can count on. Even Wright, a former minister, gives little attention to God in the utopian church he envisions in *God and the Groceryman*. The absence of references to God in these novels contrasts boldly with the perception of God in many antebellum popular novels. God is an absolute ruler and a vivid presence in the experience of harsh Puritans and fanatical Calvinists. Harriet Beecher Stowe's Dr. Hopkins is so certain of the justice and providence of God that he is willing to be damned for all eternity if that serves God's purpose. God is a formidable factor even for Herman Melville, who struggles to the end of his life to rid himself of a sadistic perception of God as one who makes impossible demands on humans. Even Nathaniel Hawthorne's psychologically misshapen clergy argue for the cosmic reality of God.

After the Civil War, God seems less fearsome to most fictional ministers. Stowe, whose life spans the nineteenth century, chronicles the shrinking God in her fictional clergy. The equivocating Mr. Lothrop and the angler minister Mr. Avery lack the sense of a formidable God that turns the Edwardsian Moses Stern into an equally formidable preacher. During the nineteenth century, there is a profound erosion of belief in a providential God in American fiction. Social gospel novels reflect a negative perception of orthodox Calvinist theology that affirms such an omnipotent God. In these novels, orthodox believers are usually portrayed as reactionaries and obstructionists. Most fictional ministers who embrace the social gospel reject orthodox theology. For good reason. A theology that suggests the status the poor have in this world is a reflection of God's judgment, and that implies that no human effort in their behalf can alter God's will for them, has little appeal to those who feel called to improve the lot of the poor or to reform the social order.

Social ministers and social activists in American fiction are human heroes; they are rarely held up as people of faith. The contrast between James Fenimore Cooper's Parson Amen and J. Herbert Quick's Emerson Courtright is quite revealing. Amen prays for his enemies as the executioner's tomahawk is about to fall on him; he is an admirable believer, a paragon of faith. Courtright dies protesting the slaughterhouse owners' treatment of their workers; he is an admirable actor, a paragon of morality. Amen's Christian faith is absolutely central to his significance, whereas Quick never identifies Courtright's Christian faith as the explicit cause of his action. Courtright's actions stem from his moral concern. They carry a moral, not a theological, message. While Emanuel Bayard and Emerson Courtright's heroic deaths are compared with Christ's sacrifice, their deaths are not similarly redemptive. No salvation for anyone issues from their martyrdom. No one is moved to faith in *God* by their witness. They, like all social ministers and social activists in popular fiction, are morally strong, *human* heroes. God is hardly a factor in their experience or their ministry.[17] In fact, God is rarely mentioned in most of the popular novels I discuss in this chapter.

This perceived displacement of the divine in large segments of popular culture has immense significance.[18] While theologically liberated ministers like John Hodder no longer feel oppressed by the orthodox Calvinist God, they have lost the divine authority that God provides.[19] The loss has profound implications. Ministers are, after all, ministers of *God*. Without a potent Divine standing behind them, some divines can still be heroic moral figures, but all divines are significantly less compelling.

VII

CHAMPIONS OF THE FAITH

Church Images

Muscular Believers

Testifying to the faith was the central concern of the courageous Methodist circuit riders who ministered along the Middle Border (the Middle West) west of the Appalachians and south of the Great Lakes during the early decades of the nineteenth century. They were muscular believers. They had to be. Circuits were commonly three hundred to five hundred miles long. Circuit riding ministers served these extended parishes regardless of the weather—through driving rain in the spring and blowing snow in the winter. Few of them married; itinerant ministry paid poorly and provided little time or space for a family. A worn Bible and a faithful horse were the circuit ministers' prized and often only personal possessions.[1]

Law enforcement was sparse in the territory that circuit riders traveled. Local rowdies sometimes mingled with those who gathered for open-air preaching services. These hecklers came not to dispute the preacher's theology; they feared the civilizing effects of his message. They knew that Methodist classes were the first step in a civilizing process that would soon lead to schools and local government. Law and order would then replace the unregulated society that gave the rowdies an upper hand. The more effective a preacher was, the more likely local rowdies were to disrupt meetings where he preached. Sometimes they ambushed the preacher on his way to or from a circuit meeting, hoping to prevent his return. Circuit riders who survived were as strong in body as they were in faith. Though biographers are clear that itinerant preachers never initiated a fight, when the rowdies attacked, they discovered an adversary who could fight as well as pray.[2]

Edward R. Eggleston's *The Circuit Rider* (1874) offers what is probably the most accurate and realistic fictional account of the challenges early circuit riders faced. The experiences Eggleston recounted in *The Circuit Rider* are based on stories he heard his mother tell the family when he was a young boy and on recollections former Middle West circuit riders shared with him when he became a Methodist minister in 1856.[3] The central characters in the novel are Mort Goodwin and Hezekiah (Kike) Lumsden, two young men who are converted by Methodist circuit riders and then become circuit riders themselves. Mort and Kike live in the Hissawachee settlement in southern Ohio during the "reign of Madison"—the years when James Madison served as U.S. president (1809–17). Kike is converted by a circuit rider named Magruder. Eggleston describes Brother Magruder as "a short, stout man, with wide shoulders, powerful arms, shaggy brows, and bristling black hair . . . [who] prayed with the utmost sincerity, but in a voice that shook the cabin windows and gave the simple people a deeper reverence for the dreadfulness of the preacher's message" (102).

Magruder begins his preaching ministry in the Hissawachee settlement at the Wheeler home. Mrs. Wheeler is willing to host these meetings because she was an active Methodist before she married and moved to the settlement. Magruder's preaching ministry leads to the formation of a Methodist class—a meeting that gathers weekly, even when no preacher is available. As is to be expected, Magruder's success is not received favorably by everyone in the settlement. Two of those who are unhappy with his ministry, Bill McConley and Jake Sniger, confront Magruder early one morning as he travels alone on his way to conduct the Sunday service. They hold the bridle of his horse and demand that he dismount. When he asks, "What for?" they reply, "We're goin' to lick you tell you promise to go back and never stick your head into the Hissawachee Bottom agin." Noting that there are two of them, he asks them to give him time to remove his coat—which they do. "Never seeking a fight," after Magruder ties his horse, he tells Bill and Jake, "my friends, I don't want to whip you. I advise you to let me alone." But they are intent on thrashing him.

As soon as Bill and Jake attack Magruder, they realize they are fighting a trained boxer! With one blow, Magruder knocks Jake down. The preacher turns quickly and lands a second punch squarely on Bill's nose. Jake picks himself up and, fists flying, rushes at the preacher. Magruder stops him with a single punch that fractures two of Jake's ribs. Jake decides he has had enough and retreats into the brush. With Jake out of the fight, Bill recognizes that alone he is no match for Magruder. He turns away from Magruder and follows Jake into the woods.

Magruder's encounter with Jake and Bill leaves him with a swollen lip and stiff jaw and brings an unexpected challenge to the newly converted Kike Lumsden. Unable to preach to the gathered worshippers, Magruder calls on Kike to take his place. Kike is seized by fear. He is certain that he has a call to preach, but he had assumed he would fulfill that call first among strangers—not in front of the large crowd of friends and neighbors who have now gathered in the yard in front of Wheeler's cabin. He kneels in prayer in the leaves behind the house and prays for courage. But the terror remains. As Kike stands up to give his first sermon, Magruder sees the fear in Kike's eyes. "If you get confused, tell your own experience," he advises. Kike quickly exhausts the few thoughts he had time to write down on the fly leaf of his Bible. In six minutes he has nothing more to say. Some of those gathered begin to snicker. Suddenly Kike recalls Magruder's advice, and it comes to his rescue:

> Now you have all seen that I cannot preach worth a cent. When David went out to fight, he had the good sense not to put on Saul's armor. I was fool enough to try to wear Brother Magruder's. Now, I'm done with that. The text and the sermon are gone. But I'm not ashamed of Jesus Christ. And before I sit down, I am going to tell you all that he has done for a poor lost sinner like me. (128)

The honest recital of "his own sins . . . with a trembling voice and simple earnestness [is] absolutely electrical." The trembling Kike is transformed into a "fiery boy whose contagious excitement . . . [sets] the whole audience ablaze." Among those converted is a man with a badly bruised nose, Bill McConkey, one of the two men who had accosted Brother Magruder earlier in the day.

While Kike preaches, his friend Mort Goodwin sits symbolically on the fence, listening "half in anguish and half in anger" to Kike's public recital of his sins (130). In the hours that follow, the forces of sin and grace at work in Mort contend with each other. By Sunday night, it appears that the old nature will triumph. Mort loses all of his money, his pocketknife, his watch, his hat, his coat, and, finally, his horse in a card game with a local character named Burchard. Burchard turns out to be a generous winner. He returns Mort's hat and coat. He returns Mort's gun and horse after exacting a bill of sale that requires Mort to redeem them for $125 at the end of six months "so that I may be sure you won't gamble them away to somebody else." A series of misadventures ends up with Mort in jail, accused of stealing his own horse. The accusers are about to hang him when help arrives from an unexpected source: Mr. Donaldson, an old Presbyterian minister, passes by on his way to a Presbytery meeting in Cincinnati. Parson Donaldson is so deep in thought over the theological address he expects to deliver at the impending Presbytery meeting that he fails to hear Mort Goodwin's cries for help. Finally, one of Goodwin's accusers agrees to chase after the divine. After several attempts, the pursuer manages to break through Donaldson's theological reverie. When the runner describes Mort Goodwin's dilemma, Donaldson immediately recognizes that the condemned prisoner is Goodwin—and that Dolly is Goodwin's horse. The preacher's testimony establishes Mort's innocence. After the accusers disperse, the Presbyterian preacher subjects Mort to a long discourse on the sinfulness of gambling and the errors of the Methodist religion. Mort feels so indebted to the divine that he suffers patiently under his scolding.[4]

Once Donaldson leaves, Mort Goodwin resumes his journey. Late in the day, he finds lodging with a family who are hosting the celebrated Methodist preacher, Valentine Cook. The elderly Cook, who suffers from poor health, is making a farewell tour of Methodist "classes" he founded. At the evening worship service, the fragile preacher delivers what all remember as a formidable final sermon. One of the converts at the service is Mort Goodwin—who resolves not only to become a Christian but also to give his life to preaching.

When the next chapter opens, two years have elapsed. Mort Goodwin and Kike Lumsden have completed their probationary period and are full-fledged circuit riders. Eggleston describes how their preparation for ministry differs from the formal seminary education required of Presbyterians like Mr. Donaldson. The fact that they share the life experience of those to whom they preach equips circuit riders for ministry on the frontier. Mort and Kike are like Brother Magruder, who "had not been educated for his ministry by years of study of Hebrew and Greek, of Exegesis and Systematics; but he knew what was of vastly more consequence to him—how to read and expound the hearts and lives of the impulsive, simple, reckless race among whom he labored" (103).[5]

As another year passes, the demands of a frontier ministry weigh heavily on the physically fragile Kike. When Mort visits Kike's tent as Methodist clergy from several districts gather for their annual conference, he finds a sick and nearly debilitated man. Mort takes Kike to a local doctor. The doctor forces Kike to take a long rest. After his convalescence, Kike refuses to heed the Presbyterian doctor's warning that a return to circuit-riding ministry will bring another collapse. Even as his body wastes away, Kike continues to serve. Soon his strength is entirely dissipated. Late one evening, Mort brings the ailing Kike back to the doctor who had treated him before. The next morning when Mort asks the doctor for a diagnosis, the physician replies, "Absolute physical bankruptcy, sir. . . . Wasted life, sir, wasted life. It is a pity but you Methodists had a little moderation in your zeal" (301). The physician's words of caution fail to deter Kike; for him, there can be no compromise. He leaves his sick bed to return to ministry. Within a few weeks, he is dead. His passing is recorded in the conference journal with a few simple words: "Hezekiah Lumsden was a man of God, who freely gave up his life for his work. He was tireless in labor, patient in suffering, bold in rebuking sin, holy in life and conversation, and triumphant in death" (312).

A number of postbellum novels describe the difficulties Southern ministers faced when they refused to compromise their faith during the Civil War. Even before the war had begun, Griffith Davenport, the Methodist preacher who stands at the center of Mrs. Helen Hamilton (Chenowith) Gardener's novel *An Unofficial Patriot* (1894), decides that as a Christian he cannot own slaves. But when he marries Katherine, the daughter of a local major and a wealthy Presbyterian plantation owner, he suddenly finds himself the owner of twenty-two slaves. His dilemma is compounded when the major decides to sell a slave named John to a new owner in Georgia. John is married to Sallie, who is one of the slaves Griffith acquired when he marries Katherine. Either John will be sold and separated from his wife, or Griffith must buy John. After a painful struggle with his conscience, Griffith decides to break his vow never to buy or sell a slave; he purchases John.

The pain Griffith suffers when he is forced to purchase John convinces him that he must free all of his slaves. The only way he can accomplish their freedom is to move north, so he decides to take his entire household to Indiana. When the travelers reach Washington, Griffith discovers that by law in Indiana freed slaves cannot be employed—as in most other Northern states—out of fear that they will work cheaply and displace white workers from their jobs. The only way he can free his slaves is to set up a trust that will provide their care and leave them in Washington. And so he does.

In *Inside: A Chronicle of Secession* (1866), William Mumford Baker offers an equally powerful portrait of a faithful and uncompromising Civil War pastor. War breaks out just as the Rev. Edward Arthur begins his ministry as the founding pastor of a Presbyterian congregation in a small town in South Carolina. Arthur's study of the scripture leads him to believe that both slavery and secession are wrong. He never uses his pulpit as a platform to promote his political views, but he makes no attempt to hide his conviction that slavery is morally wrong. As the war persists and the plight of the South becomes more difficult, Arthur's open opposition to slavery and to the South's "rebellion" to protect it become more and more costly. Arthur stays at his post but refuses to compromise his convictions, even when friends fade away and parishioners withdraw their support.

Arthur's reluctance to use his pulpit to promote his political views contrasts sharply with the local Methodist minister's approach. The author holds up that minister, Mr. Barker, as an example of those Southern clergy whose "eloquent appeals for Secession . . . accomplished more for Secession than all other instrumentalities combined" (27). Barker repeatedly twists scripture to support his view that "the Confederacy is the last, lingering abode on earth of pure religion" (71). Arthur is mortified by Barker's accommodating: "If ever there was a time when religion and the ministers of religion should hold themselves aloof from the infatuation of the hour it is now," he tells one of his parishioners (71).

Baker argues that, at least in part, his Presbyterian protagonist's uncompromising faith is a product of superior preparation for ministry. Mr. Arthur approaches the study of scripture with the tools of a theological scholar. His well-considered understanding of scripture protects him against the temptation to accommodate his faith to the cause of the moment. "To me the *side* the minister happens to be on is a mere nothing in comparison [with] his abandoning the Gospel; that is his [Barker's] deadly sin," he tells a friend (88).

Baker's novel shows that the demands placed on ministers in the Old South during the Civil War were much different from those placed on ministers in the Middle West earlier in the century. In the early decades of the nineteenth century, Methodist ministers like Mort Goodwin were much better prepared for the challenges of ministry on the less-settled Middle West than were scholarly clerics like the Presbyterian Mr. Donaldson in Eggleston's *The Circuit Rider*. The challenges ministers faced forty years later in wartime Somerville were equally as demanding but qualitatively different. The rowdies in Baker's Civil War–era novel demand that local preachers adapt their religious convictions to help them defend what is clearly an unjust social order. The rudely educated Brother Barker is unable to resist. The seminary-trained and more theologically mature Mr. Arthur refuses to compromise—even when they threaten him with physical harm.[6]

The uncompromising preacher in *From Jest to Ernest* (1876) by New York State writer E. P. Roe faces challenges much less threatening than those that test circuit riders and Civil War pastors like Presbyterian minister Mr. Arthur. A femme fatale, Lottie Marsden, is the primary antagonist in Roe's novel. Lottie is an affluent and sophisticated young woman from New York City who decides to visit her country relatives during the Christmas holidays. After she arrives, Lottie discovers that the Rev. Frank Hemstead, a recent seminary graduate who is soon to begin ministry in the West, will be a guest in the same household. She and her irreverent friends believe the young minister is certain to be naive and a boor. They decide to toy with him. Lottie, who is an accomplished flirt, will pretend to be a pious young woman, the type who would be an ideal companion for a missionary pastor. The minister is certain to fall in love with her. When Frank arrives, he does seem to fit the players' vision: he is awkward and ill-dressed, but he is also handsome, physically strong, and very bright. Lottie plays her role well, and the minister is soon smitten by her. But Frank Hemstead is no fool. In a repartee with Mr. Harcourt, a local lawyer and brazen atheist, he demonstrates that he is not only genuinely pious but also quite sophisticated.

Hemstead's physical prowess is as impressive as his ability to debate. When Lottie's sister and father are trapped in an ice jam while they are crossing the Hudson River, Hemstead becomes their rescuer. He and the estate handyman wend their way through the ice floes in a small boat. They reach the trapped young woman and her father just as their damaged boat is about to sink. Hemstead leaps into the sinking boat and lifts the barely conscious father and daughter to safety. When all reach the shore safely, the rescuer is nearly overcome by hypothermia. But the doctor who examines him assures the obviously worried Lottie that Hemstead will recover completely: "Now he is the right kind of dominie—not all white choker and starch. No fear about him, Miss Marsden. He's made of good stuff, well put together. A night's rest and a warm breakfast, and he will be himself again" (300). The story climaxes predictably: Frank and Lottie declare their love for each other. Frank is tempted to compromise his call to the mission field and, instead, accept a call to a city church where Lottie could be comfortable as his wife. But his struggle to overcome temptation turns out to be unnecessary. His long talks with Lottie lead to her conversion. She gives up her rich and comfortable life to join him in the mission field.

Frank Hemstead seems to me to be a more contrived character than the other muscular believers that I discuss in this chapter. Roe's story follows many of the formula elements that appear in popular religious novels at the time: flighty rich young woman meets naive dedicated young minister, falls in love with him, and is converted. Frank also obviously serves as a platform to expound the theological views of his minister-author creator. The long didactic passages designed to correct Lottie's theology probably challenged even the most sympathetic nineteenth-century readers. Frank Hemstead exhibits traits generally associated with muscular ministers, but he is much more controlled than they are. He is physically strong, but muscular believing is by far his strongest attribute.

Social Evangelicals

From the perspective of those who affirmed both traditional theology and the social gospel, social evangelicals represented the most appropriate and effective response to the challenges posed by the new urban, industrial world that dominated American society after the Civil War. Social evangelical ministers in fiction are convinced that God gives those who trust him the resources they need to live as Christians in the modern world. In their view, total commitment to God is essential for an effective social ministry because God is the primary agent of ministry. Social evangelicals are preeminently ministers *of God*. They bear witness to what God expects and to what God can do.

Sip Garth, a young woman in Elizabeth Stuart Phelps's *The Silent Partner* (1871), is to my knowledge the first social evangelical minister featured in American fiction. As Phelps's story begins, Perley Kelso learns that her father has been killed in a train accident. Perley is his only heir; his death makes her a partner in the Hayle and Kelso fabric mill in Five Falls. Perley wants to be an active partner in the firm, but the men who dominate it refuse to take her request seriously because she is a woman. Perley is frustrated by their decision to make her only a silent partner, but she is no less determined to take an active role in the mill. She decides to see for herself how the mill is run and what kind of life it leads to for the workers. When she goes into the workers' homes and sees how the meager wages they receive for working twelve hours a day six days a week leave them poor and debilitated, she is appalled. She shares her concern about the workers' condition with Maverick Hayle, the senior partner's son, who has become her suitor. Maverick is not sympathetic. He points out that during a recent recession her father and the other partner kept the workers on even though the mill was losing money. That seems charity enough to him; the workers should be grateful (135).

Defeated in her efforts to bring about change within the mill, Perley Kelso concentrates on relieving the workers' personal suffering. Her charitable work leads to a friendship with Sip Garth, a twenty-one-year-old mill worker. Sip works eleven and one-half hours six days a week in the mill to support herself and her deaf sister, Catty. When Catty's eyesight begins to fail, Perley arranges a visit to an occulist. The occulist says Catty's lost vision results from working in the mill: "There's a disease of the hands those people acquire from wool-picking sometimes; an ugly thing. The girl rubbed her eyes, I suppose [and spread the disease that will soon make her completely blind]. The mischief has been a long time in progress, or she might have stood a chance" (186). After Perley leaves, Sip tries to explain to Catty in sign language what is happening. When Catty wonders why, "what God means" by the adversity, Sip has no answer. After Catty goes to sleep, Sip stumbles over an old book Catty had taken from the mission Sunday school and never returned. Flipping through the pages, she happens on a picture of the crucifixion. Gazing at the picture quiets Sip: "For some reason—the Cross with the Man upon it put a finger on the bitter lips of Sip's trouble. She could not ask a Man upon a Cross, 'What was the sense of it?'" (195).

The following spring, a devastating flood strikes Five Falls. Feeling the water begin to rise around her, the now blind and deaf Catty wanders onto a bridge that is then swept away by the deluge. Catty's death confirms Sip's growing conviction that she is called to become a preacher of the gospel among the mill workers. The novel ends as Sip preaches to a crowd of workers gathered outside the mill. Her street congregation heeds this humble preacher's words because she is one of them. "I undertood to help her at the first," Perley Kelso tells a bystander as they listen to Sip preach, "but I was only *among* them at best; Sip is *of* them; she understands them and they understand her" (293): "It ain't a rich folks' religion that I've brought to talk to you [Sip tells her congregation]. Rich religion ain't for you and ain't for me. We're poor folks, and we want a poor folks' religion or none at all. . . . The religion of Jesus Christ the Son of God Almighty is the only poor folks' religion in all the world" (296). In her sermons Sip offers an honest and yet hopeful gospel. There will be no reordering of society in this world. But those who suffer are not without hope. Jesus understands and takes their suffering as his own. And in his good time there will be his way to "unsnarl us all."

In *We and Our Neighbors* (1873), Harriet Beecher Stowe presents a fictional Methodist preacher whose approach to ministry is similar to Sip Garth's. The Rev. Mr. James serves a storefront mission. In the same manner as Sip, he shares the life of those among whom he ministers. His sermons are based on texts like the parables of the Lost Sheep and Prodigal Son. His listeners are moved by James's preaching because they feel he knows and speaks to their condition.

By the 1890s when Charles Sheldon began to write fiction, the social evangelical image had become a favorite among writers who wished to affirm both traditional theology and the social gospel.[7] Sheldon was probably the most widely read turn-of-the-century novelist who used this cultural image in his fiction. Sheldon's descriptions of the plight of the urban poor, like Phelps's, came out of direct contact with them. Phelps learned about the difficulties of poor factory workers when she worked in the slums of Abbot, Massachusetts.[8] In 1889, shortly after Sheldon moved to Topeka, Kansas, to become the pastor of the Central Congregational Church, he donned shabby clothes and spent several days with those who wandered the streets of the city looking for work. Sheldon's novels reflect his experiences among the poor of Topeka and his attempts to motivate members of his congregation to minister to the poor and unemployed.[9] Sheldon first preached them a chapter at a time as sermons to his own congregation during Sunday evening services. The short chapters read like episodes in a serial. Many of them have cliffhanger endings designed to build suspense that would encourage listeners to return the following Sunday to hear the next installment.

Sheldon's best-known novel, *In His Steps* (1897), is certainly one of the best-selling, if not the best-selling, church novels of all time.[10] When the story opens, the Rev. Henry Maxwell has almost finished preaching a sermon on the atonement to his affluent and mostly disinterested congregation. Suddenly, a poorly dressed young man stands up, walks to the front of the church, and begins to speak. He tells the congregation that he is a printer and has been out of work for ten months. He has wandered the streets of Raymond (a fictional city that resembles Topeka) hoping to find work, but, like countless others, without success. He concludes his short speech by describing the wide gap he sees that separates people like him from those who attend the city's churches: "It seems to me sometimes as if the people in the big churches had good clothes and nice houses to live in, and money to spend for luxuries, and could go away on summer vacations and all that, while the people outside the churches, thousands of them, I mean, die in tenements, and walk the streets for jobs, and never have a piano or a picture in the house, and grow up in misery and drunkenness and sin" (9). After speaking these words, the young man faints. Henry Maxwell closes the service quickly and insists that the young man be carried to his house. During the week that follows, Maxwell and a local doctor do their best to care for the young man, but he is so weakened from hunger that he never rallies. On Saturday afternoon he dies.

After the young man dies, Maxwell discards the sermon he had planned to preach the following morning. Instead, he speaks extemporaneously and challenges the members of his congregation to join him in a Christ-centered social ministry. He asks for volunteers who "will pledge themselves, earnestly and honestly for an entire year, not to do anything" in their personal and public lives "without first asking the question, 'What would Jesus do?' And after asking that question, each one will follow Jesus exactly as he knows how, no matter what the result may be" (15). At the close of his remarks, Maxwell invites those who want to take this pledge to join him in the parish house.

Nearly one hundred members of the congregation respond to their minister's invitation. During the discussion that follows the service, some of the volunteers question how they will know they are doing what Jesus would do. Rachel Winslow, the lead soprano in the church choir, asks, "Who is to decide for me just what He would do in my case? It is a different age. There are many perplexing questions in our civilization that are not mentioned in the teachings of Jesus. How am I going to tell what He would do?" (17, 18). Maxwell tells Rachel that he is confident that each of those present can discover what God wants him or her to do through prayer and inspired faith: "There is no way that I know of except as we study Jesus through the medium of the Holy Spirit."

Asking "What would Jesus do?" in every circumstance brings dramatic changes to the lives of those who agree to live by the answer, regardless of the personal consequences. Edward Norman, editor of the town's leading newspaper, decides to omit any reference in the Monday paper to a prizefight held on Sunday—because Jesus would not support violence as entertainment, especially on Sunday. When the newsboys complain that hardly anyone buys their papers, Norman buys all the unsold copies himself. The next day, he decides to drop all liquor and tobacco ads and then to discontinue the paper's Sunday edition. Finally, he tells his readers that the paper will examine all political questions within a moral context and evaluate all candidates according to moral standards. The paper is soon in financial crisis, but, against the advice of all his junior editors, Norman persists; he is committed to ask prayerfully what Jesus would do and to live according to the inspiration he receives, regardless of the consequences.

Alexander Powers, general manager for one of the railroads that serve Raymond, discovers that the local freight office has been violating Interstate Commerce Commission rules. The freight agent has been accepting rebates and passing them along to the company. Powers asks what Jesus would do if he discovered such illegal practices and decides he must expose the practices publicly. The railroad rewards Powers's ethical decision by firing him. Edward Norman responds by running an editorial in support of Powers's decision.

Rachel Winslow, the lead soprano in the First Church choir, turns down a concert career so she can continue to sing at the church. Her mother is appalled by her decision and accuses her of being a fanatic. Rachel responds that she is simply doing what Jesus would do. When Rachel begins to sing at evangelistic tent meetings held in the "Rectangle, the most notorious district in Raymond," her mother becomes even more inflamed.

Though Henry Maxwell tells those committed to follow Jesus' example that they can expect to suffer for their faith, some of those who make the commitment receive unexpected benefits. One afternoon, Edward Norman describes the reverses his paper has suffered since he decided to operate it strictly as Jesus would to Virginia Page, one of the more affluent members of First Church. He tells Virginia that he is seeking support from subscribers who share his vision for the paper, but he realizes that only an endowed paper is free to serve its community responsibly. Virginia responds to Edward's dilemma by asking what Jesus would do if he had wealth like hers. She decides to invest a half million dollars to provide an endowment that supports Norman's paper "on one condition, of course, that it be carried on as it has been" (108).

When Virginia Page becomes involved directly in relief work in the Rectangle, she decides to use some of her money to improve the lives of streetwalkers who live there. She even hires one of them, Loreen, a prostitute she meets outside a saloon, to work as a maid in her own household. A week later during a riot that follows a hotly contested election, Loreen repays Virginia's faith in her when she sacrifices her life for Virginia by pushing her out of the path of a liquor bottle someone has hurled at Virginia. The bottle misses Virginia, but it strikes Loreen and kills her. After the incident, Virginia decides to buy up a large parcel of property in the Rectangle: "My money—I mean God's, which he wants me to use—can build wholesome lodging-houses, refuges for poor women, asylums for shop girls, safety for many and many a lost girl like Loreen" (125).

As the novel closes, Henry Maxwell and some others from the Raymond church visit a settlement house in Chicago. At an open meeting, they listen patiently as those who are poor and out of work describe their struggles. One of the speakers, Mr. Carlsen, a socialist leader, offers a particularly scathing criticism of the church. He says it is dominated by aristocrats who live off the backs of the poor. Ministers "as a class are their slaves" (229).

Ministers and church members preserve and benefit from a social system that keeps the workers poor. None of those present seems able to respond directly to Carlsen's accusations. A former local bishop who is now ministering at the settlement house simply calls time and asks Rachel Winslow to sing. Her golden voice captivates the assembly; it moves even the hardened Carlsen to tears. As he watches how Rachel's singing affects the meeting, the bishop says that preaching the gospel "to the world of sinful, diseased, depraved, lost humanity . . . by consecrated prima donnas and professional tenors and altos and bassos . . . would hasten the coming of the Kingdom quicker than any other one force" (226).

Philip Strong, the title character in Sheldon's next novel, *The Crucifixion of Philip Strong* (1898), is Sheldon's most impressive social evangelical minister. When the novel opens, Philip is struggling to decide between two calls: one invites him to become the pastor of a comfortable church in a university town; the other invites him to become the pastor of a downtown church in the industrial city of Milton. Though his wife urges him to accept the call to the university town, Philip decides God wants him to go to Milton. Within only a few weeks, Philip discovers why God wanted him to go to Milton. He walks through one of the poorest sections of Milton and is appalled by the conditions he finds there. He is even more startled when he discovers that many of the "saloons, gambling houses and dens of wickedness" in this section of Milton are owned by prominent members of his own church. He resolves to confront his congregation with the social responsibility they have as Christians. He decides to devote one sermon each month to "Christ and Modern Society": "It will be my object in these talks to suppose Christ himself as the one speaking to Modern Society on its sins, its needs, its opportunities, its responsibilities, its every-day life" (18, 19).

While some members of his congregation support Philip's ministry among the poor in Milton, most oppose his social gospel. Matters come to a head when Philip proposes moving the church building to the tenement district as a symbol of the congregation's willingness to serve those who live there. When the church board refuses his request, Philip redoubles his personal efforts to bring the gospel to the working poor. Before long, he realizes that the bias his church members have against workingmen discourages local union members from attending his church. Philip decides to offer himself as a speaker at union meetings. Union leaders invite him to give a series of talks on "Christian socialism." As the series proceeds, more and more workers attend. Though Philip cautions the workers against strikes and violence in his talks, their growing frustration with low wages and poor working conditions finally boils over into a riot. Rioting workers break through police barriers, surround the owner of the local mill, and threaten him with bodily harm. Philip places himself between the rioters and the owner and convinces them to disperse and to use peaceful means to resolve their dispute.

As the weeks pass, more and more workers from the local mill begin to attend services at Philip's church; more than thirty of them become members. Philip begins a series of Sunday night services designed specifically to appeal to mill workers. At the final sermon during this series of services, Philip tells his congregation that they, like the rich young man in the gospel, must "renounce all to follow Jesus." After the service, the church board meets and decides their minister has gone too far. They ask Philip to resign. A few Sundays later as Philip preaches his farewell, he has a heart attack and dies. After his funeral, a "great procession" of the poor gather about his grave. When all have left except Sarah, his wife, and a close friend, Sarah bursts out, "But Philip, Philip, my beloved, they killed him!" The close friend, a poor man who visited Philip and Sarah in their home, responds, "Yes, they crucified him. But he is with his Lord now. Let us be glad for him. Let us leave him with Eternal Peace" (256).

Novels like *The Crucifixion of Philip Strong* and *In His Steps* are obviously intended to show how people with faith can live as Christians even in the new urban, industrialized society. This purpose is clear in Philip Strong's addresses to the local labor union, as well as in conversations among those who decide to take the Raymond pledge at the beginning of *In His Steps* (17–19). The necessity of conversion is always in the forefront of social evangelical ministers' preaching. Absolute, unqualified faith is essential. Only grace that is appropriated through faith can equip believers for ministry in modern society.[11]

God, not the human minister, is the primary actor in novels that feature a social evangelical minister. In Charles Sheldon's significantly subtitled *Richard Bruce, or Life That Now Is* (1892), the Rev. John King and Adam Tower, a labor organizer, compete for the loyalty of union members. King gains the workers' confidence, and Tower (who is not a Christian believer) becomes increasingly distressed by the minister's success. In an act of desperation, Tower ambushes the minister one night in a dark alley. When Tower strikes King, the minister responds as he thinks Jesus would: he tells Tower that he loves him and turns the other cheek. The minister's courageous act of faith startles Tower. It opens him to God and God acts. Tower is converted and immediately joins King's effort to convince the workers to become Christian believers (278, 279, 343).[12]

Conversion is the first step in a three-step process that leads to moral reform and acts of charity. Moral reform and charity that follow conversion often provide additional opportunities for evangelism—which begins the process over again. Programs at settlement houses in *In His Steps* and *The Redemption of Freetown* (1898), for example, encourage moral reform and provide relief for the poor and unemployed who live in the neighborhoods where they are established. But their primary purpose is to provide points of contact for evangelistic ministry. Following the familiar pattern, David Dowling, the social evangelical minister in Cortland Myer's *Would Christ Belong to a Labor Union?* (1900), shows genuine concern for local workers when he accepts invitations to speak at labor union meetings. But Dowling is always clear that faith in Christ is what the workers need most (128–40). Workers who attend the meetings where Dowling speaks appreciate his sympathetic support, but the fact that many of them respond to his evangelistic appeal and become members of Dowling's church is obviously more important.

Unlike social ministers and social activists who often step outside roles prescribed for clergy, social evangelical ministers always honor socially accepted and ecclesiastically defined roles for clergy. Toward the end of *In His Steps*, the former bishop and Dr. Bruce give up lucrative ministry positions and even spend some of their own money to establish a church presence in the slums. But they keep their clerical status and even their titles in their new work. They engage in social ministry, but in their new work they present themselves and are viewed as ministers. They *preach* against social evils and *call* for reform. But they *never* leave the ministry like Emerson Courtright does (J. Herbert Quick, *The Broken Lance*), or reject traditional theology like John Hodder does (Winston Churchill, *The Inside of the Cup*), or turn their backs on the church like Dan Matthews does (Harold Bell Wright, *The Calling of Dan Matthews*) to further their ministry. Social evangelical ministers like Philip Strong, David Dowling, and Murvale Eastman (in Albion Turgee's *Murvale Eastman, Christian Socialist* [1891]) press against social and ecclesiastical boundaries defined for ministers. They reach out to the poor with acts of caring that are costly, but they always do so as ministers of the gospel. Bringing others to Christian faith is always the primary purpose of their ministry.[13]

Social evangelical ministers do press for reform in the world around their churches, but their objective is always *moral* reform, never *social* reform. There is never an explicit or even an implicit message in these novels that Christians should seek to change the social order. People need to change, not the social order. References to socialism and socialists are always negative.[14] Socialism is antagonistic to Christian belief; socialists are enemies of the Christian faith; socialists are dangerous radicals.[15] Katharine Woods's *Metzerott, Shoemaker* (1889) seems designed specifically to show the dangers of socialism that is not Christian socialism. Karl Metzerott is a self-employed shoemaker who provides handmade shoes for those who live in his ethnic German neighborhood. In his personal life, Metzerott is a contentious atheist and radical socialist. He believes that those who hold economic power in America will never give it up voluntarily. He sees the church as an agency that supports the status quo. Metzerott is very outspoken; he even challenges the pastors who serve neighborhood churches to debate his revolutionary ideas.

The introduction of less-expensive machine-made shoes threatens Metzerott's livelihood and confirms his belief that, under capitalism, a few always gain at the expense of the majority who are workers. When Mr. Clare, an Episcopal clergyman who is also a socialist, moves to the area and begins to preach in the local Episcopal church, he becomes Metzerott's primary antagonist. Clare believes that the New Testament supports communism but does not advocate establishing a communist order through violent revolution. He believes that God will bring a more just social order into being and urges faith and patience. Both Metzerott and Clare want a more just social order, but they are very much at odds about how to achieve it.

After Karl Metzerott's wife dies, he raises their son Louis to embrace the same revolutionary socialist views that he holds. Fate (or, more likely, in the author's view, providence) challenges Karl's vision for Louis when Louis falls in love with the daughter of Mr. Randolph, who owns the local mill. Events climax when a poorly paid millworker's daughter dies after a long illness, likely because her millworker father cannot afford proper nourishment or medical care. Karl is infuriated. He decides the time for revolution has come. At a union meeting, he urges the workers to seek revenge. At first, they propose burning Randolph's mill, but someone observes that destroying this one mill will hurt Randolph very little: he has many other mills. So the workers decide to burn Randolph's house, instead. They plan to surround the house and force Randolph and his family to stay inside so they will be killed in the fire. When Louis Metzerott accidentally discovers what the workers intend, he goes immediately to the Randolphs' house to warn them of the workers' plan. But Louis's warning is not in time; rioting millworkers arrive within minutes. During the ensuing confusion, Louis is shot and killed by a bullet intended for Randolph, the mill's owner.

When the crowd realizes that Karl's son has been killed, they quickly disperse. Karl who witnesses the tragedy is overwhelmed by grief, but he insists on taking Louis's body home to prepare it for burial. Mr. Clare calls to give Karl support. Karl vents his frustration and his anger at this minister who has opposed his radical socialism. But as he and Pastor Clare talk, Karl suddenly dissolves in tears. He realizes that he is partly to blame for Louis's death. His pursuit of violent social revolution may have led to Louis's death. His son would probably still be alive if he had advocated moral reform rather than social revolution—if he had trusted God to work through converted individuals to bring about social change. Overcome now by guilt, Karl confesses the "error" in his thinking to Mr. Clare. When Clare tells Karl that God forgives him, Karl becomes a Christian believer.

Social evangelical ministers in fiction are confident that charity like moral reform follows naturally from conversion. Virginia Page acts out this conviction in Sheldon's *In His Steps* when she buys a large parcel in the infamous Rectangle and builds institutions that will benefit young women like Loreen who saved her life. She makes the purchase with "My money—I mean God's, which he wants me to use." Often a woman of means like Virginia exemplifies charity in social gospel novels. Helen S. Campbell's *Mrs. Herndon's Income* (1886) traces Mrs. Herndon's effort to spend her income responsibly on charitable causes. When Perley Kelso is unable to convince the male partners to allow her to become an active partner in the local mill, she uses her money to provide relief for workers in need. In *Would Christ Belong to a Labor Union?* Grace Chalmers, a member of David Dowling's church, uses her vast resources in a philanthropic ministry among the poor. Both Dr. Bruce and the bishop who appear in the closing chapters of Sheldon's *In His Steps* possess significant resources, which they commit to provide services to the poor when they take the Raymond pledge. The very rich are simply examples. Social evangelicals assume that those who ask what would Jesus do will be inspired to commit whatever resources they possess to charitable purposes.

The social and economic views social evangelicals hold sometimes seem naive. They exhibit little understanding of social and economic systems as *systems*. Affluent clergy and church members who are converted share their wealth, often generously, but there is no leveling. There is not even a hint in these novels that social and economic *systems* need to be reordered. Conversion leads to charity, and charity is sufficient. Some individual converts show courage and suffer for their Christian convictions, but they never facilitate, even by peaceful means, changes in the social and economic order.

Believers lose some of their wealth, but they never lose their status. Affluent, inspired individuals share their wealth with others, but the social and economic order remains much the same.

Businessmen who appear in social gospel novels often see themselves paternalistically: as custodians of wealth. In *The Silent Partner*, Phelps offers a scathing criticism of the existing class system (and sexism) when Perley Kelso questions whether she and the other partners in the local mill have the right to be so affluent while workers in their mill are so poor. But as the title of the novel suggests, a woman is supposed to be a *silent* partner. Maverick, the new managing partner, points out to *Miss* Kelso that the male owners possess wisdom that leads them to exercise a stewardship that justifies their wealth. They exhibit that superior wisdom and stewardship when they keep the mill going during a recession, paying the workers even when the mill is losing money (135). Perley is not convinced: "There is *something* about the relations of rich and poor, of master and man, with which the state of the market has nothing whatever to do" (141; italics in the original). Perley's critique fails to impress Maverick and the other partners. Their views are closer to those expressed by George F. Baer, the nineteenth-century railway magnate: "The rights of laboring man will be protected and cared for, not by labor agitation," Baer says, "but by the Christian men to whom God in His infinite wisdom has given control of the property interests of the country."[16]

It rarely occurs to anyone in these novels that church members like Baer might support a moralistic approach to social reform in order to protect their own social and economic position. No Eldon Parr recognizes and then admits he is using conservative theology to justify business practices that support his affluence at the expense of others. Business owners who are obviously selfish have not yet seen the full light of the gospel. When they do see the light, as the traction company leaders do in Myers's novel, they immediately become altruistic and generous.

Social evangelicals seem to be as naive about their racial bias as they are about social and economic systems. In Sheldon's *The Redemption of Freetown*, Burke Williams, a young black man from Freetown, the district in the city of Merton where all African Americans are forced to live, is implicated in a shooting. Williams protests that he is innocent—and actually he is—but he is nonetheless convicted and sentenced to twenty years in prison. Whites who have the power to judge Williams see him as a symptom of the moral decay they associate with residents of Freetown. During Williams's trial, the Rev. Howard Douglass decides that God wants him and his congregation to help those who live in Freetown. While he is discussing his proposal with some church leaders, including Judge Vernon who presided at Williams's trial, news arrives that Williams has escaped from jail. This information is soon followed by even more frightening news: those searching for Williams have found the judge's son, Claude Vernon, seriously injured, obviously the victim of an assault. The authorities conclude immediately that Williams is to blame for the assault on Vernon. Williams is soon recaptured and again protests that he is innocent. The evidence against him is entirely circumstantial. But when Claude Vernon dies a few days later, Burke Williams is charged with his murder.

The violent acts blamed on Williams encourage members of Howard Douglass's congregation to support the social ministry he proposes in Freetown. His plan follows the usual social evangelical pattern. Those who commit themselves to the ministry Douglass calls for ask themselves what Jesus would do in Freetown. They decide to build a settlement house that will offer ministries of evangelism and social service. Mrs. Carlton, a wealthy church member, provides the funds. The program at the settlement house includes a kindergarten and day nursery to care for babies of mothers who must go out to work, a kitchen where cooking can be taught, a reading room, other rooms for classes in sewing and music, and space in the basement to teach trades. The plan also offers "premiums or prizes . . . to encourage neatness, thrift and industry." Prizes will be offered "for the best gardens . . . , the neatest-looking front and back yard and alley . . . , the best flowerbeds . . . , and the most improvements on any place in a year." The plan also provides for regular "Sunday work, a Sunday school, preaching services, good music" (39). Finally, Mr. Douglass encourages leading members of his congregation to follow his example and agree to live for several weeks of the year in the settlement house in Freetown. He believes the presence of Christian men and women will encourage moral reform among the residents there.

The members of Douglass's church who support the mission work in Freetown are obviously dedicated Christians ready to make significant personal sacrifices to help the residents there. But nothing they propose or accomplish challenges the existing racial hierarchy of Merton. Church members who work at the settlement house assume that black people who live in Merton will always be socially and economically subordinate to white people who live in Merton. As members of the church's young people's organization discuss the roles they will play in the settlement house, for example, they decide that cooking classes are essential for the young African American women who live in Freetown. One member, "a tall, energetic-looking girl," argues, "And some of us girls think the best thing we could do to help in the social settlement will be to volunteer our services as cooks in the housekeeping department, and teach the colored girls over there the best ways, *and fit them for service*" (53; italics mine). The possibility that "colored girls" might be fit for something other than service and that the program at the settlement house should prepare them for that possibility never surfaces in the discussion.

The systematic bias of Merton's white community takes a final tragic turn when Burke Williams decides that none of those who will judge him will believe he did not murder Claude Vernon. Williams is overcome with despair and commits suicide before his case goes to trial. At the end of the novel, Sheldon reveals that Williams really is innocent: Claude Vernon was killed in a fight with a friend when both were drunk. But Sheldon draws only a moral lesson from the incident: Vernon's death at the hand of his friend points up the evil of drinking. Neither the pastor nor any of the church members who work at the settlement house recognize that Williams hangs himself to avoid the indignity of a public execution.[17]

Many novels that feature social evangelical ministers reflect what seem to me to be idealistic perceptions of both churches and ministers. Fictional clergy who mirror this cultural image *never* perceive the church as the villain.[18] The "good minister/bad church" formula that often appears in novels that reflect popular culture never appears in novels that reflect church culture. A congregation may resist their social evangelical minister's leadership for a time, but eventually some or all of its members recognize that their minister is inspired by God. The possibility that churches in their present form may not be able to address the realities people face in the new urban, industrialized society never emerges in novels that reflect church culture. No social evangelical minister finds the church so defective that he leaves it, like John Gaunt does to found an alternative secular League of Service to promote the social ministries his congregation refuses to consider. Social evangelicals may not know what to do, but they have absolute faith in God, as well as in the church as God's instrument of redemption. They may not know when or how God will act. But they wait in faith. They trust God.[19] They are courageous *believers*.

The most admired ministers in novels that reflect the values of late-nineteenth- and early-twentieth-century popular culture are courageous *actors*. Waiting in faith for God to act seems far too passive to social ministers and social activists. Ministers like James Cameron in *That Printer of Udell's* and Smith Boyd in *The Ball of Fire* are particularly put off by reactionary pastors and church members who use their commitment to traditional styles of ministry and theology to protect themselves.[20] Ministers who see "what needs to be done" and who have the courage and physical strength to do it reflect a popular culture that respects ministers who act.

These two cultures—a popular subculture that has high regard for ministers who act and is less concerned about their theological pedigree, and a church (evangelical) subculture that has the highest regard for ministers who are uncompromising believers—are well-defined by the late-nineteenth century—and they persist into the twentieth century and beyond.[21] The ideal minister in popular culture (which included then as now many of those who view themselves as moderate or liberal Christians) is a person of open faith who advocates social justice and human betterment—for example, Henry Ward Beecher in real life and John Hodder in fiction.[22] The ideal minister in evangelical church culture is one who promotes explicitly Christian beliefs, along with personal morality and charity—for example, Charles Grandison Finney in real life and Henry Maxwell in fiction.[23] As might be expected, fiction that affirms the norms of one subculture tends to parody ministers who reflect the norms of the other. For example, ministers cast as good humans in popular fiction are often presented as equivocating believers in evangelical church fiction. Ministers perceived positively as uncompromising believers in fiction that reflects evangelical church norms are characterized as naive in fiction that reflects popular culture.

The well-documented blossoming of evangelical Christians during the last half of the nineteenth century and early decades of the twentieth century can give the impression that they were and are the most significant religious group in American society.[24] However, this evangelical Christian subculture was by no means the only significant or always the most influential subculture in American society during this period. It is worth noting that the most famous preacher in America in the middle and latter nineteenth century, Henry Ward Beecher, was *not* an evangelical. Beecher, who drew thousands to Plymouth Church in Brooklyn, was a convinced evolutionist who read both Darwin and Herbert Spencer. He was also an admirer and covert friend of Ralph Waldo Emerson. Beecher was not only a theological liberal; he was a social and political activist and often took politics into his pulpit at Plymouth Church.[25] The popularity of the novels I discuss in chapters 4 through 6, especially the social gospel novels I review in chapter 6, testifies to the size of the liberal Protestant subculture that admired preachers like Beecher. During the twentieth century, it was this subculture of social Christians, not the evangelical subculture, that "came to be defined as the American mainstream."[26]

In chapters 8 and 9, I consider fiction that reflects cultural images of ministers within yet a third subculture that blossomed during the closing decades of the nineteenth century—the subculture of disbelievers. This radical subculture was smaller and less apparent than either the evangelical religious or mainstream popular cultures. The relative lack of organizational affiliation related specifically to their disbelieving has made disbelievers more difficult to identify and track than evangelical and mainline Christians. But their emergence as a challenging subculture in the late-nineteenth century and their continued growth in American society since that time is nonetheless real.[27] Images of clergy formed within this subculture challenged the accuracy of many popular and most church images of Protestant clergy. When placed alongside ministers that dominate the fiction of this radical subculture the heroic ministers of popular and church fiction seem like wishful thinking.

VIII

FOUNDERING DIVINES

Radical Images (1)

In the middle of the nineteenth century, only a handful of authors based their fictional clergy on radical images. By the end of the century, dozens of American writers drew on radical images to create fictional clergy. In fewer than four decades, writers and readers who accepted radical images as accurate reflections of real-life ministers became a significant subculture in American society. What produced such a dramatic development?

Profound social, economic, and cultural changes at home and abroad during the last half of the nineteenth century challenged the credibility of traditional viewpoints and encouraged the growth of an openly secular and increasingly irreverent subculture in American society. The long Civil War of the 1860s bled America spiritually, as well as physically. While the years of suffering encouraged a stronger faith in some, they generated irreversible doubt and skepticism in others. In his study of the sources of naturalism in America at the end of the nineteenth century, Lars Ahnrbrink says the Civil War dealt "a fatal blow to romanticism and Emersonian idealism."[1] After more than four years of seemingly endless slaughter, many Americans could no longer hold on to their conviction that the world is ordered by a provident, loving God.

The religious doubt and confusion that pervaded postbellum America helped to create a receptivity to faith-challenging intellectual developments from abroad. On November 24, 1859, Charles Darwin's *On the Origin of Species by Means of Natural Selection, or The Preservation of Favoured Races in the*

Struggle for Life was published in England. The title itself is provocative; it suggests that the fate of individual living things is determined more by chance and competition that favors the strong and able than by divine providence. In the 1870s, Herbert Spencer extended evolutionary thinking to human society. His work describes a social world that is also dominated by the privileged and able. Emerging psychology on the continent, especially the work of Sigmund Freud, also defined humans as creatures *within* a natural order, shaped by their human nature rather than by a divinely given soul.

These radical perspectives represented significant breaks with the past. Humans, whose fate is determined by natural selection like all other living things, lose any individual or special relationship to a Creator God. On the analyst's couch, soul is transformed into psyche. What had long been the exclusive province of priests and preachers now became the province of the analyst. Religion became an "illusion."[2] An epistemological search for self-knowledge displaced the belief that one discovers the purpose of life through faith.[3]

Developments in the physical sciences, new philosophical perspectives, especially Comte's positivism, and the emergence of higher criticism in biblical studies also challenged the authority of Christian beliefs, first in Europe and then at the close and turn of the century in America. For generations, physical sciences and theology had formed a partnership in American public life that recognized the preeminence of Protestant Christian faith. Calvinist theology mediated through a Scottish commonsense realist epistemology and a Baconian philosophy of science offered a comprehensive, rarely disputed, scripture-based metaphysics. When coupled with Newtonian physics, that metaphysics provided a providential view of the cosmos that was grounded both scientifically and scripturally. According to the dominant Baconian perspective, God wills *and equips* humans to appreciate nature, both scientifically and devotionally. Those who are truly reverent are inspired to observe nature accurately. If humans err in their observation, they do so because they lack faith. A similar inspiration informs the faithful when they consult scripture. Theological facts about God can be discovered from reverent study of the Bible, just as facts about the creation can be discovered through the reverent study of nature. Scientific research and the study of scripture provide compatible and mutually reinforcing factual data. Princeton professor Charles Hodge affirmed the Baconian outlook that dominated American educational institutions at midcentury in his *Systematic Theology:* "The Bible is to the theologian what nature is to the man of science. It is his storehouse of facts."[4]

The philosophy of Auguste Comte that European intellectuals embraced during the nineteenth century and developments in physics at the century's end challenged the Baconian science-theology construct. Comte argued that humans can have no certain knowledge of a divine being—if such a being exists—because they have no access to a supernatural dimension; they can know only about the phenomenal. The phenomenal world in and of itself offers no clear evidence of an overarching, ordering God. In fact, emerging perspectives in the world of physics at the time suggested quite the opposite. This new thinking climaxed in 1905, when Albert Einstein published papers that introduced his special theory of relativity. Relativity and uncertainty (especially after Werner Heisenberg) are inherent in the new physics. The new conception of the natural order holds out little possibility of a provident God; it posits mechanics without a mechanic. The new philosophy and science challenged rather than supported traditional religious beliefs.[5] The dispute was much more than a theological disagreement. The detractors were not simply questioning the Christian view of God. The challenge was more basic: it displaced the likelihood that there is a God.

During the nineteenth century, especially after the Civil War, these European perspectives began to infiltrate American society. A recent study edited by Christian Smith indicates that this infiltration was more like a gush than a trickle—and an intentional gush, as well.[6] In the period between the Civil War and World War I, thousands—in fact, many thousands—of American students traveled to Europe for graduate study.[7] During their stay in Europe, many (perhaps, most?) of these graduate students lost their Christian faith and embraced emerging European philosophical perspectives. They brought back "a set of German philosophical and theological systems that effectively undermined the existing American view of the intellectual authority of religious knowledge."[8]

These scholars not only discovered new radical perspectives that displaced their religious faith; their new knowledge emboldened them. When they returned home, they fomented a "secular revolution." They began a sustained and largely successful attempt to transform the institutions of American public life into secular institutions. As they assumed key leadership roles in American society, especially those who became teachers in American colleges and universities, these European-educated Americans made an *intentional* effort to "push religion out of the universities and to convince Americans that the dawn of science had made religion obsolete":[9]

> The secularization of American public life was in fact something much more like a contested revolutionary struggle than a natural evolutionary

> process. . . . The secularization of the institutions of American public life did not happen by accident or happenstance. . . . The people at the core of these secularizing movements, at least, knew what they were doing, and they wanted to do it. They were activists, secularizing activists.[10]

When the secular revolution climaxed in the early twentieth century, the revolutionaries had effectively secularized American intellectual culture, as well as American universities, public schools, and publishing, and had made deep inroads into the law, politics, psychology, and other aspects of American public life. Radical philosophical, social, and religious perspectives that were once confined to a handful of intellectual elite now permeated American society. In less than half a century, a sizeable and powerful subculture emerged and threatened to displace Protestant religious perspectives that had long dominated American public life—and the clergy who represented these perspectives.[11]

Consider the wide-ranging influence that just one of these returning students, G. Stanley Hall, exerted in several areas of American life. Just after the Civil War, Hall graduated from Williams College and entered Union Theological Seminary to prepare for the ministry. Financial support from Henry Ward Beecher made it possible for Hall to study in Germany in 1868. While he was a student in Germany, Hall encountered positivist philosophy and, what is most important, became a devoted student of psychology. He gave up his intention to become a minister and returned to the United States to study under William James at Harvard, where he earned the first American doctorate in psychology. Hall's study of developmental psychology convinced him that religious belief in its traditional form is an immature stage of human development. In 1917, he published *Jesus*, a collection of essays on the historical Jesus. *Jesus* "corrects" traditional theology that keeps Christians in a state of immaturity. Hall's essays envision Jesus as a human peer rather than as a divine authority. Believers appropriate the benefits of believing only as they understand Jesus scientifically through the lens of psychology. In Hall's view, Jesus is a charismatic figure who has a magnetic effect on his followers. This psychologically correct interpretation of Jesus is essential because, over time, doctrinally entangled Christianity has become "less and less a solution, and more and more a problem."[12] Hall's influence reached far beyond the specific discipline of psychology. His emphasis on applied psychology anticipated the self-help movement of the twentieth century. His belief that applied psychology, particularly his conviction that the psychology of child development should shape the education of children, had a significant and lasting influence on public education in the United States. Hall's thinking and his work challenged both Christian theology and pedagogy.[13]

Developments within the theological world during the nineteenth century that weakened the Bible's credibility posed as great a threat to practitioners of faith as social and cultural changes did from without. Even before the Civil War, some comparative religion scholars in Europe, especially Germany, proposed that the Bible is a collection of "myths" like those that appear in the sacred texts of many religions.[14] Biblical scholars on the Continent also began to employ "higher" criticism to interpret the Bible. These developments challenged the Bible's unique authority. When the Bible is examined through the lenses of comparative religion and higher criticism, it loses its special sacred status; it becomes simply another human, cultural product, shaped as much (or more) by human authors as by the inspiration of God. The Bible can still be viewed as a sacred text, but it loses its uniqueness when it is considered as only one among many sacred texts. It becomes a book that contains *our* cultural mythology. It is *our* sacred literature. It embodies *our* cultural perceptions of God.

Classifying the Bible as literature, albeit sacred literature, also raises the possibility that it may be fiction. Reading the Bible like fiction does not necessarily discredit it, but it opens up the possibility that the Bible, either in part or as a whole, may not be true. It discounts the authority of scripture because it invites readers to judge for themselves whether, or in what ways, the Bible is true. Fiction *invites* belief, it does not *require* belief. Readers typically approach a work of fiction skeptically, with disbelief—with the notion that it is probably something an author made up. To be accepted as true, a work of fiction must convince readers to suspend their disbelief. If a story seems convincing to readers, they may suspend their disbelief as they read it, but—and the qualification here is significant—never completely. They always know in the back of their minds that the story is fiction, that it is not quite true. At best, they accept it as true with reservations:

> Precisely what is a danger in religion is the very fabric of fiction. In religion, a belief that is only "as if" is either the prelude to a loss of faith, or an instance of bad faith (in both senses of the phrase). If religion is true, one must believe. . . . Once religion has revealed itself to you, you are never free. . . . Fiction asks us to judge its reality; religion asserts its reality.[15]

"Fiction [is always] the place of not-quite-belief"; religion that does not demand belief has lost its reality and its credibility.[16] What is inherent in fiction is a threat to faith. The concept of comparative religion poses a similar threat. *Comparative* religion marks the end of believing. Religious pluralism renders faith into religion: "Religion is culture rather than belief, religion is literature that attests . . . unbelief."[17]

These developments in comparative religious studies and higher criticism raised serious issues for believers, especially Christian ministers. Christianity is a revealed religion. The Bible is the primary source of that revelation, as well as the foundation of ministers' authority. Ministers are credentialed ambassadors of the God who is revealed in the Bible. If the unique reality of scripture and of the God that scripture reveals become uncertain, then both God's and ministers' authorities are precarious. Preachers fall to the level of fiction writers. To become credible, they first have to convince others to suspend their disbelief. To exercise their authority as representatives of God, they have to establish the Bible's credibility, as well as their own.

European thinking shaped the world of American literature just as it did other aspects of American intellectual life during the nineteenth and early twentieth centuries. The literary realism and naturalism that dominated nineteenth-century European literature made a deep impression on the postbellum generation of American writers who read that literature—especially those who experienced these radical perspectives firsthand. American authors like William Dean Howells, Mark Twain, Henry Adams, Henry James, and Harold Frederic traveled to Europe in a pilgrimage similar to that of the graduate students that Christian Smith describes. Their discoveries in Europe encouraged the new generation of American writers to reframe their own personal and cultural perspectives according to positivist, realist, and naturalist frames of reference they encountered in European culture and literature.

As they integrated European perspectives into their own experience, American authors gave them a distinctively American shape. The specifically American realism that resulted reflected the frontier and urban Middle American origins of many late-nineteenth- and early-twentieth-century American authors. Writers like Edward Eggleston, Hamlin Garland, E. W. Howe, William Dean Howells, Joseph Kirkland, and Mark Twain, who came originally from the Middle West, received little formal education; most of their education took place in the school of experience. When they began to write fiction, the reality they noted from *their own* present and past experience, not classics out of the past, shaped their writing. This immediate, experiential approach was especially pronounced in writers like Twain, Frederic, and Dreiser, who began their careers as newspaper reporters, often assigned to cover the underside of frontier and urban life.[18] The grimy life that was the lot of so many who lived on the frontier or composed the urban working poor was always the central concern in the works of American naturalists like Theodore Dreiser and Robert Herrick.[19]

"The frontier, having no tradition, worked on images of the past like acid," Alfred Kazin observes in an essay devoted to Mark Twain.[20] Michael Davitt Bell describes the acidic difference between the older generation of writers and the new frontier, urban-bred nineteenth-century realists like Twain: "The most significant distinction [between the older and newer generations of writers] is not between modes of literary expression or representation but between kinds of men. On the one side is the artist, overwhelmed and enervated by 'literary consciousness,' metaphorically feminized by his concern with 'preening and prettifying,' with 'fashion.' On the other side are 'real' men, 'men whose lives have been passed in activities,' men who handle language as a burly carpenter hefts his tools."[21] In nineteenth-century America, an often rough initiation to authorship joined with the perspectives of realism and naturalism to nurture a different breed of writer. As they wrote fiction, American realists were concerned above all to represent people—including ministers—*as they are*, not as they should be, according to some preconceived model or ideal.

Many of the women who produced literary novels between the 1880s and the 1920s echoed a similarly rough realism in their writing. In addition, their work reflects a feminist viewpoint that rails against the limited and subordinate social roles that popular culture defined for women. Kate Chopin's *The Awakening* (1899), for instance, became one of the most unsettling novels of the time. *The Awakening* describes the self-discovery of Edna Pontellier, an affluent but emotionally fettered New Orleans woman, who breaks out of the polite restraints of her oppressive marriage to experience sexual and aesthetic awakening. The novel ends as Pontellier wades into the surf to drown beneath the waves because she believes that society cannot tolerate the awakened person she has become.

Late-nineteenth- and early-twentieth-century women authors like Chopin portrayed the declining respect for American clergy in their writing with the same penetrating realism they employed to describe the strengthening image of women. In stories like Mary Wilkins Freeman's "A Village Singer" (1891) and in novels like *The Country of the Pointed Firs* (1896) by Sarah Orne Jewett, *Virginia* (1913) by Ellen Glasgow, and *The Song of the Lark* (1915) by Willa Cather, the strong woman is often a foil to the inept minister. Women were not the only writers who embraced these opposing perceptions of ministers and women in turn-of-the-century America. In fact, strong, independent women and weak, inept ministers appear in novels by male writers as well. The formidable Esther Dudley, who dominates Henry Adams's novel *Esther* (1884), is typical. The talented, well-educated, and socially privileged Rev. Stephen Hazard is no match for her. When he proposes marriage, with characteristic male bias, he expects she will modify her beliefs and behavior to suit him. He is totally dismayed when Esther refuses to compromise either her beliefs or her personhood. At the end of the novel, Esther prevails both against the minister and against his faith.[22]

Historical evidence points to a dramatic discrediting of both divines and the Divine in American culture during the closing decades of the nineteenth century. Major social, economic, and intellectual developments destabilized the Christian faith, undermined ministers' authority, constricted ministers' influence, and reduced ministers' significance. Ministers in literary fiction between the 1870s and the 1920s mirror this discrediting. They are either culturally disabled or personally inept, or some combination of the two. They founder at least as often because the secular world overwhelms their attempts to minister as they do from their own weakness. Committed to beliefs defined in traditional, premodern categories, and burdened with obsolete images of their own authority, many ministers are cognitively crippled, as well. They are not able either to believe or to minister in this place and time.

Ministers in literary fiction from the 1870s through the 1920s reflect cultural images that grew out of the new radical subculture. These images depict ministers as inept contenders and obsolete clerics, as well as inferior and deceiving humans. I discuss fictional clergy that reflect the first two images in this chapter and fictional clergy that mirror the other two in chapter 9. Though I treat them in separate chapters, the four images are interrelated. The first two reflect the social and cultural changes I discuss in the opening pages of this chapter; the last two reflect the lower quality of candidates entering the ministry after the Civil War.[23] The combination, which is quite clear in contemporary fiction, contributes to the discrediting of divines and reflects the discrediting of the Divine. Just when society demands ministers who can do more, the available ministers seem able to do less.

Inept Contenders

The fact that so many ministers founder in William Dean Howells's novels is significant in itself. Howells was probably the most influential nineteenth-century American realist. During his long literary career, this "dean of

American letters" published over thirty novels and held prestigious editorial positions at both *Atlantic Monthly* and *Harper's Magazine*. In their study of literary changes that signal the transition from Puritanism to postmodernism in America, Richard Ruland and Malcolm Bradbury describe Howells as the spokesperson for changes "in stylistic assumptions which were direct responses to deep changes in national experience." Howells gave the international movement of realism a "special American application." Novels by Howells and other American realists who shared his literary outlook are most often located at a "place of change—the altered farming community, the new practices of business and politics, the modern city, the changing region." They most often reflect the pieties of "skepticism and science."[24] They describe ordinary humans struggling to survive in a changed America.

Ministers appear as important characters in more than half of Howells's novels.[25] Howells's fictional clergy mirror the limited social role and declining respect awarded ministers in his time. Howells was deeply influenced by this changed intellectual and religious climate. In 1919 as an old man looking back over his life, he recalled the atmosphere of doubt that entered American culture after the Civil War. There was an "almost universal lapse of [Christian] faith in the prevailing agnosticism of the eighteen-seventies and 'eighties."[26] Most of the clergy in Howells's novels reflect this lapse. They function like social aliens struggling unsuccessfully to minister in an unfamiliar world. The new physical sciences, biology and psychology, that surround them are at odds with the divine order they represent. The social worlds of business, industry, and the frontier within which they minister offer only limited roles for clergy. Most ministers in Howells's novels are bystanders: they offer moral advice but have no other significant social or even religious influence. In their best moments they offer pertinent critical comments, but they seem able to do little else. Their foundering suggests that those who hold on to the old faith are ill-equipped to contend in the modern world.[27]

In Howells's novel *A Modern Instance* (1882), the present and former social orders are represented by Bartley Hubbard and the Halleck family. Hubbard, who represents the new order, rises above humble beginnings by his own wits. He begins life as an orphan, makes his way through college, and enjoys some success in the newspaper business. Though he is successful as a businessman, Hubbard lacks many of the moral restraints associated with the Calvinist faith that still lingers in a few old families like the Hallecks. Mr. and Mrs. Halleck reflect the old theocratic order and are nondescript players in present-day Equity, Maine, where the novel is set. Their disciplined life and firm commitment to the old faith are living reminders of a once-integrated social and theological world. But the church in present-day Equity is only a pale reminder of the church the Hallecks' faith recalls: "Religion there had largely ceased to be a fact of spiritual experience, and the visible church flourished on condition of providing for the social needs of the community" (18).

The perfunctory religious observances of Squire and Miranda Gaylord reflect the eroded faith that now prevails in Equity. The Gaylords maintain the socially prescribed outward forms of religion but have lost its spirit. The squire is a covert agnostic, and when they marry, Miranda gives up her own Christian faith out of a sense of duty to accommodate to her husband's skepticism. Their marriage survives only because divorce is not a possibility in the social order they honor—and because they live apart much of the time. Their daughter Marcia is the real casualty of their relationship. As she grows into adulthood, Marcia internalizes and becomes a victim of the emotional and spiritual ambiguity that characterizes her parents. When Marcia marries Bartley, the failure of their marriage is already determined by their blighted characters. The combination of her emotional instability and his moral opportunism cripples the marriage from the beginning; after only three years, it ends in a nasty divorce.

Ben Halleck, the inept minister, is even more crippled than Marcia Hubbard—though his origins suggest he should be a stronger person than he actually becomes. As a member of the Halleck family, Ben is nurtured by parents who still believe and practice Calvinist Christian faith. These origins, which would have served him well in another time, now cripple Ben. Though he is internally committed to the old faith, Ben finds it difficult to apply it to daily life in the contemporary world. As a result, Ben finds himself caught in a dilemma: he is unable to live by orthodox beliefs completely as his parents do, yet he is unable to cast the old faith off like the irreverent squire and Bartley Hubbard do. Ben's religious quandary actually reflects a crippled personality. His entire life is shaped by equivocating. He is unable to give himself fully to anything or anyone. He fails to take advantage of the opportunity to attend Harvard College; he is unable to declare his love to Marcia Hubbard, the woman he wants to marry—and spends many hours mooning over her picture. When Marcia is ostensibly again available for marriage after her divorce, Ben is unable to set aside his traditionalist opposition to divorce and declare his love for her. Adrift without any clear commitments or convictions, Ben Halleck retreats into the ministry: "He freely granted that he had not reasoned back to his old faith; he had fled to it as to a city of refuge. . . . He did not ask if truth was here or there, anymore; he only knew that he could not find it for himself, and he rested in his inherited belief" (359).

The equivocating Halleck is no more able to function successfully as a minister than he can in other parts of his life. The fact that he is physically lame makes his intellectual and spiritual lameness even more apparent. Howells characterizes Ben with the same qualities as the orthodox faith to which Ben retreats: he is unable to offer anything substantive to those who live in the contemporary world. After Ben completes his preparation for ministry, he visits Equity on the way to his first assignment. When he stays over a Sunday and attends worship in the village church, as a courtesy, the resident minister invites him to offer the opening prayer: "It was considered a good prayer, generally speaking, but it was criticized as not containing anything attractive to young people. He was understood to be on his way to take charge of a backwoods church down in Aroostook County, where probably his prayers would be more acceptable to the popular taste" (359).[28]

In *The Rise of Silas Lapham* (1885), published three years after *A Modern Instance*, Howells offers side-by-side portrayals of an inept businessman and an inept minister. Silas Lapham is the new American businessman who rises—and falls (a favorite Howells character); Mr. Sewell is the inept pastor. Neither man is equipped to compete in the modern world. Lapham is a crass, ill-mannered, poorly educated Vermont paint manufacturer who has made enough money to move to Boston where he has gained some reputation for his business success. Silas's lack of social grace is painfully obvious at a dinner party hosted by the Bromfield Coreys. Bromfield's son Tom, viewed as a possible suitor for Lapham's daughter Irene, is newly employed in Lapham's business. The Coreys are an upper-class, old-moneyed Boston family. Silas's social awkwardness stands in stark contrast to their gentility. His dinner conversation is shallow: his expressions are marked by bad grammar—which only worsens as he consumes more and more wine. Even Persus, his country-bred wife, recognizes that Silas is not fit for polite company.

Silas Lapham's good fortune in business is only short-lived. A West Virginia competitor discovers a vein of natural gas on its property and also discovers how to process the paint that Lapham's company makes. The competitor's source of cheap energy allows them to produce paint for one-tenth of Silas's costs. Within months, the competing company dominates the market. The loss of market share is fatal to Lapham's company. He is forced to shut down his factory. The fact that he has made other poor investments compounds his difficulty. It soon becomes clear that Lapham will lose everything—and he does.

During his downfall, Silas Lapham consults Mr. Sewell, on several key occasions. But each time Sewell turns out to be as inept as Lapham is. An especially pathetic exchange between Lapham and his pastor closes the novel. Several months after the financially ruined Laphams return to their farm in Vermont, the Sewells visit them and spend the night. In the morning as the two men inspect the farm in "an open buggy long past its prime," Silas shares his questioning with Sewell, hoping the minister can offer some insight:

> "Sometimes . . . I get to thinking it all over, and it seems to me I done wrong about Rogers [the business partner he wronged] in the first place; that the whole trouble came from that. It was just like starting a row of bricks. It tried to catch up and stop 'em from going, but they tumbled, one after another. It wan't in the nature of things that they could be stopped till the last brick went. . . . I should like to know how it strikes you." (336)

An old-line Calvinist divine would have seized the opportunity to interpret Lapham's falling bricks analogy as an example of the workings of providence. But the orthodox theology is emasculated in Sewell. He can offer only feeble moralisms to his former parishioner. And those are stated so obscurely and couched "with that subtle kindness of his" that the unscrupulous but now broken Lapham feels no condemnation—and gains no insight. Sewell continues in his hesitant manner:

> "I should be inclined to think—nothing can be thrown quite away; and it can't be that our sins only weaken us—that your fear of having possibly behaved selfishly toward this man kept you on your guard, and strengthened you when you were brought face to face with a greater"—he was going to say temptation, but he saved Lapham's pride, and said—"emergency." (336)

Sewell then asks "delicately . . . , 'And do you have any regrets?'"

> "About what I done? Well, it don't always seem as if I done it," replied Lapham. "Seems sometimes as if it was a hole opened for me, and I crept out of it. I don't know," he added thoughtfully, biting the corner of his still mustache. "I don't know as I should always say it paid; but if I done it, and

the thing was to do over again, right in the same way, I guess I should have to do it." (336, 337)

Lapham obviously has no clear perception of the universe as a moral system ruled by a provident God. Bereft of any conviction that affirms such a cosmic ruler, Lapham needs a minister who can at least speak with personal authority. But the inept Sewell founders both theologically and personally; at every point where he might be morally or theologically direct, he equivocates. If he does have clear theological convictions, he never shares them. He is so unsure of his personal authority that he feels compelled to sugarcoat his comments. Without any clear indication from his former pastor that his fall may have been either the work of a provident God or the end result of his own unethical behavior, Lapham decides it must have been fate—just unfortunate circumstances, the luck of the draw. Sewell's inability to speak with authority to Lapham reflects on the God Sewell represents. His equivocating suggests weakness in God; an inferior divine suggests an inferior Divine. Lapham has neither a strong guiding faith nor a strong spiritual guide.[29] Without either an internal or an external moral compass, he is a morally vulnerable person. If a similar situation arises in the future, he will likely be a victim again.

Sewell exhibits the same foibles and seems even more inept when he reappears two years later in *The Minister's Charge* (1887). The novel's opening scene takes place in rural Willoughby Pastures where the Reverend David Sewell and his wife Lucy have been vacationing. During their stay, David is what Lucy terms "recklessness" in praising the poetry of Lemuel Barker, a young, aspiring but unfortunately untalented local poet. David tries to make light of his dishonesty: "I dare say the boy will never think of my praise again." But Lucy's assessment of the effect the minister's praise will have is more accurate: "I could see that he pinned his faith to every syllable" (2).

The Sewells return to Boston the following day. David is quickly immersed in the rush of pastoral duties and soon forgets about his conversation with the young poet. Then, late in October, a letter arrives from the aspiring Lemuel Barker. It includes a sample from a long poem the poet has composed. Barker hopes that Mr. Sewell will help him find a publisher. The letter then describes serious illnesses that afflict various members of the Barker family. Lemuel hopes that publishing his poem will bring in some much-needed money. When Sewell reads the new poem, he is even sorrier that he praised Lemuel's work; the verse is of such poor quality that he immediately resolves to send a reply that offers a more realistic estimate of the poet's talent. But it's Saturday, and he has a sermon to write—and a funeral to conduct in the afternoon. He puts the letter aside and resolves to respond on Monday when he has time to compose a proper and honest reply. By the end of the day, he has again forgotten about the young man.

A few weeks later, the still-hopeful poet appears at Sewell's parsonage. He reiterates his artistic dreams and tells the minister in great detail about the continuing sicknesses that now afflict nearly everyone in his family. After listening to Lemuel's dreary account, Sewell decides he must act on his resolve to tell Barker the truth about his poetry. But the minister's truth-telling is as clumsy as his former evasiveness. He is blunt and harsh when he tells the young poet he should have told him months ago that he has no talent—and that the present long poem gives "me even less reason to encourage you than the things you read me at home" (15). When the devastated Barker can make no reply, Sewell's old nature regains control and he tries to soften the blows he has just dealt. He promises to go with Barker the next day to see a publisher who can give Barker a "professional judgment" of his work. But he never does. The rest of the novel traces Barker's continuing misadventures in the city and Sewell's inept attempts to minister to him. Sewell tries repeatedly to be helpful to Barker, and at times it seems he succeeds, but nothing he offers compensates for his ill-advised praise that drew Barker to the city. Barker never prospers, but he never goes under completely, either. Like many novels shaped by realism, Howells's story never climaxes, it just stops.[30] The characters are average people who muddle on.

Several other Howells novels offer extensive portraits of clergy patterned on the image of the inept pastor. They include Julius Peck (a minister I mention in chapter 6), Conrad Dryfoos in *A Hazard of New Fortunes* (1890), and Clarence Ewbert in the turn-of-the-century novella, "A Difficult Case" (1901). Ministers in Howells's fiction tend to become weaker and weaker characters as his novels progress. They reflect Howells's growing conviction that clergy in general are consigned to the role of bystanders who offer only moral observations and advice but rarely act in significant ways themselves.[31]

The Rev. Clarence Ewbert is probably the saddest fictional cleric Howells creates. Mr. Ewbert is a minister of the Rixonite church. Though the sect has a formal name, most people identify it with the name derived from the name of its founder, the Rev. Adoniram Rixon. Rixon's theology encourages passivity among his followers. He conceived of "the religious life as a patient waiting upon the divine will. He put as great stress as could be asked upon the importance of realizing faith in the life to come, and an implicit trust in it for the solution of the problems and perplexities of this life" (149).

The story unfolds in a series of exchanges between Mr. Ewbert and Ransom Hilbrook, an unbelieving parishioner. Hilbrook is not at all like the arrogant agnostics who appear in so many nineteenth-century novels. Hilbrook is a defeated man who has lost out so many times that he simply wants no more of life. He tells his pastor that, when he was a young man, a close friend named Josiah "got the girl" who was the love of his life. After four or five years of mourning, he married another woman and they had one child, a boy. His wife died while he was away fighting in the Civil War, and his son died soon after he returned from the war. Hilbrook then went into business and made a good deal of money but soon lost it. An extremely successful cousin saved Ransom from poverty by willing him the large house where Ransom now lives, as well as enough income to maintain himself. But the reclusive Ransom simply survives there. His life experience, especially in the war, deprived him of both the desire to live in this world and any wish for immortality. As Mr. Ewbert explains to his wife following one of his visits to Hilbrook, "the overwhelming presence of death [he saw on the battlefield] extinguished his faith in immortality; the dead riders were just like their dead horses" (160).

Ransom Hilbrook's unbelief intrigues and challenges Clarence Ewbert. The pastor spends hour after hour in conversation with Hilbrook, trying to help him move from doubt to faith. He discovers that Hilbrook's doubt is not rooted in ignorance: Hilbrook is well acquainted with the literature on immortality. Ewbert then turns away from philosophical argument and proposes that Hilbrook should have faith in immortality because human character is immortal—and then discovers that Hilbrook's doubt is a matter of conscious choice. Hilbert doubts because he *wants* to doubt! His life has been so unhappy that he looks forward to death as a time when he can cease to be conscious: "Why, man, you don't suppose that I *want* to live hereafter? . . . I'm tired. I've had enough. I want to be let alone. I don't want to do anything more, or have anything more done to me. I want to *stop*" (176–77).

Ewbert is appalled by the outburst. Though the conversations with his parishioner are beginning to exasperate him and wear him down, Ewbert decides he must continue no matter what the personal cost. He counters Hilbrook's despair of surviving into a new life by arguing that the immortal person is "a creature . . . in effect newly created" (177). Hilbrook is still not convinced. Ewbert closes the conversation in frustration. He tells

 Hilbrook, "You've presented a problem that would give any casuist pause." Later, a very weary Ewbert tells his wife that he left Hilbrook with what amounted to a jab: Hilbrook should at least hope for enough consciousness in the afterlife to enjoy his unconsciousness!

This offhand remark cracks Holbrook's defenses. When they next meet in Ewbert's study, Hilbrook says, "I see that I can't prove that we shan't live forever any more than you can prove that we shall. . . . What I want you to do *now* is to convince me, or to give me the least reason to believe, that we shan't live again on exactly the same terms that we live now." Ewbert struggles to respond. He offers scripture as a source of the assurance Holbrook seeks; scripture promises that "if we live rightly here we shall be happy in the keeping of the divine Love there. That assurance is everything to me." The reference backfires. Holbrook retorts: "It isn't to me! We are in the keeping of the divine Love here, too and are we happy?" (183–85). Ewbert casts about for a convincing argument—and fails to find one. When Hilbrook leaves, Ewbert is completely exhausted. He spends a sleepless night and is even unable to nap the next day. Then much to his surprise, when he next meets Hilbrook, the parishioner says he has become a believer. He would be happy if he woke up any morning in the other world: "You've made me want to meet my boy again" (199).

Clarence Ewbert is relieved but so debilitated by the series of conversations with his parishioner that he is forced to take a month's rest. When he returns, he is surprised to discover a wan-looking Hilbrook confined to his bed. Obviously the old man has not eaten, and though it is a cold fall day there is no fire in the heating stove. When he asks what is wrong, Ewbert discovers Hilbrook has lapsed into his old apathy. He is in bed because "I ha'n't any call to get up":

> "What was that you said about my wantin' to be alive enough to know I was dead?"
>
> "The consciousness of unconsciousness?"
>
> "Ah!" the old man assented, as with satisfaction in having got the notion right; and then he added with a certain defiance: "There ain't anything *in* that. I got to thinking it over, when you was gone, and the whole thing went to pieces. That idea don't prove anything at all, and all that we worked out of it had to go with it." (211)

Ewbert pulls up a chair next to the bed and says, "Let's see if we can't put that notion together again."

"*You* can, if you want to," the old man responds dryly; "I got no interest in it any more; 'twa'n't nothing but a metaphysical toy, anyway." With these words Hilbrook turns his face to the wall. In less than a day he dies.

In this story, Howells combines a revealing portrayal of an inept minister with a surprising critique of theological liberalism. The arguments Ewbert draws on to help Holbrook find faith are actually "mere toys of their common fancy which they had constructed together in mutual supposition" (211). His analogies to the world awakening each spring and the plants and trees blossoming anew, along with the vague assurance that God loves us, lack the assurance once provided by the powerful Calvinist faith and cosmology that pastors and parishioners shared. The shallow suppositions Ewbert offers collapse. Inadequate theology renders an unable pastor even more inept: "Religious liberalism of the sort which Ewbert espouses has irretrievably destroyed any reliable basis for conviction once and for all."[32]

Howells's fictional clergy struggle to minister effectively in a world of conflicting cultures; Mary Wilkins Freeman's pastors struggle to serve those who live in a blighted rural world that change has left behind. Freeman was born in 1862 in Randolph, Massachusetts, a village west of Boston. When she was eleven years old, her family moved to Brattleboro, Vermont. What young Mary Wilkins saw and experienced over the next decade in Brattleboro is reflected in the stories she began to write in her mid twenties. Urbanization, a shifting economy, and technological improvements that led increasingly to mechanized farming (which is possible on the rockless land in the Middle West, but not in most of New England) encouraged a massive outmigration from rural New England after the Civil War. The younger and more able, especially younger and more able men, left the area in droves to seek their fortunes elsewhere. Those left behind, like the Wilkins family, inhabited what became an economic and cultural wasteland. Between Mary Wilkins's eleventh and twenty-first birthdays, her family moved at least four times to humbler and humbler dwellings as her father went from job to job, each job paying less than the last. Sickness accompanied poverty. Mary's mother, sister, and father all succumbed; at age twenty-one, she was left with only an old aunt who was dependent on her for support.[33]

The blighted human landscape Freeman observed in Brattleboro shaped the characters who appear in her stories. In the words of Fred Lewis Pattee, they are "like plants that have sprung from sterile soil . . . : tillers of rocky hillsides, their nature warped by their poverty-stricken environment; old maids, prim and angular . . . ; workhouse inmates, forlorn children, work-worn wives of driving men."[34] They have stayed where they are because they could not go elsewhere.

Ministers who served the churches of these barren villages tended to be either young and inexperienced or old and worn. They founder in Freeman's stories because they are as inept in the changed world that Freeman observed as Howells's clerics are in the modern world that he perceived. Mr. Sands, the weak-kneed minister in the short story "Life-Everlastin'" (1891), is typical. He is completely intimidated by the strong-willed Luella Norcross, a doubting parishioner. The entire community is aware of Luella's consistent absence from church services. But they are equally aware of her good works: she often provides food and other care for the needy of the community, including Liza, an old woman who lives with her. After no little procrastination, Mr. Sands, the new parish pastor, decides he must confront Luella with her lack of orthodox believing. With no advance notice, he appears at her side door one afternoon. Old Liza who lives with Luella grins as she tells Luella who the caller is. Luella goes to the door: "There in the entry stood a young man, short and square-shouldered, with a pleasant boyish face. He looked bravely at Luella, and tried to speak with suave fluency, but his big hands twitched at the ends of his short coat sleeves."

Luella invites the pastor in. An awkward conversation punctuated by even more awkward silences ensues. They talk about the weather, the condition of several parish invalids, and recent funerals. Then, without warning, as "a blush flamed out to the roots of his curly hair," straining to make his voice sound casual but slipping "into his benediction cadences," the minister bursts out: "I don't see you at church very often, Miss Norcross." "You don't see me at all," she replies. There is a long silence. Then Luella speaks:

> "I may just as well tell you the truth, Mr. Sands . . . , an' we may just as well come to the point at once. I know what you've come for; my sister told me you was comin' to see about my not going to meetin'. Well, I'll tell you once for all, I'm just as much obliged to you, but it won't do any good. I've made up my mind I ain't goin' to meetin', an' I've got good reasons."
>
> "Would you mind giving them, Miss Norcross?"
>
> "I ain't going to argue."
>
> "But just giving me a few of your reasons wouldn't be arguing."

The young minister has now regained his composure. He has "acquired the tone which he wished." He looks at Luella "with an innocent patronage." She looks back at him; he looks very young to her:

> "The fact is . . . I'm not a believer, an' I won't be a hypocrite. That's all there is about it."
>
> The minister looked at her. It was the first time he had encountered an outspoken doubter, and it was for a minute to him as if he faced one of the veritable mediaeval dragons of the church. This simple and untutored village agnostic filled him with amazement and terror. (350–51)

Mr. Sands loses ground steadily as the conversation continues. He asks Luella if she realizes her soul's salvation depends on believing. She responds, "I'd be dreadful priggish to make goin' to heaven any reason for believin' a thing that ain't reasonable." He tries another approach: certainly she has read the New Testament, and she must agree that there was never any man like Jesus. Luella responds, "I know there wa'n't . . . , that's just the reason why the whole story don't seem sensible." Luella realizes that continuing to converse is pointless; she interrupts the exchange by asking the minister if he likes apples. He says he does, and she fills his pockets with apples. He tries to reopen the argument. She refuses. As he leaves, she says, "Try that big Porter; I guess it's meller."

Mr. Masten, the minister who calls on Anne Sparrow in Joseph Kirkland's *Zury: The Meanest Man in Spring County* (1887), is a Middle West version of the inept contender. Mr. Masten is even more of a fumbler than Mr. Sands: he fails not only as an apologist but also as a suitor. The fact that Anne Sparrow is a stronger character than this self-described "unworthy champion of a worthy cause" is apparent from the beginning of their conversation. As Masten's appeal becomes increasingly personal, he asks Anne Sparrow to kneel next to him and accompany him "to the throne of grace." She is quite aware of his ulterior motives: "Now is my time to put up the bars," she thinks to herself. She tries to deflect the minister become suitor with subtle comments. He fails to catch her drift. Finally, she says simply, "I'm a heretic!—not even so much as a Unitarian in faith." Masten redoubles his efforts, but none of his arguments gain any ground with Ms. Sparrow. He leaves having extracted a promise that she will attend his preaching services the following Sunday.

Masten crafts his sermons for the day to speak to this one "ewe-lamb" who has become both the object of his evangelism and his affection. She attends worship, hears them both, and leaves unimpressed. During their next conversation, he offers a clumsy and convoluted proposal, which serves only to convince Miss Sparrow even more that she should reject him. Mr. Masten is totally undone by her combined refusal and rebuff:

> "You are not sent to call sinners to repentance by marrying them—at least not this sinner! You orthodox saints seem to think that we heterodox sinners are only waiting for you to come along and tell us the news—to unfold your scheme of redemption that we may subscribe to it. You are mistaken—we decline your views because we know all about them and think they are *foolish*." (284; italics in the original)

At the end of this conversation, the minister retreats in defeat.

The unnamed Lutheran pastor who appears in O. E. Rolvaag's *Giants in the Earth* (1927) may be the most provocative characterization of an inept contender in American fiction. Rolvaag, who was born in Norway in 1876 and emigrated to the United States in 1896 at the age of twenty, wrote several powerful novels in Norwegian that describe the experiences of Norwegian Americans who settled in the Dakotas following the American Civil War. After he arrived in America, Rolvaag traveled immediately to South Dakota where he worked on the farm of the uncle who had paid for his passage and at a variety of other jobs. Remnants of the generation of Norwegians who were the first settlers in the Dakota Territory during the 1870s and 1880s were still alive in the 1890s. Rolvaag learned about the grim reality of an earlier frontier life from these surviving settlers. He drew on these recollections as he wrote several of his novels, including *Giants in the Earth*.[35]

Giants in the Earth describes a world far different from the romanticized frontier life pictured in most twentieth-century fiction. Per and Beret Hansa and their neighbors emigrate from Norway in the 1870s to escape poverty, only to discover even harsher misery in their sod houses scattered across the Dakota prairie. Per and Beret embody "the loneliness, the disappointments, the renunciations [of this] great army of derelicts who failed and were laid away . . . in forgotten graves."[36] Some, like Beret Hansa, break under the strain. Beret emigrates against her will when she becomes pregnant and is forced to marry Per, who carries her away from Norway because he sees no future there for them. Cut off from her family and friends, Beret feels desperately alone on the Dakota prairie—especially during the relentless winter blizzards that isolate her and her husband from all other humans. An introspective person by nature, the lonely Beret is overcome by dark and sometimes demonic beliefs that translate the old Norse gods into a retributive and unforgiving Christian deity.

After several years, a Norwegian Lutheran pastor visits the scattered settlement that includes the Hansas and their neighbors. When the pastor finishes preaching, he offers to baptize those who have not received this sacrament. The last child to be baptized is Per and Beret's son Peder. Peder is brought forward by Sorine, his godmother. The pastor asks by what name the child is called and then repeats Sorine's response in a loud voice. "Peder Victorious" resounds throughout the room. The sound of her son's middle name, given to him by his father, is too much for Beret. She forces her way through the crowd to face the pastor. "This sin shall not happen!" she shouts at him. "How can a man be *victorious* out here, where the evil one gets us all! . . . Are you all stark mad?" "Take your wife outside," the pastor commands. Per picks Beret up; she strikes out wildly. "This is the work of the devil!" she screams as he carries her out. "Now he will surely take my little boy! . . . God save us—we perish!" (378–79).

After the others leave, Per and the pastor sit and talk. Per shares the desperation and guilt he feels. Perhaps he and Beret are being punished because they conceived their oldest child before they were married. Perhaps they should never have come to America—she was opposed to going, he forced her to come with him. Per pleads with the pastor for answers: When a husband and wife cannot agree, what is the husband to do? The pastor feels the depth of Per Hansa's "aching need." But he responds impersonally—by quoting a scripture text. Per hears the text, but it does not speak to his despair. Does the man of God have no more to offer him than this? He presses the minister for a better answer. Again the pastor responds with a text, given this time with full ministerial authority: "He shall humble himself before the Lord his God, and shall take up his cross to bear it with patience." The seeming dismissal is too much for Per; he responds with a bitter laugh:

> "That's too scanty a fare for me to live on. You'd better put that kind of talk aside. . . . I ask as an ignorant man, and I must have an answer that I can understand: Did I do right or did I do wrong when I brought her out here? . . . We find other things to do out here than to carry crosses. . . . I have sweat blood over this thing—and now I'm no longer equal to it. . . . Have you ever thought what it means for a man to be in constant fear that the mother may do away with her own children—and that, besides, it may be *his* fault that she has fallen into that state of mind?" (384–85)

The pastor is sympathetic. He and Per talk on. He tries again and again to reassure the troubled man. But he has no answers.

The unnamed pastor's failure is real, but he is not entirely to blame for it. Rolvaag suggests that this minister's inability to be helpful to Per and Beret stems from the fact that he has nothing *substantive* to bring to them. The depth of their continued suffering flies in the face of the hope he offers. The scriptural analogies he cites do not hold. The resources of the faith he represents are insufficient for those who live on the Dakota prairie.[37]

The struggling pastors in novels by authors like Howells, Freeman, Kirkland, and Rolvaag are typical of the inept preachers who dominate fiction shaped by realism. The fictional ministers these American realists create often seem less able than ministers in the past. According to cultural perceptions shaped by an earlier time, they should be more capable than they are. But most of them founder, and the fault is not entirely, or even mostly, theirs. As the nineteenth century passes into the twentieth, ministers struggle not only with their own human limitations but also against social and cultural contexts that defy their faith. This radical testing brings forth a troublesome possibility: ministers may be *constitutionally* unable. Maybe the basic fault is not theirs. Maybe they founder because faith as they have been given it founders.

Anachronisms

In the summer of 1883, Henry Adams took a respite from his work as a historian to concentrate on a novel he had begun some time before. By late fall he sent the completed novel, *Esther*, to Henry Holt, his publisher. He instructed Holt to publish the book under the pseudonym Frances Snow Compton and to refrain from advertising or promoting it in any way. Adams did not want to be identified as the author because he wanted the novel to stand on its own merit. His strategy turned out to be ill-advised: *Esther* had limited appeal as a work of fiction. Two years later, in deep depression after his wife Marian committed suicide, Adams tried to suppress the novel. Fortunately he was not successful; *Esther* provides a revealing picture of the changing religious climate and emerging perceptions of upper-class American ministers in the closing decades of the nineteenth century.[38]

Ministers like Stephen Hazard, who shares center stage with the title character in Adams's novel, are anachronisms. Even when they are intellectually capable—as the sophisticated, urban, upper-class, well-educated

Episcopal clergyman Stephen is—they still falter. When the novel opens, Stephen has just become pastor of St. John's Episcopal Church, a fashionable Fifth Avenue, New York congregation. The differing, sometimes even contradictory, aspects of Stephen's personality engage and perplex both his old and his new friends. In a social setting, Stephen stands out as a broadly cultured man. "He is the most rational, unaffected parson in the world. He likes fun as much as any other man, and is interested in everything," his old friend George Strong explains (194). After graduating from college, Stephen studied at a German university and traveled throughout Europe. He even lived in Paris for a time, where he became acquainted with members of the artistic community. Stephen's library reflects his diverse interests. It includes "classics of every kind, even to a collection of Eastern literature; a mass of poetry in all languages, not a few novels; . . . an elaborate collection of illustrated works on art, Egyptian, Greek, Roman, Medieval, Mexican, Japanese, Indian, and whatever else had come in his way" (196).

But there is another—and, as it turns out, dominant—side to Stephen Hazard. When Esther Dudley begins to be attracted to the Rev. Mr. Hazard, her cousin George Strong warns her about his other side: "Even at college he would have sent us all off to the stake with a sweet smile, for the love of Christ and the glory of the English Episcopal Church. . . . At college, we used to call him St. Stephen. He had this same idea that the church was everything, and that every thing belonged to the church" (191, 194).[39] Though he is clearly an urbane and cultured person, the church and the faith are Hazard's primary loyalties.

George Strong, who warns Esther about the risk of getting close to the aptly named Mr. Hazard, is an empirical thinker who epitomizes the man of science in the late-nineteenth century. Strong is as rich as he is brilliant. His professorship reflects his genuine interest in science more than a need to earn a living. He is a professor of paleontology and, like Esther's father, at least skeptical, if not openly disbelieving, of the faith that Stephen Hazard defends. Though Mr. Dudley embraces none of its teachings personally, he still defers to the church. He keeps, but never occupies, a pew at St. John's Church. Dudley is a lawyer by profession, but a sizeable inheritance he received as a young man has made him indifferent to the practice of law. His frequent banters with George Strong reveal that Esther's aging and increasingly sickly father is still a skeptical man with a keen mind and a sharp wit.

Esther Dudley is both socially and intellectually her father's daughter. Her mother died when Esther was ten years old, and for the past fifteen years she has been "absolute mistress of her father's house." Esther is a well-educated but not a disciplined scholar. She is acquainted with contemporary knowledge in a variety of fields. Like her father and her cousin, Esther is a free thinker—a comfortable agnostic who is naturally skeptical of the claims of orthodox religion. As all the men in the novel discover, Esther is a strong woman, accustomed to having her own way and unwilling to be controlled or dominated by anyone.

During the time he lives in Paris, Stephen Hazard becomes acquainted with Mr. Wharton, the artist he has now engaged to complete the decorative murals in St. John's Church. The very talented Wharton is quite equal to the assignment. He also knows how to get on with his patrons: when he becomes aware of Esther Dudley's artistic ability and notes her interest in Stephen Hazard, he invites her to paint the figure of St. Cecelia in one of the murals. And she happily accepts.

Though Esther has little sympathy for the faith Stephen Hazard represents, and Stephen has only a shallow appreciation of Esther Dudley's agnostic convictions, they find themselves more and more attracted to each other. The relationship soon poses dilemmas for both of them. Esther realizes she cannot have a relationship with Stephen apart from his faith and his church—both of which repel her. Stephen realizes that his congregation will never accept the free-thinking, agnostic Esther as his wife.

Stephen's developing relationship with Esther brings out his dominant side. She represents a kind of person he must convince if he is to be a success at St. John's: "Hazard's instinct told him that his success, to be lasting, depended largely on overcoming the indifference of people like the Dudleys" (217). Esther and her father and George Strong are prizes to be won for the church. But Stephen soon realizes he has underrated the strengths of his contenders—especially Esther. When Esther's father becomes seriously ill, Stephen offers to stay with her "on the chance of your needing help." She tells him she can get along and sends him away: "Do not feel alarmed about me. Women have more strength than men." After he leaves, the minister is puzzled: "Most women would have asked him for religious help and consolation. She had gently put his offers aside. . . . 'I almost think . . . that she could give a lesson in strength to me. It seems rather unnecessary, my offering to give in to her'" (263). Stephen similarly misreads Esther's agnosticism; he assumes it is a weakness—an emptiness that he can fill with Christian faith. As William Merrill Decker observes in his study of Henry Adams's writings, Hazard fails to see the "conviction" with which she maintains it.

The frustrated lover becomes desperate. In a move that that seems like a breach of pastoral ethics, shortly after her father dies, Stephen tells the mourning Esther that he loves her. With little regard for her vulnerability as a mourner, Stephen presses Esther repeatedly to tell him that she loves him. She finally capitulates—and immediately warns him against pursuing the relationship: "You do not know me! You must not love me! I shall ruin your life! I shall never satisfy you!" He ignores her warning. "Promise to love me," he reassures her, "and I will take care of the rest" (267, 268).

Esther's protest is prophetic. Taking care of the rest is not as simple as Hazard envisions in his moment of passion. Esther is neither a weak, dependent woman nor a person without religious conviction. Their relationship is not developing according to the plan Stephen envisions. After a week, he finds Esther "not only unaffected by his influence but actually slipping more and more from his control" (294). He begins to be alarmed—for good reason. The Sunday morning after she confesses her love for Stephen, Esther attends worship at St. John's. As she listens to Stephen read the service he becomes Mr. Hazard—even to her. She looks around at the gathered congregation and is overcome by a depressing reality:

> He belonged not to her but to the world; a thousand people had rights of property to him, soul and body, and called their claim religion. What had she to do with it? Parts of the service jarred on her ear. She began to take a bitter pleasure in thinking that she had nothing, not even religious ideas, in common with these people who came between her and her lover. (271)

When the service ends, Esther rushes home. There she confesses her dilemma to a friend: "Catherine! What am I to do? I don't like church" (272).

Stephen not only wants to succeed with Esther, he *needs* to succeed with her. His conviction that "all human energies belonged to the church is on trial," and if it breaks down "in a test so supreme as that of marriage, the blow would go far to prostrate him forever" (290).[40] But Esther is not willing to compromise her beliefs to become a trophy that testifies to Stephen's evangelical prowess. The impossibility of their situation becomes inescapable to Esther. Esther not only dislikes church, she realizes that the church is the third party in a triangle with her and her lover. As much as Stephen may want to, he cannot give himself unreservedly to her: "He believes in his church more than he does in me. If I can't believe in it, he will have to give me up. . . . He must give me up, if I am jealous of his congregation, and won't believe what he preaches" (273). She tries again and again to make Stephen understand her feelings and respect her beliefs, but he is too single-minded to give up his relentless pursuit of her. In desperation, Esther flees with Catherine and her cousin George to Niagara Falls. At night, alone in her room, she is overwhelmed with feeling as she listens to the water flowing over the falls: "'If he could only hear it as I do,' and of course 'he' was Mr. Hazard; 'how he would feel it!' She felt the tears roll down her face as she listened to the voice of the waters and knew that they were telling her a different secret from any that Hazard could ever hear. 'He will think it is the church talking!'" (314). For Stephen, every human experience is a triangle that includes God.

The next day, Stephen arrives at the hotel where Esther is staying. He has followed her to make one last, desperate attempt to convince her to marry him. Almost as soon as they begin to talk, they both recognize that the differences that separate them are not negotiable. Esther is now fully conscious that Stephen's love for her has *always* been conditional—that he has always expected she will recognize his obligations to God and his calling as primary and that she will modify, or at least restrain, her thinking and behavior to conform to his and his church's beliefs and expectations. Esther tells him once again that such a relationship is impossible for her. He pleads with her to understand the nature of his calling and how that limits the commitment he can make to her. "Ah, be generous!" she responds: "It is not my fault if you and your profession are one; and of all things on earth, to be half-married must be the worst torture" (331).

They now throw off all restraints. He demands to know why she has run away:

> "Well! I will tell you. It was because, after a violent struggle with myself, I found I could not enter a church without a feeling of—of hostility. I can only be friendly by staying away from it. I felt as though it were part of a different world. You will be angry at me for saying it, but I never saw you conduct a service without feeling as though you were a priest in a Pagan temple, centuries apart from me." (332)

Surely she can disregard the ceremonies, he responds, "and feel the truths behind them." His statement only takes Esther deeper into the mire: "The ceremonies are picturesque and I could get used to them," she admits, "but the doctrines are more Pagan than the ceremonies." His retort is even more personal than hers. He warns her that her lack of Christian faith means she has no hope of ever seeing again those she has loved in this life—an obvious reference to the recent loss of her father. Esther feels the cheap shot: "Why must the church always appeal to my weakness and never to my strength!" At that moment, Esther's cousin George Strong enters the room. Stephen directs his anger at Strong momentarily and then leaves Esther with a bitter forecast: "I am beaten. You have driven me away, and I will never trouble you again, till, in your days of suffering and anguish you send to me for hope and consolation. Till then—God bless you!" (334–35).

Henry Adams's novel is much more than a story about two people who discover they are personally incompatible. The profoundly different beliefs that separate Stephen Hazard and Esther Dudley reflect their different worlds—his premodernist and hers modernist. The different priority each gives to God finally undermines the affection they feel for each other. In his literary biography of Adams, William Merrill Decker points out that Adams's characterization of Stephen Hazard shows that Adams "had begun to develop an active, principled antipathy to Protestant claims, a repugnance for much of the substance and application of church dogma."[41] Hazard embodies an arrogance Adams perceives in the Christian church's claims. He is unwilling to enter into a true *dialogue* about beliefs with someone who is not a Christian believer. In conversations with agnostics like Esther Dudley and George Strong, Hazard advocates his own beliefs dogmatically but doesn't listen seriously to others' beliefs. He sees no reason to listen; only Christians are true believers.

Faith for Stephen Hazard is an institutionalized dogmatic reality. The church's claims are absolute and normative. *True* believers belong (commit themselves) to the church and accept the church's faith. Faith for Esther is personal and tentative. Her refusal to capitulate to Stephen's demands is much more than a feminist affirmation—though it is that. She is baffled by Stephen and his congregation's insistence that she must conform her personal believing to the church's beliefs to be an acceptable wife. She insists that beliefs are a personal matter and remain so even in marriage. In a conversation with her friend Catherine the day after she and Stephen confess their love to each other, Esther already senses that holding beliefs that are different from Stephen's and his church's beliefs will make it impossible for her to function as Stephen's wife. He has no personal identity separate from his identity as a minister-believer, and if she becomes his wife, neither would she.

Stephen Hazard is an anachronism in the nineteenth-century world reflected in Henry Adams's novel.[42] While Stephen is well acquainted with the artistic and scientific perspectives others espouse in the novel, there is no evidence that his broad acquaintance with contemporary culture has any substantive impact on his beliefs. His doctrinal theology binds him to a *specific* past; it is conceptually frozen. But this rigid commitment does not seem problematic to believers like Stephen. He thinks the historical faith of the church is absolute truth and that it has absolute authority for *all* time.[43]

Esther and her friends are modernists. They advocate a "scientific," contemporary approach to believing. What they believe is real at any given moment in time stems from the empirical knowledge available to them *at that moment*. That knowledge is always approximate and tentative; it never embodies absolute truth. Their "belief" involves them in a continuing search for truth rather than in a defense of absolute truth—as George Strong explains when he bids Esther, "Ask me whether science is true!" She complies, and asks:

> "Is science true?"
> "No!"
> "Then why do you believe in it?"
> "I don't believe in it."
> "Then why do you belong to it?"
> "Because I want to help in making it truer." (284)

Ministers like Stephen Hazard are quite different from people like George Strong. They represent ways of thinking and believing and living that have become obsolete among citizens of the modern world. Hazard embodies the perspectives of the Scottish realism I discuss at the beginning of this chapter. The world as he sees it is simply a theater for the activity of God. Faithful humans look for the hand of God in every experience and relationship. Empiricists like Esther Dudley and her friends engage directly with the people and things around them. Esther Dudley wants a direct and exclusive marriage relationship with Stephen Hazard. But Stephen can't enjoy or experience people or things simply in and of themselves. No one and no thing is an end. To him, everything and everyone is a means to an end. They all gain significance only as he can relate them to God (as he and the church perceive God). When Esther is unwilling to submit to Stephen's beliefs, he can't include her in his world. He can't join her time, and she won't join his.[44]

The image of ministers as anachronisms develops as the years pass. In some novels, the traits that make a minister an anachronism are more personal than social. In Ellen Glasgow's novel *Virginia* (1913), for example,

Gabriel Pendleton who serves St. James Episcopal Church in the southern town of Dinwiddie lives his life wholly governed by the memory of what he once was as a military officer in the Civil War. As he ages, he continues to imagine himself as a battlefield hero. Pendleton's anachronistic self-perception has deadly results. One night when he is out walking, two men accost him. Foolishly, he views them through his past prowess; he assumes not only that he can defend himself but also that he can do them in. In the reality of the present, the minister is no match for the assailants, and they kill him.

The Rev. Joseph Mahon, the Episcopal priest in William Faulkner's *Soldiers' Pay* (1926), is a Victorian adrift in a post–World War I world. When friends bring his mortally wounded and severely disfigured son Donald home after the Armistice, Mr. Mahon is unable to cope with the reality Donald represents. Though Donald is obviously dying from wounds he has suffered in the war, and his face is so contorted by scars that no one can bear to look at him, his minister father keeps insisting that Donald will recover and marry Cicely, his fiancée. When Donald does die, his father is no more able to deal with the fact of his death than he could with the fact of his life. The army friends who bring Donald home and stay on with his family for a time accept the "soldiers' pay" Donald represents. They are far more capable of coping with the reality of his injury than is the anachronistic Joseph Mahon.

Harold Frederic's *The Damnation of Theron Ware* (1896) offers what I think is at once the most convincing and the most damning portrayal of the minister as an anachronism in American fiction. In fact, I think Frederic's novel is one of the most significant novels in American literature.[45] Frederic was a product of central New York where *Theron Ware* is set. He began his writing career in Utica, New York, as a newspaper reporter and editor. Frederic's experience in the newspaper world served him well when he became a novelist. He brought a reporter's skill to his fiction writing. Like Theodore Dreiser and other American naturalists, he used the naturalistic technique of documentation to authenticate the fictional characters he created. Frederic spent five years painstakingly researching and authenticating the material he used in *Theron Ware*:[46]

> After I had got the people of my novel grouped together in my mind, I set myself the task of knowing everything they knew. All four of them happened to be specialists in different professions, the task has been tremendous. For instance, one of them is a biologist, who, among other

> things, experiments on Lubbock's and Darwin's lines. Although these pursuits are merely mentioned, I got up masses of stuff on bees and cross-fertilization of plants. I had to teach myself all the details of a Methodist minister's work, obligations, and daily routine, and all the machinery of his church. In the case of Father Forbes, who is a great deal more of a pagan than a simple-minded Christian, and loves luxury and learning, I have waded in Assyriology and Schopenhauer, pored over palimpsests and pottery, and in order to write understandingly about a musician who figures in the story, I bored a professional friend to death to get the technical stuff.[47]

The novel begins on the concluding day of the local Methodist Annual Conference, an annual gathering of ministers and lay delegates that culminates with the reading of appointments—churches the ministers will serve during the coming year. Frederic's description of the tense group of clergy waiting to hear their names called suggests a portentous decline in competence among them:

> The effect of these faces as a whole was toward goodness, candor, and imperturbable self-complacency rather than learning or mental astuteness, and curiously enough it wore its pleasantest aspect on the countenances of the older men. The impress of zeal and moral worth seemed to diminish by regular gradations as one passed to younger faces, and among the very beginners, who had been ordained only within the past day or two, this decline was peculiarly marked. (3)

Theron, who is one of the younger, less-impressive members of the conference, has nonetheless had the honor of preaching at one of the many worship services held during the conference. After that service, several of his colleagues compliment him on his sermon. Though their compliments represent politeness more than genuine esteem, Theron is full of confidence that he will be appointed to Tecumseh, one of the area's largest and most-sought-after churches. But when the bishop reads the list of appointments, one of the oldest members of the conference is assigned to this prized pulpit. Theron is appointed to "miserable Octavius," one of the smallest and most-troublesome congregations in the area. As his appointment is announced, Theron can't fathom why the bishop has given him such a lowly assignment.

When the conference adjourns, Theron encourages his wife Alice to make the best of their appointment. Octavious, however, turns out to be even more miserable than Theron anticipates. A meeting with the church's three trustees on Wednesday of his first week in Octavius reveals what the Octavius congregation expects of their minister and his wife. Brother Loren Pierce acts as spokesperson for the group. There will be no milk deliveries to the parsonage on Sunday, he announces; it is not fitting for anyone to work on the Sabbath, especially at the minister's house. The cheery flowers Alice inserted into the hat she wore to the church service the previous Sunday will have to go: "'We walk here,' [he continues], eying the minister with a sour regard, 'in a meek an' humble spirit, in the straight an' narrow way which leadeth unto life. . . . No new-fangled notions can go down here. Your wife'd better take them flowers out of her bunnit afore next Sunday.'" The "pale-faced," knit-browed Theron agrees to see that she does. Brother Pierce then continues with words that dash Theron's dreams of becoming an erudite preacher: "Another thing: We don't want no book-learnin' or dictionary words in our pulpit. . . . Some folks may stomach 'em; we won't. Them two sermons o' yours—p'haps they'd do down in some city place, but they're like your wife's bunnit here—they're too flowery to suit us. What we want to hear is the plain, old-fashioned Word of God" (27).

In the weeks that follow, Theron chafes under the restrictions imposed on him by the trustees. But one day as he is out for a walk, he discovers another side of Octavius. As he makes his way along the edge of the town's Irish neighborhood, he comes upon a crowd following four men carrying a mortally injured man on a litter. Someone explains what has happened. The injured man is employed at Jerry Madden's wagon shop. Earlier in the day, Madden asked the worker to trim dead limbs out of the top of an elm tree in front of his house. He slipped and fell to the ground, breaking nearly every bone in his body. When the procession reaches the injured man's house, a messenger is dispatched, not for a doctor as Theron anticipates but for Father Forbes, the local priest. Within minutes, an attractive, well-dressed woman appears, followed by the priest. As Father Forbes administers extreme unction to the dying man, Theron is captivated by the scene—the priest dipping his finger in the oil and tracing patterns on the dying man's head, the smell of burning incense, the sound of the priest's Latin chant.

Theron's encounter with the mysterious Father Forbes and the elegant Celia Madden spurs his resolve to become something more than an ordinary Methodist minister. When he returns home, he decides to write what he believes will become the authoritative work on the origins of the biblical patriarch, Abram, among the Chaldeans. Unfortunately, Theron cannot begin the work he projects because he has no information on his chosen subject. But he has heard that the priest in Octavius is a very learned man. Theron decides to pay a call on Father Forbes. When he arrives at the rectory and announces who he is, the housekeeper invites him in. He finds the priest having supper with his good friend, the biologist and physician Dr. Ledsmar. They invite Theron to join them at the table, and soon he is telling them about his proposed book. The conversation begins well, but it is quickly apparent that Theron is not in any way the equal of these two men who constitute the intellectual community in Octavius. When they retire to an upstairs library for cigars, they continue to discuss Theron's book. Dr. Ledsmar can be very helpful, Father Forbes tells Theron: "There is perhaps not another man in the country who knows Assyriology so thoroughly as our friend here, Dr. Ledsmar." The doctor protests the compliment but then goes on to reveal it is justified:

> I follow only at a distance—a year or two behind. But I daresay I can help you. You are quite welcome to anything I have: my books cover the ground pretty well up to last year. Delitzsch is very interesting, but Baudissin's 'Studien zur Semitischen Religionsgeschichte' would come closer to what you need. There are several other important Germans—Schrader, Bunsen, Duncker, Hommel, and so on. (68)

Theron responds that unfortunately he doesn't read German. "That's a pity," the doctor replies, "because they do the best work." The best work in English is Sayce: "I daresay you know him." Theron replies mournfully, "I don't seem to know anyone." After this comment, "the others exchange glances."[48]

Theron's efforts to develop a relationship with the priest's woman, Celia Madden, are equally awkward. He is aware that gossip among the Protestants in the town suggests that Celia and her priest have an "inappropriate" relationship—though no one has been able to confirm the accusation. These salacious rumors make Theron even more determined to pursue a relationship with the intriguing Celia. He hears her playing the organ in the Catholic church one evening and steals inside, thinking she will not notice his presence. But she does, and much to his surprise, invites him to walk home with her. As they walk along in the dark, Theron shares his admiration for Dr. Ledsmar. Celia tells him that she despises "that Doctor and his heartless, bloodless science." Theron hardly knows how to respond. After an awkward silence, he says, "I can readily see how such a cold, material, and infidel influence as that must shock and revolt an essentially religious temperament like yours." Celia replies that she is not religious in the usual way that Christians use the word; she's a Pagan, "an out-and-out Greek." "Why, I had supposed that you were full-blooded Irish," Theron responds. Celia tries again, "I take more stock in Plato than I do in Peter." He still doesn't get her drift.

Some days later when a promised parcel of books from Dr. Ledsmar arrives at the parsonage, Theron chooses to read first Renan's *Recollections of My Youth*, a memoir in which the author describes how he lost his faith. The innocent minister quickly imbibes Renan's apostasy as his own. This growing disbelief amplifies the stress Theron already experienced between the ministry to which he is committed and the doubt that now threatens to overwhelm him. The tension soon proves too much for Theron. He suffers a nervous collapse.

After he recovers from his collapse, Theron visits Dr. Ledsmar to talk about the books he has borrowed. During their conversation, Theron hints that Celia and Father Forbes appear to have a relationship that is inappropriate between a priest and a parishioner. Ledsmar will not be drawn into such a conversation. He feigns a sudden, painful attack of rheumatism in his right shoulder. Noticing the grimace on the doctor's face and that his right hand hangs helplessly, Theron graciously leaves. After Theron is out of sight, Ledsmar opens the door to his house with the supposedly affected right hand. He goes into his laboratory and carefully picks up a lizard "with a coiling, sinuous tail and a pointed, evil head." A "grim smile" comes across his face as he looks at the lizard. "Yes, you are the type," Ledsmar says to the lizard. "Your name isn't Johnny any more. It's the Rev. Theron Ware" (226).

Soon after Theron's faux pas with Dr. Ledsmar, the area Methodists hold a camp meeting. On the fifth day of that gathering, a weary Theron decides to take a walk in the woods. Much to his surprise, he discovers that the Octavius Catholics are having a picnic not far from the Methodists' camp meeting. Theron quickly notices the contrast between the two groups: instead of praying prayers and singing hymns like the Methodists, the Catholic are drinking beer and dancing. Theron spies Father Forbes and Celia Madden, walking arm in arm. They invite him to join the party and send someone to bring lager beer for all of them. Their laughing and drinking is interrupted suddenly by an ugly incident. Celia's drunken half-brother Theodore staggers into the group and accuses her of being too intimate with Father Forbes: "You can at least keep your hands off the priest." Theron immediately comes to Celia's defense and is rewarded with a similar attack: "Why don't you leave our girls alone?" Theodore barks out. "You're a married man into the bargain." Father Forbes's hand clamped over Theodore's mouth stops the outburst.

After the incident with Theodore, an embarrassed Celia invites Theron to take a walk with her. As they walk alone, Theron pleads with Celia to dissociate him from the role of a minister. He asks her to regard him simply as a man. He tells her how cramped he feels, both as a minister and in his marriage to Alice. Celia senses where the conversation may go and asks Theron to move on to some other topic. He misses her cue. He goes on to suggest that there is no suitable person for her to marry in Octavius, that perhaps she will go to Europe and marry some nobleman. Celia responds that needing to be someone's wife is not how she thinks of herself: "That is an old-fashioned idea . . . that women must belong to somebody, as if they were curios or statues, or race-horses" (254). As they walk along through the sunlight, Theron notices Celia's "disordered hair" and begins to fumble with one of the ribbons that falls from her hat. Suddenly he spies a young lad with a gun, carrying two dead gray squirrels. "Heavens above!" he groans. "Know him?" Celia asks. Theron is mortified at their being seen: "He spades my—wife's garden. . . . He works in the law office of one of my trustees." Celia gazes at him, the color gone out of his face. He looks like a guilty schoolboy. "Somehow, I fear that I do not like you quite so much just now, my friend," she says (260). She realizes that Theron is not only completely lacking in culture, she sees also that he is not much of a man. Determined now that this meeting will be their last, she lets him kiss her. In her mind, it is a kiss good-bye; in his, it signifies that she loves him.

Some days later, Theron discovers by accident that Celia has taken the train to New York City. He envisions her trip as an opportunity for a tryst. He tells Alice a made-up story about needing to go to Albany on church business and follows Celia. After spending the night in New York and discovering that Father Forbes has gone to the city with Celia, Theron finds out the number of her hotel room and boldly knocks at the door. Thinking he is Father Forbes, she bids him enter. The scene that follows is painful. Celia tells Theron that she and Father Forbes have come to New York to seek the assistance of a lawyer because her hot-headed half-brother has gotten himself into serious trouble. Theron's presence is extremely inappropriate; she asks him to leave. He insists on staying and hints that the two of them could go off together. The bold suggestion is too much for Celia; she commands him to sit down. It is time for him to face reality:

> "We were disposed to like you very much when we first knew you," [Celia tells Theron]. . . .
>
> "We liked you . . . because you were unsophisticated and delightfully fresh and natural. Somehow we took it for granted you would stay so. But that is just what you didn't do—just what you hadn't the sense to try to do. Instead, we found you inflating yourself with all sorts of egotisms and vanities. We found you presuming on the friendships that had been mistakenly extended to you. . . . I can [now] understand that all the while you really fancied that you were expanding, growing, in all directions. What you took to be improvement was degeneration. . . .
>
> "It is all in a single word, Mr. Ware," she said in low tones. "I speak for others as well as myself, mind you—we find that you are a bore. (321–23)

At this point, Father Forbes enters the room. Celia explains that the obviously distraught Theron discovered her name in the registry by accident. Theron's explanation simply adds to the awkwardness: "I just dropped in to make a friendly call." The priest looks at the minister sharply: "Then you have a talent for the inopportune amounting to positive genius." After he leaves Celia's hotel room, the despondent Theron seeks haven with the Soulsbys, the pragmatic couple who raised the funds to pay off his church's mortgage. Once inside their house, he completely collapses. Though in a few weeks he regains his health, he is forced to leave the ministry.[49]

Harold Frederic's Theron Ware is an even more pathetic anachronism than Henry Adams's Stephen Hazard. Stephen doesn't fit the new age in which he finds himself, but he is at least cultured and capable. Theron Ware is neither. Theron's fumbling reflects not only his own personal shortcomings but also the ineptness and obsolescence of the Methodists he represents, and probably, in Frederic's view, of other Protestants as well. Sophisticated Roman Catholics like Father Forbes escape Frederic's general condemnation only because modernism is still a permitted viewpoint among them. But even that will end in 1907 (less than a decade after *Theron Ware* is published) when Pope Pius X declares modernism unacceptable as a theological approach for Roman Catholics.

Ministers like Theron Ware were not simply victims of their own foibles. While some like Theron were exceedingly unable, the credibility of all ministers was compromised by the social and cultural changes that engulfed American society during the last half of the nineteenth and the beginning of the twentieth centuries. Even the most capable were often not able to meet the demands of the new time. As the intellectual and social revolutions associated with modernism swept through American society, they struggled to stand their ground. In reality, many of them were pushed aside and left behind. And in the minds of some, perhaps many, of their contemporaries, so was the God they represented.[50]

IX

FLAWED DIVINES

Radical Images (2)

Radical cultural images of Protestant clergy reflected in late-nineteenth- and early-twentieth-century fiction mirror not only the diminishing social status and waning authority of clergy in American society but also the declining quality of contemporary ministers.[1] Contemporary sources indicate that the quality of candidates seeking ordination to the ministry weakened significantly after the Civil War. Ann Douglas cites several late-nineteenth-century observers who bemoan the decrease in the quality of candidates for the ministry. Notable among them is President Charles Eliot of Harvard, who in 1883 observed that "the ministry had declined greatly in the preceding forty years principally because educated men no longer found the 'intellectual qualities' in clergy which they expected in a guide." Eliot goes on to note that "multitudes of educated men" now question the intellectual abilities of ministers.[2]

Two likely related trends support Eliot's observations: fewer of those enrolling in seminaries were graduates of leading universities after the Civil War, and a greater proportion of seminary students came from smaller denominational colleges. In an article published in 1904, Everett T. Tomlinson also noted this phenomenon: the total number of graduates from Yale doubled between 1850 and 1895, but the number who entered the ministry during the same period fell by more than 60 percent.[3] The preferences of contemporary church members may even have encouraged the declining quality of contemporary clergy. As early as 1859, the Rev. C. van Santvoord, president of the General Synod of the Reformed Church in America, complained that "churches of the present times . . . show . . . a proclivity toward calling young men in preference to teachers of riper experience and more solid attainments."[4] Church members likely found these younger, less-seasoned ministers more eager to please—and willing to serve for less money.

Characters in popular fiction also lament the declining quality of candidates entering the ministry. In the early pages of Winston Churchill's novel *The Inside of the Cup* (1914), the entrepreneur Eldon Parr observes that people who want to do something significant no longer choose to become ministers; they choose a career in business (40, 41). One of the characters in William J. Dawson's *A Prophet of Babylon* (1908) offers a similarly pessimistic assessment of the contemporary clergyman's role in society and the diminishing quality of those seeking to become ministers (211–12). In Harold Bell Wright's *The Calling of Dan Matthews* (1909) when the fictional Dan Matthews leaves the ministry for what he believes will be a much more important career in business, he describes his disappointment with the ministry in great detail (209, 346).[5]

When these observations by educational and ecclesiastical authorities and by characters in popular fiction are viewed in the context of the social and intellectual shifts I discuss in chapter 8, it is not surprising to discover that portrayals of ministers as weak and ineffective humans abounded in literary fiction during the last quarter of the nineteenth century and the first quarter of the twentieth. If becoming a minister means being relegated to a precarious and even impotent social position, only those who are willing to accept such a diminutive role are likely to become ministers. And when intellectual developments make believing more difficult to sustain, it is not surprising to discover that some ministers only pretended to believe—and that others became out-and-out deceivers to take advantage of those foolish enough to trust them.

Weak and Impotent Men

Putnam May, who appears in James K. Hosmer's *The Thinking Bayonet* (1865), is one of the earliest examples of a minister who is a weak man. Hosmer's novel traces the experiences of four friends, beginning with their years as students at Havenbridge College and continuing into the Civil War. The contrast between brash Herbert Lee, who is the hero of the novel, and faint-hearted May, who becomes a minister, stands at the center of the story. After

Lee is expelled from college for misbehaving, he goes west to seek his fortune. He finds work as a miner. When a cave-in after an explosion buries a coworker, Lee risks his life to rescue the man from the rubble. During the Civil War, Lee shows similar courage. He enlists in the Union army and distinguishes himself on the battlefield, especially during one engagement when he continues to fight even after he is seriously wounded. May, the minister, is Lee's opposite in every respect. He is a small, unimpressive man who cringes in the face of every challenge. Even during their student days, May recognizes that he is a lesser man than Lee: "He towers over me—little puny fellow that I am!" (15).[6]

In *Sevenoaks* (1875), J. G. Holland presents the Rev. Solomon Snow as a typical example of the weak men who served as ministers in New England factory towns after the Civil War. Snow's antagonist in the novel, the unscrupulous Robert Belcher, owns the mill, the local water source, and almost every other significant piece of property in Sevenoaks. Belcher also controls all of the institutions in Sevenoaks: the town meetings and the poorhouse, as well as the churches and their ministers.

Solomon Snow, the weak-kneed pastor in Sevenoaks, offers only feeble protests against the injustices Robert Belcher perpetrates. When Miss Keziah Butterworth confronts Belcher about the deplorable conditions that Belcher's handpicked overseer Tom Buffin maintains in the poorhouse, Belcher refuses to take any steps to force him to improve them. Miss Butterworth turns hopefully to Mr. Snow. As a woman, she cannot speak or vote in the town meeting, but the minister can. Will he? Mr. Snow equivocates. He explains that it would be pointless to oppose Mr. Belcher in the town meeting; everyone is intimidated by him, no one would vote against him: "I wish it were otherwise; but we must take things as they air." This revealing phrase galls Mrs. Snow as much as it does Miss Butterworth. The two women press the minister to take action—but he is afraid:

> "To take things as they air," was a cardinal aphorism in Mr. Snow's budget of wisdom. It was a good starting-point for any range of reasoning, and exceedingly useful to a man of limited intellectual and little moral courage. The real truth of the case had dawned upon Miss Butterworth. . . . [Mr. Snow] was afraid of offending Robert Belcher, for not only did his church need repairing, but his salary was in arrears, and the wolf that had chased so many up the long hill to what was popularly known as Tom Buffum's Boarding House he had heard many a night, while his family was sleeping, howling with menace in the distance. (18)

Near the end of the novel, Mr. Snow does finally take a public stand against Belcher in a town meeting. But this late-in-the-day protest reflects little courage; by the time Snow speaks out, the unscrupulous factory owner has already been exposed and fled.

Mr. Pollard, the local pastor in Mary Wilkins Freeman's "A Village Singer" (1891), is even wimpier than Mr. Snow. When Freeman's story opens, Candace Whitcomb, the lead soprano in the village church choir for forty years, has been summarily dismissed from her position. The entire choir stops by on Thursday evening to give Miss Whitcomb what she presumes is a surprise party—the first ever for her. After they leave, Candace discovers a photograph album they have left behind. A letter inside thanks her for her long service and informs her that she is no longer needed. Three days later on a warm, spring Sunday, her replacement, Alma Way, sings her first hymn as lead soprano. Miss Way has unexpected competition: a warm breeze drifting through the open windows of the church building bears the surprisingly strong voice of Candace Whitcomb into the sanctuary. Candace is seated at the parlor organ in her cottage next door to the church, singing a competing hymn with power and purpose. She is determined to prove that she can still sing as well as the younger woman employed to replace her. Each hymn during the service at the church draws another competing rendition from Candace.

After the worship service concludes, Mr. Pollard, the local minister, is dispatched to restrain the errant soprano. He calls at her next-door cottage immediately after the service. They exchange the usual pleasantries, and the diffident preacher comes haltingly to the point of his visit:

> "Well, Miss Whitcomb, I suppose I—may as well come to—the point. There was—a little—matter I wished to speak to you about. I don't suppose you were—at least I can't suppose you were—aware of it, but—this morning, during the singing by the choir, you played and—sung a little too—loud. That is, with—the windows open. It—disturbed us—a little. I hope you won't feel hurt—my dear Miss Candace, but I knew you would rather I would speak of it, for I knew—you would be more disturbed than anybody else at the idea of such a thing."
>
> Candace did not raise her eyes; she looked as if his words might sway her through the window. "I ain't disturbed at it," said she. "I did it on purpose; I meant to." (24)

The wimpy minister tries repeatedly to reason with the discharged soprano—to no avail. In desperation, he suggests they kneel and seek the guidance of the Lord. Candace refuses: "I don't see any use prayin' about it. . . . I don't think the Lord's got much to do with it, anyhow" (29). As the hymns are sung during the afternoon service, the minister's failure is obvious: during each of them, Candace Whitcomb raises her voice in discord. During the evening service, she is silent. There is no more need to compete; her rival has withdrawn.

In novels published after the turn of the century, the weak minister's inability to confront his antagonists often has more serious consequences. In *A Circuit Rider's Wife* (1910), Corra Harris offers an angry semiautobiographical description of the abuse her self-effacing circuit rider husband suffers during thirty years of ministry. An upper-class Episcopalian by birth, Mrs. Harris is shocked by the stark severity of life in a Methodist parsonage "where every piece of furniture . . . contradicts every other piece, each having been contributed by rival women or rival committees in the society" (137). Unmatched chairs ring the dining table; threadbare church-aisle carpet deemed no longer good enough for the church sanctuary stretches down the parsonage hallway. But Mrs. Harris is most troubled by the mistreatment her preacher husband William receives at the hands of the Methodist congregations he serves. They reward William's relentless humility by repeatedly taking advantage of him. William never protests the humiliation and privation he suffers. As his life is about to end, his wife is overcome by sadness and regret as she gazes at his wasted form: he has "a weary look [she thinks] . . . like that of a man who has made a long journey in vain. This is always the last definition the itinerancy writes upon the faces of its superannuates. They are unhappy, mortified, like honorable men who have failed in business" (300).

The compliant Methodist minister in Willa Cather's *The Song of the Lark* (1915) is equally pitiful. Pastor Kronberg serves the Swedish Methodist Church in Moonstone, Colorado. Cather describes Mr. Kronberg as a diffident and always nervous man who "coughed behind his hand, and contracted his brows. His face threatened at every moment to break into a smile of foolish excitement" (5). Mr. Kronberg and his family are undone again and again by his chronic need to please: "When he spoke to his family about matters of conduct, it was usually with a regard for keeping up appearances. . . . The fear of the tongue, that terror of little towns, is usually felt more keenly by the minister's family than by other households. Whenever the Kronbergs wanted to do anything, even to buy a new carpet, they had to take counsel together as to whether people would talk" (159, 165).

Cather offers what is perhaps her most caustic portrayal of a weak cleric in her description of Lars Larsen in *The Song of the Lark*. Larsen makes only a cameo appearance in the novel, but it is sufficient to establish him as one of the weakest candidates for ministry in American fiction:

> Lars was the fourth son, and he was born lazy. He seemed to bear the mark of overstrain on the part of his parents. Even in his cradle he was an example of physical inertia; anything to lie still. When he was a growing boy, his mother had to drag him out of bed every morning, and he had to be driven to his chores. At school he had a model "attendance record," because he found getting his lessons easier than farm work. He was the only one of the family who went through the high school, and by the time he graduated he had already made up his mind to study for the ministry, because it seemed to him the least laborious of all callings. In so far as he could see, it was the only business in which there was practically no competition, in which a man was not all the time pitted against other men who were willing to work themselves to death. His father stubbornly opposed Lars's plan, but after keeping the boy home for a year and finding how useless he was on the farm, he sent him to a theological seminary—as much to conceal his laziness from the neighbours as because he did not know what else to do with him. (208–9)

Christopher Malling, the Episcopal priest who is the focus of Basil King's novel *Pluck* (1928), is an even more pathetic cleric than his fictional Methodist colleagues—though his capitulation to servility comes, at least initially, as a complete surprise to his family and friends. When he first meets the woman who becomes Mrs. Malling, Christopher is a "handsome, clever, lighthearted Harvard graduate." Those who know Christopher well are certain that he is destined to become a highly successful attorney. But, for some unknown reason that he never shares, Christopher suddenly turns his back on that future. He renounces the study of law and begins to prepare for the Episcopal priesthood. When he graduates from seminary, he commits himself to a life of poverty and accepts a call to Walmer, a small coastal parish.

Mrs. Malling, who was raised in a prosperous Massachusetts family, probably suffers most from her husband's decision. The strains of living as a poor minister's wife and of bearing five children in quick succession bring on a mild stroke at an early age. The Mallings' children are a mixed blessing. The two oldest are a credit to their parents: as an adolescent, the firstborn, Felicia, assumes her invalid mother's responsibilities in the household; the eldest son follows in his father's early footsteps and studies law. The three youngest children are constant burdens: one son is a ne'er-do-well who is caught stealing an automobile and ends up in jail; the other son is developmentally disabled and requires continuous care. The younger daughter resents her father's inability to provide, along with the privation of their family life. She tries to compensate for a lack of comfort and affection at home by seeking attention from others. The results are predictable: at an early age she is forced to flee the community to bear a child out of wedlock. The other daughter, Felicia, is the only strong presence in the Malling household. After she leaves home to pursue a life of her own, her pastor father's fragile world crumbles. Members of the vestry meet and decide to terminate his services. His personal life is more to blame for their decision than his performance as a priest. A son in jail for stealing a car and a daughter bearing a child out of wedlock is more scandal than the church and community leaders can tolerate. Mr. Malling protests their decision in his letter of resignation, but his protest has the same feeble and self-deprecating character that compromises his entire ministry in Walmer.

Arthur Bainbridge, who is the focus of Basil King's earlier novel *The Lifted Veil* (1917), is a much stronger character than Christopher Malling. When the novel opens, Arthur has just begun to serve as an Episcopal priest at fashionable St. Mary Magdalen's Church (the name is significant) in Manhattan. Clorinda Guildersleeve, a young widow, comes to see him to confess her "sin": she is in love with a married man, in fact, has been his mistress. During their initial conversations, Clorinda wears a veil to conceal her identity. But she is ready to repent, and Arthur's counsel helps her accept forgiveness and move on with her life. As the counseling sessions progress, Clorinda lifts her veil both literally and symbolically. Before long, she and Arthur admit they are attracted to each other. From the beginning, Arthur has some discomfort about their relationship—whether this woman who had been another man's mistress can accept the role of a minister's wife, "going to church and being a gentle, comforting hostess to dull parishioners" (190). Clorinda is even more uneasy: "That I should be the wife of a clergyman is inconceivable" (208). Arthur ignores his own doubts about Clorinda's suitability and her resistance to serving as a minister's spouse; he is too intent on having her for his wife—and soon they are engaged.

The engagement intensifies Clorinda's apprehension. In a revealing conversation, she tells a surprised Arthur the real source of her struggle: she is unable to move past her image of him as a minister to accept him as a human lover:

> "But—but the kind [of love] you can feel for me? What kind *is* that?"
>
> . . . "I suppose—I suppose the kind one can feel for a—for a clergyman."

> He flushed to a deeper shade of red. "But I'm not a clergyman—in this relation. I'm only a man."
>
> She continued to finger the paper-weight. "You're a clergyman before you're anything else to me. If you hadn't been a clergyman—"
>
> "Well? What then?"
>
> "Oh, then—I don't suppose I should have cared anything about you. . . . I care for you, because—because you're the best man I've ever known. It's precisely because you are the best man that I do care. You've been wonderful to me—from that—that very first time we talked. You remember? But you wouldn't have been so if you hadn't been what you are professionally. . . .
>
> "And so," she went on, tremulously, "you'll always be a clergyman to me." (214–16)[7]

Arthur Bainbridge is abashed and nearly undone by this conversation. Later the same day, he asks a trusted parishioner, Leslie Palliser, whether he sees any reason why ministers should not marry—without mentioning Clorinda specifically. Much to his chagrin, Palliser affirms Clorinda's view of the clergy: "The marriage of a clergyman isn't different from that of any other man—to *him*. It only is to us—his people. It—it brings him down. He's never the same to us afterward" (230).

Arthur is shaken by the conversations with Clorinda and Leslie, but he is still determined to move ahead. Though most people in the parish hold the same heroic view of the celibate minister as Leslie Palliser does, Arthur chooses to ignore them. He presses Clorinda to agree to a date for their marriage. She consents to the Monday before Ash Wednesday. The ceremony is never completed. In the midst of it, Clorinda feels faint and has to be taken to her home. Day after day, Clorinda remains confined to her home. For weeks she refuses to see Arthur. Finally she relents. As they talk, she tries once more to make him understand that she loves him but with "a special kind of love . . . the kind of love . . . that Mary Magdalen and the other women in the New Testament must have felt toward the Saviour" (327). Arthur refuses to accept her statement; he is even more determined to complete the marriage ceremony. He will return tomorrow with Dr. Galloway. He never has the opportunity. The morning paper carries an item: "Sir Malcolm and Lady Grant, who were married yesterday afternoon, left by the night train for Montreal, where they will take up their residence" (334). Clorinda has married the recently divorced banker who was her lover.

Arthur Bainbridge is dumbfounded. He slowly recognizes how blind he has been to reality. He realizes that his colleague's wife and Clorinda's friend, Mary, tried to help him understand Clorinda's feelings for him right after the aborted marriage ceremony:

> "She said—she said she'd told you something—she didn't say what it was—and I've no idea—but she told you—and you'd taken it—I forget the exact word she used—but I think it was—too leniently. . . .
>
> "She said she'd told the same thing to another man—she didn't say who—but I guessed—and he almost—trampled her under his feet."
>
> "And she liked that better? . . ."
>
> "No; she didn't like it better; she only thought—oh, why do you make me say it?—she only thought it was the way a man who was going to marry a woman would feel—naturally—and the way he would act—brutally was the word she used there—I remember now—she said that if he didn't think and act brutally—in such circumstances—it was a sign that he wasn't wholly a man—or something like that—but that he was too much—too much like God—." (302)

Clorinda cannot imagine Arthur in a sexual relationship with her. To enter a sexual relationship with him would taint him; it would downgrade him as a minister. To protect her image of Arthur and his standing as a godly minister, Clorinda transforms her feelings for Arthur from love into gratitude—and marries another man.[8]

The socially prescribed denial of his sexuality has even more serious consequences for the Rev. Curtis Hartman, the Presbyterian minister who appears in Sherwood Anderson's *Winesburg, Ohio* (1919). Repression as a way of life and its effects in small-town America is one of the overall themes of Anderson's novel. Most of the characters in the series of portrayals in the book suffer from personal and social inhibitions that stifle their humanity. The Rev. Mr. Hartman is typical of these residents of Winesburg who lack the resources, and sometimes the will, to break free from the cultural restraints that prevent their emergence into full humanity. The chapter in which Hartman appears is ironically titled "The Strength of God." Hartman exhibits little strength, either of his own or derived from God. He is a scholarly, quiet man who raises little enthusiasm with his sermons. He sometimes dreams of a time when the spirit will burn in him and add power to his preaching—but he has become resigned: "I am a poor stick and that will never happen to me" (172).

A dilemma enters Hartman's life one summer Sunday morning as he sits in the church's bell tower, the pages of his sermon spread across an open Bible. The only window in the tower is a stained glass portrait of Christ laying his hand on the head of a child. As the pastor looks across the Bible through a section of the window that is open, he sees a partly undressed woman in the house next door, lying on her bed, reading, and smoking a cigarette. He quietly closes the window, but he trembles as he realizes that his eyes "just raised from the pages of the book of God, had looked upon the bare shoulders and white throat of a woman" (173). Later the same morning, the distress Hartman suffers after seeing the partly exposed body of a woman overwhelms his preaching; he can think only of the woman as he delivers his sermon. The image of bare-shouldered, thirty-year-old Kate Swift, a local schoolteacher, becomes an obsession to Hartman. During the early hours of another Sunday morning as he wanders the streets of Winesburg because he cannot sleep, Hartman suddenly picks up a stone and rushes up to the bell tower. He locks the door and breaks a hole in the stained glass window—knocking out the heel of the child staring with enthralled eyes into the face of Jesus.[9] He then sits down at the desk and stares across the Bible through the hole in the window into the window of the house next door, waiting for a naked Kate Swift to raise the shade. When it does go up, it is her aunt who raises it!

In the days that follow, Hartman discovers by chance that the schoolteacher often lies on her bed in the evening and reads. He climbs the bell tower regularly, often waiting for hours, hoping for a glimpse of a bare-shouldered Kate. He now realizes he has become obsessed. He prays repeatedly to be delivered from his obsession, but no delivery comes. He wanders the streets night after night, trying in vain to stay away from the bell tower. One bitter cold January night, he leaves home so hurriedly that he forgets his overshoes. He climbs the bell tower, wet and cold. He is at his wits' end. "I want to look at the woman and to think of kissing her shoulders and I am going to let myself think what I choose," he says bitterly, tears in his eyes. He resolves to leave the ministry; he cannot continue as a hypocrite. He tells himself that he has a right to the passion his wife has never given him. He almost hates her. Then, suddenly, a light shines in the upper room in the house next door. As Hartman gazes through the stained glass window, he sees only an empty bed. Then he sees a naked Kate Swift standing by the bed. He watches as she throws herself face downward on the bed and beats the pillow with her fists and begins to weep. "With a final outburst of weeping," she kneels and begins to pray. As Hartman gazes at her praying, her slim and strong figure resembles the figure of the boy looking into the eyes of Christ in the stained glass window.

Hartman stands up abruptly, upsetting the desk and knocking the Bible onto the floor. Hardly conscious of what he is doing, he stumbles down the stairs and into the streets. He enters the office of the *Winesburg Eagle* where George Willard, the editor, is at work. "I have found the light," Hartman cries: "After ten years in this town, God has manifested himself to me in the body of a woman. . . . God has appeared to me in the person of Kate Swift, the school teacher, kneeling naked on her bed." He turns and runs toward the door. He stops and holds up a bleeding fist. "I smashed the glass of the window," he cries: "Now it will have to be wholly replaced. The strength of God was in me and I broke it with my fist" (182–83).

The ironic symbolism in Anderson's portrayal is profound. Curtis Hartman looks across the Bible through the stained glass window at a young woman. He cannot admit to the sexual feelings that rise up inside him. The constraint of God he experiences, manifested in the repressive office of the minister, keeps him sexless. Both his public and personal lives are contained. As a minister, he is permitted to see Kate Swift's nakedness only as she prays. Maintaining his identity as a minister requires him to be a weak and impotent man. When he stands up in despair and accidentally throws the Bible to the floor, without fully realizing what he is doing, he smashes the stained glass window with his fist. Hartman can affirm his manhood including his sexuality only by breaking out of the ministerial identity that constrains him.

Constrained or repressed by an imposed or self-inflicted cultural image that defines them as weak and impotent men has serious consequences for fictional clergy. Enforced impotence thwarts the manhood of clerics like Curtis Hartman and Arthur Bainbridge. Wimpy preachers like Solomon Snow (*Sevenoaks*) and self-deprecating ministers like William (*A Circuit Rider's Wife*) and Christopher Malling (*Pluck*) enable base elements to dominate their congregations. Snow's inability to stand up publicly against Robert Belcher enables Belcher's abuse to continue unimpeded in Sevenoaks. Malling's failure to seek adequate compensation for his family condemns them to poverty. His daughter Felicia is nearly forced to compromise her personal integrity with their benefactor to gain some relief for them.

Whether the ministry as portrayed in these novels forces those who enter it into a self-deprecating role or whether it attracts those who are self-effacing to begin with is an open question. Ministers like Christopher Malling and Curtis Hartman do seem to have more than just a poor self-image; they may have psychological issues as well. Out of what seems to me to be a confusion of calling and sickness, they expect and sometimes even seek to be abused. The common assumption that ministers are often weaker, less-virile humans may make their abuse likely. The terrible cost of accepting this abuse is clearest in Corra Harris's semiautobiographical novel, *A Circuit Rider's Wife*. Her minister-husband William capitulates to his abusers again and again because he views his capitulation as a godly act. He sees submission as Christ-like. Actually it is neither Christ-like nor healthy. While ministers like William may tell themselves they are modeling Jesus in their suffering, actually their suffering is quite different. Their suffering comes out of weakness—out of an inability to confront those who take advantage of them. Jesus' suffering comes out of strength and virility; he chooses it for a redemptive purpose and endures it with courage. Impotent ministers are false and even dangerous models of godliness. Suffering brought on by weakness turns clergy into victims and serves no redemptive purpose. Quite the opposite: it demeans ministers and enables their abusers.

Pretenders, Deceivers, and Commercial Preachers

The influx of weak men into the ministry is not the only or perhaps even the most-significant flaw that characterizes American ministers at the end of the nineteenth and beginning of the twentieth century. Two other radical images suggest that some ministers are deceptive, either by necessity or by choice. "Pretenders" are ministers who become deceptive by necessity; "deceivers" are clerics who become deceptive intentionally. Most pretenders become deceptive reluctantly because they feel they have no other choice. Deceivers and "commercial preachers," in contrast, have a character flaw; they become deceptive on purpose to take advantage of those they are supposed to be serving.

I think clergy who reflect both of these radical cultural images emerged in part as a result of the secular revolution I describe in chapter 8. Especially among intellectuals, that revolution challenged a dominant worldview that took the reality of God and the supernatural for granted. Within that displaced paradigm, Christian believing was the assumed norm and unbelievers were deviant. From the perspective of the displacing paradigm, Christian believers are the ones who are deviant. Christian believers are viewed as naive, cultural relics who refuse to give up a discredited and obsolete perception of reality.

When the social consensus that respected Christian faith as *the* given norm falls apart, maintaining that faith becomes a more difficult and lonely undertaking. Christian belief is no longer *generally* accepted and validated but is regarded as a perspective that individuals validate and adopt *if* they are Christian believers. Christian believers are now marked off as a subculture; they are a variety, not the norm. Christian faith is still a vital force in society, but its authority is more limited. It is still normative within church groups and among those who sympathize or identify with them. But in the intellectual community that is now a significant cultural competitor, Christian believers and their churches are viewed as behind the times, as cultural laggards.

Some communities of faith respond to this social displacement by becoming more exclusive. They close ranks to protect themselves. They harden and narrow their theological positions. Those who assume this defensive posture tolerate little, if any, flexibility, especially on the part of ministers and theological professors. Individuals who weaken or compromise in matters of faith are viewed as a danger to the community of faith.[10]

Such a climate puts immense social pressure on ministers. Because ministers are usually viewed as normative believers within the community of faith, doubting ministers feel compelled to pretend they are still unwavering believers. They know the community of believers will cast out any who openly doubt. The denial that goes with pretending becomes a heavy burden that sometimes breaks fictional clergy who feel they must shoulder it. The Rev. John Westlock in E.W. Howe's *The Story of a Country Town* (1884) is one of these struggling pretenders. Westlock suppresses all human feelings that might compromise his commitment to a harsh and inflexible faith. He presents a consistently strong face to the world.

Only when he becomes an adult does John's son Ned realize that his father's religion "never did afford him the peace he professed." The truth bursts forth unexpectedly one day when John Westlock's pretense crumbles. He runs away, taking Mrs. B. Tremaine with him. A letter Ned and his mother find reveals that John Westlock and Mrs. Tremaine have carried on a covert affair for seven years! The letter explains, but doesn't justify, John's leaving. The cause is "discontent," he writes. The pressure of denying and keeping feelings within has become unbearable: "I believe that were I compelled to remain here another week, I should murder somebody—I don't know who; anybody—and for no other reason than that I cannot control myself." He can no longer maintain his mask: "I go because I cannot remain as I am. I cannot explain to you what I mean by such a strange assertion, but it is true—I am running away from myself" (204). John Westlock feels he can no longer be a minister because he can no longer pretend to be the believer everyone thinks he is.

Several pretenders appear in the stories of Hamlin Garland. One of them is a reluctant pretender named Elder Pill, who appears in *Other*

 Main-Travelled Roads, a collection of stories Garland wrote between 1887 and 1889. Elder Pill, like John Westlock, discovers that his believing is not as solid as others need to think it is to accept him as their minister. In his sermons, Pill's faith comes across as severe as John Westlock's, but in personal relationships Pill is much more relaxed than Westlock. When Pill introduces himself to "old man Bacon," a local farmer, for example, Bacon is surprised and a bit intrigued by the large stature of the man who stands before him: "You look like a good, husky man to pitch in the barnyard; you've too much muscle f'r preachun'." Pill accepts the challenge and counters with one of his own: "Come and hear me next Sunday, and if you say so then, I'll quit" (31–32). Pill's response to an incident that occurs during worship the following Sunday is as convincing to Bacon as Pill's sermon. Some rowdies attempt to disrupt the service. Pill is not at all intimidated: "He pulled off his coat and laid it on the table before him, and, amid a wondering silence, took off his cuffs and collar, saying: 'I can preach the world of the Lord just as well without my coat, and I can throw rowdies out the door a little better in my shirt-sleeves'" (39). And he does. The muscular Pill with his equally muscular religion makes quite an impression in the area.

But much to everyone surprise, Pill's faith is not as sturdy as his physical frame. It turns out that his "whole system of religious thought" is "like the side of a shelving sand-bank—in unstable equilibrium—needing only a touch to send it slipping into a shapeless pile at the river's edge" (54). The touch comes unexpectedly and suddenly one day as a reflecting Pill rides along on his horse. His faith simply slips away. He tries for a time to pretend that he is still a firm believer, but the effort fails. He is forced to confess his doubts to the church—and they cast him out. They have no tolerance for a doubting preacher. Though some of Pill's friends hope he will return to preaching some day, he cannot because he is unable to recover his lost faith.

Frank Shallard in Sinclair Lewis's *Elmer Gantry* is probably the most tragic pretender in late-nineteenth- and early-twentieth-century American fiction. Shallard is a timid, scholarly man who becomes a pretender because he is afraid (with good cause, it turns out) to confess his doubts publicly. Even during his student days, Frank begins to question the literalistic theology imposed on Baptist students at Mitpah Seminary. During his middle year at seminary, he senses quite rightly that Dr. Bruno Zechlin, the Old Testament professor, is a sympathetic soul. The two spend many hours together and finally share their questions and their fears of exposure. During one of their many conversations, a troubled Shallard wonders aloud whether he should stop pretending and simply leave the church. The Baptist Church will never accept one who questions like he does. The venerable professor responds by describing his own dilemma: he is sixty-five years of age and "too sorry a preacher" and "too lumbering a writer" to consider leaving his teaching post. He has no alternative but to pretend. He advises his student to do the same: "Stay in the church. Till *you* want to get out." Frank accepts his professor's advice and sets himself the goal of "liberalizing the church from within" (122–23).

After Frank Shallard becomes an ordained minister, he discovers that the ministry offers much less opportunity to reform the church from within than he had envisioned as a student. The congregations among whom he ministers prove much more resistant to progressive theological ideas than he anticipated they would be during his talks with Dr. Zechlin. Most church members are unwilling or unable to consider the questions that trouble him. Shallard survives in the ministry by befriending understanding, like-minded clergy colleagues in each of his parishes. But in public he holds fast to the course of pretension he resolved to follow as a student—partly because he is afraid to disappoint his minister father, and partly because he witnesses the quick downfall of his mentor Dr. Zechlin when Zechlin's liberal beliefs are exposed. The seminary fires Dr. Zechlin immediately. The discredited professor is then, as he himself predicted, unemployable. He is forced to depend on a sister for support; within two years, he dies. Dr. Zechlin's demise impresses Frank profoundly.

For a time, Frank is a successful pretender. His reputation as a preacher grows, and he is rewarded with calls to larger churches. Eventually he becomes pastor of a significant Baptist congregation in the city of Eureka. After only a few years in Eureka, Frank makes a courageous decision: he leaves his Baptist congregation to become a minister in the somewhat more liberal Dorchester Congregational Church, located on the edge of the large Midwestern city of Zenith. Though he is still forced to temper his theology as he preaches to this Congregationalist congregation, at least some of them are not shocked by his suggestions that socialism may be more in line with the teachings of scripture than capitalism and that modern biology may offer a more reliable record of human origins than the book of Genesis.

But Frank Shallard's relief is short-lived. When his liberal preaching comes to the attention of conservative business leaders in Zenith, they determine to discredit him. Their effort succeeds in forcing Frank to resign his pulpit, and he soon finds work as an outreach worker with the Charity Organization Society (COS). Shallard is actually more comfortable as a social worker than he was as a minister. He has an enjoyable three years with the COS. During his third year, the Dayton evolution trial occurs. Local conservative clergy in Zenith and prominent business owners in their congregations view the trial as an omen. They organize to oppose the forces of liberalism. Frank secures a leave from the COS in order to become a spokesperson for those who support the teaching of evolution, and he embarks on a lecture tour. With great anticipation, he travels to his first assignment, a lecture in the Central Labor Hall in a large Southwestern city.

Ominous signs greet Frank as soon as he arrives in the city. Posters that announce the topic of his lecture—"Are the Fundamentalists Witch Hunters?"—are defaced. He finds an anonymous threatening note in his hotel room. A threatening telephone call follows. But Frank refuses to be intimidated. He begins his lecture with a bold criticism of Fundamentalists. Within minutes after he starts to speak, hecklers interrupt him. When he refuses to be deterred, the hecklers rise and move toward the platform. A fight breaks out between members of the audience and the hecklers. The foolishly fearless Frank steps off the platform to join those fighting against the hecklers. The chairman restrains him: "You'll get beaten to death! We need you!" The man seems to be a rescuer. He hustles Frank out a back door, into a waiting car. Frank realizes too late that he has made a horrible mistake. An hour later, the captors push him from the car. A whip cracks across his face—again and again. When the assailants drive away, he is unconscious, bleeding, disfigured, blinded in one eye, and left only with partial sight in the other.

Frank Shallard pays a terrible price when he stops pretending. Sinclair Lewis's description of the fate that befalls him is a scathing (and, I think, intentional) criticism of what Lewis sees as the church's intolerance for ministers who espouse progressive theological and political perspectives. Lewis's portrayal implies that those who refuse to honor narrow conservative beliefs have few options: pretending is essential if they want to remain in the ministry. Radical ideas that challenge orthodox theology threaten the dominance of economic forces that benefit from this theology. These same forces control the American church. Maintaining conservative theology that affirms the status quo and quiets those who would oppose them (liberal believers, socialists, labor unions, etc.) is absolutely essential. A minister like Frank Shallard must be stopped—even brutally, if necessary—as a clear warning to other closet liberals who might be tempted to stop pretending.[11]

I call fictional clergy who reflect a related radical image "deceivers" because they deceive others *intentionally* to advance either their own religious beliefs or their own personal interests, or both. "A Day of Grace," another story in Garland's *Other Main-Travelled Roads*, describes deceiving preachers at a tent meeting. It begins on a hot August Sunday morning. Ben Griswold, a bachelor farmer, rushes through his farm chores, dresses in his Sunday best, and at noon rides off toward his neighbor Grace's home, hoping to accompany her to a camp meeting. When he arrives, he discovers that Grace has already agreed to go to the meeting with Conrad Sieger. Ben and his friend Milton invite Maud and another young woman to go to the services with them. As they approach the camp meeting, the road is crowded with wagons. By the time they reach the tent, night has fallen. Flickering torches cast shadows of swaying worshippers against the canvas. The air is filled with the shrieks of those responding to the passionate message of the preachers. "What cursed foolishness!" Ben blurts out. But he stays to watch.

As the exhorters' voices grow in intensity, more and more of the worshippers are overcome, especially the young women. A shouting preacher descends into the aisle. Ben watches him with disgust. He seems to be praying: "Foam was on his lips, but his eyes were cool and calculating; they betrayed him" (75). A man and a woman are overcome. "Why, it's Grace," Maud cries out. Conrad loses consciousness and falls to the ground; Grace is now defenseless. Ben is on his feet, through the crowd, his fists "like mauls" pushing people away. "Grace!" he cries out, and she hears him. "Let me go," she says, struggling against the preacher who holds her. "You are going to hell," he protests. Ben is at her side. "God damn ye," he says to the preacher. "I'll kill ye if you lay a hand on her. . . . I'd smash hell out o' you for a leather cent." The preacher retreats. Ben carries Grace and Conrad to his wagon. He bundles the exhausted, sleeping Conrad into the carryall. Conrad is soon forgotten as Ben sits next to Grace. She is his now—safe from the deceitful, mesmerizing preacher. It is a scene he will never forget: "On the long ride home, Grace lay within his right arm. . . . He talked, and his spirit grew tender and manly and husbandlike, as he told his plans and his hopes. Hell was very far away, and Heaven was very near" (78).

The exposure of deceiving preachers that Hamlin Garland begins in "A Day of Grace" becomes even more extensive in his 1905 novel *The Tyranny of the Dark*. Though Garland focuses on what he sees as the pretense of spiritualism in *Tyranny*, the novel seems designed to discredit the reality of the supernatural in *any* form. At the center of the story is the Rev. Anthony Clarke, who has recently moved from a large, prestigious Eastern congregation to become pastor of a Presbyterian Church in the Western mining town where the novel begins. After the death of his wife Adele, Clarke became so despondent that he was forced to resign his previous pulpit. As part of an effort to recover his health, he moved from the city to this more-peaceful location, where he assumed the pastorate of a less-demanding small church. Though Clark's physical health improves after his move to the West, his psychological state continues to deteriorate. Unable to accept the reality of Adele's death, Clarke becomes increasingly obsessed with the occult. He develops a domineering relationship with Viola Lambert, a local young woman who is a psychic, initially hoping that she will become the means of communicating with the departed Adele. Miss Lambert soon becomes the object of Clarke's affection, as well as the means of satisfying his obsession.

Clarke's antagonist in the novel is Dr. Morton Serviss, a biologist and teacher in the bacteriology department of Corlear Medical College in New York City. The vacationing Professor Serviss meets Viola Lambert by chance as he is riding through the countryside. He is immediately taken, not only by Viola's beauty but also because his scientist's eye recognizes that she is psychologically disturbed. When Morton meets the Rev. Mr. Clarke, he realizes that the driven minister is taking advantage of his young parishioner to serve his own needs.

The two male antagonists in Garland's novel represent two worlds in conflict: the Rev. Mr. Clarke the spiritual or supernatural world, and Dr. Serviss the new world of science—the "tyranny of the dark" (as the title suggests) versus the light of modern science. The antagonism between Clarke and Serviss (and the two worlds they represent) comes to a head when Clarke travels to New York, bringing Viola Lambert with him. The obsessed Clarke is determined to exhibit her in a public séance that will provide indisputable proof of the reality of the spirit world

Anthony Clarke's plan is frustrated unexpectedly when Viola Lambert becomes aware that he is using her. She rebels and also begins to question the reality of spiritism. As Viola's doubts grow, an increasingly desperate Anthony places more and more pressure on her to perform in a public test. Just as it appears that she will succumb, Joe Lambert, her stepfather, appears. The spiritualist minister is no match for the burly mine owner. Joe Lambert tells the minister simply to get out of their lives. He warns that Westerners bring speedy justice to bear when someone is a threat to their loved ones; he will kill Clarke if he utters "one word public or private against my wife or daughter" (383). The frightened minister retreats. Without Viola to maintain his deception, his world falls to pieces. He simply cannot cope with the possibility that Viola's "trances and all phenomena connected therewith [are] pathologic, explainable on the grounds of some obscure neural derangement" (402).[12] Clarke cannot go on without his deceptiveness. He commits suicide.

In *The Leatherwood God* (1916), William Dean Howells argues that those who *want* to believe a deceiving minister's message can convince even a deceiver who knows he is a deceiver to believe his own message. Howells's story is set in southern Ohio during the 1820s and recalls "the stomping, shouting, God-drunk" revivals that Howells's grandfather attended as a young man and years later recalled and described to his young grandson.[13] The mesmerizing preacher is Joseph Dylks. As Dylks's claims become more and more outrageous, Matthew Braile, the local squire who serves as his antagonist in the novel, is amazed to see how few of his neighbors recognize that Dylks is deceiving them. Most of the humble people of Leatherwood want to believe in Dylks. They aid and abet Dylks's megalomania. Within the span of a few days, his identity expands from teacher to prophet to messiah. It culminates one night as he preaches: "I am God and the Christ in one. . . . In me, Father, Son, and Holy Ghost are met. There is no salvation except by faith in me. They who put their faith in me shall never taste death, but shall be translated into the New Jerusalem, which I am going to bring down from heaven." Though a few in the congregation that night are revolted by Dylks's claims, most are willing believers. They shout, "We shall never die." When Dylks descends from the pulpit after his sermon, one of those present calls out, "Behold our God!" The gathered company falls to their knees and worships the Leatherwood God (75).

The Leatherwood God's fall is as quick as his rise. Dylks reaches beyond his grasp when he promises to work a miracle. A crowd gathers expectantly on the appointed night. They wait several hours, but Dylks fails to appear. As the hours pass, the congregation's mood shifts. A few men set out to search for Dylks and with the help of dogs track the frightened messiah to a local cabin where he is hiding. With their quarry in hand, the congregation becomes an angry mob. Several of them want to lynch the man they now regard as a false prophet. But cooler heads prevail; the captors agree to confine Dylks until he can be tried. The next day, the fallen divine is brought before Squire Braile. The scene in the outdoor courtroom in front of Braile's cabin is reminiscent of the trial of Jesus before Pontius Pilate. Braile asks what crime Dylks has committed. A voice from the crowd answers, "He professes to be Almighty God." When Braile asks the prisoner whether the charge is true, "Are you God?" Dylks responds, "Thou sayest." The crowd wants Dylks punished, but there is no law in Ohio against "a man's being

 God." Like Pontius Pilate in the scripture, Braile releases the prisoner. Before the captors can execute their own form of justice, Dylks escapes. There is no crucifixion of the Leatherwood God.

In a conversation with Matthew Braile the day before he leaves Leatherwood for the last time, Dylks reveals how overeager believers aid the making of a deceiver. Braile wonders how someone could achieve the level of deceiving that Dylks has. "Nobody can understand it that hasn't been through it," a sobbing Dylks replies:

> "How you're tempted on, step by step, all so easy, till you can't go back. . . . When you begin to try for it, to give out that you're a prophet, an apostle, you don't have to convince anybody. They're only too glad to believe in what you say from the first word; and if you tell them you're the Christ, didn't He always say He would come back, and how do they know but what it's now and you?" (172)

In *The Leatherwood God*, William Dean Howells argues that deceivers like Dylks succeed because believers as a class are gullible.[14] They are duped so easily because they want to believe in the visions deceivers place before them. Their eagerness to believe is contagious. The deception spreads and comes full circle. In the end, the deceiver is taken in by his own pretension. He becomes a victim of his own deceiving.

Some fictional deceivers go beyond pretending and deceiving to commercialize the ministry. These commercializing clerics turn ministry into a business. They market faith as a commodity—which is why I call them "commercial preachers." Commercial preachers preach salvation, but their main concern is to advance themselves. Like W. D. Howells's "man who has risen," they hope to become "preachers who have risen."

One of the earliest commercial preachers is the Rev. Ronald Carnaquay, who appears in Bradley Gilman's novel *Ronald Carnaquay: A Commericial Clergyman* (1903). Carnaquay is actually cast as a foil to Lawrence Freeman, the social-activist hero of the novel.[15] When Freeman's hard-hitting social gospel sermons offend a significant bloc of members at Emmanuel Church and revenues begin to fall, the church board asks him to resign. Freeman becomes a victim of what Gilman refers to as the "commercial age" of church life (28).

Not long after Lawrence Freeman resigns, Ronald Carnaquay is invited to preach a candidating sermon at Emmanuel Church. Carnaquay reads the scripture lessons confidently, with "a clear ringing voice." But when he pulls the manuscript of his sermon from his pocket, his face is covered with dismay. He slowly places the sermon back in the pocket. With a firm look of resolve, he explains his dilemma. He departed from home hurriedly, he tells the congregation, and by mistake brought the manuscript of an address he delivered before the Northwestern Annual Conference the previous month. He asks for the "kind indulgence and sympathy" of the congregation; he will preach a recent sermon as best he can from memory. It's an old trick of the smooth preacher trade. The sermon Carnaquay preaches is the one he intended to preach—a sermon he has preached many times before, a sermon that has been "revised and enriched with each delivery." The ruse succeeds. The duped congregation is so impressed that they vote immediately to call Carnaquay as their pastor; they even agree to his demand for a salary that is considerably more than they paid their previous pastor.

The commercial clergyman is a great success at Emmanuel Church. Carnaquay is soon noted throughout the city not only as an engaging preacher but also for a facility with language and ideas that marks him as "a very advanced thinker." As Carnaquay's fame spreads, Emmanuel Church becomes so crowded on Sundays that the congregation is forced to build a new wing to accommodate the large numbers attending worship. Carnaquay introduces a variety of successful innovations into the church program—all of them centered on him, including a series of weekly "smoke talks" that attract a large group of cigar-smoking men.

But praise for Carnaquay and his innovations is not quite universal. Some of the most serious criticism stems from the actor-minister's inadequacy as a pastor. When faced by the mother of a dying young man of twenty-two, the golden-tongued pulpit orator is at a loss for words. Will she and her son meet again beyond death, and when and how? Carnaquay doesn't know; he has nothing to say. Then one evening, fire destroys the church building. When the church board meets the next day, they discover that their building was not insured. The insurance agent pocketed the premium money—and now he has disappeared. When board members turn to Dr. Carnaquay for advice, he is more befuddled than they are. They realize that though he talks well, he lacks the skills needed to lead a congregation in crisis. A second revelation is even more unsettling: several church members bring forth indisputable evidence that some of Carnaquay's sermons are not his own creations. He sometimes preaches the sermons of others as though they were his own. The esteemed preacher plagiarizes. Carnaquay is forced to resign when his plagiarism becomes common knowledge. He returns to the occupation for which he is most suited and becomes a great success as the sales representative for a local mill. Carnaquay continues to maintain a connection with his former parish. In between his travels, he worships occasionally at Emmanuel Church. He even contributes $5,000 to the reconstruction of the church building.

In the foreword to *Ronald Carnaquay*, the Rev. Bradley Gilman explains his purpose for writing the book. He believes Ronald Carnaquays are unfortunately common among ministers of the day: "The fundamental idea of this book is the economic principle that 'demand creates supply.' The religious bodies of our time, who have 'Ronald Carnaquays' in their pulpits, have them because they have 'demanded' them, created them, nourished them" (vii).

Twenty-four years after Gilman's novel, a similar and somewhat more popular book, *Shoddy* (1928) by Methodist minister Dan Beardly Brummit, extends Gilman's thesis to include the larger church. Bartelmy Bonafede, the shoddy and ambitious pastor who is the focus of Brummit's novel, is a character similar to Carnaquay. Like Carnaquay, Bonafede is a golden-tongued orator who rises to the top of his profession by preaching palatable religion. But unlike the hapless Carnaquay, Bonefede succeeds. He has his difficult moments, but he recovers from his missteps and even becomes a Methodist bishop.

Fred B. Fisher, a sitting Methodist bishop at the time *Shoddy* was published, reviewed the book for *Christian Century*. Fisher's review is mostly a mea culpa exercise. He commends Brummitt for the moral lashings the book delivers to the back of what Fisher agrees has become a deplorably bureaucratic church served by similarly deplorable bureaucratic clergy. He applauds Brummit as "one of us," an author who deserves to be listened to because he knows the church from the inside.[16]

Fisher has no similar appreciation for Sinclair Lewis's *Elmer Gantry*, a novel that appeared in 1927, the year before *Shoddy*. In the bishop's mind, Elmer Gantry "was merely a slimy boomerang. His unwise creator just picked up an ordinary criminal and dressed him in a white tie and Prince Albert coat for a holiday orgy in the home of the saints."[17] Actually, Elmer Gantry is still well remembered, whereas Ronald Carnaquay and Bartelmy Bonafede are largely forgotten, because his "unwise creator" was an astute observer of ministers and the church. Ministerial authors like Gilman and Brummitt are friendly critics; the Revs. Carnaquay and Bonafede, their fictional clerics, are tame examples of the commercial preacher. Sinclair Lewis is not a friendly critic, and his fictional clergy are not sanitized in any way. The faith-selling clergy Lewis creates are as true to life as Gilman's and Brummitt's, but they probably offend ministers who read his novels because Lewis's fictional ministers are not shaped to fit the biases of contemporary mainstream clergy like the affronted bishop. Lewis's parody of contemporary clergy in novels like *Babbitt* and *Elmer Gantry* is blatant, intentional—and very skillful.

Harry Sinclair Lewis was a contrary, sometimes cynical and consistently irreverent, post–secular revolution, post–World War I American literary naturalist. He was also a superb social critic who did his homework thoroughly before he crafted his characters. Much of the authenticity readers perceived in Lewis's characters stemmed from his uncanny ability to assimilate the characteristics of people he met and to duplicate those characteristics in the fictional characters he created. His ability to identify common character traits and then package them into memorable characters that engage readers was exceptional.[18] Lewis's often-caustic novels published during the 1920s struck a familiar chord with a surprisingly large number of contemporary readers; they were enormously popular.[19] One of his biographers recalls that "Lewis was able to 'absorb' or 'memorize' people to such an astonishing degree that, like Dickens, to whom he has often been compared, he could virtually become them—speak as they spoke, walk the way they walked . . . and render with eerie accuracy their facial expressions, hand gestures, even eye movements."[20] In personalities like Carol Kennicott, the semisophisticated doctor's wife who is trapped in Gopher Prairie, Minnesota, and George Babbitt, the tired businessman who lives in Zenith, Winnemac, a fictional city in a fictional Midwestern state that closely resembles Ohio, Lewis captured "types" who represent what many of his sympathetic readers recognized as frighteningly common national averages. In his 1920s novel of the same title, Lewis raised Main Street from a place to a "state of mind," a cultural attribute. What one critic describes as "'the village virus,' . . . [or] small-town . . . 'dullness made God,'" Lewis associated with a state of mind he believed held American culture hostage.[21] George F. Babbitt, the Zenith real estate broker who stands at the center of *Babbitt*, the novel that follows *Main Street*, has so many authentic small-town businessman qualities that he seemed to many contemporary readers like a real person they had met somewhere.

Actually, Babbitt and the other characters in the 1922 novel that bears his name are composites based on scores of small-town Americans Lewis met during an eight-week fact-finding trip through small cities of the American heartland.[22] The commercialism that infects every aspect of life in provincial, middle-American Zenith is based on his recorded observations of daily life in the cities he visited. The need to be and appear successful dominates the lives of everyone who lives in Zenith. It encompasses their personal lives, their community, and their church. Church life in Zenith is as shallow and manufactured as any other business there; religion is "reduced to the observance of a kind of industry standard against which 'success' is measured. Christianity is engineered like an assembly-line product and is managed like a business."[23] Zenith's leading ministers mirror their leading parishioners. All the esteemed and successful ministers in Zenith are commercial preachers. Mike Monday, a prizefighter become evangelist, exemplifies the kind of successful preacher-businessman that business leaders like Babbitt admire. The accounts of Monday's evangelistic activities read like reports from a successful business. One of them boasts that Monday "has converted over two hundred thousand lost and priceless souls at an average cost of less than ten dollars a head" (87). When the business owners and bankers who make up the majority of lay leaders in Zenith's churches suggest that Monday be invited to conduct one of his crusades in Zenith, a handful of local clergy argue against issuing the invitation. But their opposition is quickly quelled when the committee composed of leading manufacturers points out that, in every city where Monday appeared, he "had turned the minds of workmen from wages and hours to higher things, and thus averted strikes" (87). Monday's sermons in Zenith match their expectations. He preaches a pure, Bible-based gospel. No social gospel religion or higher criticism, or any other notion associated with "secular thinking," creeps into his sermons.

Babbitt's own pastor, the Rev. John Jennison Drew, approaches his ministry with a similar, though more-refined, commercialism. The Rev. Dr. (the appellation is very important to him) Drew is "eloquent" in the pulpit and "efficient and versatile" in the rest of his ministry. Babbitt and other business owners who attend Dr. Drew's Presbyterian church are pleased to note that their pastor presides regularly "at meetings for the denunciation of unions or the elevation of domestic service." Dr. Drew is "proud to be known primarily as a business man." On one occasion he justifies his overt efforts to publicize his church by explaining that he is not willing to "permit the old Satan to monopolize all the pep and punch." Local newspapers offer extensive coverage of the activities of Dr. Drew's church and often print his sermons. These reports help to attract even more worshippers to his church services and Sunday school. Dr. Drew's campaign to promote himself and his church succeeds admirably; within the city and throughout his denomination, he is considered to be the quintessentially successful minister.

However, Dr. Drew, like most of the pretentious business leaders he emulates, is not entirely as he appears. An incident that occurs toward the end of the novel reveals Dr. Drew's phoniness even to Babbitt, his like-minded parishioner. Midway through the novel, Babbitt experiences what would now be termed "a midlife crisis." His life begins to feel hollow to him. In what turns out to be a futile attempt to fill the void, Babbitt seeks the companionship of a fast crowd. But fear of discovery and the business ruin that is certain to accompany that exposure soon overwhelms him, and he quickly retreats. A lingering sense of guilt plagues the repentant Babbitt. He makes an appointment to see his pastor. Perhaps an open confession of his misdeeds will bring forgiveness and release from the remorse he suffers. When Babbitt enters Dr. Drew's office, he finds the busy pastor talking animatedly on the telephone, berating the local printer for being late with the proofs for next Sunday's church bulletin. As Dr. Drew hangs up the telephone, Babbitt comes right to the point. He explains that for a few weeks he was "kind of slack," had a few drinks too many and strayed, but he has come back to his senses. Does repentance even the score?

Dr. Drew's response to Babbitt's honest confession is a prurient quizzing, such as inquiring whether Babbitt's wanderings included escapades like "squeezing girls in cars." When Babbitt will offer no such juicy details, Dr. Drew recalls his schedule: he tells Babbitt that there is "a deputation from the Don't Make Prohibition a Joke Association coming to see me in a quarter of an hour, and one from the Anti-Birth-Control Union at a quarter of ten." But he will take five minutes to pray with Babbitt:

> "Kneel right down by your chair, brother. Don't be ashamed to seek the guidance of God." Babbitt's scalp itched and he longed to flee, but Dr. Drew had already flopped down beside his desk-chair and his voice had changed from rasping efficiency to an unctuous familiarity with sin and with the Almighty. Babbitt also knelt, while Drew gloated:
>
> "O Lord, thou seest our brother here, who has been led astray by manifold temptations. O Heavenly Father, make his heart to be pure, as pure as a little child's. Oh, let him know again the joy of a manly courage to abstain from evil. . . ."
>
> As his pastor drones on a squinting Babbitt catches him looking at his watch. He quickly concludes and asks the organist who has just entered the room, "Has the deputation come yet, Sheldy?" (348–49)

Many ministers who read *Babbitt* were understandably offended by Lewis's pejorative characterizations of ministers in the novel. In the summer of 1922, one of these offended clerics, the Rev. William L. Stidger, a prominent Methodist minister from Detroit, met up with Sinclair Lewis when both of them happened to be in Terre Haute, Indiana. Stidger raised strong objections to Lewis's characterization of the Rev. Dr. John Jennison Drew. He challenged Lewis to visit him in Detroit where he could show Lewis what ministers are really like. Though Lewis was intrigued by Stidger's offer, he was busy with research for a book on the labor movement. Four years passed before he and Stidger were able to get together. By then Lewis was actively gathering material for *Elmer Gantry*, his "preacher book," and was very interested in what Stidger had to show him. Stidger himself had moved from Detroit to Kansas City to become pastor of the Linwood Boulevard Methodist Church. This new pastorate in the heartland of Fundamentalism was actually a better location for Lewis to gather information on the kind of ministers he would portray in *Elmer Gantry*. After a short visit with Stidger in Kansas City in January, Lewis agreed to return in the spring for a more extended stay. Stidger was a real find; he was precisely the kind of minister Lewis would fictionalize in *Elmer Gantry*.

In his correspondence with his publisher during the early months of 1926, Lewis states repeatedly that he intended to provide a representative portrayal of contemporary Protestant clergy in his new book.[24] Actually, a wide variety of preachers appear in the published novel, but the majority of them are deceiving commercial preachers. Though the characteristics that all the ministers in the novel embody are based on living ministers Lewis met, he featured commercial preachers to advance his view that commercial clergy, especially Fundamentalist clergy, dominated the contemporary American Protestant church.[25] Lewis's letters to his wife during the winter and spring of 1926 show that he viewed the upcoming novel as an opportunity to expose the phoniness of Fundamentalists in particular.[26]

During late March when Lewis returned to Kansas City, he immersed himself in the local minister culture. With the help of Leon Birkhead, a Unitarian minister with whom he developed a warm friendship, Lewis assembled a collection of two hundred books representative of those ministers would likely have read either during seminary or afterward.[27] He met weekly on Wednesdays with a group of local clergy in his suite at the Ambassador Hotel. Between fifteen and twenty ministers attended what came to be known as "Sinclair Lewis's Sunday School Class." Those in the group were admittedly some of the more liberal clergy in Kansas City. But the "class" brought together representatives from most of the major Protestant denominations in the city. Ministers who participated regularly included Methodist, Baptist, Presbyterian, Unitarian, Congregational, and Christian (Campbellite) pastors, as well as one member who was identified simply as a "rationalist" and another who was a local rabbi.[28] Birkhead described the preachers in the class as "good sports" who could be "'razzed' and would take no offense." During class sessions, they "talked about nearly every phase of the work of the preacher." Lewis prepared for the weekly sessions by careful reading in his ministerial library. Each week he assembled a list of provocative theological and moral questions and challenged his Sunday school class to respond to them. The questions covered a wide range of topics: "Who will literally follow Jesus into loneliness, ridicule and death? . . . Why don't you tell your congregations that you are agnostics?"[29] Lewis challenged the ministers both personally and professionally with questions like "What are you fellows trying to do? Are you anything more than parasites? If you preachers believe in the meek and lowly Nazarene, the One who had not where to lay his Head, who said 'Blessed are ye poor,' why don't . . . you give up your comfortable homes, your fine motor cars, your big fat cigars, and your good food and become real Christians?"[30]

Lewis's overall purpose during the weeks he spent in Kansas City was to experience the ministry from the inside. In protected settings like his Sunday school class where ministers felt safe and expressed themselves freely, he carefully noted their personal and professional views on a wide range of subjects. Lewis attended several worship services each week. He even convinced some of his newfound ministerial friends to let him preach or offer prayers in their pulpits. On these occasions, he literally acted the part of a minister. And if contemporary reports are accurate, he was a credible preacher. "I went in and preached a fine sermon, I did," Lewis wrote from Kansas City to his wife, Grace, "and there were five preachers in the front row, there were, and they all said I was a swell preacher, they did."[31] Though he may have been convincing when he acted the role of a minister, Lewis's letters to Alfred Harcourt show that he was not at all sincere: "All of this damned fool preaching in pulpits and so on which I have been doing has been largely to give me a real feeling of the church from the inside. . . . You probably realize that most or all of this idiotic appearing in pulpits and general hell-raising is to have a chance to be behind the scenes, completely in, with church matters, and it has worked like a charm."[32]

Lewis drew on his experiential research in Kansas City, as well as his ministerial library and the wider data he has already accumulated on American ministers, to create the characters and plot of *Elmer Gantry*. Many of the ministerial phrases recorded in Lewis's notebooks during 1926 and before come through directly in ministers in the novel.[33] Elmer Gantry and Sharon Falconer, the main characters in the novel, closely resemble real-life evangelists like Billy Sunday and Aimee Semple McPherson, as well as real-life pastors like William Stidger, John Roach Straton, and J. Frank Norris. The illuminated revolving cross that Sharon Falconer affixes to the steeple of her coastal tabernacle, for example, is similar to those that topped McPherson's Angelus Temple and Stidger's Methodist Church in Detroit. The eye-catching titles Elmer Gantry uses for his sermons and many of his commercializing methods of ministry were lifted directly from similar titles and methods that appeared in Stidger's books. Elmer's vice-exposing sermons sound much like those the Rev. John Roach Straton preached when he served the Yorkville Methodist Church in New York City (which is to be Elmer's next pastoral appointment as *Elmer Gantry* ends). Elmer's personal actions against dens of prostitution in Zenith resemble those employed by the vigilante-like preacher from Fort Worth, Texas, J. Frank Norris, also known as "the Texas tornado" and "the pistol-toting divine." Sharon Falconer's career includes several incidents that resemble similar incidents in the life of Aimee Semple McPherson.[34] Even the most offensive preachers in *Elmer Gantry* (including Elmer himself) have true-to-life characteristics that make them credible characters.

Elmer Gantry epitomizes the commercial preacher image Lewis wanted most to parody in the novel that bears his name. Originally from a small town in Kansas, Elmer attends the Baptist-affiliated Terwillinger College, where he distinguishes himself as a football star and hell-raiser. During his student days, Elmer makes a concerted effort to separate himself from anything religious. The highly clericalized faculty and the most passionate evangelical students view the openly irreverent Elmer Gantry as a special challenge. They engage Judson Roberts, a former All-American athlete now become evangelist, as the main speaker for the college's annual evangelism crusade. During the week-long series of meetings, Roberts and the evangelical students press Gantry to join Jesus' team. He resists initially, but they badger him until he finally caves in and goes forward as a convert.

The testimony Elmer gives immediately after his conversion gives him his first taste of preaching. It also launches an internal struggle between faith and doubt that will plague him for the rest of the novel. Elmer can't decide whether what he experiences during his conversion was real or phony. Perhaps it was genuine: "If the Holy Ghost really was there and getting after me? I did feel different!" But, "Jud Roberts kidded me into it. With all his Big Brother stuff. Prob'ly pulls it everywhere he goes." Then he recalls the experience of preaching after he was converted: "The whole crowd! Turned to me like I was an All-American preacher!" (51).

This irresolvable conflict between wanting to believe and wondering whether there is any reality to faith, along with the inability to be open about this core dilemma, plagues Elmer and many of the other ministers in the novel. Even the evangelist Roberts who converts Gantry struggles with doubt as he smokes "an illegal cigarette" in the vestibule of the train after his successful crusade at Terwillinger College. He recalls the scene at the conversion of "that Elmer what's-his name." He wonders, "Suppose there *isn't* anything to it. Won't hurt him to cut out some of his bad habits for awhile, anyway. And how do we know? Maybe the Holy Ghost does come down. . . . I do wish I could get over this doubting! . . . I don't think I'm hurting these young fellows any, but I do wish I could be honest" (60–61). But a successful faith seller cannot give even the appearance of doubt.

Judson Roberts manages to overcome his doubt and temptation. Elmer Gantry never does: doubt and the desires of the flesh repeatedly gain the upper hand in his life. After graduating from Terwillinger, Elmer enrolls in Mizpah Seminary. During his second year, the dean gives Elmer the opportunity to serve as a student preacher at a country church located in the small village of Schoenheim. The appointment gives him a chance to try out his gifts as a preacher. It also provides an opportunity to seduce Lulu Bains, the daughter of a local deacon. Lulu is the first in a succession of women who Elmer will seduce during his career as a minister. Though Elmer manages to seduce Lulu and escape from Schoenheim unscathed, he is not as fortunate when he is sent to preach in Monarch. He gets to drinking at the local tavern after his arrival on Saturday afternoon and fails to wake up in time to keep his preaching appointment on Sunday. This time the seminary dean discovers the truth, and Elmer is expelled from seminary.

The now-discredited Elmer Gantry becomes a "not unsuccessful" traveling salesman. After two years of selling, he arrives one evening at Sautersville, Nebraska, where he notes placards advertising tent meetings to be held by one Sharon Falconer, a woman evangelist. Though Elmer dismisses the thought of a woman as an evangelist, he decides to attend the evening service anyway. He is surprised and completely smitten by what he sees. Sharon is not only the most beautiful woman he has ever seen; she epitomizes the commercial cleric Elmer hopes to become. He resolves immediately to join her evangelistic organization. When Elmer goes to see her the next day and tries to con her into thinking that he is really a prestigious evangelist, she recognizes him for the con artist that he is. But Sharon is not put off. She realizes that she and Elmer Gantry are soul mates. "I like you!" she tells him: "You're so completely brazen, so completely unscrupulous, and so beautifully ignorant!" (165).

Within days of their meeting, Elmer joins Sharon's "operation." In town after town, he poses as a salesman who is converted and testifies to the power of Sharon's preaching. In the months that follow, he and Sharon learn from each other. Sharon shows Elmer how a profitable evangelistic organization functions. In return, Elmer, the consummate salesman, helps Sharon improve the advertising and promotion of her evangelistic meetings. The team is highly successful. Converts increase, and the crusades become even more profitable. Sharon is able to stop traveling. She builds a huge tabernacle (topped by a lighted, revolving cross) on a pier over the ocean to serve as a permanent home for her evangelistic meetings. Then tragedy strikes. The crowded tabernacle catches fire one evening; scores of those attending the worship service perish in the fire, including Sharon Falconer.

After the tragedy, Elmer is again at loose ends. He tries to develop an evangelistic organization of his own but has little success. Then, one evening, the Rev. Wesley R. Toomis, the Methodist bishop in the Zenith area, hears Elmer Gantry preach. The congregation is not large, but Bishop Toomis recognizes Elmer's gifts and offers him a chance to become a Methodist preacher. As Elmer sits for the first time in the sanctuary of the small Methodist church of Banjo Crossing, his first assignment as a Methodist preacher, he feels humble and grateful. He prays sincerely, asking God to look past his unworthiness and equip him to become a pure servant of the gospel. For a time, Elmer's newfound dedication to the ministry seems genuine. He is "assiduous, but careful, in his pastoral calls on the women" (279). He devotes himself to the scholarship he neglected as a seminary student. He even conducts a mostly honorable courtship with Cleo Benham, who becomes Mrs. Elmer Gantry.

But Elmer Gantry's reform is only temporary. The modest fruits of his ministry at Banjo Crossing are not enough reward for him. He begins to employ more and more catchy stunts to increase the size of his congregations. Elmer's methods may be crass but they produce results, and the increasing size of his congregations catches the attention of Bishop Toomis. The bishop rewards the successful Elmer with appointments to bigger churches in larger towns: from Banjo Crossing with 900 people to Rudd Center (pop. 4,100) for only one year; then on to Vulcan (pop. 47,000) for three years; on to Sparta (pop. 129,000) for two years; and then in 1920 the apex, a church in Zenith (pop. 400,000).

Elmer puts his well-honed self-advancement skills to work immediately. Within weeks, "the Rev. Elmer Gantry" and "Wellspring Methodist Church" are household words in Zenith. His eye-catching sermon titles stand out in the Saturday religious advertisements. As the months pass, Sunday congregations at Wellspring Church grow larger and larger: "I'll take the crowds away from all of 'em," Elmer gloats. I'll be the one big preacher in Zenith. And then—Chicago? New York? Bishopric? Whatever I want! Whee!" (328).

But behind the public face of Zenith's most successful man of the cloth is a fallen man of the flesh. Elmer's hunger for women is as great as his hunger for success—and nearly undoes him. The femme fatale is Hettie Dowler, who becomes his private secretary. Within weeks after he hires her, Elmer is enjoying Hettie's bed and the applause of her kisses as he rehearses his sermons in her flat. The ax falls one evening as Elmer and Hettie sit on the couch in her apartment. The door to the hall opens suddenly, and a grave-looking man confronts them. He says he is Hettie's husband! He is aware of their affair and demands $50,000 hush money, or he will expose the Rev. Dr. Elmer Gantry and sue him in court for that amount to compensate for the loss of his wife's affections. Elmer responds to the threat with typical bravado, but actually he despairs. When he leaves Hettie, he makes a midnight call on his old friend and confidant, T.J. Rigg. Fortunately, Lawyer Rigg knows con artists when he sees them. He hires a detective and soon has enough incriminating information about Hettie and her accomplice to rescue Elmer. In a tense meeting, Riggs recites a long list of charges pending against them. They have skipped out of innumerable towns. All the police departments in those towns would be delighted to find them. Rigg offers Hettie a chance to gain their freedom by recanting her charges against the Rev. Dr. Gantry. She and her "husband" are eager to escape and quickly sign a statement retracting all their accusations of immorality against Elmer Gantry. They swear that all the rumors about the minister published recently in the newspapers are false.

Elmer Gantry is relieved and grateful. The next Sunday as he watches the choir filing into the auditorium, he feels sincerely repentant. "I've learned my lesson. I'll never look at a girl again," he tells God prayerfully. He gazes through an open door at twenty-five hundred worshippers gathered for the morning service. He realizes how much he loves the church, how much he would miss "the choir, the pulpit, the singing, the adoring faces," if they did not believe in him. Will they believe he is innocent? He enters the sanctuary. They rise and cheer! "Oh my friends! [a sobbing Elmer cries]. Do you believe in my innocence, in the fiendishness of my accusers? Reassure me with a hallelujah!" And they do; a hallelujah thunders through the auditorium. As he turns to include the choir in the prayer that follows, he notices for the first time that there is a new singer, "a girl with charming ankles and lively eyes, with whom he would certainly have to become acquainted. But the thought was so swift that it did not interrupt the paean of his prayer" (431–32).

Though Elmer Gantry is clearly the central character in Lewis's novel, the book is much more than the fictional biography of an unusually opportunistic American faith seller. Elmer is not one of a kind but one of a class. All the *successful* clergy who appear in *Elmer Gantry* are commercial preachers. Sharon Falconer, by far the most-sophisticated commercial preacher in the novel, teaches Elmer Gantry how to be a successful commercial preacher.[35] From Sharon, Elmer learns how appearance helps make a minister successful. Sharon's public identity is entirely constructed. Her real name is Katie Jonas; she is from Utica, New York, not old Virginia as she pretends to be; the daughter of a brick worker, not a converted southern belle. Katie invents Sharon Falconer when she is working as a stenographer and looking for some way to better herself. Katie can become the highly successful Sharon Falconer because she learns how to calculate her appearance to gain exactly what she wants in every situation. When she preaches, she wears a flowing white robe and gives the appearance of an angel. When she negotiates financial arrangements for a crusade, she dresses in a gray business suit. She swings a pair of pince-nez, "with lenses made of window-glass," and exudes "an air of metropolitan firmness" as she presses the local sponsors—until they grant exactly the financial arrangements she wants (193).

Though Sharon Falconer is clearly the most successful commercial preacher in the novel, Sinclair Lewis takes great pains to show that she is not unique. Sharon is one of a class. A "shop talk" session that includes Sharon, Elmer, and Dr. Howard Bancock Binch, another traveling evangelist, demonstrates that *all* successful traveling evangelists employ sales-like methods in their ministries:

> "What methods, Dr. Binch," asked Elmer, "do you find the most successful in forcing people to come to the altar when they resist the Holy Ghost?"
>
> "I always begin by asking those interested in being prayed for to hold up their hands."
>
> "Oh, I believe in having them stand up if they want prayer. Once you get a fellow to his feet, it's so much easier to coax him out into the aisle and down to the front. . . . We've trained our ushers to jump right in the minute anybody gets up, and say 'Now, Brother, won't you come down front and shake hands with Sister Falconer and make your stand for Jesus.'"
>
> "No," said Dr. Binch, "my experience is that there are many timid people who have to be led gradually. To ask them to stand up is too big a step. But actually, we're probably both right. My motto as a soul-saver, if I may venture to apply such a lofty title to myself, is that one should use every method that, in the vernacular, will sell the goods." (207–8)

When local ministers in Zenith get together, their shop talk is similar to shop talk among traveling evangelists. On one occasion, Zenith's Methodist pastors discuss the relative worth of suggestions put forth in church "trade papers," including "the comparative values of a giant imitation thermometer, a giant clock, and a giant automobile speedometer, as register of money coming in during special drives; the question of gold and silver stars as rewards for Sunday School attendance; the effectiveness of giving the children savings-banks in the likeness of a jolly little church to encourage them to save their pennies for Christian work" (324).

Sinclair Lewis seems to attribute the success of commercial preachers like Elmer Gantry to two factors: their lack of scruples, especially their willingness to serve the interests of business leaders in the congregations and communities where they minister, and the naïveté of typical church members. The same provincialism and gullibility that *Main Street*'s Carol Kennicott finds in Gopher Prairie is present in the congregations Elmer Gantry preaches to on Sundays. The Rev. Dr. Gantry takes advantage of their willing gullibility. He gives them a vision of religion that matches their cultural biases, and they reward him with devotion and loyalty. They might have seen through Gantry, but Lewis's characterization implies that they don't want to. They don't want to question the conventions that he honors. Theirs is a blind faith. Elmer Gantry succeeds, in part, because he ministers to naive and willing believers.

Elmer Gantry also succeeds because he is willing to serve the entrenched and powerful in his community. Elmer is corruptible; he permits those who use religion to repress others to use him to pursue their own advantage. Lewis connects those who maim Frank Shallard directly to what he views as the evils of Fundamentalism (389–93).[36] Shallard's liberal social and theological views mark him as a dangerous person and justify the horrendous mutilation he suffers. Those who attack him will employ even the most dastardly methods to protect their interests. They would much rather support a morally questionable, orthodox-sounding minister like Elmer Gantry—especially if they can use ministers like him to help them destroy a "dangerous" liberal like Frank Shallard.[37]

Sinclair Lewis's description of Elmer Gantry as a commercial preacher, as overpowering as it sometimes is, does not seem to me to be his main concern in the novel. Lewis's stated goal in this "minister novel" is to describe the real experience of being a minister *from the inside*.[38] While ministers like Elmer dominate the novel, not all the ministers in *Elmer Gantry* are commercial preachers, and those who are *not* successful commercial preachers seem as authentic as, and at times even more authentic than, the commercial ministers Lewis castigates. There are moments in the novel when Lewis seems surprisingly sympathetic to the plight of ordinary, dedicated, faithful ministers. Lewis captures the simple, profound, and authentic devotion of the country preachers who ordain Elmer and Eddie Fislinger. Elmer is genuinely moved as they lay their hands on his head:

> On his head were the worn hands of three veteran preachers, and suddenly he was humble, for a moment he was veritably being ordained to the priestly service of God.
>
> He had been only impatient till this instant. In the chapels of Mizpah and Terwillinger he had heard too many famous visiting pulpiteers to be impressed by the rustic eloquence of the Kayooska Association. But he felt now their diffident tenderness, their unlettered fervor—these poverty-twisted parsons who believed, patient in their bare and baking tabernacles, that they were saving the world, and who wistfully welcomed the youths that they themselves had been. (79–80)

Later in the novel when Elmer visits Eddie Fislinger after Eddie has served as a minister for several years, Lewis again shows his sensitivity and appreciation of ordinary preachers. The formerly fervent YMCA student leader is now a mediocre minister who feels trapped in a congregation that isn't responding to his ministry. As Elmer travels away from their meeting, he feels the defeat Eddie feels: "Eddie had lost such devout fires as he had once shown in the Y.M.C.A.; already he was old, settled down, without conceivable adventure, waiting for death" (155).

Lewis's description of Elmer Gantry's unsuccessful struggle to become a faithful believer is similarly poignant and seems equally authentic. As Elmer feels the weight of the hands of the ordaining ministers on his head, he prays "not as an exhibition but sincerely, passionately, savoring righteousness: 'Dear God—I'll get down to it—not show off but just think of thee—do good—God help me!'" (80). Midway through the novel, when Sharon is dead and the Methodist bishop has given him a chance to begin again, as Elmer kneels in the empty church at Banjo Crossing, he prays with equal sincerity: "Lord, thou who hast stooped to my great unworthiness and taken even me to thy Kingdom, . . . make me whole and keep me pure, and in all things, Our Father, thy will be done. Amen" (265). At the end of the novel, even after all his despicable behavior in Zenith, Elmer still yearns for grace: "He knelt. He did not so much pray as yearn inarticulately. But this came out clearly: 'I've learned my lesson. . . . I'm going to be all the things I want other folks to be'" (431).

But grace never comes to Elmer Gantry. Perhaps the most damning aspect of Lewis's novel is the fact that neither Elmer's prayers nor those of any other minister in the novel are answered. Elmer prays for strength to overcome his sin and never receives it. Elmer prays, and he falls. He falls again and again, not only because he lacks moral character but also because there is in Lewis's view no Higher Power to uphold him.[39] He is a casualty of the displaced Divine. *Elmer Gantry* is a tragedy. Elmer falls because no God exists that can prevent his fall. Within the post-secular revolution, radical culture Lewis reflects in the novel, both the Divine and the divine are flawed. Gantry's God seems as counterfeit as Gantry.

PART III

The Legacy

1930s–2000s

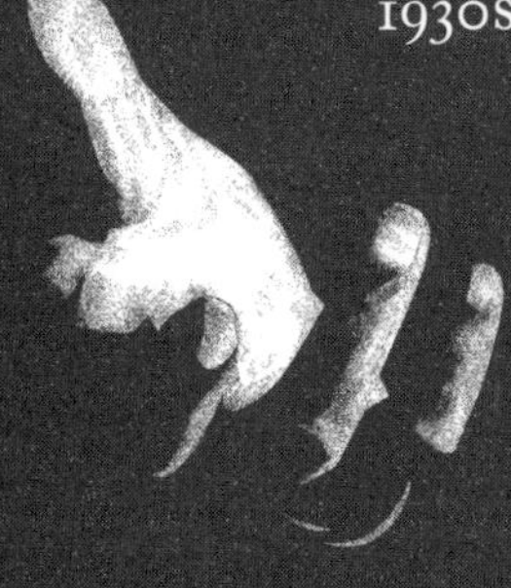

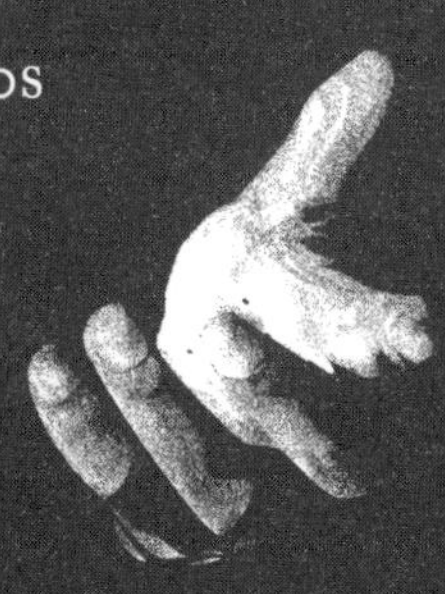

The final belief is to believe in a fiction, which you know to be a fiction, there being nothing else.

—Wallace Stevens, "Adagia"

I ain't preachin' no more much. The sperit ain't in the people much no more; and worse'n that, the sperit ain't in me no more.

—The Rev. Jim Casy in John Steinbeck, *The Grapes of Wrath*

X

FALLEN DIVINES

Some Contemporary Images

The displacing of divines in American society produced a cultural legacy that has shaped and still shapes cultural images of ministers mirrored in American fiction. Though not every work of fiction published after the 1920s reflects the fall of Protestant ministers and their God, as the years pass, the effects of this cultural transformation are apparent across the spectrum of cultural images. As noted in chapter 8, the actual displacement culminated during the cultural movement known as modernism. Modernism represented a rejection and turning away from the past, including theological perspectives associated with traditional faith. The previous integrating reality of traditional beliefs was still apparent and many Americans continued to embrace it, but modernism discredited that reality.

During the twentieth century as modernism moved into postmodernism, not only were past realities rejected but also individuals and groups began to construct new perceptual worlds in place of discredited, premodern worlds. These new worlds often embodied remnants of the old worlds—traditional views and experiences of God and community, for example—but these remnants now appeared as fragments of lost realities. The harmonized world in which the fragments cohered to form a unified whole was lost. The fragmented nature of this postmodern perception of reality still shapes cultural images of ministers of God.

Deprived Preachers: A Radical Image

As the old, traditional world was discredited, fictional divines were deprived of a worldview that lent them credibility and gave them authority. Like their real-life counterparts, they struggled to minister in a society that questioned their faith and discounted their significance. The cultural legacy of displacement is most apparent in art or literary fiction during the twentieth century. Within the new perceptual worlds encouraged by displacement, it is difficult to imagine how anyone could have believed in the stable, integrated reality of the premodern world. Doubt becomes incredulity.

This cultural discrediting of Christian faith is already anticipated in William Faulkner's modernist portrayal of the Rev. Joseph Mahon, the anachronistic Victorian minister in *Soldiers' Pay*, Faulkner's 1926 novel I discuss in chapter 8. Mahon is an obsolete divine who has no adequate word to speak to his mortally wounded and severely disfigured son Donald, a victim of the Great War. The friends who bring Donald home carry with them the reality of the war, a reality that overwhelms and displaces the only world Donald's minister father understands. As Donald slips slowly out of life, his father's faith falters completely. When Donald dies, the quiet order of the rural village world and parish the Rev. Mr. Mahon serves also dies. Neither the minister nor his God seems sufficient now. Even their assumed adequacy in the past seems doubtful. The old world and the old God seem distant from present experience. When the old world and God slip away in *Soldiers' Pay*, no new world that includes God emerges to take their place.

In *The Sound and the Fury*, Faulkner's 1929 novel that appears three years after *Soldiers' Pay*, the characters' worlds of experience are even more disconnected from a lost past. This new novel embodies both postmodernist and modernist perspectives.[1] Benjy, Quentin, Caddy, and Jason Compson and their mother live simultaneously in two worlds. They all inhabit the fictional world of Yoknapatawpha County, and each also lives within a unique world of his or her own construction. The Yoknapatawpha County world they all inhabit is Faulkner's invented "geography of imagination, a self-contained, imagined 'world' that vies to replace the lost world of political, cultural, and theological order that vanished with . . . [the] 'disappearance of God.'"[1] The individual worlds each Compson constructs and inhabits are as distinctive and disconnected from each other as Faulkner's imagined world is from other social worlds.

Except for a flashback to 1910, all the action in *The Sound and the Fury* takes place in fictional Jefferson, Yoknapatawpha County, Mississippi, during the three days of Easter weekend, 1928. The different sections of the novel reveal each sibling's unique perceptions of himself or herself and his or her world. The only perception of reality available to each Compson is her or his own. Faulkner establishes the limited and idiosyncratic nature of these individually constructed realities with great force. He opens the novel with a long and demanding chapter that forces the reader into the perceptual world constructed by the developmentally disabled Compson son, Benjy. Each of the chapters that follow describes the perceptual world of another Compson. These other worlds are not as difficult to fathom as Benjy's is, but they are just as limiting and idiosyncratic.

Though all the Compsons (with the exception of son Quentin, who attends Harvard and lives in Cambridge, Massachusetts, during the time of his narrative) live in and around Jefferson, there is no overall world of *common* experience that all of them perceive that might interconnect their individual worlds. The Compsons interact, but they never interconnect. There is no larger, broader world that includes some common reality like God or family or place that either informs the Compsons' individual experiences in some common way, gives them a solid anchor in the past, or provides them with solid roots in the present. The traditional pasts of God, culture, family, and place continue to shape the Compsons, as they do characters in Faulkner's other novels set in Jefferson, but they cannot access these pasts in any helpful way. Elements of these larger worlds are present only as figments within the experience of each individual, more haunting than helpful.

Dilsey, the Compsons' African American servant, is the one character in *The Sound and the Fury* who is not afflicted by the displacing and distorting effects associated with modernism. Unlike the Compsons she serves, Dilsey's personal, social, and spiritual worlds are still intact and interconnected. Family, faith, place, and community form an integrated social and personal reality in Dilsey's experience. That reality includes both the Divine and divines; God and ministers are powerfully present and integrated into Dilsey's world.[2] The guest preacher on Easter Sunday at Dilsey's church witnesses to the integrated wholeness of Dilsey's experience. Very little of this preacher's strength stems from personal characteristics. In fact, when he is first introduced, members of the congregation wonder why he was invited to give the Easter sermon. Faulkner describes him as "undersized" with a "wizened" face. Next to the tall, muscular local preacher, he looks "like a small, aged monkey."[3] "En dey brung dat all de way fum Saint Looey," Frony, Dilsey's daughter, whispers when she sees him.

But the small man's massive voice quickly counters these first impressions. As he stands at the reading desk and begins to preach, his resounding "Brethren" startles the gathered congregation: "The preacher had not moved. His arm lay yet across the desk, and he still held that pose while the voice died in sonorous echoes between the walls. It was as different as day and dark from his former tone, with a sad, timbrous quality like an alto horn, sinking into their hearts and speaking there again when it had ceased in fading and cumulative echoes" (175). The sermon that follows permeates the gathered congregation with the spirit of the resurrected Jesus. As Dilsey and her family walk away from the service, her children talk about the preacher:

> "He sho a preacher, mon! He didn't look like much at first, but hush!"
>
> "He seed de power en de glory."
>
> "Yes, suh. He seed hit. Face to face he seed hit."
>
> As they continue on in silence tears roll down Dilsey's face. Frony tells her to stop crying. People are staring.
>
> "I've seed de first en de last," Dilsey said. "Never you mind me."
>
> "First en last whut?" Frony said.
>
> "Never you mind," Dilsey said. "I seed de beginnin, en now I sees de endin." (177)

No secular revolution has displaced the Divine and divines in Dilsey's world. Past, present, and future, God and creation and ministers, individual and social experiences are all integrated and interconnected. The living God is still powerfully present in both Dilsey's individual world and her social world. But even a Dilsey filled with the spirit cannot bring the benefits of her world to the Compsons. When she arrives home after the church service, she walks quietly past Mrs. Compson's bedroom door, thinking the sick woman is asleep. But Mrs. Compson calls out to her, "Where's Jason?" (Jason has gone to look for his daughter Quentin, who has run away with a drifter.) There's no word. She asks Dilsey to pick up the Bible that has fallen off her bed. Dilsey finds it, lying (significantly) face down on the floor. She places it back on the bed, where Mrs. Compson can reach it. But the gesture seems futile. Dilsey reminds the old woman, "You cant see to read, noways." But dim eyesight is not the only obstacle. The book that testifies to a living God for Dilsey is only a relic from a lost world to Mrs. Compson. Dilsey goes back down to the kitchen. She notices the stove is almost cold. She sets out some cold food. She sings a hymn as she walks back and forth, repeating the first two lines over and over. She is alone, but she is not alone. The hymn recalls God who was and is and will be present in all of Dilsey's worlds. It has ultimate meaning. "Ise seed de first en de last," Dilsey says out loud. The Compsons see neither.

Divines deprived of their faith are much more common figures in American literary fiction after the 1920s than powerful believers like the guest preacher in Dilsey's church. The effects of displacement that burden the Compsons also burden many of the ministers who appear in American literary fiction throughout the twentieth century and beyond. As the decades pass, the social and cultural world that supported believing slips further and further into the past. As the gap between the now of disbelief and the then of faith widens, preachers who lose their faith are less likely to recover it. Like the Compsons, they not only don't believe anymore; they can't believe. They have become bereft believers.

Jim Casy, the preacher in John Steinbeck's *The Grapes of Wrath* (1939), is one of these bereft believers. On a hot day, Casy and Tom Joad meet as they both travel the same road. As they talk, the preacher recognizes the boy become a man; he baptized him years before in an irrigation ditch. He longs for that time when he "used to get an irrigation ditch so squirmin' full of sinners half of 'em like to drownded. But not no more. . . . Just Jim Casy now. Ain't got the call no more. Got a lot of sinful idears—but they seem kinda sensible. . . . I ain't preachin' no more much. The sperit ain't in the people much no more; and worse'n that, the sperit ain't in me no more" (27). Jim Casy never recovers that lost faith. The world that supports that faith has blown away, like the soil from the land that surrounds him. The people Casy served when he did have the spirit have been forced to leave their homes to travel the same road west as Casy. Like Casy, they are bereft. All the places where they and Casy knew how to believe have been reduced to dust. The familiar world that integrated God with human experience has blown away.

The image of ministers as bereft believers persists in American fiction throughout the twentieth century. It is reflected in John Updike's 1996 novel *In the Beauty of the Lilies*. Significantly, the opening date of the novel is 1910. On a hot summer day in Paterson, New Jersey, the Rev. Clarence Wilmot, a Presbyterian minister who serves the Fourth Presbyterian Church in that city, loses his faith. He has been reading Robert Ingersoll's *Some Mistakes of Moses* (1879) in order to gather evidence to refute Ingersoll for a troubled parishioner. As he walks along, he is suddenly overwhelmed by the thought that Ingersoll is not wrong but right. The Old Testament God is an "absurd bully. . . . There is no such God, nor should there be." This final loss is the culmination of a vain attempt in Wilmot's mind to hold on to believing—"like a many-legged, wingless insect that had long and tediously been struggling to climb up the walls of a slick-walled porcelain basin; and now a sudden impatient wash of water swept it down the drain" (5–6). The secular revolution, represented specifically in Ingersoll's *Some Mistakes of Moses*, displaces Wilmot's faith and washes it down the drain.

The loss leaves Clarence Wilmot bereft. Facts like "cruelty and death" that before raised questions now become simply facts. There is some relief: Wilmot is out from under the "riddle of predestination" and the burden of wondering how God can condemn people when all their actions "from alpha to omega are His very own." But this small sense of relief hardly mitigates the overwhelming sense of loss and emptiness that Wilmot experiences. Humans lose any special value. Without God's providence as the energizing force, the physical universe becomes "horrible and disgusting" (7). Clarence Wilmot never recovers his faith. The rest of Updike's novel describes how Wilmot's immediate family and the generations that follow him suffer under the legacy of his loss.

Deprived divines who are victims of the disconnection of all human experiences and activities from faith as a result of the secular revolution are common figures in American literary fiction after the 1920s. David Treadup in John Hersey's novel *The Call* (1985) recalls Harold Frederic's *Theron Ware*. Treadup not only fails to reconnect science and faith, he loses his own faith in the process. After a life-changing conversion during his student days at Syracuse University early in the century, Treadup goes to China as a missionary under the auspices of the YMCA. As a young missionary, Treadup uses only preaching evangelism to present Christianity to the Chinese. But after years of limited success, he begins to employ literacy education, programs of social benefit, and references to science to gain the interest of the Chinese he seeks to convert. He hopes that better-educated Chinese will associate literacy and western scientific advancement with the Christians who give them education and bring other social benefits:

> Mr. Hsiao makes the introduction, but this time Treadup is the main speaker—in Mandarin. He puts on a show. He has brought blind-man posters, but he has brought something else, too, which doesn't seem to have much to do with literacy, at least in an immediate way. It is the battered old Wrestling Gyroscope. He has decided to amaze first and persuade afterward. (376)

Treadup spins the large gyroscope. Two men from the village try to move the spinning wheel. They cannot. Do those gathered understand why they cannot? No. Do they know why Mr. Hsiao and David understand? It is because they can read and write. And because they can read and write, they have learned about science. Members of the village agree that they would like to learn to read and write so they can understand about science.

Treadup's efforts to bring social betterment and scientific demonstrations gain the attention of his Chinese audiences, but members of these audiences fail to connect social improvements and scientific knowledge to the faith Treadup seeks to promote. As the years pass, an increasingly frustrated Treadup suffers through the Japanese occupation and then the Communist revolution in China. He questions not only the wisdom of his social gospel approach but also the truth of the Christian faith he is pledged to represent. In his old age, Treadup becomes a cynic, bereft of the faith that originally spurred him to China.

Dale Kohler, the idealistic born-again theological student in John Updike's *Roger's Version* (1986) makes an even more sophisticated attempt to bring science into the service of faith. Kohler wants to use a computer-simulated model to demonstrate the existence of God. Science, he promises, will soon be able to offer a physical description of the universe, a description, Kohler is convinced, that is certain to testify to the existence of God. With some help from a computer model, Kohler believes he can anticipate that actual description. Though Kohler fails to persuade the somewhat cynical, middle-aged theological professor Roger Lambert to support his effort (Lambert predicts quite accurately that Kohler will lose his faith when the effort fails), he is finally able to convince the theological faculty to give him a grant to support his research. Dale spends hours in front of the computer screen, attempting to ring meaning from the numbers and images in the simulation. One long night he thinks he has a breakthrough: in the confusion on the screen he sees what appears to be the image of a hand. The hand seems relaxed. Why? Is it relaxed because it is the hand of someone slain, perhaps someone who has died on a cross? He requests a printout; it is disappointing. He returns to the screen. Perhaps a rerun will produce a better image, or—he hardly dares to hope—even more of the body to which the hand is connected. He types "repeat." The computer strains. The hand vanishes. Again he types "repeat." The computer strains again. Then a gray screen appears, with black letters: "Insufficient heap storage."

The committee renews Dale Kohler's grant, but his research is never successful. At a party, an almost sadistic (and somewhat intoxicated)

Professor Myron Kriegman, "a real scientist," delivers the mortal blow that kills what remains of Kohler's faith. In a long conversation, the obviously superior thinker plays with Kohler's notion of simulation as a demonstration of the providence of God in the universe. It's all the result of chance. From a "Big Bang." Finally, a desperate Dale asks the life scientist, "How about the origin of life? Those odds are pretty impossible to get a self-replicating organism with its own energy system" (328). The unwitting student has now placed the argument on the life science professor's home turf. Dr. Kriegman has had just enough alcohol to lose all restraint. The speech that follows is overwhelming. Life comes from clay. The professor details all the steps. All life, including human life, is simply the result of an evolutionary process. God has nothing to do with it. God isn't needed. Dale has found nothing in his computer search because there is nothing to find.[4]

Disconnection from God makes Jack Eccles, Harry "Rabbit" Angstrom's pastor in John Updike's *Rabbit, Run* (1960), an even more pathetic figure than Dale Kohler. Eccles stands on the edge of the other character's lives, included only because he represents some significant functions ministers had in a former time. But in the present he is useless: "His big fair head seems stuffed with a gray mash of everybody's precious secrets and passionate questions, a mash that nothing, young as he is, can color" (106). Eccles keeps having conversations with Rabbit Angstrom, but none of them help prevent the steady disintegration of Rabbit's life. He has only companionship to offer Rabbit, nothing of spiritual substance. Actually, Rabbit's relationship with Eccles contributes to Rabbit's deterioration. Eccles's wife Lucy exposes her husband's hollowness in a conversation after they discover Rabbit's despondent wife has drowned her baby. "Where was *he* [Rabbit]?" when it happened, she asks after Eccles receives the telephone call informing him of the tragedy. No one knows. The caller has asked Eccles to try to find Rabbit. Janice looks at her minister husband, completely exasperated: "Why must you spend your time chasing after that worthless heel?" "He's not worthless," Jack protests. "I love him." The statement seems ludicrous to Janice. "You love him. That's sickening. . . . Why don't you try loving me, or your children?" "I do," he replies. The meaninglessness of the reply angers Janice. "You *don't*, Jack. . . . You couldn't bear to love anyone who might return it" (265–66). There is nothing in Eccles that could connect him to another. The pastor is an empty vessel.

In novels published during the 1970s and 1980s, the results of spiritual deprivation are even worse: spiritual emptiness often leads to depravity. Tom Marshfield, the theologically orthodox preacher in John Updike's 1974 novel *A Month of Sundays*, and Ed Parsley, the clumsy liberal minister in Updike's

1984 novel *The Witches of Eastwick*, are both deprived and depraved. Like Roger Lambert in *Roger's Version*, Marshfield tries unsuccessfully to fill his spiritual emptiness with sex. Sex fails the even more pathetic Parsley as well; in desperation, he leaves his wife and runs off with a hippie woman to join a radical movement. Parsley's ultimate demise is more spectacularly symbolic than his promiscuity: he accidently blows himself up while trying to assemble a homemade bomb. Once he is gone, hardly anyone misses Ed Parsley—including his wife, who becomes the local preacher in his stead. He had nothing substantive to offer; as his name suggests, he was never more than a garnish to life.

Spiritual emptiness that characterizes corporate clerics in radical fiction during the early-twentieth century becomes increasingly typical of clerics in popular and even church fiction as the century progresses. The Rev. Fred Worthington, the cynical Methodist district superintendent nicknamed "Beloved" in the pseudonymous Gregory Wilson's *The Stained Glass Jungle* (1962), reflects a church version. He nearly disillusions the Rev. Jack Lee, a young, idealistic minister on fire for the cause of Christ. Midway through the novel, Lee asks the superintendent to arrange with the bishop for a lesser appointment, at a salary lower than the one he receives presently. The very bureaucratic Worthington is flabbergasted by the request: "I know that in all my years in the superintendency I have never yet had a man deliberately seek out a church beneath his salary bracket simply because it offered greater opportunity for service" (176). Worthington can't believe Lee would want to place service above salary and prestige.

In Cassandra King's 2002 novel *The Sunday Wife*, the Rev. Benjamin Lynch is the spiritually empty ambitious minister; Dean Lynch, his spouse, is the suffering Sunday wife. When Lynch is assigned to a large church in Florida, he sees success there as a stepping-stone to the episcopacy. Already an insensitive and neglectful husband, he has even less time for his wife in this new parish. Her friend Augusta Holderfield encourages Dean to develop her musical talent. Dean begins to play her dulcimer and sing in local clubs. Church members complain she is not acting like a minister's wife. When their complaints reach Ben, his only concern is the effect they may have on his career. The ever-compliant Dean gives up her public performances—and becomes increasingly depressed. Ben arranges for her to see a church-affiliated marriage counselor, who tells her that her primary obligation is to be a supporting wife to her minister husband. The novel climaxes when Dean discovers that the successful minister who is her husband's mentor stole affection from her best friend Augusta when he needed it—and then cast Augusta aside when he feared their affair might threaten his career ambitions. When Dean finally breaks free of the emotional bonds her husband and his ministerial colleagues place on her, she recognizes that she too has been victimized by an abusive divine. Sitting on a beach at the end of the novel, she realizes why she has finally been able to leave her spiritually empty and relentlessly ambitious minister husband: "I know now—without any doubt—that God has not left me. I have left God instead" (384). The play on words is clear: she treated this divine like he was a Divine—and he didn't deserve it.

The disappearance of God and the spiritual emptiness that results for a minister of God are painfully apparent in Reynolds Price's post-9/11 novel *The Good Priest's Son* (2005). Mabry Kincaid, an independent art conservator, is flying home from Europe to New York on September 11, 2001. While he is en route, terrorists crash airplanes into the towers of the World Trade Center in New York. The ensuing devastation renders Mabry's lower Manhattan apartment uninhabitable. After Mabry's plane is diverted to Nova Scotia and he realizes he will be unable to return to New York for several days, he decides to travel south to visit his father, the Rev. Tasker Kincaid, an eighty-three-year-old retired Episcopal priest. Tasker, who is confined to a wheelchair by injuries suffered in a recent fall, is living in Arbay's childhood home in Wells, a small town in North Carolina.

Actually, Mabry welcomes the unexpected chance to go home again. Since leaving Wells, he has been much less successful personally than he has professionally. After a series of affairs, his marriage to Frances collapsed. Soon after their divorce, Frances developed terminal cancer. Mabry set aside his career and returned to their home to care for her during the last months of her life. This sincere act of kindness is not sufficient to repair Mabry's relationship with his adult daughter Charlotte; she is still unable to forgive him for his unfaithfulness to her mother. Since Frances's death, Mabry has stumbled on through a series of relationships with women, none of them really satisfying. Perhaps a return to his roots will refresh him.

But the Wells Mabry finds is not idyllic. In Price's novel, neither God nor his minister's faith is intact—and any recovery is unlikely. An angry exchange that occurs between father and son soon after Mabry's return confronts both of them with the fact that the ideal world they recall is no longer what it was:

> "You didn't hear this, son—*you should have stayed here*. You can stay here now. It's not too late."

> "Pa, what in the world is waiting for me here? Have you looked at the actual present? It's a nearly dead village with half as many people as when I was born." (44; italics in the original)

Mabry's assessment is correct. Life is no more intact in Wells than it is in the world beyond the town. Mabry's old buddy Vance is wasting away, drinking and shooting pool in the tavern he owns. Mabry's high school sweetheart Gwyn, recently divorced, is back in Wells trying to put her life together. The old house she's living in will cost more to repair than she can afford. Mabry's father Tasker nearly exhausted his savings to buy back Mabry's childhood home. But this house also is badly in need of repair: the leaking roof is symbolic of Tasker's leaking life. What Mabry discovers in Wells is more than the usual "you-can't-go-home-again" reality. There is no haven for anyone here. The global cultural roof is leaking even here.

There are not even any ideal images left in the Rev. Tasker Kincaid's memories of his priestly life. Tasker's recollections are dominated by compromises. He confesses to Mabry painful, unforgivable lapses that marred his ministry: "I fucked three women six or seven times—women in my churches who were meant to be in my spiritual care, though I all but ruined them. *Forevermore*." Mabry is taken aback by his father's confession. Were they minors? he wonders. No, but the ruin is no less: "Son, a lot of women all but worship their priest. Or they did back when I was young enough to want them. So *ruin* is the word, and don't try to change it" (111; italics in the original).

Irrecoverable personal losses are rendered even worse by lost faith. During a visit to the cemetery, as Mabry and his father look at Mabry's brother's grave, Tasker confesses to Mabry that the dead brother, Gabe, killed more than thirty years before in a shooting accident, "was the one human being I ever truly loved." Mabry is wounded by Tasker's admission: "You wish I'd been the boy that got shot," he wonders, hoping for some affirmation from his father. No direct response is forthcoming. Tasker's evasive reply is devastating—and he knows it is. When they are together the next day, he tries to soften the blow:

> "What I said there [in the cemetery] seemed the truth at the moment—and even back here, later that night. But surely you're old enough now to know the truth shifts and slides from hour to hour, if not by the instant."
>
> "Yes sir, I am. . . . But aren't you in the business of *eternal truth*?"

> "Oh, I was," Tasker said. "I was, back when."
> "And you don't believe it now?"
> "On and off," Tasker said, "like most human beings." (183)

Equivocating faith is the best the good priest can muster.

Soon after this conversation, Tasker suffers a major stroke. Within a few days, he dies. The instructions he leaves for his funeral reflect his diminished faith. He requests that his body be "inexpensively burned" and interred between his wife and Gabe, that there be no service in any church and no presiding clergy, and that "my son Mabry and my granddaughter Charlotte stand in the graveyard on the brightest day convenient and read aloud, to one another and whoever else might care to be present, whatever words from the Book of Common Prayer seem beautiful to them and have some chance of being true" (270). In Price's novel, God survives neither in the divine's experience nor anywhere in the world in which he lives. Not even in memory.

A few deprived divines become disturbed divines. The displacement of the divine that erodes the reality of God leaves them only with warped imaginings of God. Deprived of any socially rooted and shared perception of God, they retreat into their own misguided believing. They struggle not with the emptiness that afflicts other bereft believers but, rather, with fragmentary and confused recollections. These residual perceptions are often haunting recollections of the Divine, "some version of the cultural past that defies renovation, that insists on repeating itself as the 'return of the repressed.'"[6] This haunting God that remains is not a shared common reality but exists only within an individual's constructed reality.

The warping potential of such a haunting past is especially clear in the Rev. Gail Hightower, a Presbyterian cleric who appears in William Faulkner's *Light in August* (1932). Hightower is drawn to serve the Presbyterian church in Jefferson in part because he (and only he) carries the haunting memory of his grandfather as a Civil War hero who was killed at Jefferson. Soon after Hightower begins his preaching ministry there, the ghost of his grandfather begins to appear in his sermons. This grandfather who haunts Hightower's memory is a savior of the South, shot defending the honor of the South during a skirmish in Jefferson. In Hightower's sermons, this haunting memory of his grandfather becomes entangled with his perception of Jesus as the heroic, fallen savior God. Years after he has been forced out of the ministry, the townspeople in Jefferson still recall how the young Hightower seemed "wild in the pulpit, using religion as though it were a dream. . . . It was as if he couldn't get his religion and that galloping cavalry and his dead grandfather shot from the galloping horse untangled from each other, even in the pulpit . . . with his hands flying around him and the dogma he was supposed to preach all full of galloping cavalry and defeat and glory" (56–57).

Actually, neither the Jesus nor the grandfather in Hightower's memory was the hero he recollects. In truth, Hightower's grandfather was *not* a hero. He was not shot while liberating Jefferson but while attempting to rob a local henhouse. The recollection of Jesus that appears all tangled up with his grandfather in Hightower's sermons is equally confounded. Even when members of Hightower's congregation point up the foolishness in his preaching, Hightower still cannot break free from his haunting memories. Sunday after Sunday, he reiterates a tangled and distorted message of salvation enabled by Jesus and his grandfather. As the Sundays pass, the members of his congregation stop attending services; finally, no one is present to listen. Hightower continues to preach the same tangled gospel week after week to empty pews. After a tragic incident reveals that the minister's personal life is as disturbed as his ministry (his despairing wife dies from an apparent suicide), the trustees lock the doors of the church building to prevent him from preaching. Members of the congregation and community hope the discredited divine will leave Jefferson, but he does not. Hightower ends up living on a side street, doing artwork and developing photos. As the years pass, he becomes a local curiosity, watching but not participating actively in the life of the village, symbolizing a God who is as disconnected from the present world as he is.[7]

The deprived and disturbed divine who is out of touch with any reality also appears in Joyce Carol Oates's 1978 novel *Son of the Morning*. At one point in her story, the Rev. Nathan Vickery finds he is unable to resist looking lustfully at a woman. He knows that such a sin, especially if he acts on it, is unacceptable in a minister. In desperation, he follows the scriptural exhortation literally. While preaching, he confesses his temptation and then plucks out the offending right eye in full view of the gathered congregation. It is better to be maimed and blind than seeing and sinful. (In another 1970s' novel, Martin Gardner's *The Flight of Peter Fromm* [1973], the meltdown is still pathetic but also humorous. Peter goes berserk while preaching. He rips off his clothes, recites some lines from the Jabberwocky, and urinates on the organist [251–52].)

Oates's Nathan Vickery recalls Arthur Dimmesdale, the minister who is Hester's lover in Nathaniel Hawthorne's *The Scarlet Letter*. Like Vickery, Dimmesdale withdraws into his own disturbed believing when he fails to live up to the community's ideal image of a minister. He knows that a minister having sex with a woman other than his wife, especially one who is a member of his congregation, is guilty of an unforgivable sin in the eyes of the community. The faith Dimmesdale's congregation espouses includes forgiveness for those who repent, but retributive morality overwhelms faith in the actual community where Dimmesdale serves. When Vickery is unable to live with his sin, unlike Dimmesdale, he confesses it publicly and then tries to prevent its recurrence by plucking out the offending eye. Dimmesdale chooses a less-violent but ultimately even more self-destructive resolution. Both ministers suffer because they are unable to find either social or personal evidence of a God who can dispel their sin. They are left entirely at the mercy of their own deprived and disturbed believing. The court of popular opinion that rules in their minds shows no mercy. It condemns them to solitary confinement in the prison of their own misbelieving.[8]

Comic Calvinists: A Popular and Church Image

Some mid- and late-twentieth-century fictional clergy seem to be neither disturbed nor displaced divines. These fictional clerics assume that the biblically based, Christian paradigm is still valid. They not only don't contest the fallout from the secular revolution; they function as though it never occurred.[9] Pastors created by Grace Livingston Hill, Hartzell Spence, and Agnes Sligh Turnbull are early examples of fictional clergy who reflect this cultural image. Ministers in their novels are exemplary humans and firm believers. They have human feelings and face human temptations, but they always keep their faith and do their ministry, no matter what the challenge may be. Hilary Laurens, the minister at the center of Agnes Sligh Turnbull's *The Bishop's Mantel* (1947) exhibits both moral fortitude and strong faith. He steadfastly resists the advances of Diana Downes, a rich, young widow in his congregation. Diana is as attractive as she is bold, but Lauren's moral fortitude is never in doubt. He rejects her advances so forcefully that she realizes he will never compromise his morality.

Unwavering faith rather than unwavering morality is the central focus in Margaret Echard's *The Unbelieving Wife* (1955). The Rev. Bruce Cameron is so smitten with Vicki Sanderson, a young woman in the community, that he marries her even though he knows she is not a Christian believer. As the months pass, the unbelieving Vicki finds it increasingly difficult to play the role of a minister's wife; church members expect her to be the same kind of inspiring believer that her husband is. But Bruce refuses to cave in to their criticism. He stands by his unbelieving wife, and the example of his steadfast faith and loyalty finally leads Vicki to faith herself.

Within the more sophisticated, diverse, and secular cultural context that developed during the 1960s and 1970s, the idealized world peopled with hero ministers like Bruce Cameron that characterizes popular and church fiction published during the 1940s and 1950s seems naive and simplistic.[10] Writers who reflected images of ministers as heroic believing pastors continued to publish during the 1960s and after, but there were comparatively fewer of them.[11] The plausibility of Christian belief was not something that even popular writers could take for granted. Beginning in the 1970s, Americans in general were less certain that the *typical* minister was an upright character and unquestioning believer than they were during the 1940s and 1950s. Simply presenting a hero minister whose own experience testified to the reality and efficacy of Christian faith was no longer sufficient to move sophisticated readers of popular fiction to suspend their disbelief. The fact that God can work in the life of one individual divine was no longer convincing evidence that God is active and present in the world at large. Popular novelists still created fictional ministers they hoped would seem like real humans to their readers. But to make their fictional divines credible, writers now found it necessary to create entire imaginary worlds where the Christian paradigm was still in place, and then to convince their readers that these imagined worlds mirrored the real world. The tactic was often quite successful. Ministers in some of the most popular novels published during the 1980s and 1990s are convincing characters precisely because they live in premodern imaginary worlds where the Divine is still very much a present reality. I call these ministers "comic Calvinists" (an oxymoron) because they inhabit imaginary premodern worlds where a pervasive and benevolent God rules. Because they live under a comic order, the misadventures of comic Calvinists are never fatal. Readers can safely laugh at their foibles. A benevolent God always overcomes human missteps. Everything always comes out all right in the end.[12]

Garrison Keillor and Jan Karon are two current popular writers who create comic Calvinists and comic Calvinist worlds in which their divines live. Keillor's imaginary world is Lake Wobegon, a fictional small town in Minnesota. Two of his novels, *Lake Wobegon Days* (1985) and *Leaving Home* (1987) appeared on lists of best-selling books in the years they were published. Since the middle 1970s (with a short break during the late 1980s), Keillor has been a popular fixture on National Public Radio. His program *A Prairie Home Companion* features folk music, skits, "commercials," and a twenty-minute monologue during which he gives "the news from Lake Wobegon."

These twenty-minute monologues form the basis for many of the stories that appear in his books. Keillor ends each of them with the same familiar refrain, "And that's the news from Lake Wobegon, where all the women are strong, all the men are good-looking, and all the children are above average."[13] And, one might add, where God is still in his heaven; and ministers and everyone else who lives in Lake Wobegon can count on that.

The pervading reality of the Divine that undergirds the imagined world of Lake Wobegon guarantees that even the most ordinary fumbling clerics will witness to the reality of the Divine. "Pontoon Boat," a story included in *Leaving Home*, testifies to the powerful and benign God that pervades Garrison Keillor's imagined world. Twenty-four Lutheran pastors are on a five-day professional development tour and make a stop in Lake Wobegon. The purpose of the tour is to equip ministers for "Meeting the Pastoral Needs of Rural America." They are visiting typical rural towns throughout the Middle West to experience firsthand the problems people face in rural America. When Clint Bunsen hears about the purpose of the tour (to study problems), he wonders how it can be successful: "If a minister visits, you hide your problems, and shine up your children and put them through their paces. And you talk about other people's problems." But he recognizes that just being in Lake Wobegon may give the visitors the insights they need.

The tour's organizer, J. Peter Larson, is a seminary classmate of the Lutheran pastor in Lake Wobegon, the Rev. David Ingqvist. Pastor Larson's overly confident and very academic description of the tour suggests that the pastors who take it won't actually be equipped to meet the pastoral needs of rural America in any practical way. However, nothing is actually at stake in this tour; in the comic world of Lake Wobegon, the pastors' likely lack of effectiveness in dealing with the problems of rural America doesn't ultimately matter.

Pastor Ingqvist decides to welcome his visitors at a social gathering: a barbecue and cruise aboard the *Agnes D.*, a pontoon boat owned by Wally, who operates the Sidetrack Tap, the local bar in Lake Wobegon. The visitors are weightier divines than the hosts anticipated; twenty-four portly Lutheran clerics together on board the *Agnes D.* stress the capacity of the boat. When Wally casts off, the *Agnes D.* is already riding low and threatening to take on water. The flaming charcoal cooker growing hotter and hotter at the stern makes matters worse; the growing heat forces the group to shift toward the bow of the boat, and it begins to scoop up water. Wally decides a bit more speed will bring the bow of the boat up. The remedy is ill-advised: suddenly, the left pontoon goes under and the boat rolls, pitching eight Lutheran ministers into the water. The abrupt lurch also upsets the grill. With hundreds of burning coals rolling toward them, "the book of Revelation come to life," the remaining pastors plunge into the water. Fortunately, the lake is shallow, only five feet deep at the site of the disaster. Most of the pastors are short, just a bit more than five feet tall. They stand in the water, smiling, with "faces upturned, in prayerful apprehension." Feeling the weight of their water-soaked clothes and not knowing whether the water that surrounds them is deeper than where they stand, they are afraid to move. Clint's young nephew, who has been watching the unfolding drama, wades out to them. When the young boy stands in water only up to his waist, fifteen feet away from the frightened clerics, he calls to them: "It's not deep this way." In fulfillment of the scripture, "and a little child shall lead them" (Isaiah 11:6), the young boy leads twenty-four frantic Lutheran pastors to safety (103–8).

Jan Karon's imagined Mitford is qualitatively similar to Keillor's imagined Lake Wobegon. "It's easy to feel at home in Mitford. In these high, green hills, the air is pure, the village is charming and the people are generally lovable," the dustcover on the first book in the Mitford series boasts. Divine providence in Mitford is more explicit and overtly Christian than it is in Lake Wobegon. The central character in Karon's small town is Father Tim, a sixty-year-old Episcopal rector, whose blissful bachelorhood is challenged first by Barnabas, a stray black dog "the size of a Buick," whom Father Tim adopts, and then by Cynthia, a neighbor, who eventually becomes Father Tim's wife. As the Mitford series unfolds, Father Tim, like Pastor Ingqvist in Lake Wobegon, faces significant challenges in his personal life (a heart attack) and ministry (for example, when he takes responsibility for Dooley, a difficult adolescent). But like his fictional colleague in ministry, Father Tim weathers all the personal and professional trials that come his way. Sometimes he struggles, but the outcome of each struggle is never in doubt because it does not really depend on Father Tim's human strength or competence. Mitford, like Lake Wobegon, rests in the hands of a benevolent God.[14]

Readers who suspend disbelief and enter into these comic worlds of Lake Wobegon and Mitford can safely laugh at the foibles of clerics like Pastor Ingqvist and Father Tim because within these imagined worlds the effectiveness of God is never in doubt, nor is it contingent on the convincing witness of ministers or any other humans. Ministers can stumble in their attempts to minister without serious consequences because God is so clearly in charge.[15]

Other pastors in recent American fiction who reflect the comic Calvinist cultural image, though with less idealism than Karon's and Keillor's, include the Rev. Harry Donner in Conrad Richter's *A Simple, Honorable Man* (1962), the Rev Mr. Maclean in Norman Maclean's *A River Runs Through It* (1976), and, recently, the Rev. John Ames in Marilynne Robinson's *Gilead* (2004). John Ames seems to me to be the most convincing and historically accurate comic Calvinist in recent American fiction. He never exhibits the nostalgic idealism that sometimes makes clerics like Father Tim and Pastor Ingqvist seem too good to be true. Ames is well aware of issues believers face as they try to hold on to their faith in a postmodern world. His brother Edward experiences the displacement of the divine firsthand. He is one of the thousands who lose their faith when they go off to Germany for graduate study during the last half of the nineteenth century. When Edward returns home, he imposes his own lost faith on his family. The first evening he rejoins the family, Edward confirms their minister father's worst fears when he refuses to say grace before the evening meal:

> My father said, "You have lived under this roof. You know the customs of your family. You might show some respect for them." And Edward replied, and this was very wrong of him, "When I was a child, I thought as a child. Now that I am become a man, I have put away childish things." My father left the table, my mother sat still in her chair with tears streaming down her face, and Edward passed me the potatoes. (26)

Though they are upset by his apostasy, John Ames and his father read some of the books that led Edward to disbelieve. These books challenge John's and his father's thinking, but they do not displace their faith. Neither John nor his father is displaced from faith like Edward is because their faith is not simply a cognitive matter. Their believing is personal and experiential, rooted in a specific place, Gilead, and nurtured by the rituals of their living in that place. John Ames resists the postmodern notion that believing *requires* convincing thought: "I'm just trying to find a slightly useful way of saying there are things I don't understand. I'm not going to force some theory on a mystery and make foolishness of it, just because that is what people who talk about it normally do" (152). Ames struggles to work out a contemporary theology, but his inability to do so is not a significant failing; theology is not the basis of faith for him, nor does he suggest it should be for others. In matters of faith, thinking has its limits.[16]

John Ames recognizes that his experience in Gilead both limits and enables his believing: "I knew perfectly well at that time, as I had for years and years, that the Lord absolutely transcends any understanding I have of Him, which makes loyalty to Him a different thing from loyalty to whatever customs and doctrines and memories I happen to associate with Him" (235). Faith is always limited by the specificity that molds it. But such a specific experiential base is also absolutely essential to faith. Arguing the reality of faith with those who lack or lose such a specific experiential foundation is futile: "It only confirms them in their skepticism. Because nothing true can be said about God from a posture of defense" (177). Even the soundest argument cannot produce faith in those who resist believing.

The postmodern culture that accompanies the displacement of the divine impinges on Gilead and John Ames. But Ames's faith still provides a protective haven for him, even in the emerging postmodern world. Ames knows that his experience of the reality of God in Gilead may not suffice for others; it may not suffice beyond him and the Gilead that nurtured him. As he walks along one evening near the end of his life, he finds himself out of breath and decides to stop inside his church building to rest. He sits alone in the quiet and recounts the conversation he has just had with a young man who left Gilead and then returned in hopes that, by returning, he could recover lost faith and put his broken life together. Ames recalls the look in the young man's face as they walked along only a few hours before. There was "a sense of irony at having invested hope in this sad old place, and also the cost to him of relinquishing it. And I knew what hope it was. It was just that kind the place was meant to encourage, that a harmless life could be lived here unmolested. . . . To play catch of an evening, to smell the river, to hear the train pass. These little towns were once the bold ramparts meant to shelter just such peace" (242). What gives Robinson's novel so much integrity is her clear recognition that neither Ames's faith nor Gilead is ideal. John Ames is a comic hero only in his season, not for all seasons. Readers may long to appropriate for themselves what appears to be an idyllic faith like Ames's and live in an idyllic place like Gilead, but Ames knows that, even in the 1950s, neither is idyllic; he and Gilead are already relics from another time. Gilead is clearly a world that was. It is not a world that others can join—though Ames's experience may inspire others to find faith in their own Gilead.[17]

Marilynne Robinson's honest portrayal of Gilead and its pastor is refreshing. While many of us may also enjoy Garrison Keillor's and Jan Karon's stories, in sober moments we realize that their comic fictional worlds do *not* mirror the everyday world accurately. We may smile at Father Tim's antics and laugh out loud at twenty-four portly Lutheran pastors struggling in the shallows of Lake Wobegon. But our laughter is in no small measure defensive: it helps us cope with the distance we feel between these fictional pastors' reality and our everyday experience. In the everyday worlds that most of us experience, the women are not all strong, the men are not all good looking, and the children are not all above average. Nor are all divines comic Calvinists.[18]

Though the comic Calvinist worldview survives intact in Mitford, in Lake Wobegon it turns out to be a façade. As Garrison Keillor's stories develop over thirty years, an ironic strain that was always present moves more and more to the forefront. In *Pontoon* (2007), his most recent novel, it is painfully apparent that neither Evelyn, the main character, nor Barbara, her daughter, has any faith in ministers or their God. After Pastor Ingqvist hears that Evelyn Peterson has died, he tries repeatedly to impose his help. Each time, Barbara rebuffs him. His efforts appear "perfunctory" to her (101). In *Pontoon*, the persistent Pastor Ingqvist is more pathetic than comic. The young California minister who is to fly in for a local wedding is even more so. She has no substance at all. Her first name is appropriately "Misty." Misty is a "Seeker": "She used to be a Presbyterian but she had a near death-experience during breast enhancement surgery . . . [and when she] returned to life, she dedicated herself to world peace and to Momentism— . . . the idea that all time takes place in one moment, there is no eternity" (124–25). Thus the eternal Divine is completely displaced in Lake Wobegon and divines are functionaries at best.[19]

Human Divines: A Popular Image

A final group of fictional clerics neither try to protect nor recover an ideal; they are unabashedly fallible humans. These very human preachers acknowledge the displacement of the divine, and struggle openly to maintain faith within the reality of that displacement. God is rarely vivid and often elusive in their experience. Their candor about both their own humanity and their own difficulty of believing commends them. When they can't find faith, they don't pretend to believe. When their own human failings cause them to falter, they falter openly. These fictional clerics seem credible because they don't pretend. They come across as ordinary people trying to believe and to minister. It is interesting and perhaps significant to note that many of these openly human divines in American fiction are women. The displacement of the Divine and divines during the twentieth century may have helped to open the ministry to women. There does seem to be evidence that more-open and less-austere perceptions of God and the re-imaging of ministers as human caregivers in popular culture have contributed to the popular acceptance of women as ministers.[20]

The Rev. Marianne Maculyea, the fictional Methodist minister in the Joanna Brady series of mysteries by J. A. Jance, is both a strong woman and a human minister. Jance introduces Marianne in *Desert Heat* (1992), the first novel in the series. Marianne is a part-Mexican, part-Irish local woman from Bisbee, Arizona, where the stories are set. Marianne left Bisbee after high school to attend college, intending to become a microbiologist. To everyone's surprise, she returned several years later as an ordained Methodist minister, "sporting braces, Birkenstocks, and a househusband named Jeff Daniels who stayed home, baked his own bread, kept an incredibly clean parsonage, and who never hinted to Marianne that perhaps they ought to share the same last name" (39). Joanna Brady's first significant encounter with Marianne comes in the waiting room of the local hospital after her sheriff husband has been mortally wounded in the line of duty. When Andy dies, Marianne gives honest, caring ministry to Joanna. After Andy's death, Marianne is one of those who encourage Joanna to run for sheriff herself. Joanna is elected, and, as the series develops, the two women demonstrate that they are strong and effective occupants of their respective offices.

Marianne Maculyea is helpful to others who struggle to believe, in part because she struggles to believe herself. As the series unfolds, Jeff and Marianne travel to China and return with adopted twin baby girls. Then in *Rattlesnake Crossing* (1998), the sixth novel of the series, one of the twins, Esther, falls mortally ill, and the pastor who has been such a source of faith to Joanna loses her own faith. Her doubt is so powerful that Marianne questions whether she will ever again be able to do ministry: "But how will I ever be able to stand up at the pulpit and preach about faith when my own is so totally lacking? How can I teach about a loving God when I'm so pissed off at Him I can barely stand it?" The roles of pastor and sheriff are reversed as Joanna ministers to Marianne: "If you're so totally lacking in faith . . . , you wouldn't even acknowledge God, much less be pissed at Him. Now, have you had any sleep?" . . . "No." "What about something to eat?" Again the answer is negative. Eat and get some sleep, Joanna advises, and we'll talk later (175–76). When Esther dies and it is time for the funeral, Jeff and Marianne ask Joanna to officiate. Her human caring matters more than any official ministerial standing. "I don't want one of the other pastors," Marianne tells Joanna. "I want you. If one of them had the nerve to mention the word 'faith' in my company or during the course of the service, I'd probably go beserk." But Marianne doesn't go beserk. Nor is there some simple fix that heals her loss. But she does go on.

Clare Fergusson, the Episcopal priest in Julia Spencer-Fleming's Clare Fergusson/Russ Van Alstyne mysteries is an even gutsier woman in ministry than Marianne Maculyea is. The fortyish Clare is a former pilot who flew helicopters during Desert Storm before she went to seminary. She now serves a parish in Miller's Kill, New York, the Adirondack town where the novels are set. When victims of abusive behavior seek ministry from Clare, she not only supports them but determines to stop the abusers. This determination leads Clare to become an amateur detective and brings her into close association with Russ Van Alstine, the local sheriff. Spencer-Fleming walks a fine line as she portrays the feelings of affection that develop between Clare and this married man. At times, Fergusson and Van Alystyne barely refrain from crossing over into forbidden territory. One of these difficult moments occurs when they are trapped together in a cellar and rising waters threaten to drown them. Clare's military training and deep commitment to her ministry provide the discipline that keeps her from giving in to her feelings for Russ (*Out of the Deep I Cry* [2004], 285–97).[21] As the series develops, Clare's humanity seems more convincing than her divinity, though her authentic humanity implies that she must be a genuine person of faith as well.

The Rev. Walter Gower, the Episcopal minister in Gail Godwin's *Father Melancholy's Daughter* (1991), is probably the most powerful and convincing example in late-twentieth-century fiction of a minister who struggles openly to keep his faith as he wrestles with his human failings. Godwin's novel takes place during the 1970s and 1980s in Romulus, Virginia, where Father Gower serves a small Episcopal parish. Gower is portrayed as an old-fashioned priest, a traditionalist in matters of theology and liturgy, not outstanding in any way, but who is nonetheless a good pastor and a good preacher. Adrian Bonner, a priest who is Walter's friend, describes his perception of Gower to Gower's daughter Margaret, who narrates the novel: "He's just himself—himself offered daily. He worries about people, he worries about himself. . . . He baptizes and marries and buries and listens to people's fears and confessions and isn't above sharing some of his own. . . . He's a dedicated man, your father. He's lonely and bedeviled like the rest of us, but he has time for it all and tries to do it right" (199).

Gower may be "what priests in books used to be like," but there is nothing idyllic or nostalgic about him. Godwin's novel takes its title from the chronic melancholia that afflicts Father Gower. Depression is so much a part of Walter Gower's life that the community nicknames him "Father Melancholy." During his most severe attacks, depression persists for weeks. A "Black Curtain" completely engulfs him. Even in better times, the blackness never goes away completely. "It's not a question of the Black Curtain *coming back*, sweetie," he tells Ruth, his wife. "The Black Curtain's always there. It's a place I *go*." . . . Why *do* I go there? I'm not sure I know, myself. It's more as if I *wander* there, or get led there . . . and suddenly, before I know it, I'm behind the curtain again and everything is dark" (39; italics in the original). Walter is no passive sufferer; even when depression overwhelms him, he still carries on his ministerial duties. He still writes his sermons, beginning on Tuesday instead of Friday, "without hope or pleasure, every sentence reexamined and found wanting. 'This is all counterfeit,'" he tells Ruth, as he hands the pages of a sermon to her for inspection. As she reads, she disagrees: the sermon "doesn't read like a fraudulent sermon. You say a lot in a very *un*-presumptuous way" (36–37).

"Unpresumptuous" and "tries to do it right" are apt descriptions of the priest nicknamed "Father Melancholy." He's no hero, this minister; he is the opposite: a human minister. He is caring of others and faithful to his belief while he copes with the chronic melancholia that eats away at him. Even as his own life crumbles. That crumbling culminates when Ruth goes on vacation with another woman, a childhood friend, and decides she prefers this relationship to her marriage to Walter. After his wife leaves, the frustrations in Gower's ministry intensify and his health deteriorates. At age sixty, he suffers a massive stroke and dies.

In much the same manner as Marianne Maculyea and Claire Fergusson, Walter Gower's faith is a postmodern expression of his humanity. The displacement of the divine is real in Gower's experience. His continuing belief is a protest against that displacement. Toward the end of the novel, his daughter Margaret recalls a conversation between Adrian Bonner and her father that reveals the protesting spirit that energizes Walter Gower's faith: "There was a Jesuit studying with me in Zurich, at the [Jungian] Institute [Bonner says]. I once asked him, 'What if you as a priest stopped believing? What would you do then?' 'Make a fist in my pocket,' he said, 'and go on with the ritual.'" "'Exactly!' agreed Daddy" (274).[22]

Marianne and Clare and Walter are above all *human* divines. Their humanity is much more convincing than their experience of God. The displacement of God that troubled only an intellectual elite during the nineteenth century has now trickled down. It afflicts honest divines.

Fictional ministers like these brave clerics mirror the admirable persistence of many contemporary thinking ministers; they carry on even as they question. They struggle, but they keep their faith. They bet their lives there is a Divine even when they doubt. They make a fist in the face of doubt.

CONCLUSION
The Legacy of the Displaced Divine

The Displacing: A Summary

Throughout this book I argue that ministers in fiction reflect much more than their creators' imaginations. They also reflect specific social contexts and cultural images of ministers that these contexts mold. When social contexts change, new cultural images emerge. The shaping effects of social change are apparent in the cultural images that emerge in the transformed social context. Between the 1790s and 1920s, cultural images reflected in American fiction were shaped by several interconnected social changes that eroded the credibility and diminished the authority of American ministers—and their God.[1]

1. *Popular approval displaced official credentialing as the primary source of ministers' authority.* No doubt, disestablishment encouraged this shift in the principal source of ministers' authority. Before disestablishment, the status of both ministers and the God they represented was officially defined. After disestablishment, the authority of ministers and their God were (and still are) subject to popular approval.

As early as the middle of the nineteenth century, even pastors accredited by the formerly established churches also had to earn the approval of their parishioners. Fiction published during the 1850s describes the distress these old-line, newly precarious pastors experienced when they were forced to seek popular approval to keep their authority. In *A Peep at Number Five,* the older Elizabeth Stuart Phelps, a minister's wife herself, describes the plight of a bewildered fictional city pastor, the Rev. Mr. Holbrook. A self-appointed committee of local businessmen who are leaders in Holbrook's congregation visits him to complain that other churches in the neighborhood are gaining more members than theirs. They tell Holbrook that he needs to make his sermons more appealing. The disconcerted pastor tells the complainers that he is fulfilling the prescribed requirements of his call; he is preaching pure doctrine. But preaching pure doctrine is no longer sufficient; he also has to earn their approval. They want measurable results. Official accreditation alone is no longer adequate; ministers must also meet "market" standards set by those they serve.

The shift toward popular credentialing of ministers had at least one unplanned but significant consequence: the ministry became more accessible to women. Even before the Civil War, women who were barred from the official ministry because of their sex began to appear as "unofficial" ministers in American fiction. Bertha, one of the title characters in Elizabeth Oakes Smith's novel *Bertha and Lily*, refuses to subject herself to "dull" doctrinal sermons delivered by officially accredited clerics. "I find it impossible to sit them out," she tells a friend. Bertha proposes a remedy: admit women into the ministry; their preaching will liven up the dreary services. When local church leaders remind Bertha that according to St. Paul women are required to be silent in church, she responds that, in this matter, St. Paul is "less inspired." When they ignore Bertha's novel exegesis and continue to deny her the opportunity to preach, Bertha builds a chapel at her own expense and holds Sunday evening teaching services, where she serves as the preacher. Evidently, her preaching is livelier; she draws much larger congregations each week than her male counterparts do. Another popularly approved minister, Jerusha Bangs, who appears in Elizabeth Stuart Phelps's short story "A Woman's Pulpit," is similarly successful. Ms. Bangs intimidates the skeptical mission supervisor of New Vealshire into letting her serve a small congregation there. During her brief tenure, she demonstrates that she is as able a pastor as any of the officially credentialed male clergy in the area. Women who gain popular respect for their ministry even though they are not officially sanctioned as ministers are even more prominent in American fiction after the Civil War.[2]

By the last quarter of the nineteenth century, popular approval can overcome official rejection. Candidates for ministry who are denied ordination by officially constituted church bodies often overcome that rejection by demonstrating that they are nonetheless qualified to be ministers. In *A Singular*

Life, Elizabeth Stuart Phelps offers what may be the most powerful criticism in American fiction of official church bodies that use criteria based on obsolete (in her view) church doctrine to exclude otherwise-qualified individuals from the ministry. When Emmanuel Bayard admits that he is not absolutely certain he believes some essential tenets of Calvinist theology, the examining committee composed of Congregational clergy refuses to recommend him for ordination. But a group from the congregation that originally called him is still convinced that Bayard has the gifts to become a minister; they encourage him to begin a ministry among the poor in the seacoast town of Windover, Massachusetts. Bayard accepts their invitation and develops a social ministry that inspires faith in the seamen and prostitutes who live in the worst section of Windover. The success of ministers like Bayard implies that popular standards may be more adequate than the opinions of official church bodies to judge whether someone is qualified to be a minister.

The discounting of official accreditation in favor of popular approval is not without its hazards. Popular approval accredits some as ministers who are not actually worthy. American fiction from the 1790s through the 1920s abounds in examples of ministers who are really con artists—from scoundrels in collars in early American cities, to phony preachers in frontier America, to traveling evangelists like Sharon Falconer and Elmer Gantry. But the obvious risks of popular accreditation were not sufficient to reverse the democratizing trend. By the end of the nineteenth century, official accreditation by itself was no longer adequate: to be accepted as authentic, even ministers officially accredited by established church bodies also had to meet popular standards.[3]

2. *As the source of ministers' authority moved from official credentialing toward popular approval, the standard used to measure their authenticity moved from belief to action.* Godly behavior displaced adherence to particular beliefs as the primary measure of a minister's authenticity. Ministers now gained credibility not simply by affirming prescribed beliefs. They had to *act* in what are considered godly ways.

Dr. Moses Stern, the aptly named austere Calvinist preacher I discuss in chapter 4 is based on ministers who Harriet Beecher Stowe remembered from her childhood. Late-eighteenth- and early-nineteenth-century Calvinist ministers like Stern held authority because they proclaimed an approved and, at least among their colleagues and parishioners, largely undisputed body of church doctrine. They gained authority because they were loyal defenders of *the* faith. The faith they stood for gave them authority. That faith had authority *in and of itself*, quite apart from the individual minister who happened to be defending it.

In Stowe's lifetime, the primary measure of ministers' authenticity shifted from affirming an accepted body of beliefs to demonstrating the effects of believing. Keeping and defending the faith by itself no longer made a minister a credible minister. Just as holding the office of minister no longer guaranteed their authority, public adherence to an officially approved set of beliefs (the faith) no longer established their credibility. The focus shifted from theological criteria to moral criteria, from affirming the faith to living the faith, from faithful believing to faithful acting. What do this minister's beliefs lead this minister to do? Does what this minister believes make this minister a *better* believer? Do some beliefs, or some kinds of believing, lead to better behavior and others to worse behavior?

Cultural images of ministers that emerged between the Revolutionary War and the Civil War reflect the progressive discrediting of long-dominant orthodox Calvinist beliefs. The worth of inherited beliefs was no longer taken for granted; ministers' worth was judged by the positive or negative *effects* they have. Cultural images reflected in popular fiction during these decades suggest that ministers who are orthodox believers were often *not* better ministers. Many theologically orthodox ministers in early-nineteenth-century American fiction are portrayed as fumblers and misfits. Worse than that, some of the most rigidly orthodox believers do not seem to act in godly ways at all. Portrayals in popular fiction reflect cultural images of Calvinists as bigoted, fanatical, and abusive ministers. Radical images of orthodox-believing ministers offer even more troubling critiques of the inherited faith. In Hawthorne's fiction, the Revs. Digby's, Hooper's, and Dimmesdale's believing does not lead to bad behavior; it makes them sick. They are psychologically ill, and their orthodox believing aggravates their psychological dysfunction.

The ramifications of this discrediting of long-respected orthodox Calvinist theology were apparent in American fiction throughout the nineteenth century. Theological liberals attempted a recovery by suggesting that narrow Calvinism produces the bigots; clergy who are liberal believers, including liberal Calvinists, are kinder and more ethical ministers. But the attack on orthodox faith in popular and literary fiction was substantial, and the liberals' remedy gained little support.

The shift in focus from beliefs to behavior as the measure of authentic faith that lies underneath the debate was probably more significant than the specific arguments. Once critics of orthodox Calvinist theology succeeded in establishing good behavior as the preeminent measure of a minister's authenticity, the long-assumed cause and effect connection between sound belief and godly behavior became questionable. The theological fallout was profound. If holding orthodox faith is not necessary to produce godly or good behavior—in fact, does not necessarily lead to good behavior—the next logical step is to question whether there is any *essential* cause and effect relationship between faith and good or godly behavior.[4]

Contemporary fiction reflects these cultural shifts. After the Civil War, ministers who perform in godly ways but who are clearly not orthodox believers abound in popular fiction. Some of these heroic clerics spar with orthodox-believing antagonists who try to undermine their credibility by pointing to their failure to keep to the orthodox faith. The attempt often backfires: heroes of the cloth prove they are good ministers by their godly actions; their orthodox-believing antagonists' failure to match the heroes' godly actions discredits them. By the end of the century, a minister's adherence to certain essential beliefs seems increasingly irrelevant. The fact that muscular ministers like Dan Matthews (Harold Bell Wright's *The Calling of Dan Matthews*), social ministers like John Hodder (Winston Churchill's *The Inside of the Cup*), and social activists like Pastor Northmore (Elizabeth Neff's *Altars to Mammon*) lose their faith does not detract from their credibility or godliness at all. In fact, they are presented as more godly than their orthodox-believing opponents. By the early-twentieth century in most American fiction, popular approval withholds or gives authority to ministers, and their actions more than the specifics of their believing demonstrate whether ministers are godly.

3. *The paradigm shift associated with the secular revolution challenged the fundamental source of ministers' authority: the reality of God.* The displacing paradigm placed a new and significant burden on ministers: to gain credibility among those influenced by the new paradigm, ministers now had to offer empirical evidence of God's reality.[5] They not only had to prove their personal worth as ministers; they had to offer convincing evidence that God is real.

Radical images of Protestant clergy reflected in American fiction at midcentury already mirror the declining acceptance of doctrinally based perceptions of God as valid reflections of reality, as well as the challenges that this declining acceptance posed for American ministers. Consider the contrasting portrayals of Harriet Beecher Stowe's Samuel Hopkins in *The Minister's Wooing*, who reflects a church image of ministers as faithful Calvinists, and Pierre Glendinning in Herman Melville's 1852 novel *Pierre*, who suffers under a God and a minister who reflect a radical image of God and God's ministers as perpetrators of oppression. Samuel Hopkins's personal faith is a mirror of the given faith. The reality of God that Hopkins proclaims is not contingent on Hopkins's or anyone else's experience of God. The need to have a human experience of God that leads to conversion is an issue for Calvinists like Hopkins, but it is a personal issue, not a cosmic question. By contrast, when Mary Scudder's fiancé James Marvyn is feared lost at sea, his potential loss is a double tragedy. James has not had a conversion experience; if he dies unconverted, he is lost to Mary and he is lost for eternity.

Such an outcome is a given fact of the doctrinal theology or paradigm of faith they accept. It may not seem fair, but how God is does not depend on James's or Mary's or Samuel Hopkins's or anyone else's personal opinion or experience or perception of God. Their own conversion experience or lack of a conversion experience has ultimate implications for them, but it has no bearing on God's reality. Graciousness or justice or any other attributes of God do not have to be verified personally in anyone's experience to be real. God is from beyond—a revealed, cosmic, providential, and absolute reality. God does not have to meet any human test or criteria to be considered credible. Believers keep their faith in the faith, regardless of what happens to them or others personally. God is absolutely in charge, and being a person of faith means simply accepting that fact. Believers may be blessed with a conversion experience and feel assured of ultimate salvation, but having that experience does not determine one's fate: it only offers assurance of what God has decided.

After the Civil War, this long-taken-for-granted reality of God was subjected to new scrutiny. The unspeakable horror of the war raised serious questions about the existence of a providential and caring God. The century-long intellectual and scientific revolution in Europe spread to American society after midcentury and bred skepticism among American intellectuals. Under a barrage of questions, the rationale for absolute faith in God began to crumble. "Does the evidence point to the existence of God?" and "Is what God asks humans to accept fair?" are not questions that the Rev. Dr. Hopkins and his fellow believers would permit themselves to ask. But they are precisely the kind of questions that Herman Melville raised in his antebellum novels. When godly motives move Pierre Glendinning to care for his half-sister, he discovers that being godly is not possible. Not only because his mother and his minister join forces to oppose his efforts. The cosmos is stacked against the possibility. God comes across as sadistic in *Pierre:* God sets standards of performance that humans are incapable of meeting. Only God could meet them. God offers no effective help for humans in *Pierre*. There is no effective presence of God in Pierre's world. There is no helpful minister in the novel, either, only the scrap of a sermon; significantly, the ending that might have made the argument convincing is missing. There is now "no father in heaven and only the resentful memory of one on earth."[6] Melville, as one of my own sons suggests, was the first American modern.

Between the 1850s and the 1920s, the comprehensive paradigm that assured ministers' credibility was displaced by one that not only challenged ministers' credibility but also undermined the credibility of God. Ministers' failure to be persuasive among those who accepted the new paradigm reflected not simply a personal failure to be convincing; it reflected an unconvincing God. Henry Adams's Stephen Hazard (*Esther*) and Hamlin Garland's Anthony Clarke (*The Tyranny of the Dark*) fail to win over the skeptics, George Strong and Martin Serviss, because they cannot demonstrate the reality of the God they proclaim. Their claims are not independently verifiable. They can offer only testimony, not demonstration. And in the world that Strong and Serviss represent, testimony alone is no longer convincing. As the nineteenth century progressed into the twentieth, the theological foundation on which ministers relied for authority and credibility became increasingly shaky. As the physician Dr. Boynton observes in William Dean Howells's *The Undiscovered Country* (1880), "Priests in the pulpit and before the altar proclaim a creed which they hope it will be good for their listeners to believe, and the people envy the faith that can so confidently preach that creed; but neither priests nor people believe" (235).

A few fictional clergy, especially those who mirror contemporary church images, still espouse unwavering faith. But as the decades pass, even they become less convincing. In chapter 7, I describe several fictional ministers who mirror a church image I call "courageous and uncompromising believers." The most convincing reflections of this cultural image, ministers like Mort Goodwin (Edward R. Eggleston's *The Circuit Rider*), Griffith Davenport (Mrs. Helen Hamilton [Chenoweth] Gardener's *An Unofficial Patriot*), and Edward Arthur (William Mumford Baker's *Inside: A Chronicle of Secession*), are pre–Civil War or Civil War clergy. Postbellum ministers who reflect similar church images are much less persuasive. The Rev. Henry Maxwell in Charles Sheldon's *In His Steps* is typical. The faith Maxwell advocates—asking, "What would Jesus do?" in every situation, and then prayerfully following whatever inspiration comes—seems simplistic. The characters in Sheldon's novel who take up Maxwell's challenge and the outcomes they experience when they do seem contrived. Henry Maxwell seems like a pale hero next to Samuel Hopkins. His ask what-would-Jesus-do challenge seems much less persuasive than Hopkins's willingness to be damned personally, if necessary, to witness to the glory of God. What changed across the decades to produce this contrast is not only the quality of the minister but also the cultural context. The cultural context in which Hopkins serves testifies to the faith he proclaimed; the cultural context in which Maxwell serves does not. The older preacher exhorted his listeners to keep the faith; the later preacher challenges his congregation to suspend their disbelief and follow in Jesus' steps. They do, but in a post-Christian world, the adventures Henry Maxwell and his parishioners have when they follow in his steps seem like fiction.

To summarize: portrayals of ministers in American fiction during the nineteenth and early twentieth centuries reflect three shifts in American society that have eroded ministers' authority and credibility: (1) a shift from official credentialing toward popular approval as the primary source of ministers' authority; (2) a shift from convincing beliefs to convincing actions as the primary measure of ministers' authenticity; and (3) a shift from idealized concepts to experience and empirical observation as determinative measures of the credibility of any reality—including the reality of God. The third shift is an ultimate blow: when God is not perceived as credible, then neither is a minister who claims to represent God.

The accumulating effects of these social and cultural shifts that displace the Divine and divines rippled across American society during the nineteenth and early-twentieth centuries. They are reflected in the portrayals of Protestant clergy in American fiction. Early portrayals expose the personal failings of particular kinds of ministers. Misfits in the new world are incapable ministers. Bigoted Calvinists are morally reprehensible ministers. Conning clerics who proliferate in urban fiction during the early- and mid-nineteenth century are ministers gone wrong.

By the 1830s and 1840s, portrayals of ministers in fiction began to reflect the declining status and credibility of ministers as a class. After disestablishment, ministers in fiction were less likely to be presented as stable, local authority figures and were more often portrayed as itinerant professionals with limited local authority. When their authority was reduced to influence, the status of ministers became increasingly precarious. (Recall Orville Dewey's painful outburst in his letter to William Ware, as discussed in chapter 2.) As ministers' status fell, the ministry as a profession became less attractive to persons of quality. A circular pattern was set up: the lower quality of candidates entering the ministry resulted in more and more ministers who were less capable.

After the Civil War, the fall of divines was even more precipitous. Developments in science, philosophy, and biblical criticism challenged the reality of the transcendent God from whom ministers derive their ultimate authority. The bungling Theron Ware comes across as hopelessly inferior in the company of a modern woman and a modern scientist whom he mistakenly views as his equals. Even exceptional clerics like Stephen Hazard cannot keep up with strong women like Esther Dudley and men of science like her paleontologist cousin, George Strong. From the late-nineteenth century onward, ministers in fiction struggled not only with lost status but also with spiritual incapacity. In what amounts to a final blow, even fictional divines who appeal to God directly discover there is no one to help them. The unscrupulous Elmer Gantry calls on God to help him reform on several occasions to no avail. God has disappeared. With the disappearance of God, ministers lose not only their authority but also their spiritual capability. By the end of the nineteenth century and continuing throughout the twentieth, the most-credible and most-admired ministers in American fiction are morally upright pastors and social activists. They are human heroes, not representatives of a transcendent God. The possibility that ministers are ministers *of God* is now problematic.

The Legacy

The social and cultural pluralism that now marks American society poses a formidable challenge to the status and credibility of American ministers. American society is no longer composed of individuals who embrace a common culture dominated by a single belief system that esteems ministers and their God. Americans now inhabit a variety of different and competing subcultural worlds.[7] While some Americans insist the United States is (or should be) a Christian country, actually a variety of competing paradigms challenge the Christian cultural paradigm that once exerted overriding influence in American society.[8] In little more than a century, the seat of religious authority in American society has devolved from a single text-based, organized religion to individuals who identify with a variety of worldviews and subcultures. In this book, I have traced that transformation as it is reflected in portrayals of Protestant ministers and their God in American fiction. During the nineteenth century, emerging modernism launched a secular revolution that challenged the authority and credibility of American ministers and their God. Modernism dismissed the claims of traditional religion. Twentieth-century postmodernism extended the discrediting process by proposing that all perceptions of reality are subjective, including those advanced by text-based religion. Postmodernism replaces the authority of given religions and their interpreters with individual spirituality. We live with the legacy of this cultural transformation. Believing is now a varied, individual, and culturally relative phenomenon in American society. We are free to believe according to a traditional faith, to adopt or construct an alternative spirituality, or to openly disbelieve.[9]

The proliferation of diversity and pluralism that the displacement of the Divine encouraged raises the same quandary for writers and for ministers—which is why fiction writers who write about ministers so often reflect it. After the displacement of the Divine, ministers—whether in fiction or in real life—are most often greeted skeptically. Just as each author has to convince each reader to suspend disbelief to gain credibility, so each fictional or real-life minister has to convince each individual reader or parishioner she meets to suspend disbelief before they will give her credibility. In the incident I describe in the opening pages of the introduction to this book, the minister who is my neighbor is a Christian believer and he holds the office of minister in his denomination. But the parishioners who refuse to accept his ministry do not believe he is an authentic minister. He does not live up to their images of what a minister should be, and so they reject him. They believe *they* (not some official ecclesiastical body) have the right to decide who is and who is not a true minister of God.

Meeting a new minister in a world where ministers' credibility is relative and skepticism is the norm is like opening a new novel. Will this one and the world of reality she/he/it represents convince us to suspend disbelief? In the absence of a generally accepted and authoritative definition of the Divine—that is, a generally accepted text (or cultural image) that represents *the* Divine authoritatively—we try on the realities that each new minister or novel presents to us. I think there are, as some critics believe, powerful links between our perceptions of ourselves and others and our approach to fiction. If our self-perceptions and worldviews are as fluid, precarious, and relative as some contemporary critics propose, we are understandably eager to try on various characters and worldviews as possibilities for ourselves. But, as I suggest in chapter 10 in connection with my discussion of the imagined worlds of Lake Wobegon and Mitford, this tempting exercise is not without risk. As we consider character after character, we may discover "that the experimentations with various selves are all there is, that no original or authenticating self exists for the experimenter to turn to when the experimenting stops; that the experimenting in fact never ceases."[10] We may discover there is nothing beyond the particular relativity for which we settle. "The final belief is to believe in a fiction," Wallace Stevens writes, "which you know to be a fiction, there being nothing else. The exquisite truth is to know that it is a fiction and that you believe in it willingly." There is only fiction according to the perspective Stevens presents here. Within the worldview he proposes, "it is the belief and not the god that counts."[11] Every peeling away of a tentative belief reveals only another tentative belief. When the Divine is elusive, the divine's credibility is precarious. The testifying minister is reduced to arguing.[12] Displacing the Divine displaces divines. How can one model godliness when there is no God?

As much as some of us might want it to, fiction is unlikely to resolve this contemporary crisis of belief. To expect fiction writers to undo the displacement of the Divine is to expect more than they can deliver. Fiction has limits. John Updike described one of those limits in an address he gave when he received the Campion Medal from the Catholic Book Club in 1997: "Fiction holds the mirror up to the world and cannot show more than this world contains."[7] Contemporary popular and art fiction offers few credible portrayals of ministers who, like Marilynne Robinson's John Ames, are convincing believers.[14] This deficiency reflects the scarcity of convincing cultural images of ministers as sophisticated believers in American society. Serious writers who are steeped in contemporary culture find it difficult to create sophisticated believing ministers who seem authentic because contemporary American society lacks cultural images of ministers as astute, thinking believers.

The dearth of thoughtful believing clerics in American literary fiction today is a reflection of American culture today. It reveals a theological shortcoming more than a literary bias—a deficiency that I think is exacerbated by the refusal of many Christian theologians to address the theological questions of a postmodern society. The long-standing dominance of narrow and inflexible doctrinal theology among so many Christians has widened the gap between Christians and other believers. Such doctrinal theology grants credence only to "special" revelation as embodied in the Bible and codified in historical church doctrines.[15] This protective posture walls off theological discussion rather than promoting a creative dialogue between theology and culture. I think one could argue that it has actually helped to facilitate the displacement of the Divine in contemporary society. As early as the middle of the nineteenth century, Harriet Beecher Stowe foresaw the fallout from this stonewalling that has dominated Christian theology since the advent of the secular revolution.[16] It effectively renders churches into dead theologians' societies and hinders their ability to speak helpfully in a postmodern society. To paraphrase John Osborne, they come across as those who look forward to the past.[17]

This quandary recalls the thesis I stated at the beginning of this book: there is a dearth of fictional ministers who address the issues believers face in a postmodern society because ministers in fiction reflect cultural images of ministers in society. As John Updike suggests, fiction cannot show more than this world contains. It is the mirror that reflects the culture of its time. Clerics in American fiction struggle under the absence of God because so many novelists perceive ministers as unfortunate servants of a dated, discredited, and displaced Divine. Fiction cannot compensate for inadequate theology. When there seems to be no contemporary God in view for ministers to represent, their credibility and effectiveness slip away.

In *The Confidence-Man*, Herman Melville wrote, "It is with fiction as with religion; it should present another world, and yet one to which we feel the tie" (158). I think the challenge "to present another world . . . to which we feel the tie" is now at least as great to practitioners of religion as it is to writers of fiction. Among those most convinced of the displacement of the Divine (an American subculture that has increased in numbers dramatically since the late nineteenth century), any One or any Thing that purports to be a transcendent reality is suspect, and any clergyperson who claims to represent such a Being or Thing is assumed to be either unsophisticated, disturbed, or an opportunist.[18] The displacement and discrediting of ministers and their God throughout American society are profound. As modernism has penetrated American culture, disbelief has become an *established* alternative to belief. William James notes in *The Principles of Psychology* that disbelief is not the opposite of belief: the "true opposites of belief, psychologically considered, are doubt and inquiry, not disbelief."[19] Rigid belief and rigid disbelief are functionally the same. Disbelief can be as stable (and as petrified) as belief. The contemporary preacher's task is daunting. Many potential listeners are disbelievers who view all belief as fiction. Before they can feel the tie to another world, the minister must first convince them to suspend their disbelief. Then, perhaps, they can believe the Divine that this divine represents is a plausible possibility—and that there may be exquisite truth in this divine's fiction.

NOTES

Introduction: Fiction as a Mirror of Culture

1. While I realize that the term "American" properly includes those who live in the many countries in North and South America, in this book I use it to refer specifically to Americans in the United States.

2. Peter L. Berger and Thomas Luckmann, *The Social Construction of Reality* (Garden City, N.Y.: Anchor/Doubleday, 1967); the most relevant section is part 3, "Society as Subjective Reality." Other helpful sources that explore the origin, nature, and codification of human perceptions of reality include William James, *The Principles of Psychology* (Cambridge: Harvard University Press, 1983), esp. chap. 21, "The Perception of Reality"; Walter Lippmann, *Public Opinion* (New York: Macmillan, 1922); Jean Piaget, *The Construction of Reality in the Child* (New York: Ballantine, 1954); Erving Goffman, *The Presentation of the Self in Everyday Life* (Garden City, N.Y.: Doubleday, 1959); Alfred Schutz, *Collected Papers*, ed. Maurice Natanson (The Hague: Martinus Nijhoff, 1962), esp. part 3; Robert Wuthnow, *The Consciousness Reformation* (Berkeley: University of California Press, 1976), esp. chap. 2; Roland Barthes, *S/Z*, trans. Richard Miller (New York: Hill and Wang, 1974); and Douglas Alan Walrath, *Frameworks: Patterns of Living and Believing Today* (New York: Pilgrim, 1987), esp. chaps. 1–3.

3. Roland Barthes refers to the taken-for-granted cultural content that is internalized during socialization as the "cultural code" or "referential code" (Barthes, *S/Z*, 97–101, 205–7).

4. Berger and Luckman, *Social Construction*, 129–37.

5. Ibid., 153; italics theirs. Henry Adams seems to be aware of the same phenomenon when he writes: "Images are not arguments, rarely even lead to proof, but the mind craves them" (Henry Adams, *The Education of Henry Adams* [New

York: Library of America, 1983], 1167). Cultural images gain wide acceptance not because they pass empirical tests but because they seem like common sense.

6. Michael Polanyi describes how this process operates: "[The] power of a system of implicit beliefs to defeat valid objections one by one is due to the circularity of such systems. . . . [The] convincing power possessed by the interpretation of any particular new topic in terms of such a conceptual framework is based on past applications of the same framework to a great number of other topics [or individuals] not now under consideration. . . . So long as each doubt is defeated in turn, its effect is to strengthen the fundamental convictions against which it is raised" (Michael Polanyi, *Personal Knowledge* [Chicago: University of Chicago Press, 1958], 288, 289).

7. For an interesting discussion of psychosocial development and relative openness from a theological as well as a sociological perspective, see James W. Fowler, *Stages of Faith: The Psychology of Human Development and the Quest for Meaning* (San Francisco: Harper and Row, 1981).

8. Berger and Luckmann, *Social Construction*, 138–47.

9. Though he doesn't use Berger and Luckmann's terms specifically, Karl Mannheim suggests that the transition from primary to secondary socialization peaks during adolescence, between ages thirteen and nineteen (Karl Mannheim, *Essays on the Sociology of Knowledge*, ed. Paul Kecskemeti [London: Routledge and Kegan Paul, 1952], chap. 7).

10. This is another example of what Berger and Luckmann describe as a casual conversation that refines and maintains a perception of reality (Berger and Luckmann, *Social Construction*, 152–54).

11. Here I am using the term "artist" loosely, as a general term to refer to those who write fiction. When I discriminate between art fiction or literature and popular fiction, I use the term more specifically (see chapter **00**).

12. The quotes are from J. Golden Taylor, *Hawthorne's Ambivalence Toward Puritanism* (Logan: Utah State University Press, 1965), 14; italics mine. More recently, Roy Jenkins in his biography of Winston S. Churchill makes the same point that Taylor does. Jenkins writes: "Not only can fiction frequently be more vivid than fact, but it can sometimes capture as much of the truth" (Roy Jenkins, *Churchill: A Biography* [New York: Farrar, Straus Giroux, 2001], 656). Cultural images are obviously more fluid than fixed. While that lack of specificity makes them difficult to grasp, it reflects their nature. I mostly agree with the postmodern view that phenomena like cultural images do not have a separate existence apart from those who perceive them. They represent a cultural consensus as fluid and as varied as the culture of those who embrace them. However, insofar as fiction reflects cultural images, it does provide a permanent mirror. One can at least glimpse cultural images in present and past culture through fiction. For a provocative discussion of literature and religion from a postmodern perspective, see Robert Detweiler, *Breaking the Fall: Religious Readings of Contemporary Fiction* (San Francisco: Harper and Row, 1989).

13. The fact that images are somewhat ambivalent commends them as raw material for the creative process. In an essay dedicated to the relationship between art and reality, Joyce Cary writes: "It is the ambivalence of the symbol that enables the artist, as teacher or expositor, as creator of meanings, to bridge the gap between

the individual idea and the universal real of emotion, forming by art a personality which unites them both in a single active and rational will" (Joyce Cary, *Art and Reality: Ways of the Creative Process* [New York: Harper and Bros., 1958], 174).

14. Use of the phrase "real world" is a common convention that may be confusing. In my own writing, when I want to be precise, I use "actuality" to refer to the world that is actually there and "reality" to refer to the reality we construct and through which we perceive actuality. I believe we do not have direct access to actuality; our perceptions of actuality our biased by the reality through which we perceive actuality. For a more extended discussion, see Walrath, *Frameworks*, 1–49.

15. The authors who Susan Ketchin interviewed clearly describe this process (Susan Ketchin, *The Christ-Haunted Landscape: Faith and Doubt in Southern Fiction* [Jackson: University of Mississippi Press, 1994]).

16. While some authors (George Lippard, for example) base most of their clergy characters on a favorite cultural image, others pattern different clergy characters on different cultural images. For example, the late-nineteenth- and early-twentieth-century writer Mary Wilkins Freeman patterns Parson Lord, who appears in her novella *The Love of Parson Lord* (in *The Love of Parson Lord and Other Stories* [New York: Harper and Bros., 1900]), on a popular image I call the Compelled Believer. The minister who appears in Freeman's short story "A Poetess" (in A *New England Nun and Other Stories* [New York: Harper and Bros., 1891]) reflects an image I call the Inept Contender. In another story, "A Village Singer" (in ibid.), the minister is patterned on the cultural image of ministers as Weak Men.

17. The culture-challenging role that artistic writers often play does not necessarily make them disconnected, antisocial individuals. Even the most solitary authors have some audience in mind as they write—though for some, that audience may consist of only a few peers whom they respect. Initially, those who wrote and read art fiction were not as sharply defined a social group as some other social groups (church groups, for example) in American society. But from the 1850s on, they were an identifiable subculture. By the 1920s, they became a well-defined and formidable subculture with norms and cultural images that rival those affirmed by popular and church subcultures. For more, see Alfred Kazin, *On Native Grounds: An Interpretation of Modern American Prose Literature* (New York: Harcourt Brace, 1995), 205–9.

18. David S. Reynolds calls this approach "reconstructive criticism." "Ideally," he suggests, "the reconstructive critic would read *all* extant published writings of a given period with the aim of gaining a comprehensive, scientific overview." To do so, Reynolds believes, is rarely possible or practical. One can read a sufficient number of representative works and then make well-founded generalizations (David S. Reynolds, *Beneath the American Renaissance* [Cambridge: Harvard University Press, 1988], 561). I have identified nearly six hundred works of American fiction in which ministers appear as significant characters. To discuss each of these texts in detail would be overwhelming and unnecessary.

19. It is important not to confuse popular images with popular fiction or popular writers. Popular images shape characters that appear most often in popular fiction, but not exclusively in popular fiction. Sinclair Lewis, for example, is generally considered a literary author, but Frank Shallard, one of the most significant characters in *Elmer Gantry*, reflects a contemporary popular image, the Social Activist. Characters

based on the Social Activist cultural image are usually portrayed positively in popular fiction. When the very ethical Shallard shows up in *Elmer Gantry*, he is so different from the opportunistic Elmer Gantry (and most of the other ministers in the novel) that he makes Gantry seem even more despicable. I describe Social Activists in chapter 6 and Frank Shallard and Elmer Gantry in chapter 9.

The three categories—popular, church, and radical—that I use to describe cultural images of ministers from the 1790s through the 1920s are not adequate to describe cultural images of ministers after the 1920s. After the 1920s, cultural diversity becomes more accepted in American society. Especially after the social and cultural revolutions of the 1960s and 1970s, American society is recognizably pluralistic. After the 1960s, this cultural pluralism diversifies the perceptions of clergy in mainstream society, as well as the cultural images that mold these perceptions.

20. The contrasts are actually more complex than this reference to Child's work suggests. I describe them in detail in part I of this book, especially chapters 1 and 2. At appropriate points in the chapters ahead, I offer a more complete discussion of all the examples I cite in this introduction.

21. Though Hodder most likely reflects Churchill's own theological perspectives and ecclesiastical commitments (Churchill was an active Episcopal lay leader), he mirrors a popular social gospel cultural image. See chapter 6 for my discussion of Hodder. For a description of Winston Churchill's theological perspectives and ecclesiastical commitments, see his *The Uncharted Way: The Psychology of the Gospel Doctrine* (Philadelphia: Dorrance, 1940) and Robert W. Schneider, *Novelist to a Generation: The Life and Thought of Winston Churchill* (Bowling Green, Ohio: Bowling Green University Popular Press, 1976).

22. A few fictional clergy do seem to be simply eccentric; they don't appear to mirror any accepted cultural image. These unique characters stem almost entirely from a particular author's creative imagination. They may be significant as literary characters, but their tenuous connection to cultural images places them outside the scope of this book.

23. For a helpful discussion of the distinctions between popular and art fiction, see the introduction to Nina Baym, *Women's Fiction: A Guide to Novels by and About Women in America, 1820–1970*, 2nd ed. (Urbana: University of Illinois Press, 1993), ix–xlii.

24. I have given only a brief description of a complex and often-subtle process. For an extended description of the processes involved in writing and reading from a postmodernist perspective, see Detweiler. *Breaking the Fall.* The differences between more conventional popular and church images and more provocative radical images and the ways radical images may encourage revisions in popular and church images will become clearer in the examples I discuss in the chapters ahead.

25. See chapter 4 for my discussion of these novels.

26. For a discussion of Frederic's views, see Bridget Bennett, *The Damnation of Harold Frederic: His Lives and Works* (Syracuse, N.Y.: Syracuse University Press, 1997). In *Art and Reality*, Cary describes the different perspectives of those who are concerned to write art fiction and those who write popular fiction. Though Cary does not seem to be aware of "cultural images," he is aware that popular writers create characters according to some perception of what is acceptable to readers of popular fiction, while artists tend to be more loyal to their own vision: "This does not mean, of course, that the artist, the writer, should have what is called a public in

view, that he should attempt to be comprehensible to any special persons. . . . I'm not talking here about writers who try to produce the best-sellers. They are quite another category. They are producing something to sell. . . . [The artist, by contrast] wants not only to express his unique idea of things, but to communicate it. He is, in fact, almost invariably a propagandist, he is convinced that his idea of things is true and important and he wants to convert others, he wants to change the world" (Cary, *Art and Reality*, 89–91). While I agree with Cary's belief that at least some artists are "propagandists," I believe that even these artists draw on images that are cultural currency to create their fictional characters. Fictional ministers (and there are a few) that do not seem to reflect a reality readers can identify come across as entirely imagined and are not likely to convince readers that they reflect real-life clergy.

27. A description of the role that cohorts play in this process appears in Mannheim, *Essays*, chap. 7, "The Problem of Generations." For a more contemporary discussion, see Walrath, *Frameworks*, chap. 2.

28. The social and cultural divisions apparent at the infamous Scopes trial in Dayton, Tennessee, in 1925 are still with us today. One could argue, for example, that differing perceptions of ministers and the role of religion in contemporary culture evident in the 2004 presidential election reflect a theological polarization in American society that was already well defined in the 1920s. For a provocative discussion of the development of these social divisions between 1870 and 1930, see Christian Smith, ed., *The Secular Revolution: Power, Interests, and Conflict in the Secularization of American Public Life* (Berkeley: University of California Press, 2003).

29. Cultural images can be thought of as cumulative social memories that reflect the perceptions and experiences of individuals within a culture—which could explain why we identify personally with some images within our own culture. Some of Carl Jung's work suggests that he perceives cultural myths in this manner—for example, his descriptions of archetypes and the collective unconscious. For an easily accessible description of Jung's theory and review of his work, see Carl Jung, *Memories, Dreams and Reflections*, ed. Aniela Jaffe (New York: Pantheon, 1963). For a listing of Jung's texts that present these concepts more formally, see p. 394 in that volume. Fowler, *Stages of Faith*, views faith development as a psychosocial phenomenon with hierarchical, sequential, and cumulative dimensions. An individual's beliefs at any point in time are a selective and cumulative reflection of his or her faith-shaping experiences. In this volume, I am proposing that socially shaped cultural images are also a psychosocial phenomenon. They accumulate within a culture (or subculture) and together make up its corporate cultural memory. The cultural images each of us embraces reflect cultural images that are indigenous to our culture. We identify with past and present cultural images that "fit" us.

Chapter 1. Faltering Fathers and Devious Divines: Popular Images

1. For a thorough exploration of this concept of American identity, see Sacvan Bercovitch, *The Rites of Assent: Transformations in the Symbolic Construction of America* (London: Routledge, 1993), esp. chap. 2.

2. Michael Davitt Bell, *Hawthorne and the Historical Romance of New England* (Princeton, N.J.: Princeton University Press, 1971). The Europeans' perspective, of course, reflects their prejudice. The Native Americans' view of their land was—and is—quite different.

3. Winthrop S. Hudson, "The Ministry in the Puritan Age," in *The Ministry in Historical Perspectives*, ed. Richard H. Niebuhr and Daniel D. Williams (New York: Harper and Bros., 1956), 180–206. For a more recent description, see Glenn T. Miller, *The Modern Church: From the Dawn of the Reformation to the Eve of the Third Millennium* (Nashville: Abingdon, 1997), 212–13.

4. Cooper argues this point in *The Pioneers; or, The Sources of the Susquehanna: A Descriptive Tale* (1823) (New York: A. L. Burt, n.d.), chap. 28. Mr. Hardinge in Cooper's *Miles Wallingford* (1844) (New York: Putnam, 1906) may be more adaptable in some respects than Mr. Grant, but, like Mr. Grant, he is totally inflexible in matters of morality or theology.

5. For a discussion of Cooper's role in shaping popular taste, see James D. Wallace, *Early Cooper and His Audience* (New York: Columbia University Press, 1986).

6. For a description of how Lydia Child and her writing were influenced by contemporary culture, see Carolyn L. Karcher's introduction to Lydia Maria Child, *Hobomok and Other Writings on Indians* (New Brunswick, N.J.: Rutgers University Press, 1991), ix–xxxviii.

7. Bell, *Hawthorne*, 11.

8. Karcher, introduction to *Hobomok*, ix–x.

9. Bell, *Hawthorne*, 56. Bell uses the word "courage"; "fortitude" seems more appropriate to me.

10. Nathaniel Hawthorne, "Mrs. Hutchinson," quoted in ibid., 47.

11. Eliza Buckminister Lee, *Naomi*, p. 4, quoted in ibid., 60.

12. Ibid., 119. Bell comments, "The opposition of 'heart' to 'dogma' is central in this romance" (ibid., 96).

13. For more, see James E. Henretta, *The Evolution of American Society, 1700–1815: An Interdisciplinary Analysis* (Lexington, Mass.: D. C. Heath, 1973), esp. 165. Cited in Karen Halttunen, *Confidence Men and Painted Women: A Study of Middle Class Culture in America, 1830–1870* (New Haven, Conn.: Yale University Press, 1982), 21.

14. David S. Reynolds, introduction to George Lippard, *The Quaker City; or, The Monks of Monk Hall: A Romance of Philadelphia Life, Mystery, and Crime* (Amherst: University of Massachusetts Press, 1995), xxxiii.

15. Halttunen, *Confidence Men*, chap. 1.

16. Quoted in Herbert Ross Brown, *The Sentimental Novel in America, 1789–1860* (Freeport, N.Y.: Books for Libraries, 1970), 188. In popular fiction, the victim, especially if she is a woman, is often portrayed as helpless once she is in the power of the mesmerizer.

17. The Congregational clergyman and the doctor who minister to Sarah Cornell embody the moral integrity Williams associates with the old religious and social establishment. By contrast, *all* of the Methodists who appear in the novel are portrayed as questionable characters.

18. David S. Reynolds, *Faith in Fiction: The Emergence of Religious Literature in America* (Cambridge: Harvard University Press, 1981), 173.

19. Ibid.

20. In addition to the examples listed, see John Neal, *Errata; or, The Works of Will Adams* (New York: For the proprietors, 1823).

21. Taken as a whole, these novels actually form the largest body of fiction from the time. They were even more numerous than sentimental novels published during the same years. For example, David Reynolds writes, "In surveying the total range of American fiction volumes published between 1789 and 1860, I have found that although sentimental-domestic writing was popular, sensational or adventurous fiction was even more so" (Reynolds, introduction to Lippard, *Quaker City*, xxi).

22. A late-nineteenth-century collector of Thompson's fiction estimates that Thompson wrote one hundred books, most of them published as paper pamphlets or serialized (David S. Reynolds and Kimberly R. Gladman, introduction to George Thompson, *Venus in Boston and Other Tales of Nineteenth-Century City Life*, ed. David S. Reynolds and Kimberly R. Gladman [Amherst: University of Massachusetts Press, 2002], xi).

23. Reynolds and Gladman, introduction to Thompson, *Venus in Boston*, xxx.

24. See chapter 3. David Reynolds suggests that "Lippard . . . shared with Hawthorne certain character types, such as the fallen minister." It is difficult to know how directly these contemporary writers like Thompson and Lippard influenced more major literary figures like Hawthorne: "Suffice it to say that Lippard was drawing from the same repository of cultural images as the other writers and that his dramatization of these images frequently parallels theirs" (Reynolds, introduction to Lippard, *Quaker City*, xxviii–xxix).

25. Ibid., vii.

26. Ibid., xvii, xxi.

27. One of Lippard's authorial comments suggests that he had the real-life Onderdonk in mind as he created the fictional Barnhurst: "When grave gentlemen of the Church . . . assemble in Convention, and solemnly proclaim to the world, that their Bishop is guilty of all manner of uncleanliness" (Lippard, *Empire City*, 90).

28. Also quoted in David S. Reynolds, *George Lippard* (Boston: Twayne, 1982), 98, 99. Lippard believed that physicians were subject to the same temptations and corruptions as clergy. He referred to both clergy and doctors when he wrote, "Entrusted with the confidence of every member of the house, these men every day abuse that confidence, and reward blind faith with treachery and outrage" (*Memoirs of a Preacher*, 211). Lippard offered a similar comment about the vulnerability of clergy in *Empire City*, 90. George Thompson espouses a similar view of the ministers' vulnerability but adds yet another perspective. With questionable logic, he blames the victim, arguing that "the female members of a church are apt to regard their minister with the highest degree of affectionate admiration—as an idol worthy to be worshipped. They load him with presents—they spoil him with flattery—they dazzle him with their glances, and encourage him by their smiles. . . . He is very often thrown into the society of pretty women of his flock, under circumstances which are dangerously fascinating. The 'sister,' instead of maintaining proper reserve, grows too communicative and familiar, and the minister, who is but a man, subject to all the weakness and frailties of humanity, often in an unguarded moment forgets his sacred calling, and becomes the seducer—though we question

if literal *seduction* be involved, where the female so readily *complies* with voluptuous wishes, which perchance, she responds to with as much fervor as the other party entertains them. Therefore, we say that licentiousness on the part of ministers of the gospel is produced in *very many* cases by the encouragements held out to them by too admiring and too affectionate sisters" (Thompson, *City Crimes*, 213.

Chapter 2. Clerics in Contention: Church Images

1. A most helpful discussion of these phenomena appears in Ann Douglas, *The Feminization of American Culture* (New York: Knopf, 1979), esp. the introduction and chap. 1.

2. I first heard the data quoted in an address Dr. Lynn gave at a symposium at Hartford Seminary in January 1976. It also appears in Robert Wood Lynn and James W. Fraser, "Images of the Small Church in American History," in *Small Churches Are Beautiful*, ed. Jackson W. Carroll (San Francisco: Harper and Row, 1977), 7. Fraser, Lynn, and Douglas quote similar statistics. Their common source is Donald M. Scott, *From Office to Profession: The New England Ministry, 1750–1850* (Philadelphia: University of Pennsylvania Press, 1978), 74–75.

3. Scott, *From Office to Profession*, 114.

4. For a more extended discussion, see William Charvat, *The Origins of American Critical Thought, 1810–1835* (New York: A. S. Barnes, 1968), 19.

5. For a more complete discussion, see Douglas, *Feminization of American Culture*, 22, 23, and Winthrop S. Hudson, *American Protestantism* (Chicago: University of Chicago Press, 1961), 97–98.

6. The Rev. Orville Dewey describing his experience as a minister in 1852 (Orville Dewey, *Autobiography and Letters of Orville Dewey, D.D.*, ed. Mary E. Dewey [Boston: Roberts Brothers, 1883], 224; quoted in Douglas, *Feminization of American Culture*, 22). The minister's difficult position became increasingly painful as the century progressed (Douglas, *Feminization of American Culture*; see also part II in this volume).

7. For a summary, see Douglas, *Feminization of American Culture*, 114.

8. Though evangelical clergy offered a formidable challenge to those from the formerly established churches during the first half of the nineteenth century, most American fiction that reflects evangelical church images did not appear until after the Civil War. Their cultural impact occurred during the last half of the century. I discuss these images in part II of this volume.

9. The Rev. George Tracy, the staunch Calvinist and outspoken central character in the anonymous *Triumph of Religion* (Savannah: S. C. and J. Schenk, 1825), stands as the only conservative minister presented positively as a major character in an American novel published before the 1830s.

10. Michael Servetus, a physician and liberal theologian, was tried and found guilty of heresy and burned alive at Geneva in 1553. "The charitable Calvin" is a sarcastic reference to John Calvin, who was widely accused of playing a significant role in Servetus's condemnation and martyrdom. Philip Freneau's *Letters on Various Subjects* (1799) ridicules Calvinist orthodoxy in much the same manner as Tyler's *The Bay Boy*.

11. Arminius was a Dutch theologian who repudiated the strict Calvinist doctrine of predestination. Arminians believe that humans' actions on earth can have a bearing on their salvation.

12. In addition to the sources mentioned in this chapter, see those in chapters 5 and 6.

13. Jane Tompkins, *Sensational Designs: The Cultural Work of American Fiction, 1790–1860* (New York: Oxford University Press, 1986), 163.

14. For example, Douglas, *Feminization of American Culture.* While Douglas's conclusions have been sharply criticized (e.g., Tompkins, *Sensational Designs*, 162), I think her description of popular culture in the nineteenth century is largely accurate.

15. Frank Luther Mott, *Golden Multitudes: The Story of Best Sellers in the United States* (New York: Macmillan, 1947), 307. In a recent paperback edition of the novel, Jane Tompkins notes, "No novel written in the United States had ever sold so well" (Jane Tompkins, afterword to Susan Warner, *The Wide, Wide World* [New York: Feminist Press, 1987], 584).

16. Mrs. E. Prentiss, *Stepping Heavenward* (1869) (New York: Anson D. F. Randolph, 1880).

17. The suggestion that "good" ministers are dutiful and well behaved is not restricted to Unitarians. For example, Paul Creton [John Townsend Trowbridge, pseud.], *Father Brighthopes: or, An Old Clergyman's Vacation* (1853) (New York: Hurst, n.d.), a novel intended for children, embodies the same model behavior in an Episcopal priest.

18. A number of scholars believe that this novel reflects Henry Wadsworth Longfellow's religious beliefs and that his brother Samuel Longfellow is the model for the minister who is the central character of the novel (Cecil Williams, *Henry Wadsworth Longfellow* [New York: Twayne, 1964], 123, and Edward Wagenknecht, *Longfellow: A Full-Length Portrait* [New York: Longmans, Green, 1955], 296; both cited in Jean Downey's introduction to Henry Wadsworth Longfellow, *Kavanagh* [New Haven, Conn.: College and University Press, 1965], 17–18).

19. Lawrence Buell, *New England Literary Culture: From Revolution Through Renaissance* (New York: Cambridge University Press, 1989), 268. Part 3 of Buell's book offers a helpful discussion of the contrasting Arminian and orthodox perspectives.

20. James D. Wallace, *Early Cooper and His Audience* (New York: Columbia University Press, 1986), esp. chap. 2; and Charvat, *Origins of American Critical Thought.*

21. For an extensive discussion of this transition among conservatives, see Richard Rabinowitz, *The Spiritual Self in Everyday Life: The Transformation of Personal Religious Experience in Nineteenth-Century New England* (Boston: Northeastern University Press, 1989). As I read Rabinowitz's book, I was struck by how closely the perspectives of clergy in contemporary fiction mirror those of their real-life counterparts.

22. Though it is known that Stowe participated in the Episcopal Church (during her years in Hartford, for example), there is no clear evidence that she was ever actually confirmed as an Episcopalian.

23. For a helpful description of Stowe's theological struggle, see Alice C. Crozier, *The Novels of Harriet Beecher Stowe* (New York: Oxford University Press, 1969), esp. chaps. 4 and 5.

24. For more discussion, see Sandra R. Duguid's introduction to Harriet Beecher Stowe, *The Minister's Wooing* (Hartford, Conn.: Stowe-Day Foundation, 1990). Dr. Hopkins's responses to the grieving Mary probably reflect suggestions that Stowe received after her college-aged son Henry drowned while swimming in the Connecticut River. Henry also had not experienced a conversion, and the orthodox Calvinist theology Stowe inherited from her forebears offered little hope of salvation for him. In December 1855, about 1.5 years before Henry drowned, Harriet wrote to him, "I *do love* you Henry, & I know you do love me—but oh my darling, I want you to choose my Redeemer—your father's and mother's God for your own" (quoted in Joan Hedrick, *Harriet Beecher Stowe: A Life* [New York: Oxford University Press, 1994], 254). The evidence available indicates that Mrs. Stowe may have longed to accept but could not completely embrace the disinterested faith that the fictional Dr. Hopkins reflects. By 1857, when Henry drowned, Stowe had already begun to doubt some (but by no means all) aspects of Calvinist theology. These doubts moved her to refine both her theology and her fiction in the 1860s (Crozier, *Novels of Stowe*, 95, 96).

25. "If one fully acquiesces in this will of the universe, then all the apparent misfortunes of life become transformed into the most exquisite delights" (Nathalia Wright, *Melville's Use of the Bible* [Durham, N.C.: Duke University Press, 1949], 91).

26. Buell, *New England Literary Culture*, 275.

27. Tompkins, *Sensational Designs*, chap. 5.

28. Ibid., 127, 128. Some of the social roles open to women are considerably stronger by the end of the century; with the exception of social gospel ministers, those awarded to ministers are more restricted (discussed in chapters 6 and 8 in this volume).

29. Douglas, *Feminization of American Culture*, 12. For a more extended discussion, see Tompkins, afterword to Warner, *Wide, Wide World*, 584–608.

30. These include Elizabeth Stuart Phelps [H. Trusta, pseud.], *The Sunnyside; or, the Country Minister's Wife* (Boston: John P. Jewitt, 1851); Elizabeth Stuart Phelps [H. Trusta, pseud.], *A Peep at Number Five, or a Chapter in the Life of a City Pastor* (Freeport, N.Y.: Books for Libraries, 1852); Martha Stone Hubbell, *The Shady Side; or, Life in a Country Parsonage* (Boston: J. P. Jewett, 1853); and [Samuel Hayes Eliot,] *The Parish-Side* (New York: Mason Brothers, 1854). Parson Wibird Hawkins, who appears in Thomas Bailey Aldrich's nostalgic novel *Prudence Palfrey* (Boston: James R. Osgood, 1874), suffers a similar fate. Mr. Snow, who appears in Josiah G. Holland's novel *Sevenoaks* (New York: Scribner's, Armstrong, 1875), is also a weak character. He is no match for the local businessman, Mr. Belcher. Snow is vindicated when Belcher's crooked ways come to light, but he is completely under Belcher's thumb until Belcher is discredited.

31. Sidney H. Mead, "The Rise of the Evangelical Conception of the Ministry in America (1607–1850)," in *The Ministry in Historical Perspectives*, ed. Richard H. Niebuhr and Daniel D. Williams (New York: Harper and Bros., 1956), 212.

Chapter 3. Vulnerable Divines: Radical Images

1. Arthur Cleveland Coxe, "The Writings of Hawthorne," *Church Review* 3 (January 1851), 489–511; quoted in Nathaniel Hawthorne, *The Scarlet Letter*, Norton Critical Edition, ed. Seymour Gross, Sculley Bradley, Richmond Croom Beatty, and E. Hudson Long (New York: Norton, 1988), 189.

2. As recently as 2001 it was the eleventh best-selling fiction paperback book by *any* author at Amazon.com, the largest U.S. on-line bookstore.

3. Marion L. Kesselring, *Hawthorne's Reading, 1828–1850* (Folcroft, Pa.: Folcroft Press, 1969).

4. One possible exception is Herman Melville. Melville certainly portrays the effects of Calvinism convincingly in *Moby-Dick*. Melville may even feel the burden of Calvinism much more than Hawthorne does. But unlike Hawthorne, Melville seems unable to achieve a critical perspective that enables him to stand apart from Calvinism and describe its workings. Melville experiences Calvinism; Hawthorne moves beyond the experience of Calvinism to analyze it.

5. Michael J. Colacurcio, *The Province of Piety: Moral History in Hawthorne's Early Tales* (Cambridge: Harvard University Press, 1984), 7. See also David S. Reynolds, *Beneath the American Renaissance* (Cambridge: Harvard University Press, 1988), 39–40.

6. For a description of Hawthorne's religious shaping, see Colacurcio, *Province of Piety*, 22–24; Michael J. Colacurcio, introduction to Hawthorne's *Selected Tales and Sketches* (New York: Penguin, 1987), xvii; and Reynolds, *American Renaissance*, 39–40. "Sunday at Home," a tale written in 1837, probably offers the most accurate reflection of Hawthorne's personal attitude toward religion and church participation as an adult.

7. Hawthorne's sketch is titled "Mrs. Hutchinson." For an analysis of Ann Hutchinson's effect on the Puritans, see Herbert W. Schneider, *The Puritan Mind* (Ann Arbor: University of Michigan Press, 1958), 60–65.

8. My sympathy with Hawthorne's critique of Puritan Calvinism is not meant to suggest that I think all Calvinism is morbid. Hawthorne believes that the Calvinist perception of human nature and especially of human sinfulness can be destructive when believers become obsessed with their own sinfulness. I do agree with Hawthorne on this point.

9. For an extensive discussion, see J. Gordon Taylor, *Hawthorne's Ambivalence Toward Puritanism* (Logan: Utah State University Press, 1965).

10. Q. D. Leavis, "Hawthorne as a Poet," in Nathaniel Hawthorne, *Collected Essays*, vol. 2, ed. G. Singh (London: Cambridge University Press, 1985), 45.

11. I do not identify quotations and references to "The Man of Adamant" (1837) in this section and to "The Minister's Black Veil" (1836) in the next section by page number. These tales are so short that it is not difficult to find the quoted sentences in the original tale from which they are drawn.

12. Colacurcio, *Province of Piety*, 247; italics in the original.

13. Ibid., 246. See also Sidney E. Ahlstrom, *A Religious History of the American People* (New Haven, Conn.: Yale University Press, 1972), 107.

14. Perry Miller, *The New England Mind: From Colony to Province* (Cambridge: Belknap), 107; quoted in Colacurcio, *Province of Piety*, 248.

15. I recognize that "The Minister's Black Veil," which appeared in 1836, actually precedes "The Man of Adamant," which appeared in 1837. I have rearranged the order for presentation purposes.

16. Bell appears to accept this argument (Michael Davitt Bell, *Hawthorne and the Historical Romance of New England* [Princeton, N.J.: Princeton University Press, 1971], 64–68). For a biography of Moody, see Philip McIntire Woodwell, *Handkerchief Moody: The Diary and the Man* (Portland, Me.: Colonial Offset Printing, n.d.)

17. For a helpful description of Franklin's "ungodly" Puritanism, see Schneider, *Puritan Mind*, chaps. 7 and 8.

18. Michael Colacurcio offers a thorough historical and theological analysis of this story in *Province of Piety*, chap. 6. My own critique of Hawthorne's tale reflects many of Colacurcio's insights.

19. Colacurcio, *Province of Piety*, 330; see also 620 n.25.

20. As Colacurcio suggests, "There simply is no visible Community of Saints. Without some Community of Sinners, therefore, no community is possible" (ibid., 384).

21. In fact, it may be that some mark of transgression, akin to the scarlet letter, actually appears on his bare chest (*Scarlet Letter*, chap. 10, "The Leech and His Patient").

22. In November 1856, Melville visited Hawthorne who was then serving as U.S. Consul in Liverpool. On the second day of his visit, the two of them took a long walk together. On Thursday, November 20, after Melville had departed, Hawthorne reflected on their conversation: "We took a pretty long walk together, and sat together in a hollow among the sand hills. . . . Melville, as he always does, began to reason of Providence and futurity, and of everything that lies beyond the human ken, and informed me that he had 'pretty much made up his mind to be annihilated'; but still he does not seem to rest in that anticipation; and, I think, will never rest until he gets hold of a definite belief. It is strange how he persists—and has persisted ever since I knew him, and probably long before—in wandering to-and-fro over these deserts, as dismal and monotonous as the sand hills amid which we were sitting. He can neither believe, nor be comfortable in his unbelief; and he is too honest and courageous not to try to do one or the other" (Nathaniel Hawthorne, *The English Notebooks*, ed. Randall Stewart [New York: Russell and Russell, 1962], 432–33; see also Lawrance Thompson, *Melville's Quarrel with God* [Princeton, N.J.: Princeton University Press, 1952]).

23. For a recent and complete description of how his childhood and young adult experience shaped Melville, see Hershel Parker, *Herman Melville: A Biography*, vol. 1 (Baltimore: Johns Hopkins University Press, 1996).

24. Cf. Newton Arvin, *Herman Melville* (New York: William Sloane Associates, 1950): "Neither the humanitarian rationalism of the Enlightenment nor the transcendental romantic ardors of the early nineteenth century had availed in any way to soften or emasculate the austere, earnest, pessimistic orthodoxy of the Reformed Church in America" (31). Arvin's statement (which, to my knowledge, is not corroborated directly by any contemporary source) may be an overstatement. At least the Reformed Church in America does not deserve to be singled out. The personal recollections of Harriet Beecher Stowe as reflected in *The Minister's*

Wooing (1850) and of Oliver Wendell Holmes as reflected in *The Guardian Angel* (1867) suggest that the Calvinism of the Congregational Church was at least as earnest and austere as that of the Reformed Church.

25. Hershel Parker describes the details of the publication process, including Murray's cuts and revisions designed to make the book "less offensive" (Parker, *Melville*, chap. 19).

26. For a description of John Wiley's horror when he discovered some of the salacious and irreverent passages in *Typee* and his failure to excise them all in the rush to publish the book in an American edition, see Parker, *Melville*, chap. 20.

27. Reynolds, *American Renaissance*, 49.

28. Hawthorne was scrupulous in his use of historical records; Melville was not. Melville used his sources as the basis for his stories, but he often fabricated personal experiences based on information gleaned from the sources and then presented the fabrications as fact (Parker, *Melville*, chap. 22; see also John Bryant's introduction to Herman Melville, *Typee: A Peep at Polynesian Life* [New York: Penguin, 1996], ix–xxx). For a list of specific sources Melville used to write *Typee*, see Elizabeth Renker, *Strike Through the Mask: Herman Melville and the Scene of Writing* (Baltimore: Johns Hopkins University Press, 1998).

29. *Buffalo Commercial Advertiser*, July 1, 1846; quoted in Parker, *Melville*, 435.

30. It is difficult to ascertain the source of Melville's general disillusionment with the church and its leaders. Some of it may be rooted in his experience of the church as a teenager. During the Rev. Mr. Ludlow's ministry at the First Church in Albany, the Dutch Reformed Church Herman's mother attended (and which Herman also may have attended during his teenage years), the treasurer embezzled not only existing church funds but also loans he secured in the name of the church and then diverted to his own personal use. The controversy that followed the discovery of the treasurer's misconduct split the congregation into two factions: one favored punishing the treasurer according to the law of the state, the other believed the treasurer should be given an opportunity to make restitution and be forgiven. The hardliners prevailed, not only in the matter of the treasurer but also in a controversy that followed. With church funds in desperate traits, the consistory (governing board) voted to restrict access to the church's Poor Fund: instead of being available to help anyone in need, it could be used only by church members in need. This infighting among church members transpired while young Herman Melville lived across the street from the church. "If an adolescent with naïve but very lofty ideals was standing in the side-lines observing all of the bitter confrontations, it would scarcely be surprising if he came away with some very cynical views of religious institutions and their clergy." This observation by the current church historian, Robert S. Alexander, seems well founded to me. (The quoted sentence and the historical information contained in this note are based on a letter dated June 7, 2001, that I received from Robert S. Alexander, historian at the First Church in Albany.)

31. Merrell R. Davis and William H. Gilmane, eds., *The Letters of Herman Melville* (New Haven, Conn.: Yale University Press, 1960), 129; italics mine.

32. Actually, the God Melville envisions in *Moby-Dick* is not at all like the God characterized in the Book of Jonah. Melville's God would have moved swiftly to punish the sinful Ninevites, as well as the disobedient Jonah. God as portrayed in

the biblical story doesn't punish either. Everything God does with the Old Testament Jonah is designed to convince Jonah to complete a mission of mercy.

33. Personally, I do not believe that referring to God exclusively with male pronouns is either socially correct or theologically accurate. However, I think using male pronouns in the present discussion is justified. The image of God in Hawthorne's and Melville's fiction is overwhelmingly male.

34. Stowe's Samuel Hopkins is an eighteenth-century historical character who reflects the nineteenth-century theological issues with which Stowe is contending as she writes. Her choice of Samuel Hopkins as the historical model for her fictional Hopkins is significant. God for the historical Hopkins is even more disconnected from feelings than God is for Hopkins's mentor, Jonathan Edwards. The God Stowe's fictional characters perceive is more sympathetic and present than the distant, austere God of eighteenth-century Edwardsian Calvinism, especially as perceived by the real-life Samuel Hopkins. I continue this discussion of the lingering fallout of Edwardsian Calvinism in postbellum America in chapter 4.

35. A. N. Wilson, *God's Funeral: A Biography of Faith and Doubt in Western Civilization* (New York: Ballantine, 1999). Claire Tomalin makes the same point in her biography, *Thomas Hardy* (New York: Penguin, 2007), 223.

36. Allen C. Guelzo, *Abraham Lincoln: Redeemer President* (Grand Rapids, Mich.: Eerdmans, 1999), 152, 153, and 447. Guelzo describes Lincoln's theology as "providentialism." Gideon Welles, who served as secretary of the Navy under Lincoln, offers a similar view of Lincoln's faith: "There were occasions when, uncertain how to proceed, he [Lincoln] had in this way submitted the disposal of the subject to a Higher Power, and abided by what seemed the Supreme Will" (Gideon Welles, "History of Emancipation," *Galaxy* [1872], 847; quoted in Doris Kearns Goodwin, *Team of Rivals* [New York: Simon and Schuster, 2005], 482). In an 1862 conversation with Eliza Gurney, Lincoln reportedly said, "if I had my way this war would have ended before this, but we find it still continues; and we must believe that He permits it for some wise purpose of his own, mysterious and unknown to us; and though with our limited understandings we may not be able to comprehend it, yet we cannot but believe, that He who made the world still governs it" (Eliza P. Gurney, copy of interview with Abraham Lincoln [October 26, 1862], Lincoln Papers, quoted in Goodwin, *Team of Rivals*, 562).

37. No. 1551, ca. 1882, in Emily Dickenson, *The Complete Poems of Emily Dickinson*, ed. Thomas H. Johnson (Boston: Little, Brown, 1960), 646. Poems numbered 376 and 502 in that volume are examples of the despairing poems Dickinson wrote in the early 1860s. For a description of Dickinson's inability to maintain Christian faith, see Richard B. Sewell, *The Life of Emily Dickinson* (Cambridge: Harvard University Press, 1994), esp. chap. 21.

38. No doubt most of Hawthorne's contemporary readers viewed his "crazy" ministers as moral failures. Hawthorne was breaking new ground in his characterizations. The psychological categories we now draw on to describe ministers like Dimmesdale as disturbed persons were largely unavailable in Hawthorne's time.

Chapter 4. Compulsives and Accommodators: Popular Images (1)

1. By the end of the century, combined sales in the United States and England approached 200,000 copies (Frank Luther Mott, *Golden Multitudes: The Story of Best Sellers in the United States* [New York: Macmillan, 1947], 321; and Carol Farley Kessler, *Elizabeth Stuart Phelps* [Boston : Twayne, 1982], 30).

2. Elizabeth Stuart Phelps, *Chapters from a Life* (Boston: Houghton Mifflin, 1897), 97–98; quoted in Kessler, *Phelps*, 31.

3. They even shared the same first name. At birth, Elizabeth's mother named her Mary in honor of a dear friend. When Mary's mother died, Mary took her mother's name, Elizabeth Stuart Phelps, as her own.

4. In many respects, Stowe's and Phelps's fictional clergy reflect their real-life fathers, Lyman Beecher and Austin Phelps. Both authors imply that the theological views that confine their fictional creations also hinder their fathers and other Calvinist clergy from offering words of comfort, even when members of their own families lost loved ones. When Harriet Beecher was eleven years old, Alexander Metcalf Fisher, her sister Catherine's fiancé, was shipwrecked off the coast of England and drowned. Catharine was devastated by the loss. Not only was it a personal tragedy for her, Fisher had not undergone a conversion experience. According to orthodox theology, he was lost for eternity. When Catherine turned to her father Lyman Beecher for some words of hope, she found none. He told Catherine to put her grieving aside and move on with her life. Her personal loss was simply a reflection of the "human condition." When her grief persisted, Lyman told her to concentrate on her blessings—"himself included." He suggested that her continued suffering showed a lack of faith and that her effort to seek some relief from God was "causing her to remodel God's character, when in fact she should change herself, not God." Like the fictional Dr. Hopkins, Lyman Beecher "begins with a theory about God and then derives from it a prescription for how human beings should feel and act." The quotes are from Joan Hedrick, *Harriet Beecher Stowe: A Life* (New York: Oxford University Press, 1994), 40–41. Lyman Beecher's advice to Catharine appears in a letter from Lyman Beecher to Catharine Beecher, November 5, 1822, in Radcliffe College Schlesinger Library, Beecher-Stowe collection, folder 2. The quoted sections also appear in Hedrick, *Stowe*, 40–41.

Lyman Beecher was a disciple of Yale theologian, Timothy Dwight and Dwight's successor at Yale, Nathaniel William Taylor. All were leaders of a more evangelical group who saw a larger role for believers in the process of salvation than the more conservative Connecticut Calvinists led by Bennet Tyler and Asahel Nettleton. For a complete discussion, see Richard Rabinowitz, *Spiritual Self: The Transformation of Personal Religious Experience in Nineteenth-Century New England* (Boston: Northeastern University Press, 1989), chap. 9, esp. 106, 107. When he moved west to assume the presidency of Lane Seminary in Cincinnati, Lyman Beecher's concern to make Calvinism more humane led to a severe rebuke from a Presbyterian colleague, the Rev. Dr. Joshua Lacy Wilson. Wilson filed charges against Beecher accusing him of heresy. After a painful trial, Beecher was acquitted by the local presbytery. Wilson appealed to the regional synod where Beecher was again acquitted.

Wilson then filed an appeal to the General Assembly, but colleagues persuaded him to withdraw it. Beecher's treatment by his orthodox colleagues made a deep impression on both his daughter Harriet and her soon to be husband Calvin Stowe, who was a professor at Lane Seminary at the time of the trial. For a recent discussion, see Debby Applegate, *The Most Famous Man in America: The Biography of Henry Ward Beecher* (New York: Doubleday, 2006), chap. 4.

5. I do not mean to imply that these pastors, or the real-life models on which they are based, lacked feelings. In his discourse on "The Theology of the Intellect and That of the Feelings," Edwards Park of Andover Seminary describes in detail the important roles feelings play in reinforcing faith. But Park is careful to point out that theology formed by the intellect must always dominate and control that of the feelings. He speaks of the need for a "well-trained" heart and then goes on to argue that "the theology of reason derives aid from the impulses of emotion," but the theology of reason must maintain "ascendancy over" the emotions. "In all investigations for truth, the intellect must be the authoritative power, employing the sensibilities as indices of right doctrine, but surveying and superintending them from its commanding elevation." As early as 1850, when Park read his paper to an association of Congregational clergy, he seemed to be conscious of the hazards of one-sided, compelled believing and was trying to find a balance. But his task was not easy; Park was surrounded by Calvinists who were already on the defensive, and as a theological professor at Andover, an overtly Calvinist theological seminary, his views were subject to close scrutiny. In a note that appears at the bottom of the first page of the published version of his address, and that he probably hoped would disarm some critics, Park says he "he intended to avoid all trains of remark adverse to the doctrinal views of any party or school belonging to the Convention [of Congregational Ministers of Massachusetts, who composed his audience]. But, contrary to his anticipations, he was led into a course of thought which he was aware that some clergymen of Massachusetts would not adopt as their own, and for the utterance of which he was obliged to rely on their liberal and generous feeling" (Edwards Park, "The Theology of the Intellect and That of the Feelings," *Bibliotheca Sacra and Theological Review* 7 [1850], 533). Both Ann Douglas and Joan D. Hedrick describe the need Park felt to conform to strict Calvinist theology (Ann Douglas, *The Feminization of American Culture* [New York: Knopf, 1979], 149, 150; and Hedrick, *Stowe*, 276, 277). Fifty years after Park's address, William James probed the interfacing roles of intellect and feeling in religion more openly in a series of lectures designed as a popular version of his Gifford lectures (William James's notes for "Intellect and Feeling in Religion" in his *Manuscript Lectures* [Cambridge: Harvard University Press, 1988]). Stowe remained loyal much longer than Phelps. I discuss Stowe's theological journey in the present chapter and Phelps's in the next chapter.

5. Pastors Stern and Johns were most likely patterned after the highly orthodox, hard-line Tylerites, who were the most conservative pastors of the Congregational churches in Connecticut during the 1820s and 1830s.

6. Some church historians, including Glenn T. Miller, my colleague at Bangor Seminary, think that the rise of the theological seminary itself was an indication of a declining quality in candidates for the ministry. Compared with their more able predecessors, contemporary candidates needed more formal training to become

intellectually qualified ministers. For example, Glenn T. Miller, *Piety and Intellect: The Aims and Purposes of Ante-bellum Theological Education* (Atlanta: Scholars Press, 1990). Ann Douglas traces historical evidence for the decline carefully. She notes that it affected candidates in both liberal and conservative schools (Douglas, *Feminization of American Culture*, chaps. 1–5).

7. The ill-fitted Andover student is described in "An Andover Student," *New Englander* (1855), 236 (cited in Douglas, *Feminization of American Culture*, 42). The declining status and narrowing role defined for ministers is rampant in American fiction during the 1840s and 1850s, as I note in the opening pages of chapter 2.

8. Miriam Rossiter Small traces the sources and scope of Holmes's anger in her biography, *Oliver Wendell Holmes* (New Haven, Conn.: College and University Press, 1962). For example, she notes that Holmes's "early disagreement with his father's doctrine is reflected in the questions of the *enfant terrible*, as he called himself. 'When it came to the threats of future punishment as described in the sermons of the more hardened theologians, my instincts were shocked and disgusted beyond endurance'" (31).

9. Mott, *Golden Multitudes*, 323. For a description of the stir the book caused, see Margaret Deland, *Golden Yesterdays* (New York: Harper and Bros., 1941), 215–30.

10. Paul Carter, *The Spiritual Crisis of the Gilded Age* (DeKalb: Northern Illinois University Press, 1971), 82.

11. It is important to recognize that fictional preachers like Moses Stern are *idealized* portraits of the strong Calvinist. In *Oldtown Folks*, Stern seems to be designed to function as a standard against which other clergy in the novel can be judged. They are placed alongside Stern not only to show how formidable preachers like Stern are but also to show how much has been lost with the passing of Stern's generation. Stowe is not unaware of the dangers Calvinism poses to vulnerable personalities like John Ward. As early as 1859, in *The Minister's Wooing*, she writes: "But it is to be conceded that these systems, so admirable in relation to the energy, earnestness, and acuteness of their authors, when received as absolute truth, and as a basis of actual life, had, on minds of a certain class, the effect of a slow poison, producing life habits of morbid action very different from any which ever followed the simple reading of the Bible. They differ from the New Testament as the living embrace of a friend does from his lifeless body, mapped out under the knife of the anatomical demonstrator; every nerve and muscle is there, but to the sensitive spirit there is the very chill of death in the analysis" (339; also quoted in Alice C. Crozier, *The Novels of Harriet Beecher Stowe* [New York: Oxford University Press, 1969], 120, 121).

12. In his introduction to the Harper's Modern Classics edition of Freeman's *A New England Nun and Other Stories* (New York: Harper and Bros., 1919), Fred Lewis Pattee suggests that Freeman's "kinship is with Hawthorne rather than with the realists" (xxv), which would place her identity as an author in the middle rather than at the end of the nineteenth century. Many of Freeman's characters do exhibit a Hawthorne-like quality. The language in her description of Parson Lord as "welded to his faith" and "almost ossification, of spirit," for example, recalls Hawthorne's "The Man of Adamant," a story I discuss in chapter 3. Freeman's writing would seem to suggest she was influenced by Hawthorne, though she vehemently denies being influenced by any previous authors (Pattee, introduction, xix–xx.) However, I think that the Hawthorne-like quality that Freeman's characters exhibit is

more likely a characteristic of the social context they reflect than a quality that was within her as an author. Freeman's commitment to realism as a local colorist moved her to represent the reality of their belief and life as realistically as she could. That reality happened to be Hawthorne-like.

13. The transformation from compelled to compulsive believing included lay leaders as well as clergy. The rigid, compulsive, and doctrinaire parishioner, often a deacon (or elder, as in *John Ward, Preacher*) replaced the wise, though often-conservative squire as the most powerful lay leader in the local parish. Examples include Deacon Quirk, mentioned earlier in this chapter, and Deacon Trowbridge, who appears in Gideon Hiram Hollister's *Kinley Hollow* (1882). Trowbridge seeks to depose the moderate local minister by getting the court to rule that, according to stipulations in the will giving the church its parsonage, only ministers with strict Calvinist theology can reside there. A female example of a compelled believer is Deborah, who appears in Mary Wilkins Freeman's *Pembroke* (1894). Deborah engenders fear not only in the local minister but also in all the other leaders in her congregation. She is so compulsive that she beats her son when he refuses to study his catechism. He is so seriously injured that he dies from the effects of the beating. By the end of the century, doctrinal believers in American novels are almost always compulsive believers. Respected, informed, and balanced compelled believers like Stowe's Moses Stern are only a memory.

14. John Calvin's *Institutes of the Christian Religion*, trans. Henry Beveridge (Grand Rapids, Mich. Eerdmans, 1989), is considered by most Calvin scholars as the primary source of Calvin's theology.

15. For an extended description of this accountability, see Rabinowitz, *Spiritual Self.*

16. In addition to those I discuss in this chapter and elsewhere in this book, other compulsive fictional preachers include Christopher Burke in Permelia J. Parker, *The Midnight Cry* (New York: Dodd, Mead, 1886); Parson West in Edward Bellamy, *The Duke of Stockbridge* (1900) (Cambridge: Harvard University Press, 1962); and David and Gabriel Thornley, who appear in Du Bose Heyward, *Angel* (New York: Doran, 1926).

17. F. W. Dupee, *Henry James* (New York: William Sloan, 1951), 9. Ann Douglas makes a similar observation also referring to Henry James Sr. in *Feminization of American Culture*, 17.

18. Harriet Beecher Stowe, *Household Papers and Stories* (Boston: Houghton Mifflin, 1896), 436–37, quoted in Crozier, *Novels of Stowe*, 152.

19. Crozier, *Novels of Stowe*, 92.

20. Ibid., 128–29.

21. Ibid., 129. In *Kinley Hollow* (1882), Hollister also mourns the dilution of the old Calvinism and points up the implications of compromising orthodox belief.

22. Harriet Beecher Stowe, Letter to Charles Stowe, March 7, 1879, Radcliffe College, Schlesinger Library, Beecher Stowe Collection, folder 196, quoted in Hedrick, *Stowe*, 391; italics in the original. Stowe's struggle is typical of evangelicals at the time. For example, George Marsden, *Fundamentalism and American Culture: The Shaping of Twentieth-Century Evangelicalism, 1870–1925* (New York: Oxford University Press, 1980), chap. 1.

23. Stowe, Letter to Charles Stowe. Crozier quotes this material in *Novels of Stowe*, 118–19. Crozier is uncertain of the date of the letter. She speculates it was written sometime during 1881. Joan Hedrick actually located the letter in the Radcliffe College collection of Stowe materials under the 1879 date (Hedrick, *Stowe*, 391). The "Uncle Henry" referred to in the letter was Henry Ward Beecher.

24. For example, Calvin wrote to Harriet from Heidelberg that he had met Professor Creutzer, whose book *The Mythology of the Ancients* details "the formation of the various mythological ideas of the ancients to the religious element essential to man every where." The book intrigued him: "When I get home we must read the whole work together" (Hedrick, *Stowe*, 101).

25. Crozier, *Novels of Stowe*, 144.

26. The deacon refers here to the doctrine of "Original Sin." According to this doctrine, when the first man, Adam, fell from grace and became sinful, that fall contaminated all of Adam's descendents—in other words, all of humankind. Thus all humans are sinners and deserve to be condemned. No effort by humans can alter their condition. Salvation is possible only by grace.

27. Diana C. Reep, *Margaret Deland* (Boston: Twayne, 1985), 12.

5. Con Men in Collars and Heroes of the Cloth: Popular Images (2)

1. Franklin J. Meine, ed., *Tall Tales of the Southwest: An Anthology of Southwest Humor, 1830–1860* (New York: Knopf, 1930), xxxi.

2. In a discussion of Hooper's characterization of Suggs, Glenn Miller, my Southern Baptist colleague at Bangor Seminary, offered some helpful insights. Within the Southern Baptist and Southern Methodist traditions, someone does not become a qualified minister by attending seminary. One *demonstrates* first that one has received an authentic call to be a preacher and then goes to seminary. This demonstration of faith and gifts qualifies someone to be a minister, not theological education. Hooper's contemporary readers would no doubt have recognized that Suggs cons the revivalists when they don't ask him to prove his call by preaching *before* they give him money to go to the seminary.

3. James M. Cox, *Mark Twain: The Fate of Humor* (Princeton, N.J.: Princeton University Press, 1966), 103–4; italics in the original.

4. Herman Melville's and Mark Twain's fiction actually reflects a more cynical view of life than stories from popular humorists like Hooper and Harris do—a point I explore in some depth in chapter 8.

5. In her portrayal of Bangs, Phelps offers what I believe is the first portrayal of a woman as a mainstream minister in American fiction. "A Woman's Pulpit" appeared first in *Atlantic Monthly* (July 1870) and was included in *Sealed Orders*, a collection Elizabeth Stuart Phelps published in 1879 (rpt., *Sealed Orders* [New York: Garrett Press, 1969], 176–95). One could argue that Bertha who appears in Elizabeth Oakes Smith's *Bertha and Lily* (New York: J. C. Derby, 1854) is an earlier example of a fictional woman in ministry. Bertha does challenge the notion that only men can preach, but she does not seem to me to be a fully developed minister in her own right, nor does she gain ecclesiastical credentialing like Bangs does. As

 far as I know, Antoinette Brown was the first woman actually ordained by a Congregational church (1853). However, her ordination was not recognized by the denomination. She eventually left the Congregational Church and became a Unitarian.

6. Figures are for total sales of Wright's books according to an Associated Press dispatch, reported in "Harold Bell Wright Goes Back to Hills as 'Shepherd,'" *Rochester (N.Y.) Times Union*, February 6, 1934, n.p. *The Calling of Dan Matthews* (New York: A. L. Burt, 1909) sold over 750,000 copies in the year it was published (Frank Luther Mott, *Golden Multitudes: The Story of Best Sellers in the United States* [New York: Macmillan, 1947], 313).

7. "Harold Bell Wright Goes Back to Hills," n.p.

8. Mrs. Frances Hamilton Hood, *Maud Mansfield* (Macon, Ga.: J.W. Burke, 1876), offers similarly jaded characterizations of clergy and others from the North.

Chapter 6. Activist Preachers and Their Detractors: Popular Images (3)

1. For a more complete discussion of changes in the American city between 1860 and 1910, see Charles N. Glaab and A. Theodore Brown, *A History of Urban America* (New York: Macmillan, 1967), 107–228. The statistics I quote in my discussion are drawn from Glaab and Brown and U.S. Census data.

2. For an extensive discussion of late-nineteenth- and early-twentieth-century ministers' perceptions of their ministry and the social order, see Grier Nicoll, "The Christian Social Novel in America, 1865–1918," Ph.D. dissertation, University of Minnesota, 1964.

3. Ibid., 321.

4. Ibid., 4, 5.

5. Cesarea Seminary is probably patterned on Andover Seminary where Phelps's father, Austin Phelps, taught and Elizabeth lived as a child. Professor Carruth may reflect some aspects of Austin Phelps's character as a professor, and Helen Carruth, Carruth's daughter in the novel, resembles the young Elizabeth Stuart Phelps. Professor Carruth, Bayard's theology professor, is uncomfortable with some of Bayard's theology, but he admits at the end of the novel that Bayard was his favorite student (366). Carruth's scrupulous public orthodoxy but private generosity may mirror the Austin Phelps his daughter Elizabeth remembered.

6. In the Congregational tradition, an ecclesiastical council composed of area Congregational ministers examines the candidate and judges whether the candidate is fit for ordination.

7. Phelps obviously intended Emanuel Bayard to be a Christ figure. His name "Emanuel" recalls a similar appellation given to Jesus. Other references in the novel support the notion that he is a Christ figure: Professor Carruth's reaction and the scripture he quotes ("It is written that the common people heard HIM gladly" [266]). Magdalene is the formal name of Lena, the prostitute Emanuel ministers to—and she seems intended to recall Mary Magdalene.

8. Frank Luther Mott, *Golden Multitudes: The Story of Best Sellers in the United States* (New York: Macmillan, 1947), 324.

9. Harold Bell Wright probably gave the romantic role to Dick Falkner so he could portray James Cameron as a completely devoted social minister, uncompromised by a love interest. Seven years later, when Wright completed *The Calling of Dan Matthews* (New York: A. L. Burt, 1909), he was less cautious. By 1909, Wright, like the hero of this second social gospel, had left the ministry to pursue a secular vocation that he believed would afford greater opportunities to benefit people than the ministry does ("Harold Bell Wright Goes Back to Hills as 'Shepherd,'" *Rochester [N.Y.] Times Union*, February 6, 1934, n.p.). Wright became increasingly disillusioned with both the church and the ministry as the years passed. For more, see my discussion of *God and the Groceryman* (1927) in the last section of this chapter.

10. In his book *Religion in the American Novel: The Search for Belief, 1860–1920* (Lanham, Md.: University Press of America, 1984), Leo F. O'Connor writes: "The problem of resolving antithetical value systems was familiar to a sympathetic middle-class readership, because Churchill's dilemma was also faced by millions of people who supported the Social Gospel but who didn't know how to integrate the realities of church life with this new theology" (269).

11. The classic theological work that describes this phenomenon is H. Richard Niebuhr, *The Social Sources of Denominationalism* (New York: Henry Holt, 1929).

12. White's unkind portrayals may have been accurate, but he was not at all discreet as he created them: he used actual names of local people for characters in the book. The backlash from village residents after the book appeared was so severe that he was forced to move away from the village for several years. Helene S. Farrell, the current Middleburgh town historian, describes White's indiscretion in "Charles Bouck White: The Sculptor," *Schoharie County Review* (Spring 1984): "Unethically he used the actual names of friends and classmates depicting the needs and shortcomings of the living citizens" (3). Ms. Farrell based her biographical sketch of White and her description of the controversy his novel caused when it appeared on interviews with residents who knew White and on articles in a variety of New York newspapers.

13. Quoted in Nicoll, "Christian Social Novel," 204, 205. Leo O'Connor offers similar comments in connection with the same novel: "In *Caesar's Column*, the failure of the churches to bear witness against injustice is presented as the primary cause leading to the bloody revolution which concludes the novel. Shortly before the revolution occurs, Donnelly makes ironic use of a reactionary clergyman, in the mode of Beecher and Ming, delivering a sermon on the need for Christian humility and forbearance [*sic*]. . . . In his parody of the reactionary clergyman delivering a gospel of Christian passivity, Donnelly is providing a textbook sample of the Marxian indictment that religion is the opiate of the people" (O'Connor, *Religion in the American Novel*, 244).

14. O'Connor makes this point repeatedly in *Religion in the American Novel.* Nicoll also summarizes it in "Christian Social Novel." According to the perspective embodied in these novels, the typical minister in America is "no more than a hired hand, bought for a sum of money to serve the interests of the wealthy few. The modern . . . minister is chosen to serve the interests of the congregation and the ruling powers. He is, therefore, both a slave to the prevailing situation, and too often a willing perpetuator of it. . . . In the pulpit he preaches the kind of sermons his congregations will like. . . . He is careful never to say anything to

disturb his listeners' ease of mind. Preeminently orthodox in his theology, he hews closely to the accepted doctrines and the sterile teachings of the established denominational seminary, from which he is usually a recent graduate. Above all, the conservative minister of these novels teaches no disturbing doctrines; nor does he ever preach on current problems and social issues" (Nicoll, "Christian Social Novel," 98–100).

15. On the basis of his extensive study of social gospel novels, Nicoll observes that "these authors did not mourn the voluntary or forced resignations of their fictional heroes. Rather, their heroes' actions condemn the present church to perdition and free the minister for more creative ministries elsewhere" ("Christian Social Novel," 107).

16. Aristides Homos, the traveler from the futurist Altrurian Commonwealth depicted in William Dean Howells's novel *A Traveller from Altruria* (1894) (Bloomington: Indiana University Press, 1968), reflects this popular turn-of-the-century viewpoint when he describes the form of religion that exists in utopian Altruria: "We believe ourselves the true followers of Christ, whose doctrine we seek to make our life, as He made it His. We have several forms of ritual, but no form of creed, and our religious differences may be said to be aesthetic and temperamental rather than theologic and essential. We have no denominations, for we fear in this as in other matters to give names to things lest we should cling to the names instead of the things. We love the realities, and for this reason we look at the life of a man rather than his profession for proof that he is a religious man" (169).

17. Even Bayard's strong exhortation to the alcoholic Joe Slip to pray seems more heroic than an act of faith. During the rest of the novel, Slip draws his strength and inspiration from the human Bayard more than from his God.

18. The fact that so many popular novels published in the United States between 1885 and 1920 held up social gospel ministers as human heroes suggests that these cultural images had widespread popular support at the turn of the century. Elizabeth Stuart Phelps's *A Singular Life* (1894) (Boston: Houghton Mifflin, 1899) was reprinted several times. Frank Luther Mott lists Harold Bell Wright's *That Printer of Udell's* (1903) (New York: A. L. Burt, 1911) as one of the "better sellers" of 1903, and Winston Churchill's *The Inside of the Cup* (1913) New York: Macmillan, 1914) as a better seller for 1913 (Mott, *Golden Multitudes*, 324, 325). Many of these novels are readily available in used bookstores. When I last checked, ABEbooks, the largest network of used bookstores on the Internet, listed 211 copies of Wright's book for sale in affiliated bookstores. *That Printer of Udell's* is still in print in a modern edition. Thomas Nelson Page's *John Marvel, Assistant* (New York: Scribner's, 1909) is readily available in secondhand bookstores. I argue in chapter 7 that this popular appeal likely did not include more evangelical Christians.

19. Hodder begins as an orthodox believer but becomes progressively liberal as Churchill's novel unfolds.

Chapter 7. Champions of the Faith: Church Images

1. Historian F. I. Moats notes that "circuits were often three hundred to five hundred miles in circumference and each had many stations or appointments

where classes had been organized" (F. I. Moats, "The Rise of Methodism in the Middle West," *Mississippi Valley Historical Review* 15 [1928], 79; quoted in Leo F. O'Connor, *Religion in the American Novel: The Search for Belief, 1860–1920* [Lanham, Md.: University Press of America, 1984], 318). Nathan O. Hatch offers an extended description of the challenges circuit riders faced in *The Democratization of American Christianity* (New Haven, Conn.: Yale University Press, 1989), 81–97. Hatch's book includes a cover from *Harper's Weekly* 11 (October 12, 1867), 563, that features an obviously soaked circuit rider on his horse holding an umbrella against the driving rain (90).

2. Peter Cartwright, one of the most famous of the early Methodist preachers, was popularly known as "the Methodist bulldog" (Ann Douglas, *The Feminization of American Culture* [New York: Knopf, 1979], 37; see also Hatch, *Democratization of American Christianity*, 89, 138).

3. "There are those, indeed, whose sectarian pride will be offended that I have frankly shown the rude as well as the heroic side of early Methodism. I beg they will remember the solemn obligations of the novelist to tell the truth. Lawyers and even ministers are permitted to speak entirely on one side. But no man is worthy to be called a novelist who does not endeavor with his whole soul to produce the higher form of history, by writing truly of men as they are, and dispassionately of those forms of life that come within his scope" (Edward R. Eggleston, *The Circuit Rider* [New York: Scribner's, 1878], vi, vii).

4. Donaldson reflects the "Misfits in America" cultural image I describe in chapter 1. The wilderness frontier had simply moved west by the 1820s.

5. In many ways, Kike's and Mort's preparation equips them better for the ministry they face than the traditional, formal education that is required of their more refined colleagues. As Hatch observes: "There is little reason to disagree with Peter Cartwright's estimate that, of the thousands of preachers that the Methodists recruited in the early republic, not more than fifty had more than a common English education, and scores of preachers did not have even that much. The first college graduate among the circuit riders of Indiana found his education an actual disadvantage and gave up the regular ministry because of prejudice against him" (Hatch, *Democratization of American Christianity*, 89). In his autobiography, Cartwright describes the awkwardness of an educated minister who tries to read a sermon to a rowdy Methodist meeting. The wind blows out the candle, and he is unable to continue because he can't see his manuscript. When some in the meeting are caught up in the spirit, he moves among them and cautions them to be calm. They respond by throwing him bodily out of the gathering (Peter Cartwright, *Autobiography of Peter Cartwright, the Backwoods Preacher*, ed. W.P. Strickland [New York: Carlton and Porter, 1857)], 79, 360, 371; Douglas quotes some of the pertinent sections in *Feminization of American Culture*, 37).

6. Not every seminary-trained minister who appears in nineteenth-century fiction is as astute and balanced as Mr. Arthur is. In *The Ebony Idol* (New York: D. Appleton, 1860), Southern writer Mrs. G.M. Flanders portrays those who oppose slavery quite differently from the way William Mumford Baker presents the antislavery minister, Mr. Arthur. The Northern minister Mr. Cary in Flanders's novel is a crazed abolitionist. His approach is so fanatical that it alienates both his congregation and his family.

7. In addition to the works by Phelps and Stowe that I have already mentioned, these writers and their novels include the following: Amelia Edith Barr (Huffington), *The Hallam Succession: A Tale of Methodist Life in Two Countries* (New York: Phillips and Hunt, 1885); Katherine Woods, *Metzerott, Shoemaker* (New York: Thomas Y. Crowell, 1889); Albion Tourgee, *Murvale Eastman, Christian Socialist* (New York: Fords, Howard and Hulburt, 1891); Charles M. Sheldon, *Richard Bruce, or Life That Now Is* (Boston: Congregational Sunday School and Publishing Society, 1892); Charles M. Sheldon, *In His Steps* (1897) (New York: Putnam's, 1982); Charles M. Sheldon, *The Crucifixion of Phillip Strong* (1898) (New York: Grosset and Dunlap, n.d.); Charles M. Sheldon, *The Redemption of Freetown* (Boston: United Society of Christian Endeavor, 1898); Charles M. Sheldon, *The Miracle of Markham: How Twelve Churches Became One* (Chicago: Church Press, 1899); George Farnell, *Rev. Josiah Hilton: The Apostle of the New Age* (Providence, R.I.: Journal of Commerce, 1898); Elizabeth Stuart Phelps, *The Supply at Saint Agatha's* (Boston: Houghton Mifflin, 1896); Florence Converse, *The Burden of Christopher* (Boston: Houghton Mifflin, 1900); Cortland Myers, *Would Christ Belong to a Labor Union? or, Henry Fielding's Dream* (New York: Street and Smith, 1900); David N. Beach, *The Annie Laurie Mine* (Boston: Pilgrim Press, 1902); George Van Derveer Morris, *A Man for A' That* (Cincinnati: Jennings and Pye, 1902); and Gamaliel Bradford Jr., *Between Two Masters* (Boston: Houghton Mifflin, 1906).

8. Mary A. Bennett, *Elizabeth Stuart Phelps* (Philadelphia: University of Pennsylvania Press, 1939), 27, 55. See also Grier Nicoll, "The Christian Social Novel in America, 1865–1918," Ph.D. dissertation, University of Minnesota, 1964, 10.

9. Frank Luther Mott, *Golden Multitudes: The Story of Best Sellers in the United States* (New York: Macmillan, 1947), 193–94.

10. Mott lists *In His Steps* as a best seller in 1897, the year it appeared (Motts, *Golden Multitudes*, 312). Though *In His Steps* is still in print today and was unquestionably Charles Sheldon's best-selling book during his lifetime (1857–1946), it seems doubtful that the book has sold as many copies as Dr. Sheldon and its supporters suggest. The dust cover of my working copy (New York: Putnam's, 1982) states that more than "30,000,000 copies have been sold." In 1899, two years after the work first appeared in book form, a perceptive publisher discovered that it had appeared in serial form in the religious periodical *Advance* without copyright protection. At least eighteen American publishers have profited from this error, as well as publishers abroad. Mott researched actual sales figures and, on the basis of his research, estimates that sales by American publishers over the first forty years the book was available amounted to approximately two million copies, and that worldwide sales of the book likely added two or three million more copies. Most of the larger sales figures that are credited to the novel can be traced back to anecdotal evidence (Mott, *Golden Multitudes*, 193–97).

11. In addition to the two Sheldon novels I have already discussed, these works include three other Sheldon novels: *Richard Bruce, or Life That Now Is*, *The Redemption of Freetown*, and *Miracle of Markham*; as well as Elizabeth Stuart Phelps, *The Silent Partner* (1871) (New York: Feminist Press, 1983); Myers, *Would Christ Belong to a Labor Union?*; Beach, *Annie Laurie Mine*; and Morris, *A Man for A' That*.

12. Nicoll also notes this incident in "Christian Social Novel," 149.

13. The Rev. Duncan McLeod in David Beach's *Annie Laurie Mine* does work for two years as a laborer. But his purpose during those years is to gain the respect and confidence of the miners so they will respond to the preaching ministry he ultimately begins. His approach is innovative: he holds Bible classes and discussion groups for the skeptical miners. But after a two- or three-year ministry, most of the miners are converted. In advocating his approach to others, McLeod says that laboring men "are naturally religious; they want God" (191). For a discussion of McLeod's method, see Nicoll, "Christian Social Novel,"115.

14. Obvious examples include Carlsen in *In His Steps* (228–31) and, most notably, Metzerott in *Metzerott, Shoemaker.*

15. These characterizations reflect the official theology of the social gospel movement, as well as a general perception within the church that social gospel ministers should be social evangelicals, not revolutionaries. Washington Gladden is usually viewed as the foremost theologian of the social gospel movement. For an overview of Gladden's social gospel theology, see Washington Gladden, *Applied Christianity: Moral Aspects of Social Questions* (Boston: Houghton Mifflin,1886); Washington Gladden, *The Church and Modern Life* (Boston: Houghton Mifflin, 1908); and Washington Gladden, *Social Salvation* (Boston: Houghton Mifflin, 1902). For a discussion of Gladden's work, see Nicoll, "Christian Social Novel," 15–19; for a discussion of the American perception of revolution as a myth of continuing progress, see Sacvan Bercovitch, *The Rites of Assent: Transformations in the Symbolic Construction of America* (London: Routledge, 1993), esp. chap. 6.

16. The quote appears in an analysis offered by Alfred Kazin, *On Native Grounds: An Interpretation of Modern American Prose Literature* (New York: Harcourt Brace, 1995), 19. For a similar discussion, see Nicoll, "Christian Social Novel," 129.

17. At his first trial when Williams is about to be sentenced, he bursts out, "I've got only this to say, judge. The shooting was accidental. If I'd had a fair trial, I'd be let off. But everything's been against me here" (7).

18. Phelps does cast the church as the villain in *A Singular Life* (chapter 6 in this volume), and she comes close to casting the church as a villain in *The Silent Partner.* But ministers who appear in these novels reflect popular images. They also reflect an anticlericalism that grows out of Phelps's own frustration with the Congregational Church's unwillingness to ordain qualified women to the ministry. Anticlericalism seems to me to be a primary agenda in *The Silent Partner.* Emanuel Bayard is eminently more qualified for ministry (from Phelps's viewpoint) than the members of the ecclesiastical council who deny him ordination. Their legalistic commitment to church doctrine blinds them to Emanuel's human and spiritual qualities. In Phelps's view, that kind of singular vision keeps women from ministry, as well. She gives what she sees as the church's limited vision a humorous treatment in "A Woman's Pulpit" (chapter 5 in this volume).

19. The theological assumptions reflected in Sheldon's books and those of others who share his perspective seem even more simplistic within the sophisticated intellectual culture that emerges in the United States at the end of the nineteenth century. They reflect a Baconian commonsense philosophy and cosmology that is largely discredited among intellectuals by the close of the century. For discussions of this subculture, see chapter 8 in this volume; for discussion of the radical images that emerge between the 1860s and the 1920s, see chapters 8 and 9 in this volume.

20. For discussions of these fictional clergy, see chapter 6 in this volume.

21. I modified "church" with "evangelical" in parentheses because the borders that distinguish church culture from popular culture sometimes became fuzzy during the twentieth century. Especially at midcentury, mainstream culture in the United States was characterized by a "religion in general" that affirmed believing without examining the content of that believing. Will Herberg's *Protestant-Catholic-Jew: An Essay in American Religious Sociology* (Garden City, N.Y.: Doubleday, 1955) is a classic study of this phenomenon. Evangelical Christian believers maintain a clear and specific "Christian" identity.

22. John Hodder appears in Winston Churchill's *The Inside of the Cup* (New York: Macmillan, 1914), which I discuss in chapter 6. Both Beecher and Hodder offer theological as well as ethical challenges in their ministries. For a recent and comprehensive study of Beecher, see Debby Applegate, *The Most Famous Man in America: The Biography of Henry Ward Beecher* (New York: Doubleday, 2006).

23. Henry Maxwell appears in Charles Sheldon's *In His Steps*, which I discuss earlier in this chapter.

24. This documentation appears in standard church histories like Sidney Ahlstrom, *A Religious History of the American People* (New Haven, Conn.: Yale University Press, 1972), as well as in more specialized studies like Hatch, *Democratization of American Christianity*, and George Marsden, *Fundamentalism and American Culture: The Shaping of Twentieth-Century Evangelicalism, 1870–1925* (New York: Oxford University Press, 1980).

25. Historical evidence suggests that the theologically liberal Beecher was a better-known and more-popular minister than any of the other nineteenth-century conservative evangelists (Applegate, *Most Famous Man*, 291, 343, 355). The title of Applegate's book says it all: *The Most Famous Man in America*.

26. In a recent article in the *Wilson Quarterly*, Christopher Clausen writes: "The liberal Protestantism that came to be defined as the American mainstream, with its emphasis on innocuousness and respectability over clarity, has a remarkably long and stable history." Clausen cites Jean-Marie Guyau's 1897 *The Non-Religion of the Future: A Sociological Study* (New York: Schocken, 1962) to support his statement. Guyau writes, "Protestantism is the only religion, in the Occident at least, in which it is possible for one to become an atheist unawares and without having done oneself the shadow of a violence in the process. . . . According to the new Protestants there is no longer any reason for taking anything at its face value. . . . For the most logical of them, the Bible is scarcely more than a book like another; one may find God in it if one seeks Him there, because one may find God anywhere and put Him there. . . . God no longer talks to us by a single voice, but by all the voices of the universe" (Christopher Clausen, "America's Design for Tolerance," *Wilson Quarterly* [Winter 2007], 29–30). A variety of polls during the twentieth century found that for many Americans the doctrinal Christian Divine has been displaced in favor of a generalized God. A vast majority of Americans say they believe in God, but there is little consensus among them about the content of that belief. Classic studies of this generalized American religion include Herberg, *Protestant-Catholic-Jew*, and Robert N. Bellah, Richard Madsen, William M. Sullivan, Ann Swidler, and Steven M. Tipton, *Habits of the Heart: Individualism and Commitment in American Life* (Berkeley: University of California Press, 1985), esp. chap. 9.

27. While doubt and disbelief may have been widespread in American society during the mid- and late-nineteenth century, it was often not socially acceptable. Emily Dickinson and her brother Austin were typical. He struggled covertly with doubt; she was a covert disbeliever (Richard B. Sewell, *The Life of Emily Dickenson* [Cambridge: Harvard University Press, 1994], 103–6, 375, 390, 501–7). The immense popularity of Sinclair Lewis's books when they were published during the 1920s indicates that the subculture of disbelievers was large at that time. (For discussion of the popularity of Lewis's novels, see chapter 9 in this volume, esp. note 20.) In chapter 8, I describe this challenging subculture in more detail. Recent public opinion polls help clarify both the existence and growth of the subculture, identified specifically as those who check "none" when asked to specify their religious affiliation. See the National Survey of Religious Identification (1990); the American Religious Identification Survey (2001); Mark O'Keefe, "Number of 'Nones': Those Who Claim No Religion, Swells in U.S.," 2003, available at http://www.newhouse-news.com/archive/okeefe112603.html; and Patricia O'Connell Killen and Mark Silk, eds., *Religion and Public Life in the Pacific Northwest: The None Zone* (Walnut Creek, Calif.: AltaMira, 2004). A recent survey of thirty-five thousand American adults, "U.S. Religious Landscape Survey," published by the Pew Forum on Religion and Public Life in March 2008 (available at http://religions.pewforum.org/reports) found that 16.1 percent of Americans currently are unaffiliated with any particular religious faith. Among young adults, the figure is even higher: one in four contemporary young adults (aged eighteen to twenty-nine) say they are not affiliated with any particular religious faith. In an article that appeared on the Op-Ed page of the *New York Times*, John Tierney refers to a Cato Institute study of voter surveys that suggests that "libertarians," who represent a subculture to the left of liberals, account for 15 percent of American voters, a bloc about the same size as the blocs of liberals and conservative Christians. If Tierney is correct, libertarians and liberals together account for approximately one-third of American voters (John Tierney, "The Immoral Majority," *New York Times*, October 31, 2006, A27). The *New York Times Book Review* lists of best sellers support the argument. On October 8, 2006, for example, the list of paperback best sellers included Sam Harris's *The End of Faith: Religion, Terror, and the Future of Reason* (New York: Norton, 2004), which explores what Harris sees as the detrimental role of religion historically and in the contemporary world. The list of hardcover best sellers in the same issue included *Letter to a Christian Nation* (New York: Knopf, 2006), Harris's response to readers who objected to his earlier book, and *The God Delusion* (Boston: Houghton Mifflin, 2006) by Richard Dawkins, an Oxford University scientist who argues that "belief in God is irrational and . . . religion has done great harm in the world." The argument continued the following year in Christopher Hitchens's *God Is Not Great: How Religion Poisons Everything* (New York: Twelve, 2007). The ongoing popularity of books like these suggests that large liberal and secular subcultures continue to exist in American society. For a general history of disbelieving in America, see James Turner, *Without God, Without Creed: The Origins of Unbelief in America* (Baltimore: Johns Hopkins University Press, 1985).

Chapter 8. Foundering Divines: Radical Images (1)

1. Lars Ahnrbrink, *The Beginnings of Naturalism in American Fiction: A Study of the Works of Hamlin Garland, Stephen Crane, and Frank Norris with Special Reference to Some European Influences, 1891–1903* (New York: Russell and Russell, 1961), 11.

2. Freud titled his summary essays on religion *The Future of an Illusion* (*Zukunft einer Illusion*, 1927).

3. For a summary of these developments, see Peter Childs, *Modernism* (New York: Routledge, 2000). Childs offers an excellent and succinct study of the effects of modernism in the last half of the nineteenth century.

4. Charles Hodge, *Systematic Theology* (New York: Scribner's, 1871), 1:10; quoted in Eva Marie Garroutte, "The Positivist Attack on Baconian Science and Religious Knowledge in the 1870s," in *The Secular Revolution: Power, Interests, and Conflict in the Secularization of American Public Life*, ed. Christian Smith (Berkeley: University of California Press, 2003), 199. Garroutte's article provides an excellent overview of the displacement of Baconian perspectives in American intellectual life during the closing decades of the nineteenth century.

5. Albert Einstein was one of the primary contributors to this challenging worldview. Articles he published in 1905, including "On the Electrodynamics of Moving Bodies," which introduced the special theory of relativity, also demonstrated the existence of the atom and established the reality of quantum physics. Einstein's theoretical suggestions challenged long-accepted Newtonian cosmology. ("Newton, please forgive me," Einstein pleaded.) Quantum mechanics that developed in the 1920s, most especially the theoretical work of Werner Heisenberg who received a Nobel Prize in 1932, suggests that uncertainty characterizes the natural order. The fallout that came from the new physicists reached far beyond physics; it posits a worldview that leaves little room for a provident, ordering God. Interestingly, for most of his life, Einstein struggled against the belief that there is no inherent order (likely God-driven) to reality such as classical physics envisioned. For more, see Walter Isaacson, *Einstein: His Life and Universe* (New York: Simon and Schuster, 2007), 333–35, 349. For an excellent summary of Einstein's contributions and the revolutionary thinking that stems from his and other modern physicists' work, see "Special Issue: Beyond Einstein," *Scientific American* 291, no. 3 (2004). For a discussion of the epistemology and philosophy of science the new physics displaces, see Christian Smith, ed., *The Secular Revolution: Power, Interests, and Conflict in the Secularization of American Public Life* (Berkeley: University of California Press, 2003), esp. chaps. 1 and 2. For the displacing impact the new scientific view had on American religious culture, see George Marsden, *Fundamentalism and American Culture: The Shaping of Twentieth-Century Evangelicalism, 1870–1925* (New York: Oxford University Press, 1980), and George Marsden, *The Soul of the American University* (New York: Oxford University Press, 1994). Recently a physicist friend described why the new physics shook contemporary commonsense Baconian religious perspectives to the core: "What relativity showed is that what you think you know about your universe is not true. Space and time bend. If the most obvious common sense assumptions about the world can be shaken to the core, then why not ques-

tion the very core of assumption in everything else?" (Craig Lewis, personal correspondence, January 22, 2005).

6. Cultural histories that note the infiltration of European thinking into American life and literature include Malcolm Bradbury, *The Modern American Novel* (New York: Oxford University Press, 1983), esp. chap. 1; Richard Ruland and Malcolm Bradbury, *From Puritanism to Postmodernism: A History of American Literature* (New York: Penguin, 1992), esp. part III; Alfred Kazin, *An American Procession: Major American Writers, 1830–1930* (Cambridge: Harvard University Press, 1996), esp. chap. 13; Bruce Brown, *Marx, Freud and the Critique of Everyday Life: Toward a Permanent Cultural Revolution* (New York: Monthly Review, 1973). The most "recent study" I cite is Smith, *Secular Revolution*. While Smith focuses on Germany, the same secularism pervades Britain. In less than twenty years, for example, between 1886 and 1903, church attendance in London declined by 25 percent! The word "agnostic" was added to the English language and became current in the Britain during 1870s to "express the new-found conviction that to the empirical mind belief and unbelief [are] equally impossible" (Childs, *Modernism*, 46).

7. Between 1815 and 1914, almost ten thousand American graduate students studied in Germany alone (Smith, *Secular Revolution*, 56).

8. Ibid., 57.

9. Michael S. Hamilton in a review of Smith's *Secular Revolution* in *Journal for the Scientific Study of Religion* 43, no. 4 (2004), 564. The declining number of ministers serving as presidents and on boards of trustees in American colleges was one measure of the secularizers' success. In one study of twenty-six schools, 59 percent of the presidents were clergy in 1861; by 1890, the number who were clergy declined to 15 percent; by 1915, the decline reached 0 percent (Clyde W. Barrow, *Universities and the Capitalist State* [Madison: University of Wisconsin Press, 1990]; quoted in Smith, *Secular Revolution*, 101).

10. Ibid., 32–33.

11. The articles by Smith and his colleagues that make up *The Secular Revolution* describe the entire process comprehensively and convincingly. In the introduction, Smith suggests that Protestantism's complacency at the time contributed to its vulnerability: "Protestantism's Christian America in 1870 abounded in optimism, confidence, and apparent strength. The last qualifier is crucial. For although the Protestant establishment's abundant optimism and confidence were real, in retrospect we see that its strength was indeed only apparent. . . . Some of this vulnerability . . . stemmed from inattention to the kind of intellectual work in theology and philosophy that would have been needed to withstand the discursive challenges of secularism. . . . Much of Protestantism had ceased engaging in the kind of rigorous intellectual activity that would have been necessary to respond to the intellectual and cultural challenges advanced by activist secularizers" (61, 71). A kind of sloppy, pietistic, Romantic wishful thinking—most notoriously represented in Henry Ward Beecher—was one common response at the time. Careful theological thinking was rarely apparent in Beecher's wordy pronouncements. The other and probably more common response was to stonewall. At a meeting of the Evangelical Alliance held at Princeton, New Jersey, in 1873, James McCosh, president of the College of New Jersey (Princeton), proposed that Christianity and evolution could be reconciled by using the categories of Baconian Scottish Common Sense

 philosophy that most of those present would probably have affirmed. McCosh's views were clearly not those of the majority. Charles Hodge of Princeton Seminary was the most articulate spokesperson for the majority: there could be no accommodation between the new science and the Bible. Hodge's party carried the day—and forecast the future. Neither the wishful thinking that Beecher represented nor the refusal to accommodate that Hodge represented would provide a base for serious dialogue between Christian believers and those who accept the new science. For a discussion of both Beecher's and Hodge's perspectives and the widening gap between Evangelical Christians and American intellectuals, see Marsden, *Fundamentalism and American Culture*, 11–39.

12. G. Stanley Hall, *Jesus, the Christ, in the Light of Psychology* (Garden City, N.Y.: Doubleday, 1917), xv; quoted in Keith G. Meader, "'My Own Salvation': The *Christian Century* and Psychology's Secularizing of American Protestantism," in *The Secular Revolution: Power, Interests, and Conflict in the Secularization of American Public Life*, ed. Christian Smith (Berkeley: University of California Press, 2003), 288.

13. For an excellent overview of Hall's influence, see Meader, "My Own Salvation," 286–89. I am indebted to Meader for my summary of Hall's work. Hall's work reflects the influence of his Harvard mentor, William James. His *Jesus, the Christ, in the Light of Psychology*, for example, embodies some perspectives similar to those James argues in his *Varieties of Religious Experience*.

14. As noted in chapter 4, in 1836 Calvin Stowe visited Professor Creutzer in Heidelberg. In a letter to Harriet Beecher, whom he was courting at the time, he cited *The Mythology of the Ancients*, in which Creutzer describes "the formation of the various mythological ideas of the ancients to the religious element essential to man every where." Calvin could barely contain his excitement: "When I get home," he told Harriet, "we must read the whole work together." The letter is collected in the Stowe-Day Library in Hartford, Connecticut, and is referred to in Joan Hedrick, *Harriet Beecher Stowe: A Life* (New York: Oxford University Press, 1994), 101.

15. James Wood, *The Broken Estate: Essays on Literature and Belief* (New York: Random House, 1999), xiv. I am indebted to Wood for some of the insights I offer in the preceding paragraph.

16. Ibid.

17. Alfred Kazin, *Alfred Kazin's America: Critical and Personal Writings*, ed. Ted Solataroff (New York: HarperCollins, 2003), 450.

18. The suffering and crude morality that the overly sensitive Howells saw turned out to be more than he could handle; after only a few weeks, he fled from the reporter's life. For more, see Kenneth S. Lynn, *William Dean Howells: An American Life* (New York: Harcourt Brace Jovanovich, 1971), 78.

19. For examples, see Theodore Dreiser's *Sister Carrie: A Novel* (1900) (New York: Oxford University Press, 1998) and Robert Herrick's *The Memoirs of an American Citizen* (1905) (New York: Grosset and Dunlap, 1908). Herrick offers an especially disparaging portrait of a social gospel minister. Alfred Kazin discusses Herrick's perceptiveness in *On Native Grounds: An Interpretation of Modern American Prose Literature* (New York: Harcourt Brace, 1995): "Read together, Herrick's books seem to form a canon of startling unity, for they are virtually a single chronicle of the emergence of the commercial spirit from the eighteen-nineties on

to the First World War. He had a single theme, the corruption of the middle-class soul by commercialism. . . . For a novelist like David Graham Phillips the oppression of commercial civilization had been a romantic problem: for Herrick it could be understood only in terms of slavery or freedom. Slavery to business signified 'the curse of egotism,' the drive toward success as the sole end in life, the pestilential growth of fashion and greed that had poisoned the spirit. It is precisely in his comprehension of all the spiritual implications of commercialism that one marks Herrick's superiority over the muckraking novelists" (123).

20. Kazin, *Kazin's America*, 409.

21. Michael Davitt Bell, *The Problem of American Realism: Studies in the Cultural History of a Literary Idea* (Chicago: University of Chicago Press, 1993), 22.

22. There is a similar pairing of strong women with weaker ministers in many popular novels. Examples include Helen Ward and John Ward in Margaret Deland's *John Ward, Preacher* (Boston: Houghton Mifflin, 1888) and Alison Parr and John Hodder in Winston Churchill's *The Inside of the Cup* (New York: Macmillan, 1914) (though Hodder is a considerably stronger character than Ward). For my discussion of Deland's novel, see chapter 4 in this volume; for my discussion of Churchill's novel, see chapter 6.

23. I note the evidence for this declining quality in chapter 4 in this volume.

24. Ruland and Bradbury, *Puritanism to Postmodernism*, 204–5.

25. For a complete discussion of Howells's fictional clergy, see David Luisi, "The Religious Environment and the Role of the Minister in the Novels of William Dean Howells," Ph. D dissertation, University of Notre Dame, 1974. In addition to the novels I discuss in this volume, the following Howells novels include Protestant clergy as significant characters: *An Imperative Duty* (New York: Harper and Bros., 1892); *The Kentons* (New York: Harper and Bros., 1902); *Mrs. Farrell* (New York: Harper and Bros., 1921); *Dr. Breen's Practice* (Boston: James R. Osgood, 1881); and *The Day of Their Wedding* (New York: Harper and Bros., 1896).

26. William Dean Howells, "Eighty Years and After," *Harper's Monthly* 150 (December 1919), 21; quoted in Luisi, "Religious Environment," 3.

27. For a summary discussion of Howells's perceptions of clergy, see Luisi, "Religious Environment," chaps. 1 and 2.

28. Obviously Howells views Aroostook County, which is the largest and northernmost county in Maine, as the remote "backwoods."

29. When the Rev. Mr. Sewell reappears in *The Minister's Charge* (Boston: Ticknor, 1887), published two years after *The Rise of Silas Lapham* (1885) (New York: New American Library, 1963), Howell's links his weak performance directly to the lost authority of ministers in general: "He [Sewell] declared that he envied the ministers of the good old times who had only to teach their people that they would be lost if they did not do right; it was much simpler than to make them understand that they were often to be good for reasons not immediately connected with their present or future comfort, and that they could not confidently expect to be lost for any given transgression, or even to be lost at all" (5). Dr. Boynton, who appears in an earlier Howells novel, *The Undiscovered Country* (Boston: Houghton Mifflin, 1880), offers a similarly pessimistic analysis of the contemporary religious climate: "Priests in the pulpit and before the altar proclaim a creed which they hope it will be good for their listeners to believe, and the

people envy the faith that can so confidently preach that creed; but neither priests nor people believe" (235).

30. In *The Social Construction of American Realism* (Chicago: University of Chicago Press, 1988), Amy Kaplan writes, "Realistic novels have trouble ending because they pose problems they cannot solve, problems that stem from their attempt to imagine and contain social change" (160).

31. For example, the Revs. Wade and Enderby, who appear, respectively, in *The Quality of Mercy* (1891) (New York: Harper and Bros., 1900) and *The Son of Royal Langbrith* (New York: Harper and Bros., 1905) "serve mainly to advise and console the other characters involved in the wake of the evil and sometimes to comment upon the morality of the situation" (Luisi, "Religious Environment," 124). In Howells's *Ragged Lady* (New York: Harper and Bros., 1899), the other characters write off the Puritanical Frank Gregory as a leftover from a former time. Mr. March and Mrs. Faulkner, who play significant roles in Howells's *The Shadow of a Dream* (New York: Harper and Bros, 1901), find clergy in general to be disappointing humans.

32. Luisi believes that "Ewbert's well-intentioned but fraudulent manner of proselytizing . . . exposes the theological dead-end in which the [nineteenth] century had ended; and insofar as Hilbrook's—and, for that matter, Ewbert's—faith was permeated with equivocation, the narrator/Howells implies that those who do profess belief have a faith which rests on a fictional foundation" (Luisi, "Religious Environment," 145–46). The implications of this loss, which are reflected in Howells's fiction, were deeply troubling to Howells. For more, see Lynn, *Howells*, 292–96.

33. For a discussion of ways that Freeman's early personal experience shaped her fiction, see Mary R. Reichardt, *Mary Wilkins Freeman: A Study of the Short Fiction* (New York: Twayne, 1997), 3–57.

34. Fred Lewis Pattee, introduction to Mary Wilkins Freeman, *A New England Nun and Other Stories* (New York: Harper and Bros., 1919), xxi.

35. For brief biographies of Rolvaag, see both Vernon Louis Parrington, editor's introduction, and Lincoln Colcord, introduction to O.E. Rolvaag, *Giants in the Earth* (New York: Harper and Brothers, 1929), ix–xxxiv.

36. Parrington, editor's introduction to Rolvaag, *Giants in the Earth*, ix.

37. The fact that Rolvaag does not give the pastor a name may suggest that the struggles he experiences are characteristic of all clergy in a similar situation.

38. Only 514 of 1,000 copies in the initial printing were sold during the first year. Adams aborted the experiment after his wife's suicide in December 1885. At least some aspects of Esther's personality reflect Adams's perception of Marian Adams. After Marian's death, Adams wrote to Holt that he had little concern "now for anything that so-called critics could say." The Adams quote appears in William Merrill Decker, *The Literary Vocation of Henry Adams* (Chapel Hill: University of North Carolina Press, 1990), 205. The original appears in Henry Adams, *The Letters of Henry Adams*, 6 vols., ed. J.C. Levenson, Ernest Samuels, Charles Vandersee, and Viola Hopkins Winner (Cambridge: Harvard University Press, 1982–88), 3:5. For a discussion of the parallels between Esther Dudley and Marian Adams, see Decker *Literary Vocation*, 206–7.

39. The reference is probably to the young Stephen in the Bible (Acts 7), who became a willing martyr.

40. With what is obviously a bit of jealousy, George Strong describes Stephen Hazard's ulterior motives: "He sees nothing good in the world that he does not instantly covet for the glory of God and the church, and just a bit for his own pleasure. He saw Esther; she struck him as something out of his line, for he is used to young women who work altar-cloths; he found that Wharton and I like her; he thought that such material was too good for heathen like us; so he fell in love with her himself and means to turn her into a candlestick of the church" (277).

41. Decker, *Literary Vocation*, 229.

42. The juxtaposing of the thinking of one time within another time is fascinating to Adams. He develops the theme extensively in *Mont Saint Michel and Chartres* (New York: Viking Penguin, 1986) and *The Education of Henry Adams* (New York: Library of America, 1983).

43. Hazard's position recalls my previous discussion of the church's tendency to "stonewall" in the face of modernism. This tendency is especially common among Edwardsian Calvinists. See the discussion in chapter 4.

44. Though there are some similarities between Stephen Hazard and his fictional colleagues Arthur Dimmesdale and John Ward, the fact that Hazard is neither obsessed (like Ward) nor disturbed (like Dimmesdale) makes him an even more powerful and significant character. Hazard is theologically and organizationally committed, but he is not driven like Dimmesdale and Ward are. He is widely read and cultured like Dimmesdale, but he is clearly in charge of himself. Hazard is subordinate to his theology, but he is not a weak man dominated by his elders like Ward is.

45. Not everyone would agree with this assessment. No less a critic than Alfred Kazin wrote that Frederic's "most famous novel, *The Damnation of Theron Ware*, is a mischievously written museum piece, persistently overrated because it was among the first American novels to portray an unfrocked clergyman and to suggest the disintegration of religious orthodoxy" (Kazin, *On Native Grounds*, 35). To be fair to Kazin, it is important to note that he offered this opinion in 1940, which was early in his career as a critic.

46. "I am writing a novel . . . the people of which I have been carrying about with me, night and day, for fully five years. After I got them grouped together in my mind, I set myself the task of knowing everything they knew. . . . I have had to teach myself all the details of a Methodist minister's work, obligations and daily routine, and all the machinery of his church. Another character is a priest, who is a good deal more of a pagan than a simple-minded Christian. . . . I have studied the arts he loves as well as his theology. . . . I don't say this is the right way to build novels; only that it is my way" (Harold Frederic, "How the Popular Harold Frederic Works," *Literary Digest* 13 [July 25, 1896], 397; quoted in Bridget Bennett, *The Damnation of Harold Frederic: His Lives and Works* [Syracuse, N.Y.: Syracuse University Press, 1997], 89).

47. Quoted in Ahnrbrink, *Beginnings of Naturalism*, 169 n. 1.

48. These are *not* fictitious names; all the German scholars Ledsmar mentions are authentic. They are most likely Franz Delitzsch (1813–90), Wolf Wilhelm Baudissen (1847–1926), Eberhard Schrader (1836–1908), Christian Karl Josias Freiherr von Bunsen (1791–1860), Max Duncker (1811–86), Fritz Hommel (1854–1936), and Archibald Henry Sayce (1845–1933). Until recently, works by all of them that

 would have been pertinent to Theron's book were still available in the Bangor Theological Seminary Libraries in Bangor and Portland, Maine. The "best work" available in English by Sayce that Ledsmar suggests Theron consult is probably his *The Chaldean Account of Genesis* (Scribner's, 1880?), coauthored with George Smith. Informed contemporary readers at the time *Theron Ware* was published (1896) would have recognized the authorities that Ledsmar mentions as scholars associated with German higher criticism and comparative religious studies. Harold Frederic definitely did his homework.

49. Perhaps the most cynical comments in the novel appear in the closing paragraphs. "Who knows?" Theron tells Candace Soulsby: "I may turn up in Washington a full-blown Senator before I'm forty. Stranger things have happened than that."

50. Even as astute a historian as Henry Adams marvels at the extent of the displacement: "Of all the conditions of his youth which afterwards puzzled the grown-up man, this disappearance of religion puzzled him most. . . . That the most powerful emotion of man, next to the sexual, should disappear . . . seemed to him the most curious social phenomenon he had to account for in a long life" (Adams, *Education*, 751).

Chapter 9. Flawed Divines: Radical Images (2)

1. In addition to the unable ministers already discussed in chapter 8, I am aware of thirteen other fictional clergy who reflect the image of ministers as weak men. Listed in chronological order, they appear in James K. Hosmer, *The Thinking Bayonet* (Boston: Walker, Fuller, 1865); Josiah G. Holland, *Sevenoaks* (New York: Scribner's, Armstrong, 1875); Edward R. Eggleston, *Roxy* (New York: Scribner's, 1878); Henry James, *Watch and Ward* (Boston: Houghton Osgood, 1878); E.W. Howe, *The Story of a Country Town* (Boston: James R. Osgood, 1884); Mary E. Wilkins Freeman, "A Village Singer," in *A New England Nun and Other Stories*, 18–36 (New York: Harper and Bros., 1891); Mary E. Wilkins Freeman, *Pembroke: A Novel* (1894) (Chicago: Academy Press, 1978); Sarah Orne Jewett, *The Country of the Pointed Firs and Other Stories* (1896) (Garden City, N.Y.: Doubleday, 1956); Corra Harris, *A Circuit Rider's Wife* (Philadelphia: Henry Altemus, 1910); Willa Cather, *The Song of the Lark* (1915) (Boston: Houghton Mifflin, 1943); Basil King, *The Lifted Veil* (New York: A.L. Burt, 1917); Sherwood Anderson, *Winesburg, Ohio* (1919) (New York: Modern Library, 1999); and Basil King, *Pluck* (New York: Harper and Bros., 1928).

2. Ann Douglas, *The Feminization of American Culture* (New York: Knopf, 1979), 144. Douglas's well-documented study offers ample evidence of the minister's shrinking role and declining status during the nineteenth century. Eliot is quoted in Sidney H. Mead, "The Rise of the Evangelical Conception of the Ministry in America (1607–1850)," in *The Ministry in Historical Perspectives*, ed. Richard H. Niebuhr and Daniel D. Williams (New York: Harper and Bros., 1956), 244. See also Robert S. Michaelsen, "The Protestant Ministry in America: 1850 to the Present," in *The Ministry in Historical Perspectives*, ed. Richard H. Niebuhr and Daniel D. Williams (New York: Harper and Bros., 1956), 279.

3. Everett T. Tomlinson, "The Decline of the Ministry," *World's Work* 9 (December 1904), 5635; quoted in Michaelsen, "Protestant Ministry," 279.

4. *National Preacher*, new series, 2 (1859), 186; quoted in Douglas, *Feminization of American Culture*, 144.

5. As I note earlier, Wright himself offers an even more dismal assessment of roles to which clergy have been relegated through the mouth of Dan Matthews in *God and the Groceryman* (1927) (New York: Triangle, 1942). Many of the social ministers and social activists I discuss in chapter 6 complain that ministry is a limiting vocation.

6. For a discussion of Lee's and May's contrasting characters, see Douglas, *Feminization of American Culture*, 20.

7. Clorinda likely refers to the woman caught in the act of adultery who is brought to Jesus for judgment. Jesus refuses to condemn her. The incident is described in the Gospel of John, 8:2–11.

8. This need to maintain an image of clergy as sexless likely stems from the popular perception of Jesus as sexless. Clergy are supposed to reflect Christlikeness. Many Christian believers find the notion that Jesus was sexual scandalous. In teaching or public lectures whenever I suggest that Jesus was sexual (let alone sexually active), the room becomes very quiet, and many of those present are obviously uncomfortable.

9. The possible symbolism is intriguing. Is a minister's sexuality his Achilles heel?

10. In *Fundamentalism and American Culture: The Shaping of Twentieth-Century Evangelicalism, 1870–1925* (New York: Oxford University Press, 1980), George Marsden describes the specifics of this process at the end of the nineteenth and beginning of the twentieth century; see esp. chaps. 12–14.

11. I describe Lewis's views of ministers and the church more fully in the final section of this chapter.

12. In her autobiography, *Golden Yesterdays* (New York: Harper and Bros., 1941), Margaret Deland describes the wide interest in "spiritism" within the Boston intellectual community of the 1880s. Though many were skeptical of the claims of spiritualists, some of the most notable members were open to the possibility that at least a few of the many active mediums were authentic. Deland recalls a comment that William James made during one of his lectures: "To upset the conclusion that all crows are black, there is no need to seek demonstration that no crow is black—it is sufficient to produce one white crow." James then proclaimed a local medium to be his "white crow" (259–60).

13. Kenneth S. Lynn, *William Dean Howells: An American Life* (New York: Harcourt Brace Jovanovich, 1971), 319. The minister at the center of *The Leatherwood God* (New York: Century, 1916) is based on an actual evangelist, fictionalized by Howells as Joseph Dylks. Howells admits he used his imagination to enlarge upon the facts of Dylks's life as recorded by Judge Taneyhill in the Ohio Valley series: Richard Henry Taneyhill, *The Leatherwood God: An Account of the Appearance and Pretensions of Joseph C. Dylks in Eastern Ohio in 1828*, Ohio Valley Historical Series, vol. 7 (Cincinnati: Robert Clarke, 1870). However, the "drama is that of actual events in its main development." Referring to himself in the role of the author, Howells says in a publisher's note at the beginning of *Leatherwood* that "in one instance he . . . frankly reproduced the words of the imposter as reported by one who heard Dylks's last address in the Temple at Leatherwood" (iii).

14. For an explication of Howells's religious views that supports this observation, see William Dean Howells, "Eighty Years and After," *Harper's Monthly* 150 (December 1919), 21.

15. For discussion of *Ronald Carnaquay*, see chapter 6 in this volume.

16. Fred B. Fisher, review of "Shoddy," *Christian Century* 45 (April 19, 1928), 509.

17. Ibid. In 1920, an Episcopal bishop, the Right Rev. Charles H. Brent, made similar comments about *Main Street* (Richard Lingeman, *Sinclair Lewis: Rebel from Main Street* [New York: Random House, 2002], 160).

18. The detailed pictures of American life in Lewis's novels testify to his astounding powers of observation and near-flawless memory. Dr. Julian DuBois, an early mentor from Sauk Centre days, recalled that young Harry Lewis could walk through a room and later provide "a more complete enumeration of its furnishings, down to the most trivial detail, than a visitor for the weekend could put forth" (Lingeman, *Sinclair Lewis*, 12). Contemporary readers of Lewis's novels heard themselves and their neighbors in the familiar and authentic words that Lewis's characters speak and the experiences they have.

19. The popular response to *Main Street* (New York: Harcourt, Brace and Howe, 1920), for example, was astonishing for a book intended to be a serious work of fiction. The novel was published on October 23, 1920; by Christmas, just two months later, forty-seven thousand copies had been sold. Within a year, the novel sold nearly two hundred thousand copies. *Main Street* became the best-selling novel not only of 1921 but of any year from 1900 to 1925. These figures are reported in "Best Sellers in Fiction During the First Quarter of the Twentieth Century," *Publishers' Weekly* 107 (February 14, 1925), 525–27; and "The Most Popular Authors of Fiction Between 1900 and 1925," *Publishers' Weekly* 107 (February 21, 1925), 619–22; quoted in James M. Hutchisson, *The Rise of Sinclair Lewis, 1920–1930* (University Park: Pennsylvania State University Press, 1996), 42. The sales of *Main Street* (and Lewis's subsequent novels from the 1920s) in areas *away* from large urban centers like New York suggest that even many of those living in the American heartland were ready to see their Main Street in a different way (Hutchisson, *Rise of Sinclair Lewis*, 43).

20. The novelist John Hersey, who was Lewis's secretary during the summer of 1937, recalled that when Lewis launched into one of the impromptu satiric monologues that he was famous for at social gatherings, "one forgot his cadaverous face and *saw* John L. Lewis, F. D. R., Huey Long, Father Coughlin" (John Hersey, *Life Sketches* [New York: Knopf, 1989], 17; quoted in Hutchisson, *Rise of Sinclair Lewis*, 62).

21. Richard Ruland and Michael Bradbury, *From Puritanism to Postmodernism: A History of American Literature* (New York: Penguin, 1992), 67–68. "The village virus" that deadens intellectual interest like a contagious disease is a popular theme in nearly all of Lewis's 1920s novels.

22. During his trip, Lewis tried to experience firsthand every aspect of life that the characters in his novel would reflect. He visited cities in Ohio, Illinois, Wisconsin, and Michigan. He talked with people on trains, in men's clubs, at chambers of commerce. He noted their moods, their looks, and their speech and mannerisms. No detail escaped him. As Alfred Kazin observes, "Did anyone before him ever catch the American 'uh?" (Kazin, *On Native Grounds: An Interpretation of Modern*

American Prose Literature [New York: Harcourt Brace, 1995], 208). Lewis took copious notes as he traveled. Later he drew on these notes to create an entire fictional small city, Zenith. He mapped the streets of Zenith; he wrote its history; he located his characters' houses and business; he spelled out their genealogies, their social relationships—every aspect of their lives. Lewis functioned like an anthropologist intent on internalizing the characteristics of a primitive culture (Hutchisson, *Rise of Sinclair Lewis*, 62). For example, Lewis jotted down the phrase "mountains of melody" on the bulletin when he attended services at the First Congregational Church of Oak Park, Illinois. He later had the fictional Rev. Dr. Drew (who serves the Presbyterian church that the fictional Babbitt attends) use this phrase to describe the choir's singing (183). For a complete description of Lewis's research for *Babbitt*, see Hutchisson, *Rise of Sinclair Lewis*, 61–74, as well as Hutchisson's introduction to Sinclair Lewis, *Babbitt* (New York: Penguin, 1996), vii–xxviii.

23. Hutchisson, introduction to Lewis, *Babbitt*, xxiii.

24. Lewis refers to his upcoming work at least five times as either his "preacher novel" or his "preacher book" (Sinclair Lewis, *From Main Street to Stockholm: Letters of Sinclair Lewis, 1919–1930*, ed. Harrison Smith [New York: Harcourt Brace, 1952]). In a January 23, 1926, letter to Donald Brace, Lewis refers to his untitled work in progress as his "preacher novel" (193). In a letter to Alfred Harcourt dated February 3, 1926, he calls it "the preacher book" (193). In a letter to Lewis dated April 5, 1926, Harcourt seems to indicate that Lewis is thinking of ministers generically when he suggests that Lewis may want to consider "*The Reverend*" as a title for the upcoming book: "Throughout small-town America, that is the general term used in referring to the local minister and stands for ministers in the same way that *Main Street* stands for the small town" (204–5). On April 8, Lewis refers again to the "preacher book" (205), and on May 7, 1926, Lewis calls the book "my loving little volume about the preachers" (215). On August 1, 1926, after he has left Kansas City for Pequot, Minnesota, and is writing the book, he again calls it "the preacher book" (221).

25. James Hutchisson subscribes to the view that commercial preachers who dominate the novel reflect Lewis's bias and are not representative of contemporary ministers in general. For his discussion of Lewis's religious biases and how these shape *Elmer Gantry*, see Hutchisson, *Rise of Sinclair Lewis*, 127–29. Lewis's letters to his publisher during the spring of 1926 are full of sarcastic and pejorative comments about ministers in general (e.g., see the letters to Alfred Harcourt dated April 21 and April 26, in Lewis, *From Main Street to Stockholm*, 208–10). Evidence from his own writing and his biographers indicates that Lewis held disparaging views of ministers and American Protestant religion long before he began his research for *Elmer Gantry* (New York: Harcourt, Brace, 1927). The associates he chose when he prepared to write *Elmer Gantry* most likely reflected and certainly reinforced an existing bias. The group of ministers who became Lewis's "Sunday School class" in Kansas City were actually an existing group of liberal ministers in the city who had been meeting for several years before Lewis's arrival. The liberal minister Leon Birkhead, who became a Unitarian after ten years as a Methodist minister, was the "nominal president"; he introduced Lewis to the group in January. At this first meeting, Lewis proposed that the group help him gather data for his novel when he returned in March, and they agreed (Leon M. Birkhead, *Is "Elmer Gantry"*

True? [Girard, Kans.: Haldeman-Julius, 1928], 7–8). One Sunday evening during his January visit to Kansas City, Lewis held a small dinner party. The guests included Mr. and Mrs. Clarence Darrow, Gilbert Frankau, English novelist E. Haldeman-Julius, and Leon Birkhead and his wife. One could hardly imagine a more liberal group. The liberal tenor of the group is very clear: it includes not only Lewis and the Unitarian Birkhead but also the openly agnostic Clarence Darrow. Only a year before, Darrow had faced off with William Jennings Bryan at the famous Scopes or "Monkey Trial" in Dayton, Tennessee. In *Elmer Gantry*, Lewis mentions the fallout from the "Dayton evolution trial" as one of the sources of the horror that befalls Frank Shallard (389).

26. After he and Dr. Stidger visited the campus of Emporia College during January, for example, Lewis wrote a letter to Grace in which he described the college disparagingly as "a Presbyterian school with an elegant scientific library of 72 books mostly dating from 1890" (Letter from Sinclair Lewis to Grace Lewis, January 27, 1926, in Speer Morgan and William Holtz, "Fragments from a Marriage: Letters of Sinclair Lewis to Grace Hegger Lewis," *Missouri Review* 11 [1988]: 71–98; quoted in Hutchisson, *Rise of Sinclair Lewis*, 130). Lewis's decision to visit a Presbyterian school shows how well informed he was about Fundamentalism; he could expect to find usable evidence there. Early-twentieth-century Presbyterians were deeply engaged by Fundamentalism. For a description of the inroads Fundamentalism made in the Presbyterian Church during the first decades of the twentieth century, see Marsden, *Fundamentalism and American Culture*, 153–95.

27. In a small book issued soon after *Elmer Gantry* appeared, Leon Birkhead lists a large sample of the books in Lewis's ministerial library, including *One Volume Dictionary of the Bible, Bible Handbook, The Origin and Character of the Bible, Representative Modern Preachers, The American Pulpit, The History of Preaching, Yale Lectures on Preaching, The Pastoral Office, The Art of Preaching, The Preacher: His Life and Work, The Christian Ministry, The Work of the Preacher, The Work of the Minister, Preaching as a Fine Art, The Minister in the Modern World, The Cure of Souls, The Christian Ministry and the Social Order, Cyclopedia of Pastoral Methods, History of Religion in the United States, Progressive Religious Thought in America, The Circuit Rider, An Outline of Christian Dogma, Best Sermons of 1924, Best Sermons of 1925, A History of the Warfare of Science and Theology, Fundamentalism Versus Modernism, What Is Faith, Primitive Traits in Religious Revivals, The Psychology of Religion, The Varieties of Religious Experience*, and *An Introduction to the Psychology of Religion*. Lewis also read a variety of religious journals while he prepared and wrote *Elmer Gantry*, including *Word and the Way, Central Christian Advocate, Christian Century, Truth Seeker*, and *Commonweal*. These books and journals are included in a larger list that appears in Birkhead, *Is "Elmer Gantry" True?*, 14–16.

28. Ibid., 8. In a May 1926 letter to Alfred Harcourt, Sinclair Lewis named some of those who attended his Sunday school class: the Revs. Hanson and Stidger, who were Methodists; Shively and Rutherford, who were Christian (Campbellite) preachers; Birkhead, who was a Unitarian; Roberts, described as "a completely modernist preacher of the John Haynes Holmes type"; J. C. Maupin, another modernist; two lay people of unspecified denominations; Mayer, a local rabbi; Jenkins, another Campbellite; Reidenbach, a Congregationalist; Blackman, another Campbellite

and former national chaplain of the American Legion; and Samuel Harkness, a Presbyterian (Lewis, *From Main Street to Stockholm*, 216–17).

29. Samuel Harkness, "Sinclair Lewis's Sunday School Class," *Christian Century* 43 (July 29, 1926), 938–39; quoted in Hutchisson, *Rise of Sinclair Lewis*, 136.

30. Birkhead, *Is "Elmer Gantry" True?*, 9–10.

31. Letter of Sinclair Lewis to Grace Lewis, January 27, 1926, in Morgan and Holtz, "Fragments from a Marriage," 80. On Friday, June 28, 1926, Lewis and the Rev. Earl Blackman were traveling in Minnesota looking for a spot for Lewis to begin the actual writing of *Elmer Gantry*. Lewis invited Blackman to stay the night in Sauk Centre, but Blackman said he couldn't; he had to return by the night train from Minneapolis in order to arrive in Kansas City early Saturday so he could prepare for his Sunday services. Lewis pressed Blackman to stay over, but the minister explained that he had to write a prayer for Sunday morning, and that was not easy for him to do. "Hell, I'll write your prayer," Lewis responded. Between their arrival in Sauk Centre and the evening meal, a space of thirty or forty minutes, Lewis took a pad and wrote a three-page prayer. It reads, in part, "Deliver us—let us deliver ourselves—from worn-out babbling and from all wordiness—from all phrases that do not intensely bear a burden of passion for righteousness, a passion for the well-being of every living thing. Teach us simplicity in prayer. . . . Let us have so high a vision of thee that we will comprehend we are but tiny and graceless in thy vast plan. Smite our egotism and quicken our imagination until we perceive that we are but a few out of the numberless multitudes who at this moment seek to lift their spirits by this effort toward communion with thee" (quoted in Mark Schorer, *Sinclair Lewis: An American Life* [New York: McGraw-Hill, 1961], 458–59). Blackman was impressed and grateful.

32. Letters to Alfred Harcourt, April 21 and April 26, 1926, in Lewis, *From Main Street to Stockholm*, 207 and 210. Harrison Smith, who edited Lewis's letters, notes that during one of his more irreverent sermons Lewis "defied God to strike him dead." He actually held his watch in his hand for ten minutes (!) waiting for the strike to occur (Lewis, *From Main Street to Stockholm*, 207 n.1).

33. For examples, see Hutchisson, *Rise of Sinclair Lewis*, 136.

34. For a discussion of Lewis's use of factual sources in *Elmer Gantry*, see ibid., 140–46. A recent biography reveals that McPherson was nearly as colorful a character as her fictional counterpart (Matthew Avery Sutton, *Aimee Semple McPherson and the Resurrection of Christian America* [Cambridge: Harvard University Press, 2007]).

35. From a dramatic perspective, Sharon is such a strong character that Lewis has to find some way to dispose of her in order to give Elmer Gantry space to blossom. There seems little doubt that Sharon is patterned on the real-life evangelist, Aimee Semple McPherson. Lewis first intended to have Sharon drown. But McPherson's brief disappearance (perhaps to go off with a lover) and rumored drowning while he was still writing the novel forced him to change the plot and have Sharon perish in a fire (Schorer, *Sinclair Lewis*, 460–61).

36. Those who whip and maim Frank Shallard justify their actions with an appeal to religion: "Just hurt him enough so he'll remember, and then he can go back and tell his atheist friends it ain't healthy for 'em in real Christian parts" (393).

37. Frank Shallard's fate is similar to Emerson Courtright's fate in *The Broken Lance* (discussed in chapter 6 in this volume). Many of those who act according

to the social gospel meet violent ends. Those who oppose them often use theological difference to cover their real agenda, which is economic and social, not theological.

38. As stated in his letters to Alfred Harcourt, April 21 and April 26, 1926, in Lewis, *From Main Street to Stockholm*, 207 and 210.

39. Lewis's irreverence is rampant in his letters to Alfred Harcourt in 1926 when he was preparing to write *Elmer Gantry* (e.g., the letter dated April 8, in Lewis, *From Main Street to Stockholm*, 205). See also the detailed description of Lewis's irreverence in Hutchisson, *Rise of Sinclair Lewis*, 125–63. In *On Native Grounds*, Alfred Kazin describes Lewis's desire "to make Elmer Gantry an accumulative symbol of all the phoniness he hated in American life" (223; quoted in Hutchisson, *Rise of Sinclair Lewis*, 147). Presumably, the Fundamentalist religion that his novel parodies is one source of that phoniness.

Chapter 10. Fallen Divines: Some Contemporary Images

1. For a helpful discussion of modernism and postmodernism, especially as they relate to William Faulkner's fiction, see Richard C. Moreland, "Faulkner and Modernism," and Patrick O'Donnell, "Faulkner and Postmodernism," essays that appear in *The Cambridge Companion to William Faulkner*, ed. Philip M. Weinstein (New York: Cambridge University Press, 1995), 17–30 and 31–50.

2. Moreland, "Faulkner and Modernism," 32.

3. Could it be that the segregation forced on Dilsey and other African Americans protects them from the traumatic displacements associated with modernism?

4. One wonders whether Faulkner's choice of words is meant to recall the "monkey trial" held in Dayton, Tennessee, in 1925, just four years before *The Sound and Fury* appeared. That a black preacher who looks somewhat like a monkey speaks the only authentic word of God in the novel seems like ultimate irony.

5. Updike's well-known Barthian sympathies may influence his portrayal of Dale Kohler. There is no dependable general revelation to be found in the universe according to the theology of Karl Barth, only special revelation that comes from scripture. The title of his massive theology says it all: *The Theology of the Word of God*. For a discussion of religious perspectives in Updike's fiction, see James Yerkes, ed., *John Updike and Religion: The Sense of the Sacred and the Motions of Grace* (Grand Rapids, Mich.: Eerdmans, 1999).

6. Moreland, "Faulkner and Modernism," 22. For a helpful discussion of haunting divinity in Southern culture and fiction, see Susan Ketchin, *The Christ-Haunted Landscape: Faith and Doubt in Southern Fiction* (Jackson: University of Mississippi Press, 1994).

7. It seems significant to me that Faulkner casts Hightower as a Presbyterian. This association would enhance his symbolic value in the novel. The providence of God is central to Calvinist theology. The providence that appears to Hightower is particular and confused—a distorted figment. There may still be some overall providence in the world around Hightower, but the only providence Hightower knows is all tangled up with the haunting and confused images of his hero grandfather.

8. Disturbed divines also appear in George Garrett's *Do, Lord, Remember Me* (1965) (Baton Rouge: Louisiana State University Press, 1994) and *The King of Babylon Shall Not Come Against You* (New York: Harcourt, Brace, 1996); Lee Smith's *The Devil's Dream* (New York: Ballentine, 1992) and *Saving Grace* (New York: Ballentine, 1995); and Barbara Kingsolver's *The Poisonwood Bible* (New York: HarperCollins, 1998).

9. It is sometimes difficult to draw the line between church images and popular images during this period, especially as believing became fashionable in popular culture during the 1940s and 1950s. The phenomenon of fuzzy faith is well documented; Will Herberg, *Protestant-Catholic-Jew: An Essay in American Religious Sociology* (Garden City, N.Y.: Doubleday, 1955), is the best contemporary source. Within the dominant culture of the time believing per se was generally perceived as good. President Dwight D. Eisenhower's faith in faith reflects this assumption: "Every man ought to have a religion, and I don't care what kind it is." For an interesting discussion of how this original perspective changed over thirty years, see J. Edward Barrett, "Things Change in Thirty Years," *Theology Today* 43, no. 4 (1984), 183–87.

10. A late-twentieth-century source that details this transformation is Daniel Yankelovich, *New Rules: Searching for Fulfillment in a World Turned Upside Down* (New York: Random House, 1981). The early and innocent version of the comic Calvinist cultural image was the one most of my friends applied to me when I let them know in the 1950s that I planned to become a minister. Once they typecast me, they decided that as a minister I couldn't or shouldn't tolerate the real (rough) world where people swear—much less swear (openly) myself. They insisted on minister behavior for me and restrained themselves around me.

11. Hartzell Spence published his last novel during the 1940s; Grace Livingston Hill's last novel appeared in 1949. Jean Reynolds Davis's novel *Parish Picnic: A Story* (New York: Harper and Row) appeared in 1970, and Agnes Sligh Turnbull's last novel that features ministers, *The Two Bishops* (Boston: Houghton Mifflin), appeared in 1980. During the 1980s, Christians become a more self-conscious subculture (the "Moral Majority," for example, was founded in 1979), and Christian book publishing developed into a major industry serving this subculture. The development of this subculture is significant, but discussing it is beyond the scope of the present work.

12. I am using "comic" as a fictional genre in the manner described by Northrup Frye in his *Anatomy of Criticism* (Princeton, N.J.: Princeton University Press, 1971), esp. 43–52 and 163–86. According to orthodox Calvinism, everything does not always come out all right for everyone in the end. Even some of those we love may be damned.

13. For example, Garrison Keillor, *Leaving Home: A Collection of Lake Wobegon Stories* (New York: Viking Penguin, 1987), xvii.

14. In addition to Jan Karon's *At Home in Mitford* (New York: Penguin, 1994), the Mitford series now includes *A Light in the Window* (1995); *These High, Green Hills* (1996); *Out to Canaan* (1997); *A New Song* (1999); *A Common Life: The Wedding Story* (2001); *In This Mountain* (2002); *Shepherds Abiding* (2003); and *Light from Heaven* (2005), all published in New York by Viking Penguin. Karon has also written *A Continual Feast: Words of Comfort and Celebration, Collected by Father Tim*

(2006), which contains spiritual advice from the fictional Father Tim, and *Patches of Godlight: Father Tim's Favorite Quotes* (2001), both published in New York by Viking Penguin, as well as a cookbook of Mitford recipes. Recently Lynne Hinton has also created a comic Calvinist clergyperson, the Rev. Charlotte Steward, who lives in yet another comic fictional world: Hope Springs, North Carolina. See her *Friendship Cake: A Novel* (New York: HarperCollins, 2000); *Garden of Faith* (New York: HarperCollins, 2002); and *Forever Friends* (New York: HarperCollins, 2003)

15. Though at first sight the worlds in which twentieth-century comic Calvinists live may seem similar to the fictional world that nineteenth- and early-twentieth-century Christian writers like Charles Sheldon imagine, the world Sheldon and his contemporaries present in novels like *In His Steps* is fundamentally different from the worlds more recent writers like Jan Karon and Garrison Keillor imagine. (For my discussion of Sheldon's novels, see chapter 7.) Sheldon does not perceive the world presented in his novels as an invention. He may see his characters as invented, but not the world in which they live. His fiction is intended to be a *revealing* rather than an imagining; it is designed to reveal what he perceives is *the* real world. Sheldon invites readers to discover experientially—as the characters in his fiction do—that God is present and available in the everyday world. Sheldon would likely be horrified to think that readers might perceive the world he describes in his novel as his invention: that is, as fiction.

16. Recent books by A.N. Wilson, *The Victorians* (New York: Norton, 2003), and *After the Victorians: The Decline of Britain in the Modern World* (Farrar, Straus Giroux, 2005) support this appreciation for different ways of knowing and tolerance for unresolved (and, perhaps, irresolvable) questions that Marilynne Robinson weaves into her characters.

17. Her published essays as well as *Gilead* show that Marilynne Robinson is not simply a talented writer but sometimes quite theologically astute. For example, see Marilynne Robinson, *The Death of Adam: Essays on Modern Thought* (Boston: Houghton Mifflin, 1998), and Marilynne Robinson, "Credo," *Harvard Divinity-Bulletin* 36, no. 2 (2008), 20–32.

18. Even the Roman Catholic priest in Lake Wobegon appears to be a comic Calvinist. The parish he serves is called Our Lady of Perpetual Responsibility.

19. As one reviewer suggests, when its true character emerges, Lake Wobegon is closer to Winesburg than to Mayberry—or, I might add, to Mitford.(Thomas Mallon, review of Garrison Keillor, *Pontoon: A Novel of Lake Wobegon, New York Times Book Review*, September 23, 2007, 9). Garrison Keillor's ironic perspective also seems quite clear in the script he wrote for the 2006 film *A Prairie Home Companion*. I think Keillor is well aware that the comic reality of Lake Wobegon is an imagined reality, not a reflection of current everyday reality. I am less certain of Jan Karon's perspective. The purported devotional materials by Father Tim she has written suggest that she thinks the comic God and priest depicted in Mitford are closer to everyday reality than Keillor considers the God and pastors depicted in Lake Wobegon to be.

20. Women were officially admitted to the ordained ministry in many mainline Protestant churches as early as the 1950s, but they do not appear as ministers in significant numbers in American fiction until the 1990s. The lag suggests that women were not generally accepted as ministers in popular culture until the late

1980s. Mainline denominations where women have gained the most acceptance as clergy tend to be those that are either more socially progressive or theologically moderate (or both)—and therefore more directly aware of the displacement of the Divine (e.g., Unitarian Universalists and United Methodists). Mainline denominations where women are still not officially accepted as clergy tend to be conservative or Fundamentalist—and therefore less willing to recognize the displacement of the Divine as real (e.g., Southern Baptists).

21. Novels in the series include *A Fountain Filled with Blood* (2003), *All Mortal Flesh* (2006), *In the Bleak Midwinter* (2002), *I Shall Not Want* (2008), *Out of the Deep I Cry* (2004), and *To Darkness and To Death* (2005), all published in New York by St. Martin's Minotaur. In *The Tentmaker* (New York: Putnam, 1999), Michelle Blake introduces the Rev. Lily Connor, another strong and capable woman who is both an Episcopal priest and a sleuth.

22. When Margaret Gower becomes an Episcopal priest in Godwin's sequel, *Evensong* (New York; Ballantine, 1999), she exhibits the same stubborn strength that her father displays in *Father Melancholy's Daughter.*

Conclusion: The Legacy of the Displaced Divine

1. I use "diminished" here to mean both reduced and narrowed. The ministers' social influence is diminished, as well as more specialized and professional, and not as general or communal as it was in the past.

2. In Phelps's *The Gates Ajar*, when neither Deacon Quirk nor the aptly named Rev. Dr. Bland can assuage Mary Cabot's grief over the loss of her fiancé in the Civil War, her Aunt Winifred, a minister's widow, not only gives spiritual strength to Mary but is singularly able to support the grieving Rev. Dr. Bland after his wife dies a tragic and painful death. In Phelps's later novel *The Silent Partner*, Sip Garth becomes a street preacher after her deaf and blind sister is killed. The shift toward credentialing clergy by popular approval helped break down official barriers to women as ministers—though more than one hundred years passed before women gained parity as clergy in many Protestant denominations.

3. This trend continues into the present. Most of the largest churches in the present time are nondenominational "megachurches." Ministers of these congregations may be accredited by a particular denomination, but they really serve by popular approval. Megachurches that are connected to a denomination (like Garden Grove Community Church) play down their denominational identity and employ ministers whose personal appeal matters much more than their denominational or doctrinal pedigree. A recent study indicates that most megachurch pastors attended Bible colleges; only one in ten is a seminary graduate (Central Christian College of the Bible, "Prelude to Leadership: Backgrounds of Megachurch Leaders," *Review of Religious Research* 48, no. 2 [2006], 231–32). (A master's degree from an accredited seminary is required for ordination by most mainline denominations.)

4. Commenting on Emily Dickinson's experience, Alfred Kazin describes the disengagement of morality from faith: "The supernatural had been replaced by exemplary behavior" (Alfred Kazin, *An American Procession: Major American Writers, 1830–1930* [Cambridge: Harvard University Press, 1996], 164).

5. Ministers in American fiction wrestle more with the empirical demands the paradigm shift brings than with the experiential demands. The experiential demands have also received much more attention from students of American religion than the empirical demands (Nathan O. Hatch, *The Democratization of American Christianity* [New Haven, Conn.: Yale University Press, 1989], and George Marsden, *Fundamentalism and American Culture: The Shaping of Twentieth-Century Evangelicalism, 1870–1925* [New York: Oxford University Press, 1980]). The opposite is true in American fiction—as the subsequent discussion suggests.

6. Alfred Kazin, *Alfred Kazin's America: Critical and Personal Writings*, ed. Ted Solataroff (New York: HarperCollins, 2003), 345.

7. The reality that lies behind this statement is probably even more complex than the statement implies. Consider the following observation by Robert Detweiler: "What makes this relationship between self and narrative both more provocative and frustrating nowadays is the recognition by scholars of narrative that literary texts, like our individual selves are not necessarily coherent unities, totalities, wholes, but may consist also, like the self, of an aggregate of units that can be joined, shifted and rejoined in constantly changing patters to produce (to borrow a phrase from Paul de Man) 'an infinity of valid readings'" (Robert Detweiler, *Breaking the Fall: Religious Readings of Contemporary Fiction* [San Francisco: Harper and Row, 1989], 12). The quoted phrase is from Suzanne Gearhart, "Philosophy Before Literature: Deconstruction, Historicity, and the Work of Paul de Man," *Diacritics* 13, no. 4 (1983), 70.

8. As pluralism advances during the twentieth century, Christians are becoming a clearly defined subculture within American society. Christian believing is now widely regarded as one way of believing rather than the normative belief system in American culture. The progress of this shift is especially well documented in Robert Wuthnow, *The Consciousness Reformation* (Berkeley: University of California Press, 1976); Robert Wuthnow, *The Restructuring of American Religion: Society and Faith Since World War II* (Princeton, N.J.: Princeton University Press, 1988); and Robert Wuthnow, *America and the Challenges of Religious Diversity* (Princeton, N.J.: Princeton University Press, 2005). For a recent study, see Peggy Levitt, "God Needs No Passport," *Harvard Divinity Bulletin* 34, no. 3 (2006), 44–57. The overall sectarian perception of Christians is now apparent in everyday conversation. In the 1950s when people were asked what they believed, they were likely to offer an organizational response—for example, "I am a Methodist"; now, more often than not, the one questioned will respond, "I am a Christian" or "I am a Jew" or "I am a Muslim" or "I am not a believer"—all of which are more doctrinal than organizational responses. Recent court decisions regarding displays of the Ten Commandments on public property, the debate over creationism as an alternative to Darwin's theory of evolution in the public school science classrooms, and the shift to wishing friends "Happy Holidays" rather than "Merry Christmas" are all evidence of the increasing perception of Christians and Christianity as sectarian rather than normative in American culture.

9. Thus, the contemporary situation is even more challenging than I have suggested so far in this book. In a recent analysis of contemporary culture in fourteen western countries, Dick Houtman and Step Aupers identify not two but three primary perspectives: religious, scientific, and what they call "post-Christian spir-

ituality." (These might also be termed premodern, modern, and postmodern perspectives.) Those who embrace the third perspective believe that whatever may be Divine is to be discovered within human experience. They may reject both the belief that the Divine is "out there" or transcendent, as well as the belief that truth is accessible only through the use of scientific reason (Dick Houtman and Step Aupers, "The Spiritual Turn and the Decline of Tradition: The Spread of Post-Christian Spirituality in 14 Western Countries," *Journal of the Scientific Study of Religion* vol. 46, no. 3 [2007], 307). My personal experience indicates that even many of those who identify with an organized religion in the United States function as postmodern believers. See also Paul Heelas, Linda Woodhead, Benjamin Seel, Bronislaw Szerszynski, and Karin Tusting, *The Spiritual Revolution: Why Religion Is Giving Way to Spirituality* (Malden, Mass.: Blackwell, 2005). For a critical analysis of do-it-yourself spirituality, see Curtis White, "Hot Air Gods," *Harpers* 315 (December 2007), 13–15.

10. Detweiler, *Breaking the Fall*, 13.

11. Wallace Stevens, "Adagia," in *Opus Posthumous*, ed. Milton J. Bates (New York: Knopf, 1989), 188–89. Note Stevens uses a small "g" to refer to "god" to emphasize that all gods are human products. In *How to Talk About Books You Haven't Read*, trans. Jeffrey Mehlman (New York: Bloomsbury, 2007), Pierre Bayard offers an insightful discussion of the dilemma Stevens describes.

12. William Dean Howells offers a classic portrayal of the minister's reduced authority in the Rev. Clarence Ewert, who appears in "A Difficult Case," in *A Pair of Patient Lovers* (New York: Harper and Bros., 1901), 145–220. See the discussion of Ewert in chapter 8 in this volume.

13. John Updike, "Remarks upon Receiving the Campion Medal," reprinted in John Yerkes, ed., *John Updike and Religion: The Sense of the Sacred and the Motions of Grace* (Grand Rapids, Mich.: Eerdmans, 1999), 5.

14. To be sure, there are numerous popular and religious novels today that portray ministers as firm believers, but the ministers in these novels often seem contrived characterizations designed to teach moral lessons. Most are simply too good to be true. They often fail to be convincing because, as Thomas Hardy suggests in one of his essays, "the didactic novel is so generally devoid of *vraisemblance* as to teach nothing but the impossibility of tampering with natural truth to advance dogmatic opinions" (Thomas Hardy, *Thomas Hardy's Personal Writings: Prefaces, Literary Opinions, Reminiscences*, ed. Harold Orel [London: Macmillan, 1967], 118). In contemporary fiction, it is rare to find a believing minister who has literary and cultural, as well as theological, integrity. John Ames in Marilynne Robinson's *Gilead* (New York: Farrar, Straus Giroux, 2005) is one of these rare characters.

15. Holding the Bible up as canon does not make it the exclusive source of valid information about God but, rather, a standard against which all other sources are to be measured.

16. For a discussion of Lyman Beecher's difficulties with his orthodox Calvinist colleagues, see chapters 2 and 4, especially note 4 in chapter 4. I think David Tracy is one contemporary theologian whose work promotes helpful dialogue between Christian faith and postmodern thinking: for example, David Tracy, *The Analogical Imagination: Christian Theology and the Culture of Pluralism* (New York: Crossroad, 1981).

17. The reference is to John Osborne's play, *Look Back in Anger*, act 2, scene 1. Fundamentalism, including the secular fundamentalism that some committed disbelievers exhibit, is one of the more dangerous outcomes this approach encourages. The myopic we-know-it-all perspective that Fundamentalism encourages blocks dialogue that might yield helpful insights. A dose of humility on all sides would be helpful. Both doubters and believers would be better served by being less certain of themselves.

18. Contemporary critics of religion have moved from dismissing it to castigating it. For recent discussions that reflect this viewpoint, see Sam Harris, *The End of Faith: Religion, Terror, and the Future of Reason* (New York: Norton, 2004); Richard Dawkins, *The God Delusion* (Boston: Houghton Mifflin, 2006); and Christopher Hitchens, *God Is Not Great: How Religion Poisons Everything* (New York: Twelve, 2007). For my discussions of the origins of this secular subculture, see chapter 7 and chapter 8. Terry Eagleton offers a challenging critique of contemporary castigators of belief in *Reason, Faith, and Revolutions: Reflections on the God Debate* (New Haven, Conn.: Yale University Press, 2009).

19. William James, *The Principles of Psychology* (Cambridge: Harvard University Press, 1983), 914; quoted in Robert D. Richardson, *William James: In the Maelstrom of American Modernism—A Biography* (Boston: Houghton Mifflin, 2006), 288. James Carse describes the hazards of rigid believing in *The Religious Case Against Belief* (New York: Penguin, 2008).

BIBLIOGRAPHY

Primary Texts

Adams, Henry [Compton, Frances Snow, pseud.]. *Esther: A Novel* (1884). New York: Library of America, 1983.

Aesop [pseud.]. *The Hypocrite; or Sketches of American Society from a Residence of Forty Years.* New York: Thomas, 1844.

Alden, Joseph. *Alice Gordon; or, the Uses of Orphanage.* New York: Harper and Bros., 1847.

——. *Elizabeth Benton; or, Religion in Connection with Fashionable Life.* New York: Harper and Bros., 1846.

Aldrich, Thomas Bailey. *Prudence Palfrey.* Boston: James R. Osgood, 1874.

Anderson, Sherwood. *Winesburg, Ohio* (1919). New York: Modern Library, 1999.

Baker, William Mumford [Harrington, George F., pseud.]. *Inside: A Chronicle of Secession.* New York: Harper and Bros., 1866.

Barr, Amelia Edith (Huddleston). *The Hallam Succession: A Tale of Methodist Life in Two Countries.* New York: Phillips and Hunt, 1885.

Beach, David N. *The Annie Laurie Mine.* Boston: Pilgrim Press, 1902.

Bellamy, Edward. *The Duke of Stockbridge* (1900). Cambridge: Harvard University Press, 1962.

——. *Looking Backward: 2000–1887* (1887). Boston: Houghton Mifflin, 1926.

Blake, Michelle. *The Tentmaker.* New York: Putnam, 1999.

A Blossom in the Desert: A Tale of the West. New York: Scofield and Voorhies, 1836.

Brackenridge, H.H. *Modern Chivalry: Containing the Adventures of Captain John Farrago and Teague O'Regan, His Servant* (1792–97). Ed. Lewis Leary. Albany, N.Y.: New College and University Press, 1965.

Bradford Jr., Gamaliel. *Between Two Masters.* Boston: Houghton Mifflin, 1906.

Brummit, Dan Beardly. *Shoddy.* Chicago: Willett, Clark and Colby, 1928.

Campbell, Helen S. *Mrs. Herndon's Income*. Boston: Roberts Brothers, 1886.
Cather, Willa. *The Song of the Lark* (1915). Boston: Houghton Mifflin, 1943.
Chester, George Randolph, and Lillian Chester. *The Ball of Fire*. New York: Hearst's International Library, 1914.
Child, Lydia Maria. *Hobomok* (1824). Ed. Carolyn L. Karcher. New Brunswick, N.J.: Rutgers University Press, 1986.
——. *The Rebels; or, Boston Before the Revolution*. Boston: Cummings, Hilliard, 1825.
Chopin, Kate. *The Awakening* (1899). New York: Capricorn, 1964.
Churchill, Winston. *The Inside of the Cup* (1913). New York: Macmillan (1914).
The Confessions of a Magdalene; or, Some Passages in the Life of Experience Borgia. New York: Printed for the Publisher, 1831.
Converse, Florence, *The Burden of Christopher*. Boston: Houghton Mifflin, 1900.
Cooper, James Fenimore. *Miles Wallingford* (1844). New York: Putnam, 1906.
——. *The Oak Openings; or, The Bee-Hunter* (1848). Boston: Dana Estes, n.d.
——. *The Pioneers; or, The Sources of the Susquehanna: A Descriptive Tale* (1823). New York: A. L. Burt, n.d.
——. *Satanstoe; or, The Little Page Manuscripts: A Tale of the Colony* (1845). Ed. Kay Seymour House and Constance Ayers Denne. Albany: State University of New York, 1990.
——. *The Wept of Wish-Ton-Wish: A Tale* (1829). New York: John W. Lovell, n.d.
Creton, Paul [Trowbridge, John Townsend, pseud.]. *Father Brighthopes; or, An Old Clergyman's Vacation* (1853). New York: Hurst, n.d.
Croy, Homer. *West of the Water Tower* (1923). New York: Grosset and Dunlap, n.d.
Davis, Jean Reynolds. *Parish Picnic: A Story*. New York: Harper and Row, 1970.
Dawson, William J. *A Prophet in Babylon: A Story of Social Service*. New York: Fleming H. Revell, 1908.
DeForest, John. *Witching Times* (1857). Ed. Alfred Appel Jr. New Haven, Conn.: College and University Press, 1967.
Deland, Margaret. *Dr. Lavendar's People*. New York: Harper and Bros., 1903.
——. *John Ward, Preacher*. Boston: Houghton Mifflin, 1888.
——. *New Friends in Old Chester*. New York: Harper and Bros., 1924.
——. *Old Chester Tales*. New York: Grosset and Dunlap, 1898.
——. *Philip and His Wife*. Boston: Houghton Mifflin, 1894.
——. *The Promises of Alice: The Romance of a New England Parsonage*. New York: Harper and Bros., 1919.
Dixon, Thomas, Jr. *The Leopard's Spots: A Romance of the White Man's Burden—1865–1900*. Garden City, N.Y.: Doubleday, Page, 1905.
Donnelly, Ignatius [Borsgilbert, Edward, MD; pseud.]. *Caesar's Column: A Story of the Twentieth Century*. Chicago: F. J. Schulte, 1891.
Dorr, Julia Caroline Ripley [Thomas, Caroline; pseud.]. *Lanmere*. New York: Mason Brothers, 1856.
Dreisser, Theodore. *Sister Carrie: A Novel* (1900). New York: Oxford University Press, 1998.
Echard, Margaret. *The Unbelieving Wife*. New York: Longmans, Green, 1955.
Eggleston, Edward R. *The Circuit Rider: A Tale of the Heroic Age* (1874). New York: Scribner's, 1878.

——. *Roxy*. New York: Scribner's, 1878.

[Eliot, Samuel Hayes.] *The Parish-Side*. New York: Mason Brothers, 1854.

Farnell, George. *Rev. Josiah Hilton: The Apostle of the New Age*. Providence, R.I.: Journal of Commerce, 1898.

Faulkner, William. *Light in August*. New York: Harrison Smith and Robert Haas, 1932.

——. *Soldiers' Pay*. New York: Liveright, 1926.

——. *The Sound and the Fury* (1929). New York: Norton, 1987.

Flanders, Mrs. G.M. *The Ebony Idol*. New York: D. Appleton, 1860.

Foster, Hannah Webster. *The Coquette; or, The History of Eliza Wharton: A Novel Founded on Fact* (1797). Ed. Cathy N. Davidson. New York: Oxford University Press, 1986.

Frederic, Harold. *The Damnation of Theron Ware* (1896). New York: Penguin, 1986.

Freeman, Mary E. Wilkins. "Life Everlastin'." In *A New England Nun and Other Stories*, 338–62. New York: Harper and Bros., 1891.

——. "The Love of Parson Lord." In *The Love of Parson Lord and Other Stories*, 3–81. New York: Harper and Bros., 1900.

——. *Pembroke: A Novel* (1894). Chicago: Academy Press, 1978.

——. "A Poetess." In *A New England Nun and Other Stories*, 140–59. New York: Harper and Bros., 1891.

——. "A Village Singer." In *A New England Nun and Other Stories*, 18–36. New York: Harper and Bros., 1891.

Gardener, Mrs. Helen Hamilton (Chenoweth). *An Unofficial Patriot*. Boston: Arena Publishing, 1894.

Gardner, Martin. *The Flight of Peter Fromm*. New York: William Kaufmann, 1973.

Garland, Hamlin. *Other Main-Travelled Roads*. New York: Harper and Bros., 1910.

——. *The Tyranny of the Dark*. New York: Harper and Bros., 1905.

Garrett, George. *Do, Lord, Remember Me* (1965). Baton Rouge: Louisiana State University Press, 1994.

——. *The King of Babylon Shall Not Come Against You*. New York: Harcourt, Brace, 1996.

Gilman, Bradley. *Ronald Carnaquay: A Commercial Clergyman*. New York: Macmillan, 1903.

Glasgow, Ellen. *Virginia*. Garden City, N.Y.: Doubleday, Page, 1913.

Glaspel, Susan. *The Visioning*. New York: Frederick A. Stokes, 1911.

Godwin, Gail. *Evensong*. New York: Ballantine, 1999.

——. *Father Melancholy's Daughter*. New York: William Morrow, 1991.

Harris, Corra. *A Circuit Rider's Wife*. Philadelphia: Henry Altemus, 1910.

Harris, George Washington. *Sut Lovingood: Yarns Spun by a "Nat'ral Born Durn'd Fool"* (1867). Memphis, Tenn.: St. Luke's, 1987.

Hawthorne, Nathaniel. "Endicott and the Red Cross" (1838). In *Twice-Told Tales*. Centenary edition of Nathaniel Hawthorne's works, vol. 9, 433–41. Columbus: Ohio State University Press, 1974.

——. "The Gentle Boy" (1832). In *Twice-Told Tales*. Centenary edition of Nathaniel Hawthorne's works, vol. 9, 68–105. Columbus: Ohio State University Press, 1974.

——. "Main-Street" (1849). In *The Snow Image and Uncollected Tales*. Centenary edition of Nathaniel Hawthorne's works, vol. 11, 49–82. Columbus: Ohio State University Press, 1974.

——. "The Man of Adamant" (1837). In *The Snow Image and Uncollected Tales*. Centenary edition of Nathaniel Hawthorne's works, vol. 11, 161–70. Columbus: Ohio State University Press, 1974.

——. "The May-Pole of Merry Mount" (1836). In *Twice-Told Tales*. Centenary edition of Nathaniel Hawthorne's works, vol. 9, 54–67. Columbus: Ohio State University Press, 1974.

——. "The Minister's Black Veil" (1836). In *Twice-Told Tales*. Centenary edition of Nathaniel Hawthorne's works, vol. 9, 37–53. Columbus: Ohio State University Press, 1974.

——. "Mrs. Hutchinson" (1830). In *Selected Tales and Sketches*, ed. Michael J. Colacurcio, 14–21. New York: Penguin, 1987.

——. "Passages from a Relinquished Work" (1834). In *Mosses from an Old Manse*. Centenary edition of Nathaniel Hawthorne's works, vol. 10, 405–21. Columbus: Ohio State University Press, 1974.

——. *The Scarlet Letter* (1850). Centenary edition of Nathaniel Hawthorne's works, vol. 1. Columbus: Ohio State University Press, 1962.

——. "Sunday at Home" (1837). In *Twice-Told Tales*. Centenary edition of Nathaniel Hawthorne's works, vol. 9, 19–26. Columbus: Ohio State University Press, 1974.

Haynes, Emory J. *Dollars and Duty*. Boston: James H. Earle, 1887.

Herrick, Robert. *The Memoirs of an American Citizen* (1905). New York: Grosset and Dunlap, 1908.

Hersey, John. *The Call*. New York: Knopf, 1985.

Heyward, Du Bose. *Angel*. New York: Doran, 1926.

Hinton, Lynne. *Forever Friends*. New York: HarperCollins, 2003.

——. *Friendship Cake: A Novel*. New York: HarperCollins, 2000.

——. *Garden of Faith*. New York: HarperCollins, 2002.

Holland, Josiah G. *The Bay-Path: A Tale of New England Colonial Life* (1857). New York: Scribner's, 1872.

——. *Sevenoaks*. New York: Scribner's, Armstrong, 1875.

Hollister, Gideon Hiram. *Kinley Hollow*. New York: Henry Holt, 1882.

Holmes, Oliver Wendell. *Elsie Venner: A Romance of Destiny* (1860). New York: Grosset and Dunlap, n.d.

——. *The Guardian Angel* (1867). Boston: Houghton, Mifflin, 1887.

Hood, Mrs. Frances Hamilton. *Maud Mansfield*. Macon, Ga.: J. W. Burke, 1876.

Hooper, Johnson Jones. *Some Adventures of Captain Simon Suggs* (1846). Upper Saddle River, N.J.: Literature House, 1970.

Hosmer, James K. *The Thinking Bayonet*. Boston: Walker, Fuller, 1865.

Hough, Emerson. *The Way Out: A Story of the Cumberlands Today*. New York: Grosset and Dunlap, 1918.

Howe, E. W. *The Story of a Country Town*. Boston: James R. Osgood, 1884.

Howells, William Dean. *Annie Kilburn* (1881). New York: Harper and Bros., 1891.

——. *The Day of Their Wedding*. New York: Harper and Bros., 1896.

——. "A Difficult Case." In *A Pair of Patient Lovers*, 145–220. New York: Harper and Bros., 1901.
——. *Dr. Breen's Practice*. Boston: James R. Osgood, 1881.
——. *A Hazard of New Fortunes*. New York: Harper and Bros., 1890.
——. *The Kentons*. New York: Harper and Bros., 1902.
——. *An Imperative Duty*. New York: Harper and Bros., 1892.
——. *The Leatherwood God*. New York: Century, 1916.
——. *The Minister's Charge*. Boston: Ticknor, 1887.
——. *A Modern Instance* (1882). Boston: Houghton Mifflin, 1957.
——. *Mrs. Farrell*. New York: Harper and Bros., 1921.
——. *The Quality of Mercy* (1891). New York: Harper and Bros., 1900.
——. *Ragged Lady*. New York: Harper and Bros., 1899.
——. *The Rise of Silas Lapham* (1885). New York: New American Library, 1963.
——. *The Shadow of a Dream*. New York: Harper and Bros, 1901.
——. *The Son of Royal Langbrith*. New York: Harper and Bros., 1905.
——. *A Traveller from Altruria* (1894). Bloomington: Indiana University Press, 1968.
——. *The Undiscovered Country*. Boston: Houghton Mifflin, 1880.
Hubbell, Martha Stone. *The Shady Side; or, Life in a Country Parsonage*. Boston: J. P. Jewett, 1853.
Jackson, Charles Tenney. *My Brother's Keeper*. Indianapolis: Bobbs-Merrill, 1910.
James, Henry. *Watch and Ward*. Boston: Houghton, Osgood, 1878.
Jance, J. A. *Desert Heat*. New York: Avon, 1993.
——. *Rattlesnake Crossing*. New York: Avon, 1999.
Jewett, Sarah Orne. *The Country of the Pointed Firs and Other Stories* (1896). Garden City, N.Y.: Doubleday, 1956.
Judd, Sylvester. *Margaret: A Tale of the Real and the Ideal* (1845). Boston: Phillips, Sampson, 1857.
Karon, Jan. *At Home in Mitford*. New York: Penguin, 1994.
——. *A Common Life: The Wedding Story*. New York: Viking Penguin, 2001.
——. *A Continual Feast: Words of Comfort and Celebration, Collected by Father Tim*. New York: Viking Penguin, 2006.
——. *In This Mountain*. New York: Viking Penguin, 2002.
——. *Light from Heaven*. New York: Viking Penguin, 2005.
——. *A Light in the Window*. New York: Viking Penguin, 1995.
——. *A New Song*. New York: Viking Penguin, 1999.
——. *Out to Canaan*. New York: Viking Penguin, 1997.
——. *Patches of Godlight: Father Tim's Favorite Quotes*. New York: Viking Penguin, 2001.
——. *Shepherds Abiding*. New York: Viking Penguin, 2003.
——. *These High, Green Hills*. New York: Viking Penguin, 1996.
Keillor, Garrison. *Lake Wobegon Days*. New York: Viking Penguin, 1985.
——. *Leaving Home: A Collection of Lake Wobegon Stories*. New York: Viking Penguin, 1987.
——. *Pontoon: A Novel of Lake Wobegon*. New York: Viking, 2007.
Kennedy, John Pendleton. *Swallow Barn; or, A Sojourn in the Old Dominion* (1832). Baton Rouge: Louisiana State University Press, 1986.

King, Basil. *The Lifted Veil.* New York: A. L. Burt, 1917.
——. *Pluck.* New York: Harper and Bros., 1928.
King, Cassandra. *The Sunday Wife.* New York: Hyperion, 2002.
Kingsolver, Barbara. *The Poisonwood Bible.* New York: HarperCollins, 1998.
Kirkland, Joseph. *Zury: The Meanest Man in Spring County, A Novel of Western Life* (1887). Urbana: University of Illinois Press, 1956.
Lee, Eliza Buckminster. *Naomi.* Boston: W. Crosby and H. P. Nichols, 1848.
Lewis, Sinclair. *Babbitt* (1922). New York: Penguin, 1996.
——. *Elmer Gantry.* New York: Harcourt, Brace, 1927.
——. *Main Street.* New York: Harcourt, Brace and Howe, 1920.
The Life and Adventures of Obadiah Benjamin Franklin Bloomfield, M.D., Interspersed with Episodes and Remarks Religious, Moral, Public Spirited and Humorous. Philadelphia: Published for the Proprietor, 1818.
Lippard, George. *The Empire City; or, New York by Night and Day* (1850). Freeport, N.Y.: Books for Libraries Press, 1969.
——. *The Memoirs of a Preacher: A Revelation of the Church and the Home.* Philadelphia: Joseph Severns, 1849.
——. *The Quaker City; or, The Monks of Monk Hall* (1844). Intro. David S. Reynolds. Amherst: University of Massachusetts Press, 1995.
London, Jack. *The Iron Heel* (1907). New York: Regent Press, 1913.
Longfellow, Henry Wadsworth. *Kavanagh* (1849). New Haven, Conn.: College and University Press, 1965.
Maclean, Norman. *A River Runs Through It and Other Stories.* Chicago: University of Chicago Press, 1976.
Mason, Caroline Atwater. *A Minister of the World* (1895). Philadelphia: Henry Altemus, 1899.
Melville, Herman. *The Confidence-Man: His Masquerade* (1857). New York: Norton, 1971.
——. *Moby-Dick, or The Whale* (1851). Evanston, Ill.: Northwestern University Press and Newberry Library, 1988.
——. *Pierre, or The Ambiguities* (1852). Evanston, Ill.: Northwestern University Press and Newberry Library, 1971.
——. *Redburn* (1849). Evanston, Ill.: Northwestern University Press and Newberry Library, 1969.
——. *Typee: A Peep at Polynesian Life* (1846). Evanston, Ill.: Northwestern University Press and Newberry Library, 1968.
——. *White-Jacket: or, The World in a Man of War* (1850). Evanston, Ill.: Northwestern University Press and Newberry Library, 1970.
Mitchell, Donald Grant. *Dr. Johns: Being a Narrative of Certain Events in the Life of an Orthodox Minister of Connecticut.* New York: Scribner's, 1866.
Moore, John Trotwood. *The Bishop of Cottontown: A Story of the Southern Cotton Mills.* Philadelphia: John C. Winston, 1906.
Morris, George Van Derveer. *A Man for A' That.* Cincinnati: Jennings and Pye, 1902.
Motley, John Lothrop. *Merry-Mount: A Romance of the Massachusetts Colony.* Boston: J. Munroe, 1849.
Murfee, Mary Noilles [Craddock, Charles Egbert, pseud.]. *The Prophet of the Great Smoky Mountains.* Boston: Houghton Mifflin, 1885.

Myers, Cortland. *Would Christ Belong to a Labor Union? or, Henry Fielding's Dream.* New York: Street and Smith, 1900.

Neal, John. *Errata; or, The Works of Will Adams.* New York: For the proprietors, 1823.

——. *Rachel Dyer: A North American Story.* Portland, Me.: Shirley and Hyde, 1828.

Neff, Elizabeth. *Altars to Mammon.* New York: Frederick A. Stokes, 1908.

Oates, Joyce Carol. *Son of the Morning.* New York: Vanguard, 1978.

Our Parish: Annals of Pastor and People. Boston: L. P. Crown, 1854.

Page, Thomas Nelson. *John Marvel, Assistant.* New York: Scribner's, 1909.

Parker, Permelia J. *The Midnight Cry.* New York: Dodd, Mead, 1886.

Paulding, James Kirke. *Koningsmarke, the Long Finne: A Story of the New World* (1823). Ed. Daniel A. Wells. Schenectady, N.Y.: Union College Press, 1988.

——. *The Puritan and His Daughter.* New York: Baker and Scribner, 1849.

——. *Westward Ho! A Tale* (1832). Grosse Point, Mich.: Scholarly Press, 1968.

Phelps, Elizabeth Stuart [Trusta, H., pseud.]. *The Sunny Side; or, the Country Minister's Wife.* Boston: John P. Jewitt, 1851.

——. *A Peep at Number Five, or a Chapter in the Life of a City Pastor* (1852). Freeport, N.Y.: Books for Libraries, 1971.

Phelps (Ward), Elizabeth Stuart. *The Gates Ajar* (1869). New York: Regent, n.d.

——. *The Silent Partner* (1871). New York: Feminist Press, 1983.

——. *A Singular Life* (1894). Boston: Houghton Mifflin, 1899.

——. *The Supply at Saint Agatha's.* Boston: Houghton Mifflin, 1896.

——. "A Woman's Pulpit" (1870/1879). In *Sealed Orders,* 176–95. New York: Garrett Press, 1969.

Pratt, Magee. *The Orthodox Preacher and Nancy.* Hartford: Connecticut Magazine, 1901.

Prentiss, Mrs. E. *Stepping Heavenward* (1869). New York: Anson D. F. Randolph, 1880.

Price, Reynolds. *The Good Priest's Son.* New York: Scribner's, 2005.

Quick, J. Herbert. *The Broken Lance.* Indianapolis: Bobbs-Merrill, 1907.

Reed, Isaac G. *From Heaven to New York.* New York: Optimus, 1894.

Retroprogression: Being an Account of a Short Residence in the Celebrated Town of Jumbleborough. Boston: James Burns, 1839.

Reynolds, E. W. *Records of the Bubbleton Parish; or, Papers from the Experience of an American Minister.* Boston: A. Tompkins and B. B. Mussey, 1854.

Richmond, Grace S. *The Brown Study* (1915). New York: A. L. Burt, 1919.

——. *Red and Black.* Garden City, N.Y.: Doubleday, Page, 1919.

Richter, Conrad. *A Simple, Honorable Man.* New York: Knopf, 1962.

Robinson, Marilynne. *Gilead.* New York: Farrar, Straus Giroux, 2004.

Roe, E. P. *From Jest to Earnest.* New York: Dodd, Mead, 1876.

Rolvaag, O. E. *Giants in the Earth* (1927). New York: Harper and Bros., 1929.

Savage, Sarah A. *The Factory Girl.* Boston: Munroe, Francis, and Parker, 1814.

——. *Filial Affection; or, The Clergyman's Granddaughter.* Boston: Cummings and Hilliard, 1820.

Scudder, Vida D. *A Listener in Babel.* Boston: Houghton Mifflin, 1903.

Sedgwick, Catharine Maria. *Redwood: A Tale.* New York: E. Bliss and E. White, 1824.

——. *Hope Leslie* (1826). New Brunswick, N.J.: Rutgers University Press, 1989.

Sheldon, Charles M. *The Crucifixion of Phillip Strong* (1898). New York: Grosset and Dunlap, n.d.

——. *In His Steps* (1897). New York: Putnam's, 1982.

——. *The Miracle of Markham: How Twelve Churches Became One*. Chicago: Church Press, 1899.

——. *The Redemption of Freetown*. Boston: United Society of Christian Endeavor, 1898.

——. *Richard Bruce, or Life That Now Is*. Boston: Congregational Sunday School and Publishing Society, 1892.

Smith, Elizabeth Oakes. *Bertha and Lily; or, The Parsonage of Beech Glen: A Romance*. New York: J. C. Derby, 1854.

Smith, Lee. *The Devil's Dream*. New York: Ballantine, 1993.

——. *Saving Grace*. New York: Ballantine, 1995.

The Soldier's Orphan. New York: C. S. Van Winkle, 1812.

Southworth, Mrs. Emma D. E. N. *The Deserted Wife: A Novel*. Philadelphia: T. B. Peterson, 1855.

——. *Virginia and Magdalene; or, The Foster-Sisters: A Novel*. Philadelphia: T. B. Peterson, 1852.

Spencer-Fleming, Julia. *A Fountain Filled with Blood*. New York: Thomas Dunne, St. Martin's Minotaur, 2003.

——. *All Mortal Flesh*. New York: Thomas Dunne, St. Martin's Minotaur, 2006.

——. *In the Bleak Midwinter*. New York: Thomas Dunne, St. Martin's Minotaur, 2002.

——. *I Shall Not Want*. New York: Thomas Dunne, St. Martins Minotaur, 2008.

——. *Out of the Deep I Cry*. New York: Thomas Dunne, St. Martin's Minotaur, 2004.

——. *To Darkness and to Death*. New York: Thomas Dunne, St. Martin's Minotaur, 2005.

Steinbeck, John. *The Grapes of Wrath*. New York: Viking, 1939.

Stowe, Harriet Beecher. *The Minister's Wooing* (1859). Hartford, Conn.: Stowe-Day Foundation, 1990.

——. *Oldtown Folks* (1869). Cambridge: Belknap, 1966.

——. *Poganuc People* (1878). Hartford, Conn.: Stowe-Day Foundation, 1987.

——. *We and Our Neighbors*. Boston: Houghton Mifflin, 1873.

Talbot, Richard J. *The Chainbreakers*. New York: A. L. Burt, 1914.

Thompson, George. *City Crimes; or Life in New York and Boston*. In *Venus in Boston and Other Tales of Nineteenth-Century City Life* (1849), ed. David S. Reynolds and Kimberly R. Gladman, 107–311. Amherst: University of Massachusetts Press, 2002.

Tourgee, Albion. *Murvale Eastman, Christian Socialist*. New York: Fords, Howard and Hulburt, 1891.

Triumph of Religion. Savannah: S. C. and J. Schenk, 1825.

Turnbull, Agnes Sligh. *The Bishop's Mantel*. New York: Macmillan, 1947.

——. *The Two Bishops*. Boston: Houghton Mifflin, 1980.

Twain, Mark. *The Adventures of Huckleberry Finn* (1884). New York: Modern Library, 2001.

Tyler, Royall. *The Bay Boy* (1792–97). In *The Prose of Royall Tyler*, ed. Marius Peladeau. Rutland, Vt.: Charles E. Tuttle, 1972.
Updike, John. *In the Beauty of the Lilies*. New York: Knopf, 1996.
——. *A Month of Sundays*. New York: Knopf, 1974.
——. *Rabbit, Run* (1960). New York: Knopf, 1979.
——. *Roger's Version* (1986). New York: Fawcett Crest, 1987.
——. *The Witches of Eastwick* (1984). New York: Fawcett, 1996.
Varney, George R. *Out of the Depths: A Story of Western Love, Religion and Reform*. Philadelphia: Griffith and Rowland, 1909.
Ware, Henry, Jr. *The Recollections of Jotham Anderson*. Boston: Christian Register Office, 1828.
Warner, Susan. *The Wide, Wide World* (1850). New York: Feminist Press, 1986.
Waterson, Robert C. *Arthur Lee and Tom Palmer; or, The Sailor Reclaimed*. Boston: James Munroe, 1839.
White, Charles Bouck. *The Mixing: What the Hillport Neighbors Did*. Garden City, N.Y.: Doubleday, Page, 1913.
Williams, Catharine Read. *Fall River: An Authentic Narrative* (1833). New York: Oxford University Press, 1993.
Wilson, Gregory [pseud.]. *The Stained Glass Jungle*. Garden City, N.Y.: Doubleday, 1962.
Woods, Katherine. *Metzerott, Shoemaker*. New York: Thomas Y. Crowell, 1889.
Wright, Harold Bell. *The Calling of Dan Matthews*. New York: A. L. Burt, 1909.
——. *God and the Groceryman* (1927). New York: Triangle, 1942.
——. *That Printer of Udell's* (1903). New York: A. L. Burt, 1911.
The Yankee Traveller; or, The Adventures of Hector Wigler. Concord, Mass.: George Hough, 1817.

Secondary Sources

Adams, Henry. *The Education of Henry Adams*. New York: Library of America, 1983.
——. *The Letters of Henry Adams*. 6 vols. Ed. J. C. Levenson, Ernest Samuels, Charles Vandersee, and Viola Hopkins Winner. Cambridge: Harvard University Press, 1982–88.
——. *Mont Saint Michel and Chartres*. New York: Viking Penguin, 1986.
Ahlstrom, Sidney. *A Religious History of the American People*. New Haven, Conn.: Yale University Press, 1972.
Ahnrbrink, Lars. *The Beginnings of Naturalism in American Fiction: A Study of the Works of Hamlin Garland, Stephen Crane, and Frank Norris with Special Reference to Some European Influences, 1891–1903*. New York: Russell and Russell, 1961.
"American Religious Identification Survey (2001)." Graduate Center, City University of New York. At http://www.gc.cuny.edu/faculty/research_briefs/aris/aris_index.htm.
Applegate, Debby. *The Most Famous Man in America: The Biography of Henry Ward Beecher*. New York: Doubleday, 2006.

Arvin, Newton. *Herman Melville*. New York: William Sloane Associates, 1950.

Barrett, J. Edward. "Things Change in Thirty Years." *Theology Today* 43, no. 4 (1984), 183–87.

Barrow, Clyde W. *Universities and the Capitalist State*. Madison: University of Wisconsin Press, 1990.

Barthes, Roland. *S/Z*. Trans. Richard Miller. New York: Hill and Wang, 1974.

Bayard, Pierre. *How to Talk About Books You Haven't Read*. Trans. Jeffrey Mehlman. New York: Bloomsbury, 2007.

Baym, Nina. *Women's Fiction: A Guide to Novels by and About Women in America, 1820–1970*. 2nd ed. Urbana: University of Illinois Press, 1993.

Beecher, Lyman. Letter to Catharine Beecher, November 5, 1822. Radcliffe College Schlesinger Library, Beecher-Stowe Collection, folder 2.

Bell, Michael Davitt. *Hawthorne and the Historical Romance of New England*. Princeton, N.J.: Princeton University Press, 1971.

——. *The Problem of American Realism: Studies in the Cultural History of a Literary Idea*. Chicago: University of Chicago Press, 1993.

Bellah, Robert, Richard Madsen, William M. Sullivan, Ann Swidler, and Steven M. Tipton. *Habits of the Heart: Individualism and Commitment in American Life*. Berkeley: University of California Press, 1985.

Bennett, Bridget. *The Damnation of Harold Frederic: His Lives and Works*. Syracuse, N.Y.: Syracuse University Press, 1997.

Bennett, Mary A. *Elizabeth Stuart Phelps*. Philadelphia: University of Pennsylvania Press, 1939.

Bercovitch, Sacvan. *The Rites of Assent: Transformations in the Symbolic Construction of America*. London: Routledge, 1993.

Berger, Peter L., and Thomas Luckmann. *The Social Construction of Reality*. Garden City, N.Y.: Anchor/Doubleday, 1967.

Best Sellers List. *New York Times Book Review*. October 8, 2006.

"Best Sellers in Fiction During the First Quarter of the Twentieth Century." *Publishers' Weekly* 107 (February 14, 1925), 525–27.

Birkhead, Leon M. *Is "Elmer Gantry" True?* Girard, Kans.: Haldeman-Julius, 1928.

Bradbury, Malcolm. *The Modern American Novel*. New York: Oxford University Press, 1983.

Brown, Bruce. *Marx, Freud and the Critique of Everyday Life: Toward a Permanent Cultural Revolution*. New York: Monthly Review, 1973.

Brown, Herbert Ross. *The Sentimental Novel in America, 1789–1860*. Freeport, N.Y.: Books for Libraries, 1970.

Bryant, John. Introduction to Herman Melville, *Typee*, ix–xxx. New York: Penguin, 1996.

Buell, Lawrence. *New England Literary Culture: From Revolution Through Renaissance*. New York: Cambridge University Press.

Cader Books. At http://www.caderbooks.com/bestintro.html.

Calvin, John. *Institutes of the Christian Religion*. Trans. Henry Beveridge. Grand Rapids, Mich.: Eerdmans, 1989.

Carse, James. *The Religious Case Against Belief*. New York: Penguin, 2008.

Carter, Paul. *The Spiritual Crisis of the Gilded Age*. DeKalb: Northern Illinois University Press, 1971.

Cartwright, Peter. *Autobiography of Peter Cartwright, the Backwoods Preacher.* Ed. W. P. Strickland. New York: Carlton and Porter, 1857.

Cary, Joyce. *Art and Reality: Ways of the Creative Process.* New York: Harper and Bros., 1958.

Central Christian College of the Bible. "Prelude to Leadership: Backgrounds of Megachurch Leaders." *Review of Religious Research* 48, no. 2 (2006), 231–32.

Charvat, William. *The Origins of American Critical Thought, 1810–1835.* New York: A. S. Barnes, 1968.

Childs, Peter. *Modernism.* London: Routledge, 2000.

Churchill, Winston. *The Uncharted Way: The Psychology of the Gospel Doctrine.* Philadelphia: Dorrance, 1940.

Clausen, Christopher. "America's Design for Tolerance." *Wilson Quarterly* (Winter 2007), 26–32.

Colacurcio, Michael J. Introduction to Hawthorne's *Selected Tales and Sketches,* vii-xxxv. New York: Penguin, 1987.

——. *The Province of Piety: Moral History in Hawthorne's Early Tales.* Cambridge: Harvard University Press, 1984.

Colcord, Lincoln. Introduction to O. E. Rolvaag, *Giants in the Earth,* xxiii–xxxiv. New York: Harper and Bros., 1929.

Cox, James M. *Mark Twain: The Fate of Humor.* Princeton, N.J.: Princeton University Press, 1966.

Coxe, Arthur Cleveland. "The Writings of Hawthorne." *Church Review* 3 (January 1851). Quoted in Nathaniel Hawthorne, *The Scarlet Letter,* Norton Critical Edition, ed. Seymour Gross Sculley Bradley, Richmond Croom Beatty, and E. Hudson Long, 489–511. New York: Norton, 1988.

Crozier, Alice C. *The Novels of Harriet Beecher Stowe.* New York: Oxford University Press, 1969.

Davies, Horton. *A Mirror of the Ministry in Modern Novels.* New York: Oxford University Press, 1959.

Davis, Merrell R., and William H. Gilmane, eds. *The Letters of Herman Melville.* New Haven, Conn.: Yale University Press, 1960.

Dawkins, Richard. *The God Delusion.* Boston: Houghton Mifflin, 2006.

Decker, William Merrill. *The Literary Vocation of Henry Adams.* Chapel Hill: University of North Carolina Press, 1990.

Deland, Margaret. *Golden Yesterdays.* New York: Harper and Bros., 1941.

Detweiler, Robert. *Breaking the Fall: Religious Readings of Contemporary Fiction.* San Francisco: Harper and Row, 1989.

Dewey, Orville. *Autobiography and Letters of Orville Dewey, D.D.* Ed. Mary E. Dewey. Boston: Roberts Brothers, 1883.

Dickinson, Emily. *The Poems of Emily Dickinson,* vol. 3. Ed. R. W. Franklin. Cambridge: Harvard University Press, 1998.

Douglas, Ann. *The Feminization of American Culture.* New York: Knopf, 1979.

Downey, Jean. Introduction to Henry Wadsworth Longfellow, *Kavanagh,* 5–21. New Haven, Conn.: College and University Press, 1965.

Duguid, Sandra R. Introduction to Harriet Beecher Stowe, *The Minister's Wooing,* n.p. Hartford, Conn.: Stowe-Day Foundation, 1990.

Dupee, F. W. *Henry James.* New York: William Sloan, 1951.

Eagleton, Terry. *Reason, Faith, and Revolutions: Reflections on the God Debate*. New Haven, Conn.: Yale University Press, 2009.

Eggleston, Edward R. Preface to *The Circuit Rider*, v–viii. New York: Scribner's, 1878.

Farrell, Helene S. "Charles Bouck White: The Sculptor." *Schoharie County Review* (Spring 1984), n.p.

Fisher, Fred B. Review of "Shoddy." *Christian Century* 45 (April 19, 1928), 509–10.

Fowler, James W. *Stages of Faith: The Psychology of Human Development and the Quest for Meaning*. San Francisco: Harper and Row, 1981.

Frederic, Harold. "How the Popular Harold Frederic Works." *Literary Digest* 13 (July 25, 1896), 397.

Frye, Northrop. *Anatomy of Criticism*. Princeton, N.J.: Princeton University Press, 1971.

Garroutte, Eva Marie. "The Positivist Attack on Baconian Science and Religious Knowledge in the 1870s." In *The Secular Revolution: Power, Interests, and Conflict in the Secularization of American Public Life*, ed. Christian Smith, 197–215. Berkeley: University of California Press, 2003.

Gearhart, Suzanne. "Philosophy Before Literature: Deconstruction, Historicity, and the Work of Paul de Man." *Diacritics* 13, no. 4 (1983), 70.

Glaab, Charles N., and A. Theodore Brown. *A History of Urban America*. New York: Macmillan, 1967.

Gladden, Washington. *Applied Christianity: Moral Aspects of Social Questions*. Boston: Houghton Mifflin, 1886.

——. *The Church and Modern Life*. Boston: Houghton Mifflin, 1908.

——. *Social Salvation*. Boston: Houghton Mifflin, 1902.

Goffman, Erving. *The Presentation of the Self in Everyday Life*. Garden City, N.Y.: Doubleday, 1959.

Goodwin, Doris Kearns. *Team of Rivals*. New York: Simon and Schuster, 2005.

Guelzo, Allen C. *Abraham Lincoln: Redeemer President*. Grand Rapids, Mich.: Eerdmans, 1999.

Guyau, Jean Marie. *The Non-Religion of the Future: A Sociological Study*. New York: Schocken, 1962.

Hall, G. Stanley. *Jesus, the Christ, in the Light of Psychology*. Garden City, N.Y.: Doubleday, 1917.

Halttunen, Karen. *Confidence Men and Painted Women: A Study of Middle Class Culture in America, 1830–1870*. New Haven, Conn.: Yale University Press, 1982.

Hamilton, Michael S. Book review of Christian Smith, *The Secular Revolution*. *Journal for the Scientific Study of Religion* 43, no. 4 (2004), 563–64.

Hardy, Thomas. *Thomas Hardy's Personal Writings: Prefaces, Literary Opinions, Reminiscences*. Ed. Harold Orel. London: Macmillan, 1967.

Harkness, Samuel. "Sinclair Lewis's Sunday School Class." *Christian Century* 43 (July 29, 1926), 938–39.

"Harold Bell Wright Goes Back to Hills as 'Shepherd.'" *Rochester (N.Y.) Times Union*, February 6, 1934, n.p.

Harris, Sam. *The End of Faith: Religion, Terror, and the Future of Reason*. New York: Norton, 2004.

——. *Letter to a Christian Nation*. New York: Knopf, 2006.

Hatch, Nathan O. *The Democratization of American Christianity.* New Haven, Conn.: Yale University Press, 1989.

Hawthorne, Nathaniel. *The English Notebooks.* Ed. Randall Stewart. New York: Russell and Russell, 1962.

Hedrick, Joan. *Harriet Beecher Stowe: A Life.* New York: Oxford University Press, 1994.

Heelas, Paul, Linda Woodhead, Benjamin Seel, Bronislaw Szerszynski, and Karin Tusting. *The Spiritual Revolution: Why Religion Is Giving Way to Spirituality.* Malden, Mass.: Blackwell, 2005.

Herberg, Will. *Protestant-Catholic-Jew: An Essay in American Religious Sociology.* Garden City, N.Y.: Doubleday, 1955.

Herbert, George. *The Country Parson.* New York: Paulist, 1981.

Hersey, John. *Life Sketches.* New York: Knopf, 1989.

Henretta, James E. *The Evolution of American Society, 1700–1815: An Interdisciplinary Analysis.* Lexington, Mass.: D. C. Heath, 1973.

Hitchens, Christopher. *God Is Not Great: How Religion Poisons Everything.* New York: Twelve, 2007.

Houtman, Dick, and Step Aupers. "The Spiritual Turn and the Decline of Tradition: The Spread of Post-Christian Spirituality in 14 Western Countries." *Journal of the Scientific Study of Religion* 46, no. 3 (2007), 305–20.

Howells, William Dean. "Eighty Years and After." *Harper's Monthly* 150 (December 1919), 21–28.

——. Publisher's Note in *The Leatherwood God.* New York: Century, 1916.

Hudson, Winthrop S. *American Protestantism.* Chicago: University of Chicago Press, 1961.

——. "The Ministry in the Puritan Age." In *The Ministry in Historical Perspectives,* ed. Richard H. Niebuhr and Daniel D. Williams, 180–206. New York: Harper and Bros., 1956.

Hutchisson, James M. Introduction to Sinclair Lewis, *Babbitt,* vii–xxviii. New York: Penguin, 1996.

——. *The Rise of Sinclair Lewis, 1920–1930.* University Park: Pennsylvania State University Press, 1996.

Isaacson, Walter. *Einstein: His Life and Universe.* New York: Simon and Schuster, 2007.

James, William. "Intellect and Feeling in Religion." In *Manuscript Lectures,* 83–100. Cambridge: Harvard University Press, 1988.

——. *The Principles of Psychology.* Cambridge: Harvard University Press, 1983.

Jenkins, Roy. *Churchill: A Biography.* New York: Farrar, Straus Giroux, 2001.

Jung, Carl. *Memories, Dreams and Reflections.* Ed. Aniela Jaffe. New York: Pantheon, 1963.

Kaplan, Amy. *The Social Construction of American Realism.* Chicago: University of Chicago Press, 1988.

Karcher, Carolyn L. Introduction to Lydia Maria Child, *Hobomok and Other Writings on Indians,* ix–xxxviii. New Brunswick, N.J.: Rutgers University Press, 1991.

Kazin, Alfred. *Alfred Kazin's America: Critical and Personal Writings.* Ed. Ted Solataroff. New York: HarperCollins, 2003.

——. *An American Procession: Major American Writers, 1830–1930*. Cambridge: Harvard University Press, 1996.

——. *On Native Grounds: An Interpretation of Modern American Prose Literature*. New York: Harcourt Brace, 1995.

Kesselring, Marion L. *Hawthorne's Reading, 1828–1850*. Folcroft, Pa.: Folcroft Press, 1969.

Kessler, Carol Farley. *Elizabeth Stuart Phelps*. Boston: Twayne, 1982.

Ketchin, Susan. *The Christ-Haunted Landscape: Faith and Doubt in Southern Fiction*. Jackson: University of Mississippi Press, 1994.

Killen, Patricia O'Connell, and Mark Silk, eds. *Religion and Public Life in the Pacific Northwest: The None Zone*. Walnut Creek, Calif.: AltaMira, 2004.

Leavis, Q.D. "Hawthorne as a Poet." In Nathaniel Hawthorne, *Collected Essays*, vol. 2, ed. G. Singh, 30–77. London: Cambridge University Press, 1985.

Levitt, Peggy. "God Needs No Passport." *Harvard Divinity Bulletin* 34, no. 3 (2006), 44–57.

Lewis, Sinclair. *From Main Street to Stockholm: Letters of Sinclair Lewis, 1919–1930*. Ed. Harrison Smith. New York: Harcourt Brace, 1952.

Lingeman, Richard. *Sinclair Lewis: Rebel from Main Street*. New York: Random House, 2002.

Lippmann, Walter. *Public Opinion*. New York: Macmillan, 1922.

Luisi, David. "The Religious Environment and the Role of the Minister in the Novels of William Dean Howells." Ph. D dissertation, University of Notre Dame, 1974.

Lynn, Kenneth S. *William Dean Howells: An American Life*. New York: Harcourt Brace Jovanovich, 1971.

Lynn, Robert Wood, and James W. Fraser. "Images of the Small Church in American History." In *Small Churches Are Beautiful*, ed. Jackson W. Carroll, 1–19. San Francisco: Harper and Row, 1977.

Mallon, Thomas. Review of Garrison Keillor, *Pontoon: A Novel of Lake Wobegon*. *New York Times Book Review*, September 23, 2007, 9

Mannheim, Karl. *Essays on the Sociology of Knowledge*. Ed. Paul Kecskemeti. London: Routledge and Kegan Paul, 1952.

Marsden, George. *Fundamentalism and American Culture: The Shaping of Twentieth-Century Evangelicalism, 1870–1925*. New York: Oxford University Press, 1980.

——. *The Soul of the American University*. New York: Oxford University Press, 1994.

Mead, Sidney H. "The Rise of the Evangelical Conception of the Ministry in America (1607–1850)." In *The Ministry in Historical Perspectives*, ed. Richard H. Niebuhr and Daniel D. Williams, 207–49. New York: Harper and Bros., 1956.

Meader, Keith G. "'My Own Salvation': The *Christian Century* and Psychology's Secularizing of American Protestantism." In *The Secular Revolution: Power, Interests, and Conflict in the Secularization of American Public Life*, ed. Christian Smith, 269–309. Berkeley: University of California Press, 2003.

Meine, Franklin J., ed. *Tall Tales of the Southwest: An Anthology of Southwest Humor, 1830–1860*. New York: Knopf, 1930.

Michaelsen, Robert S. "The Protestant Ministry in America: 1850 to the Present." In *The Ministry in Historical Perspectives*, ed. Richard H. Niebuhr and Daniel D. Williams, 250–88. New York: Harper and Bros., 1956.

Miller, Glenn T. *The Modern Church: From the Dawn of the Reformation to the Eve of the Third Millennium*. Nashville: Abingdon, 1997.

——. *Piety and Intellect: The Aims and Purposes of Ante-bellum Theological Education*. Atlanta: Scholars Press, 1990.

Miller, Perry. *The New England Mind: From Colony to Province*. Cambridge: Belknap, 1953.

Moreland, Richard C. "Faulkner and Modernism." In *The Cambridge Companion to William Faulkner*, ed. Philip M. Weinstein, 17–30. New York: Cambridge University Press, 1995.

Morgan, Speer, and William Holtz. "Fragments from a Marriage: Letters of Sinclair Lewis to Grace Hegger Lewis." *Missouri Review* 11 (1988), 71–98.

"The Most Popular Authors of Fiction Between 1900 and 1925." *Publishers' Weekly* 107 (February 21, 1925), 619–22.

Mott, Frank Luther. *Golden Multitudes: The Story of Best Sellers in the United States*. New York: Macmillan, 1947.

"National Survey of Religious Identification (1990)." Graduate Center, City University of New York. At http://www.gc.cuny.edu/faculty/research_briefs/aris/aris_index.htm.

Nicoll, Grier. "The Christian Social Novel in America, 1865–1918." Ph.D. dissertation, University of Minnesota, 1964.

Niebuhr, H. Richard. *The Social Sources of Denominationalism*. New York: Henry Holt, 1929.

O'Connor, Leo F. *Religion in the American Novel: The Search for Belief, 1860–1920*. Lanham, Md.: University Press of America, 1984.

O'Donnell, Patrick. "Faulkner and Postmodernism." In *The Cambridge Companion to William Faulkner*, ed. Philip M. Weinstein, 31–50. New York: Cambridge University Press, 1995.

O'Keefe, Mark. "Number of 'Nones': Those Who Claim No Religion Swells in U.S." At http://www.newhousenews.com/archive/okeefe112603.html. 2003.

Osborne, John. *Look Back in Anger*. New York: Bantam, 1959.

Park, Edwards. "The Theology of the Intellect and That of the Feelings." *Bibliotheca Sacra and Theological Review* 7 (1850), 533–69.

Parker, Hershel. *Herman Melville: A Biography*. Vol. 1. Baltimore: Johns Hopkins University Press, 1996.

Parrington, Vernon Louis. Editor's introduction to O. E. Rolvaag, *Giants in the Earth*, ix–xx. New York: Harper and Bros., 1929.

Pattee, Fred Lewis. Introduction to Mary Wilkins Freeman, *A New England Nun and Other Stories*, vii–xxvi. New York: Harper and Bros., 1919.

Phelps, Elizabeth Stuart. *Chapters from a Life*. Boston: Houghton Mifflin, 1897.

Piaget, Jean. *The Construction of Reality in the Child*. New York: Ballantine, 1954.

Polanyi, Michael. *Personal Knowledge*. Chicago: University of Chicago Press, 1958.

Prentiss, Mrs. E. *Stepping Heavenward* (1869). New York: Anson D. F. Randolph, 1880.

Rabinowitz, Richard. *The Spiritual Self in Everyday Life: The Transformation of Personal Religious Experience in Nineteenth-Century New England*. Boston: Northeastern University Press, 1989.

Reep, Diana C. *Margaret Deland*. Boston: Twayne, 1985.

——. *Mary Wilkins Freeman: A Study of the Short Fiction*. New York: Twayne, 1997.

Renker, Elizabeth. *Strike Through the Mask: Herman Melville and the Scene of Writing*. Baltimore: Johns Hopkins University Press, 1998.

Reynolds, David S. *Beneath the American Renaissance*. Cambridge: Harvard University Press, 1988.

——. *Faith in Fiction: The Emergence of Religious Literature in America*. Cambridge: Harvard University Press, 1981.

——. *George Lippard*. Boston: Twayne, 1982.

——. Introduction to George Lippard, *The Quaker City; or, The Monks of Monk Hall: A Romance of Philadelphia Life, Mystery, and Crime*, iii–xliv. Amherst: University of Massachusetts Press, 1995.

Reynolds, David S., and Kimberly R. Gladman. Introduction to George Thompson, *Venus in Boston and Other Tales of Nineteenth-Century City Life*, ed. David S. Reynolds and Kimberly R. Gladman, ix–liv. Amherst: University of Massachusetts Press, 2002.

Richardson, Robert D. *William James: In the Maelstrom of American Modernism—A Biography*. Boston: Houghton Mifflin, 2006.

Robinson, Marilynne. *The Death of Adam: Essays on Modern Thought*. Boston: Houghton Mifflin, 1998.

——. "Credo." *Harvard Divinity Bulletin* 36, no. 2 (2008), 20–32.

Ruland, Richard, and Malcolm Bradbury. *From Puritanism to Postmodernism: A History of American Literature*. New York: Penguin, 1992.

Schneider, Herbert W. *The Puritan Mind*. Ann Arbor: University of Michigan Press, 1958.

Schneider, Robert W. *Novelist to a Generation: The Life and Thought of Winston Churchill*. Bowling Green, Ohio: Bowling Green University Popular Press, 1976.

Schorer, Mark. *Sinclair Lewis: An American Life*. New York: McGraw-Hill, 1961.

Schutz, Alfred. *Collected Papers*. Ed. Maurice Natanson. The Hague: Martinus Nijhoff, 1962.

Scott, Donald M. *From Office to Profession: The New England Ministry, 1750–1850*. Philadelphia: University of Pennsylvania Press, 1978.

Sewell, Richard B. *The Life of Emily Dickinson*. Cambridge: Harvard University Press, 1994.

Small, Miriam Rossite. *Oliver Wendell Holmes*. New Haven, Conn.: College and University Press, 1962.

Smith, Christian, ed. *The Secular Revolution: Power, Interests, and Conflict in the Secularization of American Public Life*. Berkeley: University of California Press, 2003.

"Special Issue: Beyond Einstein." *Scientific American* 291, no. 3 (2004).

Stevens, Wallace. "Adagia." In *Opus Posthumous*, ed. Milton J. Bates, 184–205. New York: Knopf, 1989.

Stowe, Harriet Beecher. Letter dated March 7, 1879. Radcliffe College, Schlesinger Library, Beecher Stowe Collection, Folder 196.

Sutton, Matthew Avery. *Aimee Semple McPherson and the Resurrection of Christian America*. Cambridge: Harvard University Press, 2007.

Taneyhill, Richard Henry. *The Leatherwood God: An Account of the Appearance and Pretensions of Joseph C. Dylks in Eastern Ohio in 1828*. Ohio Valley Historical Series, vol. 7. Cincinnati: Robert Clarke, 1870.

Taylor, J. Golden. *Hawthorne's Ambivalence Toward Puritanism*. Logan: Utah State University Press, 1965.

Tierney, John. "The Immoral Majority." *New York Times*, October 31, 2006, A27.

Thompson, Lawrance. *Melville's Quarrel with God*. Princeton, N.J.: Princeton University Press, 1952.

Tomalin, Claire. *Thomas Hardy*. New York: Penguin, 2007.

Tompkins, Jane. Afterword to Susan Warner, *The Wide, Wide World*, 584–608. New York: Feminist Press, 1987.

——. *Sensational Designs: The Cultural Work of American Fiction, 1790–1860*. New York: Oxford University Press, 1985.

Tracy, David. *The Analogical Imagination: Christian Theology and the Culture of Pluralism*. New York: Crossroad, 1981.

Turner, James. *Without God, Without Creed: The Origins of Unbelief in America*. Baltimore: Johns Hopkins University Press, 1985.

"U.S. Religious Landscape Survey." Pew Forum on Religion and Public Life. March 2008. At http://religions.pewforum.org/reports.

Wagenknecht, Edward. *Longfellow: A Full-Length Portrait*. New York, Longmans, Green, 1955.

Wallace, James D. *Early Cooper and His Audience*. New York: Columbia University Press, 1986.

Walrath, Douglas Alan. *Frameworks: Patterns of Living and Believing Today*. New York: Pilgrim, 1987.

White, Curtis. "Hot Air Gods." *Harpers* 315 (December 2007), 13–15.

Williams, Cecil. *Henry Wadsworth Longfellow*. New York, Twayne, 1964.

Wilson, A. N. *God's Funeral: A Biography of Faith and Doubt in Western Civilization*. New York: Ballantine, 1999.

——. *The Victorians*. New York: Norton, 2003.

——. *After the Victorians: The Decline of Britain in the Modern World*. New York: Farrar, Straus Giroux, 2005.

Wood, James. *The Broken Estate: Essays on Literature and Belief*. New York: Random House, 1999.

Woodwell, Philip McIntire. *Handkerchief Moody: The Diary and the Man*. Portland, Me.: Colonial Offset Printing, n.d.

Wright, Nathalia. *Melville's Use of the Bible*. Durham, N.C.: Duke University Press, 1949.

Wuthnow, Robert. *America and the Challenges of Religious Diversity*. Princeton, N.J.: Princeton University Press, 2005.

——. *The Consciousness Reformation*. Berkeley: University of California Press, 1976.

——. *The Restructuring of American Religion: Society and Faith Since World War II.* Princeton, N.J.: Princeton University Press, 1988.

Yankelovich, Daniel. *New Rules: Searching for Fulfillment in a World Turned Upside Down.* New York: Random House, 1981.

Yerkes, James, ed. *John Updike and Religion: The Sense of the Sacred and the Motions of Grace.* Grand Rapids, Mich.: Eerdmans, 1999.

INDEX

Index does not include the names of fictitious characters.